Study Guide Plus
for

Baron

PSYCHOLOGY
Fourth Edition

Catherine E. Seta
Wake Forest University

John Seta
University of North Carolina at Greensboro

Paul Paulus
University of Texas at Arlington

Allyn and Bacon
Boston · London · Toronto · Sydney · Tokyo · Singapore

ISBN 0-205-27290-8

Printed in the United States of America

10 9 8 7 6 5 4 3 2   01 00 99 98

TABLE OF CONTENTS

Page

TABLE OF CONTENTS

PREFACE
STUDY GUIDE OVERVIEW: ITS PURPOSE AND AIMS

It might be helpful for you to know what our goals were as we wrote this guide. First and foremost, our goal is to help you study the material that is in your text. The purpose of this guide is to supplement, not substitute for, your book. It is designed to help you review the material and includes exercises that will check for your comprehension and ability to think critically about the material in your text. Using this study guide along with careful study of your text should help you do well in the course. In addition, we have tried to provide exercises that will help you apply psychology to your everyday lives. Psychology is a useful science and your experiences in your psychology course should help you understand the world of people that we live in.

As we wrote this guide, we tried to approach it from the student's perspective. We sought the advice of a number of students in our classes concerning what kinds of exercises would be both enjoyable and beneficial for learning about psychology. In addition, we sought out what the experts have to say about effective learning strategies and incorporated many of these suggestions.

After a considerable amount of research, we developed three primary strategies. First, we decided that we would include a very active approach to learning. That is, we want to get you involved in this material! As you will see, there are many opportunities for you to analyze information and to apply psychology to your life. Second, we wanted to help you organize the material in the text. We have provided outlines with relevant learning objectives and survey/question sections that emphasize the major concepts contained in each chapter. Use these as tools for seeing how the components of the chapter fit together. Third, we wanted to give you multiple opportunities to test your knowledge of the material. Practice tests are presented for each chapter and supplemental tests are included at the end of the study guide. We have included over 500 multiple choice questions, as well as essay and short answer questions.

We will now turn to a more detailed discussion of how to use the study guide, and then consider some tips on how to improve your studying. We wish you well in your course and hope that you enjoy psychology as much as we love the field!

Integrated Chapter Outline

Using the chapter outline as a guide, this section presents the major topics and ideas of each chapter. You should read the appropriate chapter prior to completing this section. After you have read the chapter, you can use this section as a tool for seeing how the components of the chapter fit together. In this section, we also give you an opportunity to check on your comprehension of the material. Questions that relate to the major learning objectives are presented. If you can answer these questions, you have come a long way toward mastering the material.

Here's another suggestion for using this section. Review this material again several times before the exam. Along with additional reading of the chapter and studying your class notes, this section can be used as a final review for an exam.

Making Psychology Part Of Your Life: Key Terms and Concepts

Knowing the important concepts and key terms contained in each chapter is a very important part of mastering the material. In this section, we have presented some of the key terms and concepts. Check on your understanding of this material by defining those that are listed in this section. Research has also shown that providing examples of concepts is a good way to increase your memory for them. Therefore, we have provided space for you to write an example of each. Try to be as specific as possible. Research has also shown that relating material to your own personal experiences is an extremely effective learning strategy. So, whenever possible try to use your own personal experiences when thinking of an example. As you will see, the author of your book (Robert Baron) has provided many examples of important concepts from his personal experiences. Try to follow his lead and relate this material to your life.

Challenge: Develop Your Critical Thinking Skills

Robert Baron points out in your textbook that one "hidden bonus" of taking introductory psychology is that it will help you develop your critical thinking skills. We definitely agree with him! These skills are a must in today's world. In this section, we have given you exercises that will help you develop the ability to think critically. We also discuss the particular skill that the exercise is designed to develop, along with a brief discussion of why this skill is important.

The best way to use these exercises is to complete them when you feel you have a good grasp of the material in the chapter. Completing the exercise will reinforce your understanding and will also give you feedback about whether you indeed have a true understanding of the material. We consulted a number of students while developing these exercises (and those presented in the next section); they reported that they found them quite enjoyable. So, we hope that you share their impressions and will enjoy "stretching your mind."

Challenge: Taking Psychology With You

This section is designed to encourage you to use what you've learned. The exercises vary in format - sometimes we give you a situation and ask you about how you'd deal with it. Sometimes we ask you to play the role of psychologist and provide your expert opinion. In all cases, the goal is to get you to apply psychology to your life. Of course, this will help you learn the material and do better on your exams. But more importantly, it will give you an appreciation for how your knowledge of psychology can enrich your day to day life.

Challenge: Review Your Comprehensive Knowledge

In this section, we present you with 20 sample multiple choice questions. This is an opportunity to check on your mastery of the material after you have finished your studying but while you still have some time left for review. There are skills involved in taking multiple choice tests. Practicing these skills will help you develop these skills. To help you grasp the logic of multiple choice testing, we have provided explanations for why a given item is the best response to the question. We have also given you the page number in your text that corresponds with the subject of each question. If you miss a question, go back an review that material. There is also a supplementary practice quiz for each chapter at the end of the study guide.

The items on this quiz are similar to the ones that may be used by your instructor on actual class tests. It should give you an idea of how well you'll do on your exam. We have also provided you with additional multiple choice questions at the end of the study guide. You should use these as an additional check on your mastery. A strong word of caution is due at this time. Do not rely only on these questions to assess your readiness for the exam. They are only a sample of the kinds of questions you might expect. Be sure you have mastered the learning objectives, the survey material, your class notes, and the key concepts and terms.

Glossary of Difficult Words and Expressions

This section contains words and expressions that were identified by students as potentially hard to understand. We have defined these terms. This section may be especially useful for students for whom English is a second language.

Some Study Tips

In the psychology course for which you have enrolled, inevitably some students will do quite well and others not so well. This fact often leads us to assume that these students differ in their intelligence or their intellectual ability. While this may be the case to some extent, a large portion of these differences in performance is probably due to differences in the way in which students approach their studies. Some are not motivated to work hard and so spend little time in actual study. Others may spend a lot of time studying but may have poor study habits. Let's briefly discuss how each of these two problems can be overcome.

Motivation to Learn

Unless you are motivated to learn or do well in a course, you are not likely to perform well in it even if you have all the best study habits. There are, of course, many obvious reasons to be motivated to do well in a course. Personal satisfaction of doing well, approval from your instructors, and the benefits derived from good grades (e.g., getting good jobs or gaining entrance to graduate or professional schools) are often sufficient to motivate many students. If these factors are not important to you (and even if they are), you should try to learn to derive satisfaction from learning itself. The discovery of new ideas and facts and the mastery of new concepts is often an inherent source of pleasure. You can probably increase the satisfaction derived from the learning by relating these facts, ideas, and concepts to your everyday life. Another technique that may help your motivation is breaking up the material in a chapter into smaller sections. After you have read and/or reviewed a major section of your chapter, provide yourself with a reward such as a drink, a snack, a walk outside, or a brief visit with friends. Then return to your studies and cover an additional section. Be sure not to reward yourself until you have finished an entire section. This procedure should not only help motivate your studying, but also will help build good study habits.

Study Habits

Let's assume you are highly motivated to do well in a course. You should now be strongly interested in the most efficient way to study. One of the important factors is **where** you study. It's important to study in a quiet area that is free from outside distractions and interruptions. A quiet corner of the library may do. Your own room may also be fine, if you can control your roommates and/or friends. Set up definite study periods and make others respect these. Make sure your desk is not cluttered with distracting material. You can even listen to light music but avoid programs which involve talking. Do not study by the TV. It is best to study in the same place each time so that it will become a habit when you are there (don't do anything else there except study!). Also be sure you have good lighting. It is best to have your light off to the side so as to minimize glare.

The next issue is **how** to study. One concern is how long you should study at one time. All of us have a span of concentration. Some of us can study for hours without a break. Others feel the need for a break after 10 minutes of study. In general, it is best not to study too long at one time since fatigue will set in and you won't be accomplishing very much anyway. So be sure to take breaks at appropriate times. You may need one every hour or every half-hour, or even after every 15 minutes. In fact, you can use these to reward yourself for studying certain amounts of material. Again, be sure to decide how much material you plan to cover before taking a break. Then, make sure you finish this material before you do take the break.

Another tactic that may help your studying is that of working on different subjects during each study session. This will prevent you from getting bored with one kind of study. You might want to do the least preferred subjects or tasks first, so that doing the more enjoyable ones will serve as a reward for completing the less preferred ones. Another important factor is your technique of study. One frequently suggested method of study involves a number of related steps: Survey, Question, Read, Recite, and Review (Robinson, 1970; Shepherd, 1987).

Survey. When you first begin with a chapter, glance through the entire chapter briefly to note the major topics covered. Use the headings contained in the chapters since they indicate the major points of the chapter. Also read the summary at the end of the chapter. Now you will know what you will have to learn in the chapter and how to organize the material as you read it. You may want to study one section before going on to the next, especially if a section contains a lot of information. The Learning Objectives can also help you survey the chapter.

<u>Question</u>. As you now read through the chapter, turn the headings into questions. This will give you an active and receptive set as you read through each section. An active learning set is very helpful in learning the test material. Also be sure to look at the Learning Objectives and Essay Questions sections of the manual for additional questions.

<u>Read</u>. Next you should read the material in the text to answer the questions you now have. Do not read as if you were reading a novel, but read as if preparing for a test (which, of course, you are!). Read in order to remember the material at a later time. Make sure to read everything as you go along. Don't omit the graphs, tables, and boxes since they are important additions to your chapter. Organize your reading by underlying and taking notes.

<u>Recite</u>. As you finish each section, you should see if you now can answer the questions you asked yourself at the beginning. You can do this verbally or by briefly jotting down the major points of the section. Then go back and see if you were correct. As you go through the chapter, you may want to go back and recite the major points of each section. Recitation is also designed to make you an active and involved learner. It is one of the most important of the study techniques and should take up a good part of your study time (e.g., one-third). Continue to question, read, and recite until you finish the chapter.

<u>Review</u>. After you have finished the chapter, you should review all of the material immediately. You can use your notes of the main topics or the main headings for this. Try to briefly summarize the major points of each of these sections. This should take only 10 minutes or so. This review is very important. If material is not reviewed immediately, much of it is soon forgotten. This review should be repeated at spaced intervals (e.g., every few days) and just prior to the examination. The Integrated Chapter Outline, of course, can be used for this type of review. Your reviews should consist of both recitation and re-reading of the material, depending on your level of mastery.

We have only been able to make a few suggestions on how to improve your studying. If you have serious difficulties with your studying or reading, you should try to take a study skills and reading course. Many colleges and universities offer such courses, and they may be well worth the required investment of time. You should also periodically come back to this section to remind yourself about good study techniques. However, if you follow the above study suggestions carefully, you won't need to be reminded, and you should find yourself doing better than ever in your course work. Good luck and enjoy your study of psychology.

Catherine E. Seta
Wake Forest University

John J. Seta
University of North Carolina at Greensboro

Paul B. Paulus
University of Texas at Arlington

REFERENCES

Robinson, F. P. (1970). <u>Effective study</u>. New York: Harper & Row Publisher.

Shepherd, J. F. (1987). <u>College study skills</u> (3rd ed.). Boston: Houghton Mifflin Company.

<u>Acknowledgements</u>

We are grateful to a number of persons for their help with this study guide. Several students have contributed suggestions about this guide and have helped with its completion -- Laura Negel, Emily Culp, Katherine Miller, and Kenny Herbst. We very much appreciate their help! In addition, we would like to thank Rod Bedoya for helping with the glossary sections. We would like to thank Teresa Hill for preparing the text copy. We could not have done this without her. Finally, we are grateful to Beth Brooks for her suggestions.

CHAPTER 1
PSYCHOLOGY: A SCIENCE AND A PERSPECTIVE

INTEGRATED CHAPTER OUTLINE: Survey and Question

This section presents the major topics and ideas from the chapter. Use it as a tool for seeing how the components of the chapter fit together. At the end of each major topic, we have asked you a question that relates to the major learning objectives. If you can answer these questions, you have taken a major step toward mastering this material.

I. Modern Psychology: What It Is and Where It Came From

L.O. 1.1: Discuss the roots of psychology and what it is today.

A. Connections and The Emergence of Psychology

Psychology was heavily influenced by philosophy and science. The text discusses several philosophical views that were important for the emergence of psychology. These are: Empiricism -- the view that knowledge can be acquired through observation; Rationalism -- the view that knowledge can be acquired by logic and reasoning. Discoveries in the field of physiology were important for the emergence of science within psychology.

B. Psychology: From Small Beginnings...To a Thriving Field

Psychologists have defined their field in different ways during its brief history. Wundt believed that psychology should focus on analyzing conscious experience into its basic components. Wundt was a structuralist because he focused on the structure of the human mind. He used the method of introspection to analyze sensations, feelings, and images into their most basic parts. When individuals introspect they describe what is going on in their minds. This view was replaced by the idea that psychology should study only what can be observed -- overt behavior. The most radical spokesperson of the behaviorist approach was John Watson. He felt that only observable activities could be studied in a scientific manner.

Because of behaviorists like Watson and B. F. Skinner, psychology did not consider "internal" events such as thought to be part of scientific psychology. During the 1960s, however, there was a dramatic increase in the study of mental events or, stated differently, the study of cognitive processes. This reaction has been described as the cognitive revolution. It was due to advances in technology and to the accumulation of scientific findings on cognitive processes such as memory. Today, psychology is typically defined as the science of behavior and cognitive processes.

C. Modern Psychology: Grand Issues, Key Perspectives

Your author discusses three major themes or issues that have captured the attention of psychologists. One centers around the question of stability versus change -- to what extent do we remain constant over time, and to what extent do we change. The second centers around the nature-nurture question: to what extent are our actions determined by inheritance, and to what extent are they learned-influenced by our experiences. The third issue is concerned with the extent to which we behave in a rational or irrational manner. Some psychologists believe that we behave in a rational manner when our actions are consistent with the Laws of Logic or in accord with how a computer would proceed.

1

D. Key Perspectives in Psychology: The Many Facets of Behavior

Modern psychology studies behavior and cognitive processes from several different perspective. The study of overt events is the behavioral perspective. Another perspective studies cognitive processes such as thinking and deciding. A third perspective would stress biological factors such as emotions. A fourth perspective focuses on social and cultural factors. The psychodynamic perspective concentrates on factors within an individual's personality. This view, for example, might seek the conscious or unconscious motives that presumably influence a person's actions. The evolutionary perspective studies whether and to what extent a person's actions are influenced by inherited tendencies.

E. Psychology in a Diverse World: The Multicultural Perspective

Many countries are experiencing growing cultural and ethnic diversity. Our work force is also becoming more diverse in that it comprises a smaller percentage of white males. Psychology has attempted to adopt a multicultural perspective. For example, it attempts to develop tests that are valid for use with various ethnic groups. It also recognizes that ethnic background and culture are important factors for understanding psychological processes, including psychological disorders.

Questions:

1-1.   What ideas influenced the emergence of psychology? _____

_____

_____

_____

1-2.   What are structuralism and behaviorism? _____

_____

_____

_____

1-3.   Give a brief overview of how psychology developed in the twentieth century. _____

_____

_____

_____

1-4.   What are three key perspectives within modern psychology? _____

_____

_____

1-5.   Discuss the implications of growing cultural diversity for the future of psychology. _____

_____

_____

_____

II. Psychologists: Who They Are and What They Do

L.O. 1.2: Describe the background and training of psychologists and the subfields of psychology.

A. Who: The Training of Psychologists

Although many persons think that psychiatrists and psychologists are the same professions, they are quite different in training. Psychiatrists are physicians who specialize in the treatment of mental disorders after completing their medical studies. Psychologists receive their training in graduate schools specializing in psychology. This usually involves four to five years of advanced study.

B. What: Subfields of Psychology

Although nearly half of all psychologists are involved in clinical or counseling activities, there are many other specialties within psychology. These are a few of the subfields:

(1) clinical psychology: studies the diagnosis, causes and treatment of mental disorders
(2) counseling: assists individuals in dealing with personal problems that do not involve psychological disorders
(3) developmental: studies how people change physically, cognitively, and socially over the life span
(4) educational psychology: studies the educational process
(5) cognitive psychology: investigates all aspects of cognition
(6) industrial/organizational psychology: studies behavior in work settings
(7) psychobiology: studies the biological bases of behavior
(8) social psychology: studies social behavior and thought
(9) experimental: studies learning, perception, and motivation

As you can see, psychologists study a number of different things. The shared goals, values, and methods used by psychologists unifies the field. While some psychologists engage in basic research, others engage in applied research. Basic research attempts to increase our understanding of psychological phenomena. Applied research deals with practical issues.

Questions:

1-6.   Describe the background and training of psychologists. _____

_____

_____

_____

1-7.   Describe the specialties that exist within psychology. _____

_____

_____

_____

III.   Psychology and the Scientific Method

L.O. 1.3:   Describe the scientific method; explain the advantages of the method vs. a common sense approach to human behavior.

A. The Scientific Method: Its Basic Nature

Psychology is not merely common sense and intuition. It is more accurate and useful. This is because it is a science. Science uses the scientific method. The scientific method involves systematic observation and direct experimentation. The main aspects of the scientific method are objectivity, accuracy, sketicism, and open-mindedness. It also involves the development of theories -- frameworks for understanding why various events and processes occur. A theory consists of two main parts. A set of concepts and statements concerning how these concepts are related.

B. Advantages of the Scientific Method: Why Common Sense Leads Us Astray

The problem with common sense is that it often suggests contradictory answers. Research has provided a number of reasons why informal observation can be inaccurate. For example, informal observations may be inaccurate because of the confirmation bias, the availability heuristic and mood effects. The tendency to notice and remember information that confirms what we already believe is the confirmation bias. The availability heuristic suggests that the easier it is to remember an event, the more frequent or important it is. Finally, our current mood can influence the way we think.

Questions:

1-8.   Why is psychology not merely common sense? _____

_____

_____

_____

1-9.   Describe the scientific method. _____

_____

_____

_____

1-10.   What are the two major components of a theory? _____

_____

_____

_____

1-11.   Discuss why common sense can lead us astray. _____

_____

_____

_____

IV.   The Scientific Method in Everyday Life: Thinking Critically About Human Behavior

L.O. 1.4:   Understand how to think critically about human behavior.

Learning about the scientific method can help us improve our critical thinking. Critical thinking mirrors the key values of the scientific method.

Questions:

1-12.   Discuss how psychology can help improve your own critical thinking. _____

_____

_____

_____

_____

V.   Research Methods in Psychology: How Psychologists Answer Questions About Behavior

L.O. 1.5:   Compare and contrast the research methods used in psychology.

Observation, correlation, and experimentation are the three basic procedures used in the study of behavior. These methods are discussed below.

A. Observation: Describing The World Around Us

The use of systematic observation takes several different forms. Observing humans or animals in their natural settings is called naturalistic observation. An advantage is that subjects are likely to act in a natural manner. However, the data is sometimes relatively informal in nature. The detailed study of a few individuals is the case method of research. One problem with case method may be a lack of objectivity. One advantage is that when the behavior involved is very unusual, this method can uncover valuable insights.

The method that involves large numbers of individuals completing questionnaires is called the survey approach. Problems with the survey approach are that people may not answer truthfully or accurately, and the persons surveyed may not be representative of the larger population to which the findings are to be generalized.

B. Correlational: The Search For Relationships

An important goal for psychology is prediction -- the ability to forecast future events from present ones. One such technique involves examining the association of changes in one variable with those of another one. This is called the correlational method. Statistical procedures are used to determine the size of the correlation (or relationship between variables).

Advantages of the correlational method are that: (1) it is efficient, (2) it can be used in naturalistic settings, (3) it allows us to examine many variables at once, and (4) it is often the only method feasible from a practical or ethical standpoint. One drawback of the correlational method is that it is not conclusive as to cause-and-effect relationships. If two variables are correlated, it does not mean one causes the other.

C. The Experimental Method: Knowledge Through Systematic Intervention

Experimentation is the method that is preferred by psychologists because of its ability to help uncover why a relationship exists. Answering the question "why" serves the goal of explanation in science. Experimentation can provide fairly clear evidence about causality.

The experimental method involves systematically altering some factor believed to affect behavior and measuring the effects of such variations. The factor systematically varied is called the independent variable. The behavior or cognitive process studied is the dependent variable. A control condition serves as a baseline against which other conditions can be compared.

There are two requirements for the success of experiments. First, all participants in an experiment must have an equal chance of being exposed to any level of the independent variable. This is accomplished by random assignment of subjects to experimental conditions. Secondly, all factors that might affect subjects aside from the independent variable must be held constant. If this is not done, the independent variable is confounded with the other variables.

When researchers unintentionally influence the behavior of subjects, the experimenter affects the results. A procedure which minimizes these problems involves having research assistants who are unfamiliar with the hypothesis and the condition to which the subject is assigned conduct the study. This is known as the double-blind procedure.

D. Interpreting Research Results: Statistics as a Valuable Tool

Inferential statistics are used to determine whether a particular finding may have occurred due to chance. Only when the likelihood of a chance finding is low are the results described as significant.

A meta-analysis combines the results of many different studies to estimate both the direction and size of the effects of independent variables.

Questions:

1-13.   What are the naturalistic observation, case study, and survey methods of psychological research? Identify their positive and negative features. _____

_____

_____

_____

1-14.   What is the correlational method and what are its advantages and disadvantages? _____

_____

_____

_____

1-15.   What are the basic characteristics of the experimental method? Why is it frequently the method of choice in psychology? _____

_____

_____

_____

1-16.   What the two requirements that must be met in order for an experiment to be successful? _____

_____

_____

_____

1-17.   Define experimenter effects and the double-blind procedure. _____

_____

_____

_____

1-18.   What is the role of statistics in psychological research? _____

_____

_____

_____

1-19.   What is the role of theory in psychological research? _____

_____

_____

_____

VI.   Ethical Issues in Psychological Research

L.O. 1.6:   Discuss the major ethical issues that psychologists face in research and practice.

A. Deception: The Ethics of Misleading Research Participants

Sometimes it is necessary to conceal certain aspects of an experiment. This is called deception. To counteract the negative effects of deception (such as discomfort, stress, and negative shifts in self-esteem) subjects are usually given as much information as possible prior to the experiment. This is known as informed consent. Full information after the experiment is called debriefing. Those who have participated in deception experiments generally view it as acceptable. Effective debriefing seems to eliminate many potentially negative effects of deception.

B. Research With Animals

Animal research makes it possible to do important research which, for health and safety reasons, cannot be done with humans. Because of their brief lifespans, animals are also useful for studying development. Animal studies by psychologists have resulted in a variety of practical benefits. The ethical issues that confront animal research are complex and whether the "benefits outweigh the costs" is a value judgment and an important one.

C. Ethical Issues in the Practice of Psychology

Many of the ethical issues that are involved in practicing psychology center around confidentiality issues. Confidentiality problems arise when professional ethics require the psychologist to withhold information when they feel the information should be revealed. In addition, ethical issues involve situations in which the psychologist is in a conflicted relationship with a client. Practicing psychology requires adherence to the highest of professional standards.

Questions:

1-20.   What are the major ethical issues surrounding research with humans? _____

_____

_____

_____

_____

1-21.   What are the major ethical issues that psychologists face in their research with animals? _____

_____

_____

_____

1-22.   What are the ethical issues that psychologists face in the practice of psychology? _____

_____

_____

_____

_____

VII.   Using This Book: A Note on its Features

L.O.1.7:   Be aware of the ways you can use your text most effectively.

This book contains a number of features that makes it easier to read. Make notes of key terms printed in bold text. Also, note the key points in the margins. There are also a number of special sections that you'll find interesting and entertaining. BE SURE AND READ THESE SECTIONS.

- **Making Psychology Part of Your Life**

L.O. 1.8:   Learn how to study effectively.

Your text provides six guidelines for effective studying: 1) Begin with an overview; 2) Eliminate or minimize distractions; 3) Recognize the limitations of your span of concentration; 4) Set specific, challenging, but attainable goals; 5) Reward yourself for progress; and 6) Engage in active, not passive, studying.

Question:

1-23.   How will you incorporate the six guidelines for effective studying in your study routine? _____

_____

_____

_____

MAKING PSYCHOLOGY PART OF YOUR LIFE: Key Terms and Concepts

Knowing the important concepts and key terms contained in this chapter is a very important part of mastering the material. We have presented a sample of these concepts below. Define each concept and check your definition with that presented in the chapter. It will also be beneficial for you to think of an example of each concept. Whenever possible, use your own personal experience to provide an example of each term below.

1-1.   **Availability Heuristic:** _____

      Example: _____

1-2.   **Behaviorism:** _____

      Example: _____

1-3.   **Case Method:** _____

      Example: _____

1-4.   **Confirmation Bias:** _____

      Example: _____

1-5.   **Correlational Method of Research:** _____

      Example: _____

1-6.   **Correlations:** _____

      Example: _____

1-7.   **Critical Thinking:** _____

      Example: _____

1-8.   **Debriefing:** _____

      Example: _____

1-9.   **Deception:** _____

      Example: _____

1-10. **Dependent Variable:** _____

   Example: _____

1-11. **Double Blind Procedure:** _____

   Example: _____

1-12. **Experimenter Effects:** _____

   Example: _____

1-13. **Experimentation (The Experimental Method of Research):** _____

   Example: _____

1-14. **Hypothesis:** _____

   Example: _____

1-15. **Independent Variable:** _____

   Example: _____

1-16. **Inferential Statistics:** _____

   _____

1-17. **Informed Consent:** _____

   _____

1-18. **Meta-Analysis:** _____

   _____

1-19. **Multicultural Perspective:** _____

   Example: _____

1-20. **Naturalistic Observation:** _____

   Example: _____

1-21. **Psychology:** _____

   Example: _____

1-22. **Random Assignment of Participants to Experimental Conditions:** _____

   Example: _____

1-23. **Replication:** _____

   Example: _____

1-24. **Sampling:** _____

   Example: _____

1-25. **Survey Method:** _____

   Example: _____

1-26. **Systematic Observation:** _____

   Example: _____

1-27. **Theories:** _____

   Example: _____

CHALLENGE: Develop Your Critical Thinking Skills

Analysis, Induction, and Deduction

As your text points out, one "hidden bonus" of taking introductory psychology is that it will help you develop your critical thinking skills. One important element in critical thinking is the ability to use what you've learned to analyze the world around you. In addition, the ability to go from the specific case exercise to the general (induction) and to go from general principles to specific cases (deduction) are crucial skills for the critical thinker. Practice these skills in the following exercise.

It is sometimes suggested that bright stimulating colors may cause people to eat faster than duller and less stimulating colors. The fact that many fast food restaurants have brightly colored interiors is seen as consistent with this idea. These restaurants supposedly want people to eat quickly and make available space for additional customers.

1-1. What do you think of this possibility? _____

_____

_____

1-2. Can you develop a theory that might explain why such an effect might be produced? _____

_____

_____

1-3. What are some hypotheses suggested by your theory? _____

_____

_____

1-4. Design an experiment to test your hypotheses. You should decide on the experimental conditions (independent variables), dependent variables, need for deception, procedures, and random assignment technique.

_____

_____

_____

_____

_____

_____

_____

1-5.   Can you do such an experiment in actual restaurants? Why or why not? _____

_____

_____

1-6.   Would there be ethical problems? _____

_____

_____

1-7.   Can some of your hypotheses be tested with animals? _____

_____

_____

YOUR NOTES:

CHALLENGE: Taking Psychology With You

<u>Becoming a Better Consumer</u>

Newspapers, TV, and popular psychology books are filled with claims that may or may not be backed by sound research. One major benefit that you can claim from this course is a heightened sensitivity to the validity of these claims. Your text discusses some of the strengths and pitfalls associated with the various methods of psychological research. This information can make you a better educated consumer. Practice using this knowledge by critically analyzing these claims. They represent the kinds of statements we commonly hear in the media.

1-1.   Beer and soft drink ads commonly claim that those who drink their product "have more fun."

   A. Describe the relationships between variables or correlations that are claimed by these ads.

   _____

   _____

   _____

   B. Do you think these companies have scientific evidence that back up these claims?

   _____

   _____

   C. Do you think people who watch these ads actually believe that the products will be associated with favorable results?

   _____

   _____

   D. Do you think such advertising is ethical if it is not backed by strong scientific data? Why or why not?

   _____

   _____

   _____

   _____

1-2.   You read in the newspaper that recent research suggests that joggers live longer.

      A. Does this result imply that running causes increased longevity? (Hint: Remember the pitfalls of inferring causative relationships from correlations?)

      _____

      _____

      _____

      B. What alternative explanations might exist for this finding? (Hint: Are there other differences between joggers and non-joggers?)

      _____

      _____

      C. What kind of research would be required to determine whether jogging causes increased longevity?

      _____

      _____

YOUR NOTES:

CHALLENGE: Review Your Comprehensive Knowledge

SAMPLE TEST QUESTIONS

Once you have worked through the preceding sections, you should be ready for a comprehensive self-test. You can check your answers with those at the end of this section. An additional practice test is given in the supplementary section at the end of this study guide.

1-1.   Identify the two key ideas from philosophy that produced the basic ground rules of modern science.
a.   absolutism and relativism
c.   scientific method and correlations
b.   empiricism and rationalism
d.   introspection and empiricism

1-2.   Psychologists who felt that psychology should study only observable activities were the:
a.   functionalists.
c.   behaviorists.
b.   structuralists.
d.   experimentalists.

1-3.   The founder of behaviorism was:
a.   Wundt.
c.   Watson.
b.   James.
d.   Freud.

1-4.   Most psychologists believe that psychology is the science of behavior and _____ processes:
a.   cognitive
c.   correlational
b.   overt
d.   causative

1-5.   Observable behavior is to thought as:
a.   structuralism is to behaviorism.
c.   behaviorism is to psychoanalysis.
b.   structuralism is to psychoanalysis.
d.   behaviorism is to structuralism.

1-6.   The common sense approach to psychology often is characterized by:
a.   contradictory statements.
c.   systematic observations.
b.   objective evaluations.
d.   direct experimentation.

1-7.   In the 1960s there was a shift in the conception of psychology. This was called the _____ revolution.
a.   behavioral
c.   physiological
b.   cognitive
d.   emotional

1-8.   Psychologists who try to understand how we think and remember are taking a _____ perspective.
a.   physiological
c.   social-cultural
b.   psychodynamic
d.   cognitive

1-9.   When the hypothesis behind the study is communicated by the experimenter, this may be a(n) _____ effect.
a.   double-blind
c.   random
b.   survey
d.   experimenter

1-10.   The method that involves watching animals or humans in natural settings is called:
a.   survey
c.   introspection
b.   naturalistic observation
d.   case study

1-11.   Having a large number of individuals complete a questionnaire is called the _____ approach.
        a. case   c. survey
        b. natural observation   d. cognitive

1-12.   A meta-analysis allows researchers to
        a. engage in case studies.   c. perform correlational tests.
        b. confound their study.   d. combine the results of many different studies.

1-13.   If one wants to know the cause of a behavior, one should use:
        a. observation.   c. experimentation.
        b. correlation.   d. surveys.

1-14.   In an experiment, the factor that is systematically varied by the experiment is called the _____ variable.
        a. independent   c. control
        b. dependent   d. stimulus

1-15.   In experiments, it is important that the assignment of subjects to the level of an independent variable is:
        a. systematic.   c. random.
        b. natural.   d. biased.

1-16.   In an experiment, all subjects in a noisy condition are tested on Mondays and those in the no noise condition on
        Wednesdays. The noise and day of week variables are:
        a. implicated.   c. contrived.
        b. confounded.   d. interactive.

1-17.   The most important source of ideas for studies in psychology is:
        a. literature.   c. common sense.
        b. theory   d. mathematics.

1-18.   The main purpose of theories is to:
        a. explain.   c. evaluate.
        b. postdict.   d. summarize.

1-19.   Because it is often necessary to conceal certain aspects of an experiment, experimental psychologists may use the
        technique of:
        a. deception.   c. subliminal stimulation.
        b. projection.   d. conversion.

1-20.   The philosophical view that knowledge can be acquired through observation is known as
        a. behaviorism.   c. empiricism.
        b. structuralism.   d. functionalism

Answers and Feedback for Sample Test Questions:

1-1.   B   Empiricism is the view that knowledge can be gathered through careful observation and rationalism is the view that knowledge can be gained through logic and careful reasoning. These ideas are basic to modern science. (p. 5)

1-2.   C   Behaviorists believe psychology should focus on the analysis of observable actions. (p. 7)

1-3.   C   Watson is the founder of behaviorist approaches to psychology. (p. 7)

1-4.   A   Both behavior and mental (or cognitive) processes are typically thought to comprise psychology. (p. 7)

1-5.   D   Behaviorism focuses on observable behavior and structuralism focuses on conscious experience such thoughts. (p. 7)

1-6.   A   Common sense often involves contradictory claims, such as "opposites attract" and "birds of a feather flock together." The existence of these claims make a more scientific approach to psychology necessary. (p. 18)

1-7.   B   In the 1960s psychology expanded its scope to include cognitive processes. This shift was called the cognitive revolution. (p. 10)

1-8.   D   Cognitive psychologists focus on understanding the processes which underlie memory and thought. (p. 7)

1-9.   D   Experimenter effects exist when the experimenter unintentionally influences research participants. (p. 32)

1-10.   B   Naturalistic observation is the method of study that involves observation in natural settings. (p. 23)

1-11.   C   A survey involves having a large number of individuals complete a questionnaire. (p. 25)

1-12.   D   A meta-analysis is a statistical procedure that allows researchers to combine the results of many different studies to estimate the direction and magnitude of the effects of the independent variable. (p. 33)

1-13.   C   Experimentation is the method that allows us to understand causal relationships. (p. 29)

1-14.   A   We call the variable that is purposely manipulated in a study an independent variable. (p. 29)

1-15.   C   There must be random assignment of subjects in an experiment in order to be sure that manipulated variables, rather than characteristics of subjects, are responsible for the outcomes of the study. (p. 30-31)

1-16.   B   In this example, the day of the week the testing was done was not held constant. Therefore, noise and day of the week are confounded. (p. 31)

1-17.   B   Theories are the most important sources of research ideas because they represent attempts to understand why events occur. (p. 17)

1-18.   A   The purpose of theories is to explain why events occur. (p. 17)

1-19.   A   Deception is used whenever it is absolutely necessary to conceal certain aspects of a study from participants. It must be used with caution, and only when necessary. (p. 34)

1-20.   C   Empiricism is the philosophical view that assumes knowledge can be acquired through observation. (p. 5)

GLOSSARY OF DIFFICULT WORDS AND EXPRESSIONS

These terms from your text and this study guide were identified by students as potentially hard to understand. We have defined these terms and expressions.

Term or Expression	Definition
Acquainting you...	introducing you
Adamantly	strongly
Bizarre	very unusual
Capsule overview	short summary
Confounding	confusing; changing two variables at the same time
Debriefing	explaining an experiment to participants
Eclectic	having broad interests; knowing a lot
Eminently	remarkable; thought highly of
Flaws	things that are not perfect
Flock together	are seen together
Gloss over	trying to solve a problem in a way that is only temporary
Grapple	have trouble with; hard to figure out
Ground rules	basic procedures or assumptions
Harsh	not justified; overly critical
Hasten	increase the speed of your actions
High school dropouts	people who do not finish high school
Insurmountable	unable to defeat; difficult
Just around the corner	will happen very soon
Loners	people who are by themselves a lot
Nuisance	something or someone that is annoying
Ominous	creates fear
Overt	out in the open; obvious
Pine away	do poorly, sad
Pitfalls	danger that you are not aware of
Rehashing	repeating several times
Remiss	not fulfilling the expected responsibility

Term or expression	Definition
Scrutiny	to examine closely
Span concentration	amount of time that you can pay attention
Stampeded	being made to do something
Stemming from	had its origins from
Stringent	strict
Subtle cues	signals that are not obvious
Tapestry	piece of cloth used for covering walls and furniture; a picture of something
Underpinnings of...	background information
Unfurled	unfolded

YOUR NOTES:

CHAPTER 2
BIOLOGICAL BASES OF BEHAVIOR:
A LOOK BENEATH THE SURFACE

INTEGRATED CHAPTER OUTLINE: Survey and Question

This section presents the major topics and ideas from the chapter. Use it as a tool for seeing how the components of the chapter fit together. At the end of each major topic, we have asked you a question that relates to the major learning objectives. If you can answer these questions, you have taken a major step toward mastering this material.

I. Neurons: Building Blocks of the Nervous System

L.O. 2.1: Describe the structure and functions of neurons.

L.O. 2.2: Know the important role that neurotransmitters play in communication between neurons.

A. Neurons: Their Basic Structure

Biopsychology is concerned with how biological processes are related to behavior, feelings, and cognition. The following sections review what we have learned from this exciting field.

The cells within our bodies that are specialized for the task of receiving, moving, and processing information are neurons. Neurons have three basic parts: cell body, axon, and dendrites. Information is carried to the cell body by the dendrites. It is carried from the cell body by the axon. The axon is covered by a fatty myelin sheath. This sheath is made of glial cells. It is interrupted at several points by small gaps. The axon divides into small branches that end in axon terminals. The region at which these terminals approach other cells is the synapse.

B. Neurons: Their Basic Function

Information travels within a neuron by means of a change in electric charge or action potential. When a neuron is at rest, there are more negatively charged particles inside than outside. The resulting negative charge is called the resting potential. When the neuron is stimulated, the cell membrane lets positively charged ions enter, reducing or eliminating the resting potential. The neuron then pumps the positive ions inside the cell back out, restoring the resting potential. The passage of this action potential along the cell membrane is the basic signal of the nervous system. The action potential occurs in an all-or-none fashion. In neurons with a myelin sheath, the action potential passes openings known as nodes of Ranvier.

The axon terminals contain synaptic vesicles. Arrival of the action potential causes these vesicles to approach the cell membrane and empty their contents into the synapse. These substances -- known as neurotransmitters -- then reach receptors in the membranes of the other cell. The transmitter substances may either have excitatory or inhibitory effects on the neuron. After the transmitter substances have crossed the synapse, they are either taken back into the axon terminals, known as re-uptake, or they are deactivated.

C. Neurotransmitter: Chemical Keys to the Nervous System

There are at least nine universally recognized substances known to function as neurotransmitters; and many chemicals appear to function as neurotransmitters. The neurotransmitter which is at most junctions between motor neurons and muscle cells is called acetylcholine. Interference with this transmitter can cause paralysis. This transmitter is believed to play a role in attention, arousal, and memory processes. Alzheimer's disease may result from the degeneration of cells producing acetylcholine.

Negative effects can often result when an incorrect amount of a neurotransmitter is produced. For example, too little dopamine is associated with the symptoms of Parkinson's disease whereas too much dopamine is associate with the symptoms of schizophrenia.

There appear to be special receptor sites for opiates such as morphine. These sites are stimulated by similar substances in the brain called endorphins. These substances seem to reduce feelings of pain and magnify positive feelings.

D. Neurotransmitters: Using Knowledge of Synaptic Transmission to Treat Drug Addictions

Drugs affect our feelings or behavior by altering the process of synaptic transmission. A drug can mimic or enhance the impact of a specific neurotransmitter. When it mimics the transmitter, it is an agonist. A drug can also inhibit the impact of a specific neurotransmitter. In this case, it is an antagonist. Figure 2.6 in your text contains specific ways in which drugs can function as agonists or antagonists.

- **Research Methods: How Psychologists Study Synaptic Transmission**

Intracranial self-stimulation is a procedure that allows animals to provide their own brain stimulation. Animals will press a lever over and over again to provide low level electrical stimulation to the medial forebrain bundle -- a bundle of nerve fibers located in the hypothalamus. Because animals work to stimulate this area, it is often referred to as a "reward" center. When animals are given chemicals that inhibit the action of neurotransmitters in this system, their efforts to stimulate the medial forebrain bundle is sharply reduced. For example, when naturally occurring neurotransmitters like dopamine are inhibited, opiates lose much of their appeal. Conversely, chemicals that enhance the impact of dopamine and other neurotransmitters appear to be related to the rewarding effects of several drugs.

One way of combating drug and alcohol addictions is to administer drugs that prevent opiates and other substances from stimulating the reward circuits in the brain.

Questions:

2-1.   What is the basic structure of the neuron? _____

_____

_____

2-2.   How do neurons function, and how does synaptic transmission occur? _____

_____

_____

_____

2-3.   What is the influence of drugs on synaptic transmission and how is this studied? _____

_____

_____

_____

2-4.   Discuss how influences to the medial forebrain bundle may reduce drug addictions. _____

_____

_____

_____

II. The Nervous System: Its Basic Structure and Functions

L.O. 2.3: Know the basic structures and functions of the nervous system and how it is studied.

L.O. 2.4: Discuss the components of the brain involved in the basic bodily functions and survival.

A. The Nervous System: Its Major Divisions

Although the nervous system functions as an integrated whole, it is studied by divisions. The nervous system is divided into two major portions -- the central and peripheral nervous system. These systems regulate all of our internal bodily functions and enable us to react to the external world.

The two major parts of the central nervous system are the brain and the spinal cord. The spinal cord runs through bones called vertebrae. One of its functions is to carry sensory information (via afferent nerve fibers) from the receptors to the brain and to conduct information from the brain to muscles and glands (via efferent nerve fibers). Another function of the spinal cord is to regulate reflexes.

The peripheral nervous system consists of bundles of axons or nerves that connect the central nervous system with various parts of the body. Nerves that are attached to the spinal cord and serve the body below the neck are the spinal nerves. Those attached to the brain are the cranial nerves. These nerves serve the neck and the head.

The part of the peripheral system that connects the central nervous system to the voluntary muscles is the somatic nervous system. The part that connects the central system to the glands, internal organs, and involuntary muscles is the autonomic nervous system. The nervous system can be divided further. The autonomic nervous system consists of two distinct parts, discussed below.

The part of the autonomic system that readies the body for the use of energy is the sympathetic division. The part of the autonomic system which has the opposite effect and stimulates processes that conserve energy is the parasympathetic division. These systems function in a coordinated way.

B. The Nervous System: How It Is Studied

There are several methods for constructing a map that will reveal the brain structures and processes involved in mental activities and behavior. One way is to observe the behavior of persons suffering from brain or nervous system damage. Then, after the person's death, the brain can be examined, and the location of the damage can be identified. Or portions of the brains of animals are destroyed and researchers examine the behavioral effects of such damage. Another method involves introducing minute amounts of drugs directly to produce damage at specific brain sites or inducing drugs to influence neurons.

The nervous system is also studied by recording electrical activity within the brain. It can involve measuring the electrical activity of the entire brain, a procedure called electroencephalography or EEG. Researchers also measure the location and timing of brain activity while people perform various cognitive tasks. This procedure is called event-related potentials or ERPS.

Magnetic resonance imaging or MRI uses a strong magnetic field to obtain images of the brain. Superconducting quantum interference device (SQUID) produces images based on its ability to detect tiny changes in magnetic fields. Another method involves the injection of small amounts of radioactive forms of glucose that is absorbed by the most active cells. This is called positron emission tomography or PET.

One application of brain imaging procedures is to scan the brains of normal persons and compare them to those persons with a variety of mental disorders to detect differences in the activity of their brains. Persons suffering from obsessive-compulsive disorder show increased activity in several areas including the frontal cortex. Imaging procedures have also been used to reveal how the brain delegates mental tasks including language processing tasks. When tasks are novel or complex, a greater overall amount of mental effort is required -- especially in the cortex. After a task is mastered, responsibility for the task is shifted from the cortex to more automatic brain regions.

Questions:

2-5.   What are the major divisions of the nervous system? _____

_____

_____

_____

2-6.   What are the major techniques for studying the nervous system? _____

_____

_____

_____

2-7.   How have imaging techniques increased our understanding of brain-behavior relationships? _____

_____

_____

_____

III. The Brain: Where Consciousness Is Manifest

L.O. 2.5:   Know how the thalamus, hypothalamus, and the limbic system play important roles in motivation and emotion.

L.O. 2.6:   Know how the cerebral cortex involved in complex activities such as language, planning, foresight, and reasoning and be able to discuss the biological basis of gender differences.

The brain is often divided into three major components: 1) those concerned with bodily functions and survival; 2) those concerned with motivation and emotion; and 3) those concerned with complex activities such as language and reasoning.

A. Survival Basics: The Brain Stem

The portions of the brain that regulate basic bodily processes are located in the brain stem. Two of the structures in the brain stem that are located just above the spinal cord are the medulla and the pons. Major sensory and motor pathways pass through these structures. They also contain the reticular activating system which plays a role in arousal and sleep. The medulla contains collections of neuron cell bodies called nuclei that control vital functions such as breathing, heart rate, and blood pressure. The cerebellum is involved in the regulation of motor activities. The midbrain contains an extension of the reticular activating system and primitive centers for vision and hearing. It also contains structures that play a role in relieving pain and the guidance and control of motor movements by sensory inputs.

B. Motivation and Emotion: The Hypothalamus, Thalamus, and Limbic System

The hypothalamus is a small structure deep within the brain and plays a role in the regulation of the autonomic nervous system. It also helps keep the body's internal environment at an optimal level, known as the process of homeostasis. In addition, it also is involved in the regulation of eating and drinking. Damage to the ventromedial portion of the hypothalamus is related to excessive eating. The lateral hypothalamus coordinates communication between the frontal cortex (the structure responsible for planning and the execution of behavior) and those parts of the brain that monitor and regulate aspects of the body's internal state like thirst and hunger. When brain damage is specific to the lateral hypothalamus, laboratory animals continue to monitor thirst and hunger functions. However, information about thirst and hunger is not communicated to the frontal cortex which is related to the execution of behavior. Consequently, the animals do not perform the appropriate thirst and hunger behaviors.

The thalamus is located deep within the brain and receives information from all of the senses except olfaction; it transmits this information to other parts of the brain. The thalamus is located above the hypothalamus and has been called the relay station of the brain. The limbic system seems to play an important role in emotion and motivated behavior such as feeding, fleeing from danger, fighting, and sex. The hippocampus plays an important role in the formation of memories whereas the amygdala is involved in emotional control and the formation of emotional memories.

C. The Cerebral Cortex: The Hub of Complex Thought

The cerebral cortex is the thin outer covering of the brain and is involved in our mental or information processing capacities. The cerebral cortex lies on top of two nearly symmetrical halves -- cerebral hemispheres. The two hemispheres differ in function. The cerebral hemispheres have many ridges, grooves or fissures. Each hemisphere is divided into four distinct lobes or regions. These lobes or regions correspond to the largest grooves or fissures.

The area of the brain nearest the face is the frontal lobe. It is bounded by a deep central fissure. Along this fissure is the motor cortex that is concerned with the control of bodily movement. Damage to this area causes only partial paralysis because other regions of the brain may take over some of the functions. This feature of the brain is called plasticity and is greater at a young age than after maturity.

The parietal lobe is behind the central fissure and contains the somatosensory cortex which deals with information from the skin senses. Damage to the left part of this area may lead to loss of ability to read, write, or locate parts of the body. Damage to the right part leads to lack of awareness of the left side of the body.

The occipital lobe is concerned primarily with vision. Damage to one area may cause individuals to be unable to see part of their visual field. With severe damage to this lobe, a person may report complete loss of vision but be able to respond to stimuli as if they were seen. Damage to the right hemisphere leads to loss of vision in the left visual field whereas damage to the left hemisphere leads to loss of vision in the right visual field.

The temporal lobe is concerned primarily with hearing. Damage to the left hemisphere leads to loss of ability to understand spoken words. Damage to the right side is related to inability to recognize sounds other than speech.

The rest of the cortex (about 75-80%) consists of the association cortex. It plays a role in coordination of sensory systems and complex cognitive activities such as thinking and memory.

- **Exploring Gender and Diversity: The Biological Basis of Gender Differences**

  The results of many studies indicate that there are small differences between men and women on certain cognitive tasks. For example, men and women score higher on some tests of verbal ability. Because many sex-related differences have narrowed over the past several decades, it appears that these differences may be related to environmental factors. However, men and women also appear to differ in aspects of their brain structure. For example, differences in brain size can be related to differences in performance. Research on the corpus callosum — the main link between the two cerebral hemispheres — supports this conclusion.

D. Language and the Cerebral Cortex

A great deal of research has been directed at understanding how and where the brain processes language. According to the Wernicke-Geschwind model, different areas of the cortex are involved in language. According to this model, areas such as the left frontal lobe, the left temporal lobe, and the primary visual cortex are involved in language.

Research supported for the model is mixed. Little disruption of language results from removal of areas viewed as crucial by this model. The examination of the brains of persons with language-related problems do not find damage in the brain areas predicted by the Wernicke-Geschwind model. On the other hand, studies using brain imaging techniques to scan the brains of persons with language-related problems have supported predictions from the model.

Questions:

2-8.   What are the structures and functions of the brain stem? _____

_____

_____

_____

2-9.   What are the roles of the hypothalamus, thalamus and limbic system? _____

_____

_____

_____

2-10.   List the parts of the cerebral cortex and their functions. _____

_____

_____

_____

_____

2-11.   What is the role of the cerebral cortex in language? _____

_____

_____

_____

IV. Lateralization of the Cerebral Cortex: Two Minds In One Body?

L.O. 2.7: Know how the hemispheres of the brain are specialized for different functions.

The brain shows a considerable degree of lateralization of function -- each hemisphere seems to be specialized for the performance of somewhat different tasks. In most persons, the left side of the brain specializes in verbal activities and analysis of information. For most of us, the right side is concerned with control of motor movements, synthesis, and the comprehension and communication of emotion. Evidence for hemisphere specialization has been obtained from studies of people with intact brains and from research with split-brain individuals.

A. Research With Intact (Noninjured) Persons

Research with noninjured persons has been conducted in order to find out about the functions of the two brain hemispheres. Studies which anesthetize one side of the brain indicate that left hemisphere has more highly developed verbal skills. Studies of brain activity indicate that activity in the left hemisphere increases when individuals work with numbers, but it increases in the right hemisphere when individuals work on perceptual tasks. When one is trying to decide an issue, activity is high in the left hemisphere. Once a decision is made, activity shifts to the right hemisphere, which seems to play a role in global, nonanalytic thought. Signs of emotional arousal are recognized fastest by the right hemisphere. The left hemisphere is more active during positive emotions. The right hemisphere is more active during negative emotions.

B. Research With Split-Brain Participants: Isolating the Two Hemispheres

Some research has examined individuals for whom the connection between the two sides of the brain has been severed in order to relieve some disorder, such as the symptoms of epilepsy. This connection is called the corpus callosum. Research on these individuals has provided evidence on lateralization of brain function. In these participants, stimuli in the left side of the visual field stimulate only the right hemisphere. Stimuli on the right side of the visual field stimulate only the left hemisphere. Stimuli presented to the left hemisphere of split-brain subjects can be named, suggesting that the left hemisphere controls speech. Stimuli presented to the right hemisphere can be pointed out but not named, suggesting that the right hemisphere has seen the stimulus but cannot describe it in words. Research has also shown that the two hemispheres differ in the way they encode information. The left hemisphere records details and also constructs an interpretation of the details. The construction process may lead to false or inaccurate memories. The right hemisphere appears to store a more direct representation of the details.

Recent research suggests that cooperation between the two sides of the brain is based on efficiency. The brain appears to delegate its resources between the two hemispheres. These ideas form the basis of the multiple resource theory. Performance on cognitively difficult tasks is enhanced by cooperation, whereas it is more efficient to carry out simple tasks within a single hemisphere. The brain also delegates its resources within each hemisphere. Therefore, if a person performs two tasks, and if the two tasks use the same cognitive resources, a decrease in performance is likely. These results are consistent with multiple resource theory.

Questions:

2-12.   What are the different roles of the two hemispheres of the cerebral cortex? _____

_____

_____

_____

2-13.   What does the research on lateralization with intact brain persons suggest about the function of the two hemispheres? _____

_____

_____

_____

2-14. What does the research on lateralization with split-brain persons suggest about the function of the two hemispheres? [Be sure you can describe the logic of these studies' procedures.] _____

_____

_____

_____

2-15. What factors determine the delegation of resources between the two hemispheres? _____

_____

_____

_____

V. The Endocrine System: Chemical Regulators of Bodily Processes

L.O. 2.8: Describe how the endocrine system affects our behavior and basic bodily functions.

L.O. 2.9: Know the basic principles of genetics.

L.O.2.10: Be able to discuss research strategies designed to disentangle genetic and environmental effects on behavior.

The hypothalamus plays a role in regulating the endocrine glands. The endocrine glands secrete hormones directly into the blood stream. These hormones exert far-reaching effects on bodily processes and behavior. Hormones that interact with and affect the nervous system are neurohormones. Their influence on neural activity is slower, but often more long-lasting, than the influence of neurotransmitters.

The endocrine glands are controlled by the hypothalamus through its influence on the pituitary gland (sometimes called the master gland). The pituitary is comprised of the posterior and the anterior pituitary. The posterior pituitary releases hormones that regulate reabsorption of water by the kidneys and, in females, the production and release of milk. The anterior pituitary releases hormones that regulate the activity of other endocrine glands. The hormones secreted influence sexual development, metabolism, excretion, and other bodily functions. For example, if the adrenal glands of genetic females produce too much adrenal androgen, they may be born with male-like sexual organs. This is called the congenital andrenogenital syndrome. When genetic males lack receptors for androgens, they develop the androgenic insensitivity syndrome. They develop females genitals but have no ovaries and other internal female organs. The major endocrine glands and their effects are shown in Table 2.2 in your text.

Questions:

2-16. How does the endocrine system regulate bodily processes? _____

_____

_____

_____

2-17.   What is the role of biology in the behavior of males and females? _____

_____

_____

_____

VI. Heredity and Behavior

A. Genetics: Some Basic Principles

Each cell contains a biological blueprint that enables it to perform its essential functions. This information is contained in chromosomes, which are composed of the substance DNA. Most cells contain 46 chromosomes, existing in pairs. Chromosomes also contain genes that contain thousands of segments of DNA. Genes, in conjunction with environmental forces, determine many aspects of our biological makeup.

Consequently, the closer the familial tie between individuals the more similar they tend to be physically. Identical or monozygotic twins are very similar in many respects. With monozygotic twins, a single fertilized egg splits in two and forms two children. In contrast, fraternal twins are not identical and are less similar. Fraternal twins grow from two different eggs fertilized by two different sperm.

Progress has been made in detecting genetic involvement in a variety of physical and mental disorders. Recently, researchers have identified a gene responsible for Huntington's Disease -- a rare, progressive neuromuscular disorder that usually appears after age 40. Most human trails, however, are determine by more than one gene. Further, the possession of a gene does not insure that a specific effect will occur. Genes influence behavior only indirectly through their influence on chemical reactions in the brain or other organs. Therefore, these reactions may depend on certain environmental influences. For example, phenylketonuria (PKU) is a genetically-based disorder in which persons lack an enzyme to break down a substance (phenylalanine) present in many foods, leading to a build-up of this substance in their bodies and to mental retardation, seizures, and hyperactivity. Children placed on a diet low in phenylalanine do not develop the symptoms of PKU.

*   **Beyond the Headlines: As Psychologists See It**

Biology Breathes New Life Into Old Controversy (Gay Newlyweds Seek Parity With Heterosexual Counterparts)

Many studies have been conducted to determine if sexual orientation is biologically determine. Several studies have shown neuroanatomical and neurochemical differences between homosexual and heterosexual persons. For example, the size of the suprachiasmatic nucleus (a brain area involved in hormonal functions) is different between homosexual and heterosexual men but it very similar between homosexual men and women. Further evidence for a biological basis for sexual orientation has been obtained by studying twins. In these studies, the highest percentage of homosexuality was found among identical twins. There is also evidence that brothers who are homosexual share a set of "genetic markers" on the X chromosome.

A number of psychologists believe that there is no evidence supporting a purely biology explanation of sexual preference. For example, even though they examined the same anatomical structure or neurochemical process, some studies have found differences between homosexuals and heterosexuals, whereas others have not. In addition, even when consistent differences were obtained, there is no definitive evidence that links these differences to a particular anatomical structure or neurochemical process. Due to this reasoning, many researchers are again considering the possibility that sexual orientation is a product of biological and environmental factors.

A recent theory termed the "exotic leads to the Erotic" theory incorporates both biological and environmental factors. According to this view, genes do not directly determine sexual preference. Rather they shape childhood temperaments which in turn alters children's preference for male-typical and female-typical activities. Over time, those who prefer sex-typical activities (gender-conforming children) will feel different from opposite-sex peers, whereas those that prefer sex-atypical activities (gender-nonconforming children) will feel different from same-sex peers. Furthermore, children presumably experience heightened levels of non-specific arousal in the presence of exotic peers — peers from whom they feel different. Consequently, gender conforming children will experience heightened levels of arousal in the presence of opposite-sex peers whereas gender nonconforming children will experience heightened levels of arousal in the presence of same-sex peers. Finally, because this heightened level of arousal is transformed into romantic or erotic attraction, gender conforming children experience erotic attraction toward different-sex peers whereas gender nonconforming children experience erotic attraction toward same-sex peers.

B. Disentangling Genetic and Environmental Effects: Research Strategies

The concern with the relative importance of genetic versus environmental factors in behavior is the nature-nurture controversy. A way to address this issue is to study identical or monozygotic twins.

Comparisons can be made between identical twins who are separated early in life and those who are raised in contrasting environments. Because these twins have identical genes, any differences between them have to be due to contrasting experiences (an environmental factor). Similarities in the face of contrasting environments reflect the contribution of genetics. Support for genetic influence comes from findings that identical twins reared in very different environments show remarkable similarities.

Questions:

2-18. What are the basic principles of genetics? _____

_____

_____

_____

2-19. What are the research findings concerning whether sexual orientation is biologically determined?

_____

_____

_____

2-20.   What are the research strategies employed to determine the relative importance of genetic and environmental factors in behavior? _____

_____

_____

_____

•   **Making Psychology Part of Your Life**

   Traumatic Brain Injury: Using Psychology To Enhance Quality of Life

   Injuries to the brain often produce major physical and psychological problems. Severe instances of head injury, called traumatic brain injury (TBI) involve damage due to extreme forces applied to the skull. Research in biopsychology has led to the establishment of effective rehabilitation programs that focus on creating flexible environments that help TBI victims deal with their disabilities. Two ingredients for success are: (1) arranging environments in a way that reduces frustration and, (2) beginning treatment early.

Question:

2-21.   Can you apply what you have learned to think of other factors that would be helpful in helping TBI victims? _____

_____

_____

_____

MAKING PSYCHOLOGY PART OF YOUR LIFE: Key Terms and Concepts

Knowing the important concepts and key terms contained in this chapter is a very important part of mastering the material. We have presented a sample of these concepts below. Define each concept and check your definition with that presented in the chapter. It will also be beneficial for you to think of an example of each concept. Whenever possible, use your own personal experience to provide an example of each term below.

2- 1. **Action Potential:** _____

2- 2. **Afferent Nerves:** _____

2- 3. **Agonist:** _____

2- 4. **Amygdala:** _____

2- 5. **Antagonist:** _____

2- 6. **Autonomic Nervous System:** _____

2- 7. **Axon:** _____

2- 8. **Axon Terminals:** _____

2- 9. **Biopsychology:** _____

2-10. **Central Nervous System:** _____

2-11. **Cerebellum:** _____

2-12. **Cerebral Cortex:** _____

2-13. **Chromosomes:** _____

2-14. **Corpus Callosum:** _____

2-15. **Dendrites:** _____

2-16.   **Efferent Nerves:** _____

2-17.   **Electroencephalography (EEG):** _____

2-18.   **Endocrine Glands:** _____

2-19.   **Frontal Lobe:** _____

2-20.   **Genes:** _____

2-21.   **Glial Cells:** _____

2-22.   **Graded Potential:** _____

2-23.   **Heredity:** _____

2-24.   **Hippocampus:** _____

2-25.   **Hormones:** _____

2-26.   **Huntington's Disease:** _____

2-27.   **Hypothalamus:** _____

2-28.   **Lateralization of Function:** _____

2-29.   **Limbic System:** _____

2-30.   **Magnetic Resonance Imaging:** _____

2-31.   **Medulla:** _____

2-32.   **Midbrain:** _____

2-33.   **Mitosis:** _____

2-34. **Nervous System:** _____

2-35. **Neurons:** _____

2-36. **Neurotransmitters (Transmitter Substances):** _____

2-37. **Nodes of Ranvier:** _____

2-38. **Occipital Lobe:** _____

2-39. **Parasympathetic Nervous System:** _____

2-40. **Parietal Lobe:** _____

2-41. **Peripheral Nervous System:** _____

2-42. **Phenylketonuria (PKU):** _____

2-43. **Pituitary Gland:** _____

2-44. **Pons:** _____

2-45. **Positron Emission Tomography (PET):** _____

2-46. **Reticular Activating System:** _____

2-47. **Somatic Nervous System:** _____

2-48. **SQUID:** _____

2-49. **Sympathetic Nervous System:** _____

2-50. **Synaptic Vesicles:** _____

2-51. **Synapse:** _____

2-52. **Temporal Lobe:** _____

2-53. **Thalamus:** _____

2-54. **Traumatic Brain Injury (TBI):** _____

2-55. **Wernicke-Geschwind Theory:** _____

YOUR NOTES:

CHALLENGE: Develop Your Critical Thinking Skills

<u>Seeing Two Sides of Issues</u>

One of the most important elements in critical thinking is the ability to see two sides of an issue. Clearly, one controversial argument concerns whether a person's sexual orientation is determined by genes or by environmental influences (see the Research Process, pp. 77-78). Can you apply critical thinking skills to this issue?

2-1.   The basic theme of this chapter is that behavior results from complex biological processes within our bodies. Thus, it makes sense that much of our behavior is determined by hereditary factors. At the same time, it is clear that experience and the environment plays a major role in determining behavior. Using what you have learned, provide an argument for how biological factors may play a role in determining sexual preference.

_____

_____

_____

_____

_____

2-2.   Provide an argument for how environmental factors would influence sexual preference. _____

_____

_____

_____

_____

_____

2- 3.   Can you develop an analysis that integrates both biological and environmental influences on the development of sexual preference? _____

_____

_____

_____

_____

_____

_____

CHALLENGE: Taking Psychology With You

<u>Diagnosis: Playing the Part of a Neuroscientist</u>

For this exercise, let's stretch a bit and engage in role-playing. Pretend that you are a neuroscientist and that you consult with various doctors when they're having problems with a diagnosis. In each of the following cases, a M.D. has come to you with a list of symptoms. Make a diagnosis of where you believe brain damage has occurred. This will help you clarify your understanding of brain structure and function. Check your answers with those at the end of this section.

2-1.   A fifty-year old woman has suffered a minor stroke. The stroke seems to have done little damage, but she seems to have lost interest in everything around her. She is losing weight rapidly and shows no interest in either food or drink.

Your diagnosis: _____

Note the basis for your diagnosis: _____

2-2.   A 12-year-old boy fell from a tree. His collar-bone is broken, but more disturbingly, he seems to have lost control over fine muscle movements, especially of the fingers.

Your diagnosis: _____

Note the basis for your diagnosis: _____

2-3.   After a car accident, a young woman reports that she seems to have a "hole" in her field of vision. She can't see objects in a particular location, but the rest of her vision seems normal.

Your diagnosis: _____

Note the basis for your diagnosis: _____

2-4.   After a stroke, an older gentleman seems to have lost his ability to understand spoken words, but he can recognize melodies.

Your diagnosis: _____

Note the basis for your diagnosis: _____

2-5.   A woman comes to the doctor concerned that her husband routinely forgets to shave the left side of his face. She is puzzled and is concerned that he may need a CAT Scan.

Your diagnosis: _____

Note the basis for your diagnosis: _____

Feedback Answers to Taking Psychology with You

2-1.   Damage to the lateral hypothalamus.

2-2.   Damage to the motor cortex. Given his age, your estimate of his recovery probability is high; plasticity is greater when brain damage occurs early in life.

2-3.   Damage to the occipital lobe of the cerebral cortex.

2-4.   Damage to the left hemisphere of the temporal lobe within the cerebral cortex.

2-5.   Possible lesion in the right hemisphere of the parietal lobe.

YOUR NOTES:

CHALLENGE: Review Your Comprehensive Knowledge

SAMPLE TEST QUESTIONS

Once you have worked through the preceding sections, you should be ready for a comprehensive self-test. You can check your answers with those at the end of this section. An additional practice test is given in the supplementary section at the end of this study guide.

2-1.   The three basic parts of the neurons are:
    a. vesicles, gray matter, and the synapse.
    b. telodendria, nodes of Ranvier, and synaptic terminals.
    c. cell body, axon, and dendrites.
    d. myelin sheath, cell body, and dendrites.

2-2.   The stage at which the neuron has a slightly negative charge is called the:
    a. dynamic state.   c. action potential.
    b. steady-state stage.   d. resting potential.

2-3.   Which of the following is not one of the ways that drugs affect synaptic transmission?
    a. inhibit re-uptake of dopamine   c. causes leakage of neurotransmitter
    b. acts as a false transmitter   d. none of the above

2-4.   Drugs seem to affect our behavior and cognitive processes primarily by changing:
    a. thalamic structures.   c. the shape of the axons.
    b. synaptic transmission.   d. the number of axon terminals.

2-5.   Which of the following is not one of the functions of the spinal cord?
    a. regulates reflexes
    b. conducts information from receptors to the brain
    c. conducts information from the brain to the muscles
    d. connects the central nervous system to the involuntary muscles

2-6.   The part of the peripheral system that connects the central nervous system to the voluntary muscles is the _____ system.
    a. central   c. parasympathetic
    b. sympathetic   d. somatic

2-7.   A procedure for measuring the electrical activity of the entire brain is called:
    a. superconducting quantum interference device or SQUID.
    b. positron emission tomography or PET.
    c. high-tech snooper or HTS.
    d. electroencephalography or EEG.

2-8.   The part of the brain that is involved in regulating motor activity is:
    a. brain stem.   c. cerebellum.
    b. medulla.   d. pons.

2-9.   Primitive centers for vision and hearing are in the:
    a. brain stem.   c. cerebellum.
    b. midbrain.   d. pons.

2-10.   This part of the brain regulates the autonomic nervous system.
a. hypothalamus
b. thalamus
c. midbrain
d. medulla

2-11.   Damage to the motor cortex leads to:
a. complete paralysis.
b. partial paralysis and loss of control over fine movements.
c. loss of vision in the left visual field.
d. loss of the ability to read and write.

2-12.   The lobe concerned with vision is:
a. occipital.
b. temporal.
c. frontal.
d. parietal.

2-13.   The lobe concerned with hearing is:
a. occipital.
b. temporal.
c. frontal.
d. parietal.

2-14.   The following is not one of the areas involved in language processing, according to the Wernicke-Geschwind Model.
a. left frontal lobe
b. left temporal lobe
c. primary visual cortex
d. none of the above

2-15.   Research has found that during the making of a decision the _____ hemisphere is active; once the decision is made, the _____ hemisphere is active.
a. left, left
b. left, right
c. right, right
d. right, left

2-16.   Most cells contain _____ chromosomes.
a. 23
b. 46
c. 31
d. 43

2-17.   This structure connects the two sides of the brain.
a. temporal lobe
b. corpus callosum
c. limbic system
d. midbrain

2-18.   Animals will press a level over and over again to provide low level electrical stimulation to the
a. pons.
b. temporal lobe.
c. medial forebrain bundle.
d. occipital lobe.

2-19.   Men tend to score higher on _____ tests whereas women tend to score higher on certain _____ tests.
a. verbal ability, spatial ability
b. language lateralization, verbal ability
c. spatial ability, language lateralization
d. verbal ability, language lateralization

2-20.   Which statement is not true about genes?
a. They contain thousands of segments of DNA.
b. Most human traits are determined by more than one gene.
c. Genes always influence behavior directly.
d. There is evidence for genetic involvement in a variety of physical and mental disorders.

Answers and Feedback for Sample Test Questions:

2-1.   C   The three basic parts are the cell body, axon, and dendrites. (p. 45)

2-2.   D   When a neuron is at rest, there are more negatively charged particles inside than outside. The resulting negative charge is called the resting potential. (p. 46)

2-3.   D   All three are ways in which drugs can influence synaptic transmission. (p. 53)

2-4.   B   Drugs affect our feelings or behavior by altering the process of synaptic transmission. (p. 53-54)

2-5.   D   Answers A - C are functions of the spinal cord. Option D is not a function of the spinal cord. The autonomic nervous system, a part of the peripheral system, connects the central nervous system with involuntary muscles, glands, and internal organs. The spinal cord is a part of the central nervous system. (p. 55-56)

2-6.   D   The somatic nervous system is the part of the peripheral system that connects the central nervous system to voluntary muscles. (p. 56)

2-7.   D   EEG is the procedure for measuring the electrical activity of the entire brain. (p. 59)

2-8.   C   The cerebellum is involved in the regulation of motor activity. (p. 62)

2-9.   B   The midbrain contains primitive centers for vision and hearing. (p. 63)

2-10.   A   The hypothalamus regulates the autonomic nervous system. (p. 63)

2-11.   B   Damage to the motor cortex leads to partial paralysis because other regions of the brain may take over some of the functions. (p. 64)

2-12.   A   The occipital lobe is concerned primarily with vision. (p. 65)

2-13.   B   The temporal lobe is concerned primarily with hearing. (p. 66)

2-14.   D   According to the Wernicke-Geschwind model, the left frontal lobe, the left temporal lobe, and the primary visual cortex are among the parts of the brain involved in language. (p. 67)

2-15.   B   When a person is trying to decide an issue, activity is high in the left hemisphere. Once a decision is made, activity shifts to the right hemisphere. (p. 69)

2-16.   B   Most cells contain 46 chromosomes or 23 <u>pairs</u> of chromosomes. (p. 75)

2-17.   B   The corpus callosum connects the two sides of the brain. (p. 69)

2-18.   C   Animals will press a lever over and over again to stimulate the medial forebrain bundle which is located in the hypothalamus. (p. 55)

2-19.   B   Men tend to score higher on spatial ability tests; women tend to score higher on certain verbal ability tests. These gender differences have been related to differences in the size of regions in the corpus callosum. (p. 66)

2-20.   C   Genes influence behavior **indirectly** through their influence on chemical reactions in the brain or other organs. (p. 75-78)

GLOSSARY OF DIFFICULT WORDS AND EXPRESSIONS

These terms from your text and this study guide were identified by students as potentially hard to understand. We have defined these terms and expressions.

Term or expression	Definition
Compelling	convincing, persuasive, a good argument
Culprits	people who have done wrong; person who is responsible
Cumulative	add up; successive addition that increase a quantity
Cyclicity	regular and predictable patterns
Distraught	extremely upset, extremely annoyed
Dissipate	disappear; go away
Enhanced	improved, to make better
Fleeing	running or hurrying away from
Foresight	can see the future
Grooves	long indentions in a surface
Heightened activity	increased activity
Hollow	Scopped out
Immutable	will not change
Intricate	complex; complicated
Jittery	nervous, anxious
Lesions	wounds
Offset	balance, compensate for
Reared	raised
Ridges	raised areas
Secrete	release
Seizures	physical attacks
Shedding light	making it clearer, making it more understandable
Shedding of	getting rid of
Snoop	inquiring into matters
Source	starting point; the person or agent that began something
Sparked	be the immediate cause of

Term or expression	Definition
Stem (from)	come from
Striking	attention getting
Swings	forward, backward or curved move
"Take up the slack"	do extra work that someone else has not completed
Tenant	person who pays rent for a room
The onset	the beginning
Threshold	a level that must be attained for an activity or process to start or occur
"Tomboy"	girl who likes rough noisy games and play
Triggered	started; caused to happen

CHAPTER 3
SENSATION AND PERCEPTION:
MAKING CONTACT WITH THE WORLD AROUND US

INTEGRATED CHAPTER OUTLINE: Survey and Question

This section presents the major topics and ideas from the chapter. Use it as a tool for seeing how the components of the chapter fit together. At the end of each major topic, we have asked you a question that relates to the major learning objectives. If you can answer these questions, you have taken a major step toward mastering this material.

I. Sensation: The Raw Materials of Understanding

> **L.O. 3.1:** Understand why sensory thresholds and sensory adaptation are important for understanding the nature of sensation and perception.

Psychological research has found that we do not know or understand the external world in a simple, automatic way. The topic of sensation is concerned with the information brought to us by our senses. Perception refers to the process through which we interpret and organize information.

Sensory receptors are cells that convert physical energy into signals our nervous system can understand. Our experience is a product of transduction. A process in which the physical properties of stimuli are converted into neural signals that are transmitted to our brain via specialized sensory nerves.

A. Sensory Thresholds: How Much Stimulation Is Enough?

Sensory receptors code information. The task of changing the many forms of energy in the world to signals for our nervous system is called transduction. When we are deprived of all sensory input we experience sensory deprivation and our bodies often produce hallucinations to fill in the void. To determine the level of sensitivity in each sensory system, psychologists use psychophysical methods. The amount of physical stimulation necessary to experience a sensation is called the absolute threshold. For most aspects of sensation, this threshold is quite low. These thresholds have been explored by using the method of constant stimuli. Since our sensitivity varies from moment to moment, the absolute threshold is usually defined as the magnitude of physical energy we can detect 50 percent of the time.

Several factors complicate the determination of absolute thresholds. Aspects of our bodily functions are constantly changing in order to maintain our body's internal environment at an optimal level -- a state termed homeostasis. Other factors include our level of motivation and the rewards and costs related to the detection process. These last factors are taken into consideration by signal detection theory.

Difference thresholds refer to the amount of change required to produce a just noticeable difference (JND) in sensation. The ratio of the JND to a stimulus of a given intensity is a constant value termed Weber's constant.

Subliminal perception has been a source of controversy. Are we affected by stimuli that are outside our awareness? Research has explored this issue. In one study, subjects were not aware of stimuli; nevertheless, they responded as if they were. The results of several studies have indicated that subliminal messages in self-help materials do not improve performance. Rather, improvement appears to be related to other factors, such as motivation and expectations.

B.   Sensory Adaptation: "It Feels Great Once You Get Used To It!"

Sensory adaptation refers to the fact that sensitivity to an unchanging stimulus declines over time. This can be beneficial because it allows us not to be distracted by the many sensations we constantly experience. However, it can be detrimental in that we can become less sensitive to toxic stimuli, like smoke or harmful chemicals.

Questions:

3-1.   What is the difference between "sensation" and "perception." _____

_____

_____

_____

3-2.   How do researchers study sensory thresholds and what factors influence sensory thresholds?

_____

_____

_____

3-3.   What does research suggest about subliminal perception? _____

_____

_____

_____

3-4.   What is the definition and function of sensory adaptation? _____

_____

_____

_____

II.   Vision

L.O. 3.2:   Describe the basic structures and processes involved in vision.

A.   The Eye: Its Basic Structure

Light passes through the cornea and enters the eye through the pupil. The size of the pupil is controlled by the iris. Next, the light rays pass through the lens which allows us to focus on objects at various distances. The sensory receptors are found in the retina at the back of the eye. Cones are the light receptors that function best in bright light. They are involved in color vision and our ability to notice fine detail. Rods are light receptors that are most important under low levels of illumination. Information is carried from the rods and cones to the brain by the optic nerve. Once stimulated, the rods and cones transmit neural information to other neurons called bipolar cells. A blind spot exists in our visual field at this place in the eye because there are no receptors.

B.   Light: The Physical Stimulus For Vision

Visible light is only a small part of the entire electromagnetic spectrum. The distance between successive peaks and valleys of light energy is wavelength. This is related to perception of hue or color. The amount of energy or intensity of light is related to brightness. The fewer the number of wavelengths mixed together, the more saturated a color appears.

C.   Basic Functions of the Visual System: Acuity, Dark Adaptation and Eye Movements

The ability to see fine details is acuity. Our ability to discriminate different objects when they are stationary is called static visual acuity. Dynamic visual acuity is our ability to resolve detail when objects (or us) are moving. A recognition acuity test (like the eye chart test at a doctor's office) is a way of measuring static visual acuity. Our ability to discriminate objects decreases as angular velocity increases. Angular velocity refers to the speed at which an object's image moves across the retina.

If your eyeball is too long, you may suffer from near-sightedness. You see near objects clearly but distant objects appear blurry. If your eyeball is too short, you may suffer from far-sightedness and you cannot see near objects clearly.

The increase in sensitivity that occurs when we move from brightly to dimly lit environments is called dark adaptation. During the adaptation process the cones reach their peak sensitivity in about five minutes. The rods begin to adapt in about ten minutes.

Eye movement is another important aspect of visual acuity. There are two types: (1) version movements occur when the eyes move together in the same direction, (2) vergence movements occur when our eyes converge or diverge. Vergence movements influence our ability to perceive distance and depth. Three types of version movements are involuntary, saccadic and pursuit movement. Involuntary movements occur without conscious control. Eye movements that are characterized by the eye jumping from one fixation point to another are called saccadic movements. The movement that tracks moving objects is called pursuit movement.

D.   Color Vision

People who have some insensitivity to red-green and yellow-blue have color weakness. Those who see only varying shades of white, black and gray are color blind. The theory of color vision that suggests that there are three different types of cones (which are primarily sensitive to red, green, or blue) is the trichromatic theory. Research suggests that there are three different types of receptors in the retina, but they overlap in sensitivity to the three colors. This research supports the trichromatic theory.

This trichromatic theory has difficulty explaining the perception of the many different colors and negative afterimages. [Negative afterimages are the occurrence of complementary colors that occur after staring at a particular color.] These can be explained by opponent process theory. This theory proposes that there are six kinds of cells or neurons at levels above the retina. Two handle red and green, two deal with yellow and blue, and two handle black and white. For each pair, one cell is stimulated by one of the colors and inhibited by the other. A two-stage model is currently considered most accurate. According to this view, trichromatic coding occurs at the level of the cones and opponent processing occurs at higher neural levels.

E.   Vision and the Brain: Processing Visual Information

Research by Hubel and Wiesel has found that there are neurons in the visual system that respond only to stimuli possessing certain features. Cells that respond only to bars or lines in certain orientations are simple cells. Those that respond to moving stimuli are complex cells. Cells that respond to features such as length, width and shape are called hypercomplex. This research suggests that the visual system is highly selective and that these cells serve as the basis for complex visual abilities. Further, it suggests that the brain processes visual information hierarchically. Additional research supporting the idea that information is processed hierarchically comes from studying persons with visual disorders like blindsight and prosopagnosis. Prosopagnosis is a condition in which persons can no longer recognize faces but still retain relatively normal vision in other respects. Blindsight results from damage to the primary visual cortex. Persons with blindsight are able to respond to certain aspects of visual stimuli without being aware of the stimuli.

Questions:

3-5.   What is the basic structure of the eye and the properties of light? _____

_____

_____

_____

3-6.   How does the visual system work? [Include a discussion of acuity, dark adaptation, and eye movements.] _____

_____

_____

_____

3-7.   Compare and contrast the trichromatic theory and the opponent-process theory of color vision. What is the current thinking concerning these theories? _____

_____

_____

_____

3-8. How does the brain process visual information? [Be sure to include a discussion of feature detectors.] _____

_____

_____

_____

III. Hearing

L.O. 3.3:   Describe the basic structures and functions involved in auditory perception.

A.   The Ear: Its Basic Structure

The part of the ear that responds to sound waves is the eardrum. Its movement in response to sound waves causes tiny bones within the middle ear to vibrate. One of these three bones is attached to the oval window, which covers the cochlea (a portion of the inner ear containing the sensory receptors for sound). Movement of the fluid triggers nerve cells to send messages to the brain through the auditory nerve.

B.   Sound: The Physical Stimulus for Hearing

Sound waves consist of compressions and expansions of air. The faster these alternate, the higher the pitch. This speed of alternation or frequency is measured in hertz. The greater the amplitude or magnitude of these sound waves, the greater the loudness. The quality of sound is related to its timbre.

C.   Pitch Perception

Place theory and frequency theory help explain how we perceive pitch.

Place theory or traveling wave theory suggests that differences in pitch can be detected because sounds of different frequency cause different portions of the basilar membrane to vibrate. However, no portion of the basilar membrane is sensitive to low frequency sounds. In addition, place theory does not account for our ability to discriminate sounds that differ by as little as 1 or 2 Hz.

Frequency theory suggests that sounds of different pitch cause different rates of neural firing. Because neurons can only fire up to 1000 cycles per second or 1000Hz, the frequency theory includes the volley principle — the assumption that sounds above 1000Hz generate successive firings or volleys.

D.   Sound Localization

Several factors play a role in localization or our ability to detect the source of a given sound. Our head creates a sound shadow, a barrier that reduces the intensity of sound received by the ear on the side of the head opposite the source. It also increases the time it takes sound to travel to the shadowed ear. We have difficulty in determining the source of sound that is directly in front or behind us.

Questions:

3-9.   What is the basic structure of the ear? _____

_____

_____

_____

3-10.   What are the characteristics of sound? _____

_____

_____

_____

3-11.   What are the two theories of pitch perception? _____

_____

_____

_____

3-12.   How do we localize sound? _____

_____

_____

_____

IV.   Touch and Other Skin Senses

L.O. 3.4:   Describe the basic structures and processes involved in touch and the other skin senses.

There are several skin senses, including touch, warmth, cold and pain. These properties are not sensed by sensory receptors but by the total patterns of nerve impulses. Touch is perceived by stretching or pressure against the skin. Passive touch occurs when objects are placed against the skin. Active touch involves individuals bringing their body parts into contact with an object. We are most accurate in identifying objects through active touch, in part because of the feedback we receive from the movement of our body.

A.   Pain: Its Nature and Control

Pain originates in free nerve endings. Damage to the body releases chemical substances that stimulate these neurons. Pain sensitivity varies from one body region to another body region. Sharp and quick pain is carried by large myelinated sensory nerve fibers. Dull, throbbing pain is carried by small unmyelinated fibers that conduct impulses more slowly. These two receptors are the basis for the gate-control theory of pain perception. This theory proposes that neural mechanisms in the spinal cord can close and prevent pain signals from reaching the brain. Pain messages from the large fibers can activate these mechanisms or gates while those from the small ones cannot. Techniques such as acupuncture and ice packs may reduce pain by stimulating large nerve fibers and closing the spinal "gate."

Mechanisms in the brain can also affect pain perception by transmitting messages that open or close the spinal "gate." This may account for the influence of emotional states on pain perception. The brain may also produce endorphins which reduce pain perception. Changing our thoughts and feelings, as well as our overt responses before, during, and after painful episodes, can influence our perceptions of pain.

- **Exploring Gender and Diversity: Culture and the Perception of Pain**

   There are large cultural differences in the interpretation and expression of pain. These differences appear to be perceptual and not physical in nature. They aren't related to differences in pain thresholds; rather there are powerful effects of social learning on perception (e.g., some cultures teach the principle that pain should be suffered in silence) and exposure to harsh living or working conditions produce these cultural differences.

- **Research Methods: How Psychologists Study the Effects of Negative Thinking on Pain Perception**

   Cognitive processes play a significant role in pain perception. One important cognitive element is the extent to which we think negative thoughts, often termed "catastrophizing." Reducing this tendency has been shown to improve our ability to cope with pain. This has been shown in a study by Sullivan and his colleagues. They constructed the Pain Catastrophizing Scale (PCS), which measures such things as people's negative thoughts. Participants who scored high on this test (catastrophizers) reported more pain on the cold pressor task (a task that involves immersing one's hand in cold water) than non-catastrophizers. These results suggest that the PCS may be useful for predicting who will exhibit strong distress to medical procedures, such as chemotherapy.

Questions:

3-13. What is the nature of the skin senses? _____

_____

_____

_____

3-14. How does culture influence our perception of pain and how is pain perception studied? _____

_____

_____

_____

V.   Smell and Taste: The Chemical Senses

L.O. 3.5:   Describe the basic structures and processes involved in smell and taste.

A.   Smell and Taste: How They Operate

Smell is stimulated by molecules in the air that come into contact with receptor cells in the olfactory epithelium. To be smelled, substances must have molecular weights between 15 and 300. The stereochemical theory suggests that substances differ in smell because they have different molecular shapes. However, substances with nearly identical molecular structures often do not have identical smells. Receptors for taste are located in papillae on the tongue. These contain taste buds that have receptor cells responsible for taste sensations. There appear to be four basic tastes: sweet, salty, sour and bitter.

B.   Smell and Taste: Some Interesting Facts

Smell and taste have received less attention from researchers than vision and hearing. In this section, a few interesting facts are discussed. We are poor at identifying different odors. Although we may recognize a smell, we may not be able to name the odor in question -- the "tip-of-the-nose" phenomenon. However, our ability to remember specific odors is good. Although little evidence exists, some practitioners in a field called aromatherapy claim that fragrance can have positive therapeutic results. Fragrance has been shown to influence behavior. Pleasant fragrance that surrounded drivers combated drowsy driving.

Questions:

3-15. What are the basic principles and findings relating to the chemical senses -- smell and taste?

_____

_____

_____

3-16. What are the practical implications of our knowledge about the sense of smell? _____

_____

_____

_____

VI.   Kinesthesis and Vestibular Sense

L.O. 3.6:   Describe the basic structures and processes involved in our sense of balance and body movement.

Kinesthesia is the sense that gives us information about the location of our body parts with respect to each other. This sense allows us to perform movements. Kinesthetic information comes from many different sources: it comes from receptors in our joints, ligaments, and muscle fibers, as well as from our other senses. Our vestibular sense gives us information about body position in movement and acceleration -- factors that help maintain a sense of balance. The sensory organs for the vestibular sense are located in the inner ear. The two vestibular sacs provide information about the position of our head and body's axes with respect to the earth by tracking changes in linear movement (along a straight line). The three semi-circular canals provide information about rotational acceleration of the head and body along three principle axis. The vestibular system is designed to detect changes in motion.

Question:

3-17. What is the nature of the sensory systems involved in our sense of balance and body movement?

_____

_____

_____

VII.   Perception: Putting It All Together

L.O. 3.7:   Understand the processes and principles that underlie perception.

A.   Perception: The Focus of Our Attention

The process by which we select, organize and interpret information from our immediate surroundings is called perception. It is clear that we are not capable of absorbing all the available sensory information in our environment. We selectively attend to certain aspects of the environment and ignore other aspects. This process allows us to maximize information gained from the object of our attention, while reducing sensory interference from irrelevant stimuli. The cocktail party phenomenon illustrates that unattended information does have an influence on the focus of our attention. Our attention shifts, for example, when we hear our name mentioned by someone at a party even though we were not previously aware of the content of that person's conversation. Other characteristics of stimuli can cause our attention to shift; for example, features such as contrast, stimulus intensity, color, novelty, and sudden change attract our attention. Our attentional focus is also affected by higher-level cognitive processes such as expectancy and motivation. Attentional processes play an important role in our survival. Research on this topic has been applied to the development of effective warnings.

- **Beyond the Headlines: As Psychologists See It**

    WARNING (H - O - T Really Means $$$ When It Comes to Safety)

    Warnings inform people of potential hazards. To be effective they must be attention-getting, understandable, designed to overcome pre-existing beliefs and attitudes, and the potential benefits of complying with the warning must outweigh the cost of doing so. This information was important in deciding the recent law case against McDonald's. A woman was awarded $1.4 million for burns she suffered after spilling how coffee on herself. Supporters of the lawsuit argued that the printed warning message that was found on McDonald's cups was poorly designed and ineffective.

B.   Perception: Some Organizing Principles

The process by which we structure the input from our sensory receptors is called perceptual organization. The first psychologists to study this aspect of perception are known as Gestalt psychologists. They identified several principles of organization. In perception, we tend to divide the world into parts. Those that have definite shape and location in space are figure; and those that do not have definite shape are ground. This principle is called the figure-ground relationship.

The Gestaltists also pointed out a number of laws of grouping. The tendency to group similar objects together is the law of similarity. The tendency to perceive a space enclosed by a line as a simple, enclosed figure is the law of closure. When elements are grouped because they are close together, it shows the law of proximity.

Elements that are seen as going in a particular direction illustrate the law of good continuation. When elements are grouped because they occupy the same place within a plane, we see the law of common region. The tendency to perceive complex patterns in terms of simpler shapes reflects the law of simplicity. Whether these laws are innate or learned is still being debated.

C.   Constancies and Illusions: When Perception Succeeds -- and Fails

This section discusses two important perceptual phenomena: constancies and illusions. Size constancy refers to perceiving objects to be of similar size even though they are at different distances. This may be due to the fact that we take distance into account in determining size. This is the principle of size-distance invariance. When we determine size by comparison with an object whose size is known, we are using the principle of relative size.

The principle of shape constancy refers to the fact that we perceive an object as having a constant shape even when the image it casts on the retina changes. Brightness constancy is shown when we see objects as similarly bright under different lighting conditions. These and other perceptual consistencies refer to the fact that our perception of the world does not change as much as variations in the sensory information would lead us to expect.

Incorrect perceptions are known as illusions. They can be due to physical or cognitive processes. Illusions generally have multiple causes. Some illusions may be caused by the inappropriate application of the size constancy principle. This interpretation is a part of the theory of misapplied constancy. It has also been found that illusions are affected by learning. The moon illusion is an example of how size consistency can lead us astray in perceptions of shape or area. The Muller-Lyer illusion may be a result of learning. The Poggendorf illusion involves misperceptions of the positions of angled lines disappearing behind a solid figure. Therefore it's a shape illusion. Illusions are not limited to visual processes.

D.   Some Key Perceptual Processes: Pattern and Distance

Perception is a practical process that provides organisms with important information about what is in their environment. Pattern recognition is the process by which we identify what is in our environment. The template matching theory of pattern recognition suggests that we store exact representations of each pattern in memory. This theory does not account for our ability to recognize variations in visual patterns. The prototype matching theory overcomes this problem by assuming that abstract representations of stimuli are stored in memory. Prototypes are general patterns of stimuli. In either view, recognition depends upon a match between visual stimuli and stored representations.

Bottom-up theories propose that pattern recognition is built from the organization of simple perceptual abilities, such as feature detection. Perceptions are also determined by our expectations; this is the basis for top-down theories. Evidence suggests that both processes may play a role in pattern recognition. Bottom-up processes are often used in unfamiliar situations; top-down processes are often used in familiar situations.

Distance perception depends on cues that involve the use of only one eye (monocular) or both eyes (binocular). We will briefly review these. The larger the image on the retina, the larger and closer the object appears: size cue. The more parallel lines converge in the distance, the farther objects appear: linear perspective. Texture appears to be smoother as distance increases: texture gradient. Farther objects are seen less distinctly: atmospheric perspective. An object overlapping another is seen as closer: overlap or interposition. For objects below the horizon, lower ones are seen as closer. For those above the horizon, the higher ones are seen as closer. These are height cues or aerial perspectives. When we travel in a vehicle, objects far away appear to move in the same direction as the observer whereas close objects move in the opposite direction. This is called motion parallax. A binocular cue described by the inward movement of the eyes as objects come closer is called convergence. The differences between the images provided by the two eyes is retinal disparity or binocular parallax.

Questions:

3-18. What are the functions of selective attention processes? _____

_____

_____

_____

3-19. What are the ways in which Gestalt principles of perceptual organization help structure the input from sensory receptors? _____

_____

_____

_____

3-20. What are the major perceptual constancies and illusions? _____

_____

_____

_____

3-21. What are the various pattern recognition theories and what are the cues used to perceive depth and distance? _____

_____

_____

_____

VIII.   The Plasticity of Perception: To What Extent Is It Innate Or Learned?

L.O. 3.8:   Compare and contrast nativistic vs. learning perspectives on perception.

A.   Perception: Evidence That It's Innate

There is some controversy about whether perception is innate or learned. The innate position gains support from evidence that when sight is gained by individuals who were born blind, they can make sense of their visual world. Research with babies only a few hours or days old indicates that they do have a preference for color stimuli. This research supports the innate perspective on perception.

B.   Perception: Evidence That It's Learned

There is some evidence for the role of learning in perception. In one study, kittens were raised in darkness except for exposure to either horizontal or vertical stripes. Upon release from darkness, kittens tended to respond only to objects exposed in the same position as the stripes. These deficits were permanent. Recent evidence indicates that organisms may compensate for these deficits through enhanced abilities in other senses. One can conclude that both innate factors and experience are important in perception.

C.   Must We Try to Resolve the Nature -- Nurture Controversy?

Confronted with mixed evidence, most psychologists believe that perception is influenced by innate as well as learned factors. From this, Baron concludes that we do not need to resolve the nature-nurture issue, since it is clear both learning and biology play critical roles in perception.

Questions:

3-22. What evidence suggests that perception is innate? _____

_____

_____

_____

3-23. What evidence suggests that perception is learned? _____

_____

_____

_____

3-24. Why do most psychologists believe that both innate and experiential factors influence perception?

_____

_____

_____

IX.   Extrasensory Perception: Perception Without Sensation

L.O. 3.9:   Be able to discuss whether extrasensory perception is likely to exist.

Extrasensory perception (ESP) involves perception without sensation. Psi refers to unusual processes of information or energy transfer that are currently unexplained in terms of known physical or biological mechanisms. Those who study this are called parapsychologists. The ability to foretell the future is known as precognition. The ability to perceive events that do not directly stimulate the sense organs is clairvoyance. Direct transmission of thoughts from one person to another is telepathy. The ability to move objects by thought is psychokinesis. Psi has been difficult to reproduce reliably in the laboratory. These is no known physical basis for psi and much of the support for psi comes from persons who believe in its existence. The ganzfield procedure is a technique used to test for telepathic communication between a sender and a receiver. The sender is in a separate room and is asked to concentrate on a target. The "receiver" is then asked to rate several stimuli in terms of his/her imagery of what the sender transmitted. Research using this procedure is underway but most psychologists are skeptical that it will yield support of psi.

- **Making Psychology Part of Your Life: Listen While You Work: The Potential Benefits -- and Dangers -- of Stereo Headsets**

Listening to music has been found to improve performance on simple tasks -- at least for people who enjoyed the music. However, it impaired complex task performance. Stereo headsets can produce sounds intense enough to cause hearing loss. Evidence exists that the habitual use of headsets at high volume result in perceptual auditory threshold shifts and tinnitus-ringing of the ears, they increase the risk of permanent hearing loss. Be sure and keep the volume of your headset turned down; the hearing you save may be your own.

Questions:

3-25. What are the different types of extrasensory perception? _____

_____

_____

_____

3-26. What is the evidence for and against the existence of psi? _____

_____

_____

_____

3-27. What are the advantages and disadvantages associated with listening to music? _____

_____

_____

_____

MAKING PSYCHOLOGY PART OF YOUR LIFE: Key Terms and Concepts

Knowing the important concepts and key terms contained in this chapter is a very important part of mastering the material. We have presented a sample of these concepts below. Define each concept and check your definition with that presented in the chapter. It will also be beneficial for you to think of an example of each concept. Whenever possible, use your own personal experience to provide an example of each term below.

3-1.   **Absolute Threshold:** _____

       Example: _____

3-2.   **Acuity:** _____

       Example: _____

3-3.   **Binocular Cues:** _____

       Example: _____

3-4.   **Blindsight:** _____

3-5.   **Blind Spot:** _____

       Example: _____

3-6.   **Brightness:** _____

3-7.   **Brightness Constancy:** _____

       Example: _____

3-8.   **Cochlea:** _____

3-9.   **Complex Cells:** _____

3-10.   **Cones:** _____

3-11.   **Constancies:** _____

       Example: _____

3-12.   **Cornea:** _____

3-13.   **Dark Adaptation:** _____

Example: _____

3-14.   **Difference Threshold:** _____

Example: _____

3-15.   **Extrasensory Perception (ESP):** _____

3-16.   **Farsightedness:** _____

3-17.   **Feature Detectors:** _____

3-18.   **Figure-Ground Relationship:** _____

Example: _____

3-19.   **Fovea:** _____

3-20.   **Frequency Theory:** _____

3-21.   **Gate-Control Theory:** _____

3-22.   **Gestalt Psychologists:** _____

3-23.   **Hue:** _____

Example: _____

3-24.   **Hypercomplex Cells:** _____

3-25.   **Illusions:** _____

Example: _____

3-26.   **Iris:** _____

3-27.   **Just Noticeable Difference (jnd):** _____

Example: _____

3-28.   **Kinesthesia:** _____

3-29.   **Laws of Grouping:** _____

Example: _____

3-30.   **Lens:** _____

3-31.   **Localization:** _____

Example: _____

3-32.   **Monocular Cues:** _____

Example: _____

3-33.   **Nearsightedness:** _____

3-34.   **Negative Afterimage:** _____

Example: _____

3-35.   **Opponent Process Theory:** _____

3-36.   **Optic Nerve:** _____

3-37.   **Parapsychologists:** _____

3-38.   **Perception:** _____

Example: _____

3-39.   **Pinna:** _____

3-40.   **Pitch:** _____

3-41.   **Place Theory:** _____

3-42.   **Prosopagnosia:** _____

3-43.   **Prototypes:** _____

        Example: _____

3-44.   **Psi:** _____

        Example: _____

3-45.   **Pupil:** _____

3-46.   **Relative Size:** _____

        Example: _____

3-47.   **Retina:** _____

3-48.   **Rods:** _____

3-49.   **Saccadic Movement:** _____

3-50.   **Saturation:** _____

3-51.   **Sensation:** _____

        Example: _____

3-52.   **Sensory Adaptation:** _____

        Example: _____

3-53.   **Sensory Receptors:** _____

3-54.   **Shape Constancy:** _____

        Example: _____

3-55.   **Signal Detection Theory**: _____

3-56.   **Simple Cells**: _____

3-57.   **Size Constancy**: _____

          Example: _____

3-58.   **Subliminal Perception**: _____

3-59.   **Templates**: _____

3-60.   **Timbre**: _____

3-61.   **Transduction**: _____

          Example: _____

3-62.   **Trichromatic Theory**: _____

3-63.   **Vestibular Sacs**: _____

3-64.   **Wavelength**: _____

CHALLENGE: Develop Your Critical Thinking Skills

Imagining Possibilities

Critical thinking involves the ability to "play with ideas" and imagine possibilities. In this exercise, practice this skill and stretch your imagination. Imagine that a person who has been blind from birth suddenly can see. What will this person see? Will his visual world be the same as yours? As your text points out, this is an intriguing question that has often served as the basis for exploring the nature-nurture controversy. Explore this question for yourself and answer the following questions in light of what you've learned.

3-1.   Take the position that perception is innate. That is, that experience is unnecessary for the development of perception. What would the person be able to perceive if this is the case? _____

_____

_____

_____

_____

_____

_____

_____

_____

_____

3-2.   Take the position that visual experience is necessary for visual development. What would the person be able to perceive? _____

_____

_____

_____

_____

_____

_____

_____

_____

3-3.   What does the evidence suggest concerning this nature-nurture controversy? _____

_____

_____

_____

_____

_____

_____

_____

3-4.   Baron suggests that we need not resolve the "nature-nurture" controversy. Why does he take this position?
         What are your thoughts concerning this issue? _____

_____

_____

_____

_____

_____

_____

3-5.   Can you think of a way to integrate both innate and experiential factors in an analysis of how perceptual
         development occurs? _____

_____

_____

_____

_____

_____

CHALLENGE: Taking Psychology With You

<u>Everyday Sensation and Perception</u>

There are many ways in which the material in this chapter can be applied to your lives. Many dramatic examples could be provided. But the impact of the processes discussed in this chapter on our everyday behavior may be even more fascinating. Below, we present you with several situations that occur to all of us at one time or another. Practice using your knowledge of sensation and perception by analyzing these events. Check your answers with those presented at the end of this section.

3-1.   Normally, you sleep through the alarm clock and have to be dragged out of bed. But today, you have an important date and wake-up at the first buzz of your clock.

What happened? _____

_____

_____

_____

_____

3-2.   You notice even the slightest change in volume when the volume of your TV is low. But when the volume is high, changes in the sound are not as noticeable.

Why? _____

_____

_____

_____

_____

3-3.   Your little sister is happily coloring on the porch. Since you're babysitting, you'd like to let her play happily for as long as possible. But as the sun sets and the porch becomes darker, she begins to cry because she can't see the colors in the dim light.

Why? _____

_____

_____

_____

_____

3-4.   Sitting in the dentist chair, I'm acutely aware of the drill and feel the discomfort of the tooth-capping procedure. I start thinking about my recent trip to the beach and feel better.

Why? _____

_____

_____

_____

3-5.   At a party, you're having an interesting conversation with a friend. You're oblivious to everyone else around you until, suddenly, you hear someone mention your name. Now you turn your attention to this conversation.

What happened? _____

_____

_____

_____

3-6.   As you stand on the deck at night, you wonder at how huge the moon looks as it hangs above the horizon.

Why? _____

_____

_____

_____

_____

<u>Answers to Taking Psychology With You</u>

3-1.   According to signal detection theory, the costs and rewards associated with detecting stimuli affect our perceptions. The cost of oversleeping and missing an important event increased your detection of the clock.

3-2.   You're experiencing changes in difference thresholds. Our ability to detect differences in stimulus intensity depends on the magnitude of the initial stimulus. At low intensities, small changes are more noticeable then at louder intensities.

3-3.   As the porch light becomes dim, she has dark-adapted to the setting. In dim light, her rods are most effective. But rods do not register information about color. Therefore, she is frustrated because she can't see her crayons.

3-4.   Pain perception stems from both physical and psychological causes. I have used a form of cognitive-behavioral treatment to change my perception of pain by changing my thoughts.

3-5.   You've experienced what is often called "the cocktail party" phenomenon. Certain characteristics of stimuli often capture our attention. In addition, higher level cognitive processes determine what we attend to. Our name is meaningful to us; therefore, we focus attention on environmental stimuli that incorporate this meaningful stimulus.

3-6.   You're experiencing the moon illusion. When the moon is near the horizon, we can see it is farther away than trees and other objects. Such cues are lacking when the moon is overhead. This is an example of the influence of size constancy.

Now it's your turn to provide some examples of the everyday occurrences of perceptual phenomena. In the following section, write out an instance in which you have experienced each of these phenomenon.

3-1.   Figure-ground relationship: _____

_____

3-2.   Laws of grouping: _____

_____

3-3.   Size constancy: _____

_____

3-4.   Monocular cues in distance perception: _____

_____

3-5.   The influence of expectancies in shaping perception: _____

_____

CHALLENGE: Review Your Comprehensive Knowledge

SAMPLE TEST QUESTIONS

Once you have worked through the preceding sections, you should be ready for a comprehensive self-test. You can check your answers with those at the end of this section. An additional practice test is given in the supplementary section at the end of this study guide.

3-1.   The definition of perception involves:
  a. transduction.
  b. interpretation.
  c. simplicity.
  d. direct sensation.

3-2.   The definition of sensation involves:
  a. knowledge.
  b. interpretation.
  c. the senses.
  d. simplicity.

3-3.   For most aspects of sensation our threshold is:
  a. low.
  b. high.
  c. strong.
  d. weak.

3-4.   The absolute threshold is usually defined as the magnitude of physical energy one can detect _____ % of the time.
  a. 10
  b. 30
  c. 50
  d. 75

3-5.   These are most important under low levels of illumination.
  a. rods
  b. cones
  c. lens
  d. feature detectors

3-6.   The sensory receptors in the eye are found in the:
  a. pupil.
  b. lens.
  c. iris.
  d. retina.

3-7.   The distance between successive peaks and valleys of light energy are related to the perception of:
  a. saturation.
  b. brightness.
  c. hue.
  d. complexity.

3-8.   The theory of color vision that holds that there are six types of nerve cells which are stimulated by one type of stimulus and inhibited by another is:
  a. trichromatic theory.
  b. opponent process theory.
  c. complementary theory.
  d. saccadic theory.

3-9.   Fluid movement that stimulates hair cells in the ear occurs in the:
  a. oval.
  b. eardrum.
  c. auditory nerve.
  d. cochlea.

3-10. Which of the following theories suggests that sounds of different pitch cause different rates of neural firing?
  a. place theory
  b. frequency theory
  c. matching theory
  d. gate-control theory

3-11. The tendency to shift the focus of our attention toward meaningful, unattended information is known as the:
  a. risky-shift effect.
  b. cocktail party phenomenon.
  c. template-matching effect.
  d. prototype-matching phenomenon.

3-12. The size of the pupil is controlled by the:
    a. cornea.   c. rods.
    b. iris.   d. cones.

3-13. The figure-ground relationship is of interest to _____ psychologists.
    a. Gestalt   c. clinical
    b. behavioral   d. humanist

3-14. Basic ways in which we group items together perceptually are known as the:
    a. proximity principle.   c. closure laws.
    b. good continuation rule.   d. laws of grouping.

3-15. The ability to perceive stability in the face of change defines:
    a. perceptual illusions.   c. size-distance variances.
    b. perceptual constancies.   d. the Muller-Myer illusion.

3-16. Theories that propose that perceptions may be determined by our expectations are:
    a. prototype.   c. bottom-up.
    b. top-down.   d. feature.

3-17. The binocular cue derived from the inward movement of the eyes as objects come closer is:
    a. overlap.   c. parallel perspective.
    b. retinal disparity.   d. convergence.

3-18. Overt transmission of thoughts from one person to another is:
    a. telepathy.   c. precognition.
    b. clairvoyance.   d. psychokinesis.

3-19. Specific representations of stimuli stored in memory are called:
    a. features.   c. prototypes.
    b. binocular cues.   d. templates.

3-20. Which of the following theories takes into consideration that rewards and costs affect our ability to detect environmental stimulation?
    a. discrimination theory   c. Place Theory
    b. threshold analysis   d. signal detection theory

Answers and Feedback to Sample Test Questions:

3-1.   B   Perception refers to the process through which we interpret and organize information. (p. 84)

3-2.   C   Sensation is concerned with the information brought to us by our senses. (p. 84)

3-3.   A   For most aspects of sensation, our sensory thresholds are quite low, meaning that we are sensitive to relatively small amounts of sensory stimulation. (p. 85)

3-4.   C   Absolute thresholds are defined as the magnitude of physical energy we can detect 50% of the time. (p. 85)

3-5.   A   Rods are most effective with low levels of illumination. (p. 89)

3-6.   D   The retina contains our sensory receptors. (p. 89)

3-7.   C   The perception of hue or color is related to the distance between successive peaks and valleys (wavelengths) of light energy. (p. 91)

3-8.   B   Opponent process theory suggests that six kinds of cells above the retina play a role in color vision. Two handle red and green, two handle yellow and blue, and two handle black and white. For each pair, one is stimulated by one of the colors and inhibited by the other. (p. 94)

3-9.   D   Movement of the fluid in the cochlea cause hair cells to transmit messages to the brain through the auditory nerve. (p. 97)

3-10. B   Frequency theory suggests that sounds of different pitch cause different rates of neural firing. (p. 99)

3-11. B   The cocktail party phenomenon occurs when we shift the focus of our attention toward meaningful unattended information, such as when we hear someone say our name at a party. (p. 111)

3-12. B   The iris controls the size of the pupil. (p. 89)

3-13. A   Gestalt psychologists are interested in the laws of perceptual organization, such as figure-ground relationships. (p. 112-114)

3-14. D   Laws of grouping refer to the basic ways we perceptually group stimuli. (p. 114)

3-15. B   The ability to perceive stability in the face of change is referred to as perceptual constancy. (p. 115)

3-16. B   Top-down theories describe the role that cognitive factors such as expectancies, plays in perception. (p. 120)

3-17. D   Binocular (two-eye) cues are used for distance-perception. In order to see close objects, our eyes turn inward, toward one another. The greater the movement, the closer the objects. This is called convergence. (p. 121)

3-18. A   Telepathy refers to direct transmission of thoughts from one person to another. (p. 124)

3-19. D   Templates are specific representations of stimuli stored in memory. Template matching is one way of understanding pattern recognition. (p. 119)

3-20. D   Signal detection theory considers how rewards and costs affect perception. (p. 86)

GLOSSARY OF DIFFICULT WORDS AND EXPRESSIONS

These terms from your text and this study guide were identified by students as potentially hard to understand. We have defined these terms and expressions.

Term or expression	Definition
Acuity	ability to see fine details
Adage	old saying
Ailments	illness, affliction, disorder
Amiss	missing, out of place
Aversive	unpleasant, negative
Babble	meaningless talk, unable to be understood
Bassinet	type of cradle for a baby
Cast an image	to project a picture
Clamor of	loud noise
Coaxed down a path of	persuaded to take a particular stance or direction
Converge	to move toward each other
Dangle	to hang
Distress	strong feelings of discomfort or pain
Ellipse	a flattened circle
Embedded	implanted, inside
Faint spot	area in which details are difficult to see
Feats	accomplishments, deeds, achievements
Foretell	know something before it has happened
Frowning	expression to show displeasure
Fuss	bother, commotion
Gauze pad	A sterile bandage used to protect open wounds
Gaze	to look at something intensively
Goggles	glasses worn to protect eyes
Gossip	rumors
Grittiness	grainy
Hoax	trick or prank

Term or expression	Definition
Hoisted	lifted; raised
Hue	color
Immersion	putting an object into a liquid such as water
Lead us astray	to lead to believe something that is not true
Lukewarm	barely warm
Misapplied	related to something in an inappropriate way
Murky	obscure; muddy; hard to see through
Pervasive	to spread through every part of; widespread
Porpoises	sea animal resembling a dolphin
Riveted	to focus attention on something
Saturated	a very pure color; undiluted by white
Sever	to cut, to terminate, to break
Smattering	to scatter a small quantity
Snipped	to cut
Stoic	dispassionate, detached, brave
Swirl	to move something in circles
"There's no sense arguing over spilled milk"	it is useless to worry about past mistakes
Thrive	to succeed, to do well
Throbbing	pulsating
Transduce	to change
Trigger	to cause, to be responsible for something
Wintry	characteristic of a winter season

CHAPTER 4
STATES OF CONSCIOUSNESS

INTEGRATED CHAPTER OUTLINE: Survey and Question

This section presents the major topics and ideas from the chapter. Use it as a tool for seeing how the components of the chapter fit together. At the end of each major topic, we have asked you a question that relates to the major learning objectives. If you can answer these questions, you have taken a major step toward mastering this material.

I.   Biological Rhythms: Tides of Life and Conscious Experience

L.O. 4-1.   Describe the basic nature and mechanisms of circadian rhythms.

L.O. 4-2.   Be able to discuss individual differences and disturbances in circadian rhythms.

L.O. 4-3.   Know how psychologists study circadian rhythms.

Throughout a day, we are aware of ourselves and the world around us in different ways. These contrasting levels of awareness are examples of distinct states of consciousness. Although the study of consciousness is an important topic area, it was rejected by behavioral psychologists. It has now reemerged as an important topic of study.

We are most alert and energetic at certain times of the day. These regular fluctuations in our bodily processes (and consciousness) over time are called biological rhythms. These fluctuations can take place over different periods of time. If they occur over the course of a single day, they are termed circadian rhythms. Some biological rhythms can occur over longer periods of time.

A.   Circadian Rhythms: Their Basic Nature

Many bodily processes show daily, cyclical changes such as the production of various hormones. For many persons core body temperature and blood pressure are highest in the late afternoon or evening but there are individual differences in these patterns. Cyclic fluctuations influence performance on many tasks. Simple cognitive tasks and those requiring physical activity are performed best when cyclic fluctuations are at or near their peaks. The link between circadian rhythms and performance on cognitive tasks weakens as the complexity of the task increases.

B.   Circadian Rhythms: What Mechanism Underlies Them?

A biological clock is an internal biological mechanism that regulates various circadian rhythms. There is some evidence that a portion of the hypothalamus (suprachiasmatic nucleus) is sensitive to visual input and stimulates or inhibits activity in the pineal gland, which in turn secretes a hormone termed melatonin. Exposure to light decreases the secretion of melatonin. When the level of melatonin is high, people experience fatigue. Thus we feel alert and active during the day and tired at night. Research indicates that our natural day is about 25 hours, not 24 hours.

C.   Individual Differences in Circadian Rhythms: Are You a Morning Person or an Evening Person?

There are individual differences in circadian rhythms. For example, compared to "evening people" (owls), "morning people" (larks) seem to have a higher level of activation. Compared to evening people, morning people seem to have a higher body temperature early in the day and a lower body temperature at night. These differences in alertness and bodily states affect behavior. Morning persons do better in early morning classes and evening persons make better grades in classes scheduled late in the day.

D.   Disturbances in Circadian Rhythms: Jet Lag and Shift Work

There are circumstances in which circadian rhythms may get badly out of phase with our daily activities. Modern travel and shift work are examples of these circumstances.

When we travel across time zones, we often experience problems in adjusting. Our internal biological clock is set for one type of activity, while the external world calls for another type. Gradually, the adverse effect of this change goes away. Research suggests that we experience less disruption flying to a time zone where it is earlier vs. later. This may relate to a shift toward our natural "25 hour day."

Shift work is another example. In many cases, individuals must work at times when they normally sleep or must change their working schedule from week to week. These changes require constant resetting of our biological clock, which is draining.

•   **Research Methods: How Psychologists Study Circadian Rhythms -- and Disruptions in Them**

Psychologists often use the diary method to study circadian rhythms. This invokes asking participants to report on various aspects of their behavior over a period of several days, weeks, or months. Often, they are signaled by special devices, such as beepers, about when to report.

One such project involved studying nurses who worked on rotating shifts. At specific times, they provided information on their sleep, current moods, performance, stress, and mental alertness. Some of the results were that: (a) alertness, calmness, sleep quality, and mood and performance were worse on the first rest day following night shift work, and (b) adverse effects of night shift work seemed to summate overtime.

Research using these methods suggest that the best solution to swing shifts is to lengthen the amount of time people spend on each shift or to recruit employees who are willing to stay permanently on the night shift.

Questions:

4-1.   What are the different types of biological rhythms? _____

_____

_____

4-2.   Discuss the basic nature of circadian rhythms and the mechanism thought to underlie them.

_____

_____

_____

4-3.   Discuss the individual differences in circadian rhythms and the consequences of disturbances in their normal cycles. _____

_____

_____

_____

4-4.   How do psychologists study circadian rhythms and what has been learned about swing shifts using these methods? _____

_____

_____

_____

II.   Waking States of Consciousness

L.O. 4-4.   Compare and contrast controlled and automatic processes in attention.

L.O. 4-5.   Discuss the nature of daydreams and fantasies.

A.   Controlled and Automatic Processing: The Limits of Attention

Our attentional capacities are limited. How do we manage to perform two or more tasks at once? There appear to be two levels of attention. The initiation and performance of an activity with little conscious awareness is called automatic processing. Because this requires very little attentional capacity, several of these activities can occur at the same time. Activities that require more effort and conscious control are controlled processing. This type of processing does consume attentional capacity. Automatic processing is faster than controlled processing. Automatic processing, however, is less flexible than controlled processing. Automatic and controlled processing are not hard-and-fast categories; they represent ends of a continuum.

B.   Daydreams and Fantasies: Self-Induced Shifts in Consciousness

Daydreams are thoughts and images we generate internally. When these daydreams become so intense they affect our emotions, we call them fantasies. The frequency and intensity of daydreams varies greatly across persons. Some of the most common fantasy themes of daydreams include success or failure, aggression, sex, guilt, and problem-solving.

To a large extent, daydreams are induced by one's memories or imagination. But they can be influenced by external sources such as television. Developmental psychologists have concerns that TV may influence children's tendency to daydream and use their creative imagination. Research suggests that TV may have this effect. But research suggests that TV may actually increase daydreaming; it may provide them with the "raw materials" from which people construct their daydreams.

Many daydreams take the form of sexual fantasies. Men's erotic fantasies often contain more vivid images and anatomical detail; females report more submission fantasies. Such fantasies seem to function as a way to increase sexual pleasure.

Questions:

4-5.   How does automatic processing differ from controlled processing? _____

_____

_____

_____

4-6.   What are the major themes involved in daydreams and fantasies? _____

_____

_____

_____

4-7.   How are daydreams influenced by watching television? _____

_____

_____

_____

III.   Sleep: The Pause That Refreshes?

L.O. 4-6.   Understand the basic nature and functions of sleep.

L.O. 4-7.   Describe the sleep disorders.

L.O. 4-8.   Understand the nature of dreams.

A.   Sleep: How It Is Studied

Changes in brain activity during sleep can be measured by means of electroencephalograms or EEGs. Researchers also measure other changes in bodily functions such as respiration, muscle tone, heart rate, and blood pressure. These changes serve as a basic source of information about sleep.

B.   Sleep: Its Basic Nature

When we are awake, our EEGs contain many high frequency and low voltage beta waves. During a resting state, these are replaced by slower but higher voltage alpha waves. During this phase, neurons are firing individually. As we fall asleep, these alpha waves are replaced by even slower, higher voltage delta waves. This reflects the fact that increasing numbers of neurons are firing together.

Sleep onset is sudden and can be divided into four stages. These stages are associated with a slowing of bodily functions and increased frequency of delta waves. Transition from wakefulness to sleep occurs in Stage 1. Stage 2 is marked by sleep spindles -- short bursts of rapid, high-voltage brain waves. In Stages 3 and 4, we see the appearance of more slow, high-voltage delta waves and a further slowing of all major bodily functions. After about 90 minutes, we enter REM sleep. At this time, our brain resembles a wakeful but resting state. Delta waves disappear and low voltage activity returns. There are rapid eye movements and almost total muscular relaxation.

During REM sleep, individuals dream. REM sleep alternates with other stages throughout the period of sleep, with the length of REM sleep increasing toward morning. Sleep patterns change with age. Newborns sleep 16 hours or more a day; total sleep time decreases to 6 or less hours after age 50.

C.   Sleep: What Functions Does It Serve?

What benefits are gained by sleeping? One possibility is that sleep has a restorative function. Research does not offer strong support that sleep serves primarily a restorative function. A second possibility is that sleep serves a circadian function. That is, sleep is merely the neural mechanism which evolved to encourage various species to remain inactive during periods of the day. A third possibility is that only certain components of sleep, like REM, are essential. Results are mixed; most sleep researchers believe sleep serves both a restorative function and a circadian function.

D.   Sleep Disorders: No Rest for Some of the Weary

Problems of falling or staying asleep are known as insomnia. These problems increase with age. Complaints of insomnia may be related to the quality of sleep, rather than its length. Reading before sleeping, regular bedtimes, and relaxing activities aid sleep onset. Sleeping pills appear not to be helpful in the long run.

Sleepwalking or somnambulism occurs in about 25 percent of children. Another disorder of arousal is night terrors -- individuals awaken from deep sleep with intense arousal and fear without recollecting dreams. These occur primarily at stage 4. Nightmares occur during REM and involve dreams. A disturbance that involves stopping of breathing while sleeping is called apnea. Twitching while sleeping or while falling to sleep is called nocturnal myoclonus. Sleeping too much is hypersomnia. One form of hypersomnia in which individuals fall asleep in the midst of waking activities is called narcolepsy.

There is some evidence that there is a relationship between the regulation of body temperature and sleep; temperature declines as we fall asleep. Persons suffering from insomnia have relatively high body temperatures during sleep. Sleep disorders may also involve disturbances of the biological clock within the hypothalamus.

E.   Dreams: "Now Playing in Your Private Inner Theater"

All people dream; but all dreams are not remembered. Dreams run on "real time" and only seem to happen quickly. External events can be incorporated into dreams. Not being able to recall a dream does not mean you're trying to repress it. There is no experimental evidence that dreams foretell the future. And they do not necessarily express unconscious wishes (see below).

Several explanations for the occurrence of dreams have been offered. Freud believed dreams reflect suppressed thoughts, impulses, and wishes. There is little evidence supporting Freud's view. A physiological view argues that dreams are our subjective experience of random brain activity. According to this view, dreams are generated by spontaneous activity. A cognitive view assumes that neural activity forms the basis for the imagery and thought of dreams. However, this activity is not meaningless in that it reflects aspects of our memories and waking experiences.

Questions:

4-8.   How is sleep studied? _____

_____

_____

_____

4-9.   What is the basic nature of sleep? _____

_____

_____

_____

4-10.   What are the potential functions of sleep? _____

_____

_____

_____

4-11.   What are the various sleep disorders? _____

_____

_____

_____

4-12.   What are the basic facts about dreams? _____

_____

_____

_____

4-13. Compare and contrast the psychoanalytic, physiological, and cognitive viewpoints concerning dreams. _____

_____

_____

_____

IV. Hypnosis: Altered States of Consciousness or Social Role-Playing?

L.O. 4-9.   Know the techniques involved in hypnosis and be able to discuss contrasting views of its nature.

A.   Hypnosis: How It's Done and Who Is Susceptible To It

Hypnosis involves a condition in which individuals are highly susceptible to the suggestions of others. Standard hypnotic inductions usually involve suggestions by the hypnotist that the person being hypnotized feels relaxed, is getting sleepy, and is unable to keep his or her eyes open. A suggestion by the hypnotist that the person being hypnotized concentrate on a small object is also made.

About 15 percent of individuals are very susceptible to hypnosis; 10 percent are highly resistant to hypnosis. Individuals prone to fantasies are easily hypnotized. Those individuals who tend to become deeply involve in sensory or imaginative experiences tend to be high in hypnotic susceptibility. In addition, individuals who are dependent on others, those who seek direction, and those who expect to respond to hypnotic suggestions are also quite susceptible.

B.   Hypnosis: Contrasting Views About Its Nature

Systematic research has led to the formulation of two major theories about hypnosis. The social-cognitive (role-playing) view assumes that hypnotized persons are playing a social role in which they expect to lose control over their own behavior and be unable to resist suggestions. The neodissociation theory assumes that there is a split in consciousness. One part accepts suggestions from the hypnotist, while another part is a hidden observer. Of the two explanations, most psychologists believe that the social-cognitive view is more accurate. The results of recent studies suggest that hypnosis does not produce actual changes in memory or actual changes in perception. However, a recent study by Noble and McConkey suggests that hypnosis can, perhaps, produce actual changes in perception among some persons.

Questions:

4-14. How is hypnosis performed and is everyone susceptible to it? _____

_____

_____

_____

4-15. What are the two major views concerning the nature of hypnosis and what evidence supports these views? _____

_____

_____

_____

V. Consciousness-Altering Drugs: What They Are and What They Do

L.O. 4-10.   Know the basic concepts and psychological mechanisms underlying the effects of consciousness-altering drugs.

L.O. 4-11.   Discuss how cross-cultural comparisons give us insight into the effects of drugs and the nature of aggression.

L.O. 4-12.   Be able to discuss why the influence of drugs is not totally predictable.

A.   Consciousness-Altering Drugs: Some Basic Concepts

Drugs are chemical compounds that change the structure or function of biological systems. When drugs produce a change in consciousness, they are called consciousness-altering drugs. When taken on a regular basis, individuals often become dependent on their use. Physiological dependence occurs when the need is biological in nature. Psychological dependence occurs when individuals desire to continue using a drug even though there is not a physiological need. These two dependencies often occur together. Drug tolerance is a by-product of prolonged drug use. In some cases, use of one drug can increase tolerance for another drug. This is termed cross-tolerance.

B.   Psychological Mechanisms Underlying Drug Abuse: Contrasting Views

There are several views on the nature of drug abuse. According to the learning perspective, people take drugs because they expect that positive outcomes will be associated with drug use and/or they expect drug use to decrease negative outcomes. Anxiety reduction is an important cause of drug use from the psychodynamic approach. Drug use can be understood in terms of social factors from the social perspective. For example, some persons use alcohol as a tactic of impression management. From the cognitive perspective, drug use can be viewed as an automatic behavior which can be initiated by internal or external cues, even in the absence of strong urges to consume the drug.

C.   Consciousness-Altering Drugs: An Overview

There are four major categories of consciousness-altering drugs: depressants, stimulants, opiates, and hallucinogens.

Drugs that reduce the activity in the central nervous system are depressants. The most frequently used depressant is alcohol. One of the effects of alcohol is to lower our inhibitions. Alcohol may have its effects by acting on the cell membrane of neurons.

Sleeping pills and relaxants contain barbiturates, which are another type of depressant. These drugs reduce overall mental alertness. Barbiturates may reduce the release of excitatory transmitter substances at the synapses.

Drugs that increase arousal and feelings of energy are stimulants. Amphetamines and cocaine inhibit the re-uptake of transmitter substances at the synapse. They may produce a short period of pleasurable sensations followed by feelings of anxiety and depression. Continued use of cocaine can lead to psychological disorders. Caffeine and nicotine are also stimulants.

Heroin and morphine are called opiates. These produce dramatic slowing of bodily functions. They may produce very pleasurable sensations, but they are highly addictive, and withdrawal is painful. Opiates may cause the brain to stop producing endorphins. Therefore, individuals may loose their natural pain reducing mechanism.

LSD is an hallucinogen. These produce strong shifts in consciousness. For example, LSD may lead to a blending of sensory experiences known as synesthesia. They may also produce strong negative effects such as sorrow and fear. The effects are quite unpredictable. Marijuana produces a mild increase in arousal, a perceived increase in the intensity of various stimuli, a distortion in the sense of time, and a reduced ability to judge distances. Some persons report that it reduces inhibitions, increases sexual pleasures, and increases feelings of relaxation.

- **Exploring Gender and Diversity: Alcohol and Aggression -- A Cross-Cultural Comparison**

  Scientific evidence suggests that alcohol does increase aggression, especially in situations in which people are provoked. Cultural beliefs play a role in this perception. The beliefs and values of our culture act as a filter. People from countries that do believe in the link are more likely to attribute aggressive behavior to the impact of alcohol whereas people from countries that don't believe in the link between alcohol and aggression have weaker tendencies to see aggression resulting from alcohol-use.

- **Beyond the Headlines: As Psychologists See It -- "Drugged in Colombia"**

  Newspaper articles report the use of burundanga in Colombia -- a drug that is suppose to turn people into chemical slaves with no will of their own. A closer look finds that this drug is more similar to a motion sickness remedy. Baron points out that informal reports by people in newspapers are not scientific evidence and we should use caution when traveling but maintain a healthy skepticism to such sensational headlines.

D.   A Note on the Psychology of Drug Effects

The impact of a drug is strongly affected by the user's expectations concerning the drug's effect. Its impact may also depend upon the user's physical state, on the user's previous experiences with these substances, and whether the user is or is not taking other drugs.

Questions:

4-16.   What is the basic information relating to consciousness-altering drugs and their use? _____

_____

_____

_____

4-17. What are the different explanations for drug abuse? _____

_____

_____

_____

4-18. What are the characteristics of depressants, stimulants, opiates, and hallucinogens? _____

_____

_____

_____

4-19. What factors influence a drugs' impact? _____

_____

_____

_____

* **Making Psychology Part of Your Life:**

Meditation: A Technique for Changing Your Own Consciousness -- Perhaps in Beneficial Ways

Meditation is a procedure designed to alter consciousness and reduce awareness of the external world. It has been found to produce positive changes in biological processes, such as relaxation and reduced tension.

Baron provides you with several steps that are part of transcendental meditation procedure. We summarize these below:

1) Find a quiet, isolated location.
2) Choose an appropriate mantra.
3) Meditate -- gain practice in meditation.
4) Examine how you feel after meditating.
5) Continue meditating for 15-20 minutes each day or whenever you feel tense.

MAKING PSYCHOLOGY PART OF YOUR LIFE: Key Terms and Concepts

Knowing the important concepts and key terms contained in this chapter is a very important part of mastering the material. We have presented a sample of these concepts below. Define each concept and check your definition with that presented in the chapter. It will also be beneficial for you to think of an example of each concept. Whenever possible, use your own personal experience to provide an example of each term below.

4-1.   **Alpha Waves:** _____

4-2.   **Amphetamines:** _____

4-3.   **Apnea:** _____

4-4.   **Automatic Processing:** _____

       Example: _____

4-5.   **Barbiturates:** _____

4-6.   **Biological Rhythms:** _____

       Example: _____

4-7.   **Circadian Rhythms:** _____

4-8.   **Cocaine:** _____

4-9.   **Controlled Processing:** _____

       Example: _____

4-10.   **Crack:** _____

4-11.   **Cross-Tolerance:** _____

       Example: _____

4-12.   **Daydreams:** _____

       Example: _____

4-13.   **Delta Waves:** _____

4-14.   **Dependence:** _____

       Example: _____

4-15.   **Depressants:** _____

       Example: _____

4-16.   **Dreams:** _____

       Example: _____

4-17.   **Dreams of Absent-Minded Transgression:** _____

       Example: _____

4-18.   **Drugs:** _____

       Example: _____

4-19.   **Drug Abuse:** _____

4-20.   **Electroencephalogram (EEG):** _____

4-21.   **Fantasies:** _____

       Example: _____

4-22.   **Hallucinogens:** _____

4-23.   **Hallucinations:** _____

       Example: _____

4-24.   **Hypnosis:** _____

       Example: _____

4-25.   **Hypersomnias:** _____

   Example: _____

4-26.   **Insomnias:** _____

   Example: _____

4-27.   **LSD:** _____

   Example: _____

4-28.   **Meditation:** _____

4-29.   **Menstrual Cycle:** _____

4-30.   **Morning Person:** _____

4-31.   **Narcolepsy:** _____

   Example: _____

4-32.   **Neodissociation Theory of Hypnosis:** _____

4-33.   **Night Terrors:** _____

   Example: _____

4-34.   **Opiates:** _____

   Example: _____

4-35.   **Physiological Dependence:** _____

   Example: _____

4-36.   **Psychedelics:** _____

   Example: _____

4-37.   **Psychological Dependence:** _____

       Example: _____

4-38.   **REM Sleep:** _____

4-39.   **Seasonal Affective Disorder (SAD):** _____

       Example: _____

4-40.   **Self-Consciousness:** _____

       Example: _____

4-41.   **Sleep:** _____

4-42.   **Somnambulism:** _____

       Example: _____

4-43.   **States of Consciousness:** _____

       Example: _____

4-44.   **Stimulants:** _____

       Example: _____

4-45.   **Suprachiasmatic Nucleus:** _____

4-46.   **Tolerance:** _____

       Example: _____

CHALLENGE: Develop Your Critical Thinking Skills

Critical thinking is an important skill in our complex world. Practice expanding your critical thinking skills by completing these exercises which deal with hypnosis.

Thinking Critically About Hypnosis: Telling Fact From Fiction

4-1.   Baron discusses important research on the nature of hypnosis in your text. A major question concerns whether hypnosis produces actual changes in consciousness and other psychological processes. One implication of this issue concerns whether hypnosis can improve the memories of eyewitnesses to crimes or whether the extra details recalled by eyewitnesses under hypnosis reflects distortions in memory. What are the implications of these two contrasting possibilities for the use of hypnosis in legal proceedings?

_____

_____

_____

_____

_____

_____

_____

4-2.   Assume that we find that a hypnotized person can distinguish between hypnotist-induced suggestions and what they actually saw or heard. Compare and contrast what proponents of the social-cognitive and neodissociation theories of hypnosis would say about this finding.

_____

_____

_____

_____

_____

_____

_____

_____

CHALLENGE: Taking Psychology With You

Dream Diary

Dreams are fascinating. And, as your book points out, there are many contrasting views concerning their nature and function. The content of dreams often includes important life events and can also incorporate noises that occur during sleep (e.g., thunderstorms). Although some people do not remember their dreams, research suggests that everyone experiences REM sleep (the stage of sleep during which we dream). We are more likely to remember our dreams when we first wake up. A fun exercise is to keep a dream diary for a week or two. Copy our "Dream Diary" form and keep it near your bed at night. Record your dream immediately after waking...don't jump out of bed and into the shower as soon as you wake up. Rather, lie quietly for a few minutes and try to remember your dreams. After you've recorded several of your dreams, complete the "Dream Exercise" and explore what your dreams may tell you. You may want to discuss your experiences with classmates who have also completed this exercise.

DREAM DIARY

Date: _____

Have you had this dream before?   Yes   No

Was your dream in color?   Yes   No

How long do you think your dream lasted? _____

Describe your dream as clearly as possible. _____

_____

_____

_____

_____

_____

_____

_____

_____

_____

_____

Are you aware of any connection between your dream and anything that is currently happening in your life? If so, please discuss this connection below.

_____

_____

_____

_____

_____

_____

Are you aware of any connection between your dream and anything that was going on around you as you slept (e.g., telephone ringing, storms)? If so, please discuss this below.

_____

_____

_____

_____

_____

_____

List the persons that were in your dream. Label those whom you know personally, and describe those whom you do not know.

_____

_____

_____

_____

_____

_____

DREAM EXERCISE SUMMARY: What Did You Learn?

4-1.   Do you see any recurring themes in your dreams? If so, please explain.

_____

_____

_____

_____

_____

_____

4-2.   Can you relate any of your dreams or dream themes to any changes that you are currently attempting to make in your life? If so, please explain.

_____

_____

_____

_____

_____

_____

4-3.   If you answered "yes" to question #2, you may have experienced DAMIT dreams (dreams of absent-minded transgression in which people suddenly notice they have carelessly slipped into the habit they wish to break). Go back and review the feelings you noted about these dreams. Which view of dreams do these experiences best support? Discuss below.

_____

_____

_____

_____

_____

_____

4-4.   Relate your experiences in your dream diary to the basic facts about dreams discussed in your text. Do they fit?

_____

_____

_____

_____

_____

_____

4-5.   Discuss how the physiological view of dreams would interpret your experiences.

_____

_____

_____

_____

_____

_____

4-6.   How would the cognitive view interpret your experiences?

_____

_____

_____

_____

_____

_____

4-7.   How would the psychodynamic view interpret your experiences?

_____

_____

_____

_____

_____

4-8.   Discuss what you learned from keeping a dream diary.

_____

_____

_____

_____

_____

CHALLENGE: Review Your Comprehensive Knowledge

SAMPLE TEST QUESTIONS

Once you have worked through the preceding sections, you should be ready for a comprehensive self-test. You can check your answers with those at the end of this section. An additional practice test is given in the supplementary section at the end of this study guide.

4-1.   A disturbance that involves stopping of breathing while sleeping is:
  a.   hypersomnia.
  b.   apnea.
  c.   night terrors.
  d.   somnambulism.

4-2.   When we are awake our EEGs contain many high frequency and low voltage:
  a.   beta waves.
  b.   alpha waves.
  c.   delta waves.
  d.   zeta waves.

4-3.   Sleep can be divided into _____ stages.
  a.   two
  b.   three
  c.   four
  d.   five

4-4.   LSD has been associated with all but one of the following effects:
  a.   predictable effects.
  b.   synesthesia.
  c.   sorrow.
  d.   fear.

4-5.   Research examining sleep disorders suggests that there may be a relationship between these disorders and areas of the brain which regulate:
  a.   controlled processing.
  b.   body temperature.
  c.   automatic processing.
  d.   eating and drinking behavior.

4-6.   During which stage of sleep do dreams usually occur?
  a.   during REM sleep
  b.   during stage 1 sleep
  c.   during stage 3 sleep
  d.   during stage 4 sleep

4-7.   Individuals who are easily hypnotized tend to:
  a.   be old.
  b.   have negative attitudes about hypnotism.
  c.   be prone to fantasies.
  d.   be independent.

4-8.   The drugs that may stop the brain from producing endorphins are:
  a.   opiates.
  b.   amphetamines.
  c.   hallucinogens.
  d.   barbiturates.

4-9.   Research on automatic processing suggests that:
  a.   it requires a lot of attention.
  b.   it is more flexible than controlled processing.
  c.   it is slower than controlled processing.
  d.   it requires little conscious awareness.

4-10.   Which of the following is a sleep disorder characterized by uncontrollable periods of sleep during waking hours?
  a.   apnea
  b.   somnambulism
  c.   narcolepsy
  d.   hypersomnia

4-11. A hormone that seems to influence circadian rhythm is:
      a. adrenalin.   c. melatonin.
      b. endorphins.   d. testosterone.

4-12. Alcohol is classified as a(n):
      a. stimulant.   c. opiate.
      b. depressant.   d. hallucinogen.

4-13. Rapid, low amplitude brain waves that occur when individuals are in a relaxed state are called:
      a. beta waves.   c. REMs.
      b. delta waves.   d. alpha waves.

4-14. About _____ percent of individuals are very susceptible to hypnosis.
      a. 15   c. 50
      b. 40   d. 70

4-15. Which of the following is not a correct statement about stimulants?
      a. They increase arousal.   c. They inhibit the re-uptake of transmitter substances.
      b. Cocaine is a stimulant.   d. Alcohol is a stimulant.

4-16. Which of the following can influence the impact of a drug on its user?
      a. the user's expectations   c. drug interactions
      b. the user's physical state   d. all of the above

4-17. The view that people take drugs because the effects produced by the drugs are rewarding is:
      a. humanistic perspective.   c. biological perspective.
      b. psychodynamic perspective.   d. learning perspective.

4-18. Research on circadian rhythms uses the _____ method.
      a. EEG   c. cross-sectional
      b. diary   d. longitudinal

4-19. Which of the following involves the least use of attention capacity?
      a. controlled processing   c. hypnosis
      b. automatic processing   d. transcendental

4-20. If I continue to smoke cigarettes because not smoking causes me to become anxious and irritable, I am experiencing:
      a. psychological dependence.   c. cross-tolerance.
      b. physiological dependence.   d. tolerance.

Answers and Feedback to Sample Test Questions:

4-1.   B   Apnea is a sleep disorder in which people stop breathing while asleep. (p. 146)

4-2.   A   Beta waves are relatively high frequency (14 to 30 Hz) and have low voltage and they occur when we are awake. (p. 142)

4-3.   C   There are four stages of sleep. (p. 142)

4-4.   A   The effects of LSD are unpredictable. It may yield pleasant or unpleasant effects. (p. 162-163)

4-5.   B   In persons suffering from insomnia, internal mechanisms that regulate body temperature fail to operate normally, with the result that their body temperatures remain relatively high. (p. 146)

4-6.   A   Dreams occur during REM sleep. (p. 142)

4-7.   C   Persons who are highly susceptible to hypnosis tend to have vivid, frequent fantasies. (p. 151)

4-8.   A   Regular users of opiates may overload endorphine receptors within the brain. As a result, the brain ceases production of these substances. (p. 161)

4-9.   D   Automatic processing makes little demand upon our consciousness and attentional capacity. (p. 138)

4-10. C   Narcolepsy is a sleep disorder in which individuals are overcome with uncontrollable periods of sleep during waking hours. (p. 146)

4-11. C   Melatonin is the hormone that seems to influence circadian rhythms. (p. 133)

4-12. B   Alcohol is a depressant. (p. 159)

4-13. D   Alpha waves occur when people are awake, but relaxed, and are rapid, low-amplitude brain waves. (p. 142)

4-14. A   Individual differences in hypnosis exist; about 15% of adults are highly susceptible to hypnosis, while 10% are highly resistant. The rest are somewhere in between. (p. 150)

4-15. D   Alcohol is not a stimulant -- it is a depressant. (p. 159)

4-16. D   The user's expectations and physical state as well as other drugs the user takes influence the impact of a drug. (p. 164)

4-17. D   The learning perspective assumes that drug abuse is due to positive outcomes that are associated with drug use and/or that drug use decreases negative outcomes. (p. 157)

4-18. B   Researchers use the diary method to study circadian rhythms. (p. 137)

4-19. B   Automatic processing makes the least demands on attentional capacity. (p. 138-139)

4-20. B   Physiological dependence is characterized by strong urges to continue using a drug based on organic factors such as changes in metabolism. (p. 157)

GLOSSARY OF DIFFICULT WORDS AND EXPRESSIONS

These terms from your text and this study guide were identified by students as potentially hard to understand. We have defined these terms and expressions.

Term or expression	Definition
Automatic pilot	performing activities without awareness
Beeper	a device that makes a noise to signal a message
Blotting out	blocking out
Choke up	perform at a lower level than usual
Compress	get smaller, reduce in size
Cravings for	having a strong desire for
Cumulate	add together
Diligently	showing care and effort
Dimly lit	not bright
Early classes are a drag	difficult; requiring effort to go to
Enacting	performing, doing, carrying out
Feats	something difficult done well
Grooming	activities involved in looking and being clean
Hailed as	labeled as, identified as
Havoc	widespread damage; destruction
Jumbled	mixed-up, not at all clear
Mock robbery	fake robbery
Nature's way	natural process; how something would occur naturally
Onset	beginning, start
Out of sorts	irritable; in a bad mood
Perchance	to occur by accident or chance
Puzzling behavior	difficult to understand behavior
Raw material	basic ingredients
Realm of	boundaries of
Reemerged	started or began a second time
Recent decades	in the last 20-30 years

Term or expression	Definition
Safety-valve	a release; allowing pressure to escape
Self-induced	created or produced by oneself
Sexual fantasies	mental images that are sexually arousing to a person who has them
Slurred speech	confusing speech
"Shady" topic	a sinister or evil or socially unacceptable topic
Staggering	walk or move unsteadily
Submission	giving in to another's will
Summate	add together
Swing shift	working schedules in which people alternate between working day and night shifts
They...dull the senses	detract sensibility from the senses
Thoughts a thousand miles away	Not thinking about what you're doing; thinking about something else
Time slots	times available for a meeting
Tossing and turning	moving uneasily and continuously
Trance	condition-like sleep
Turmoil	based on disagreement, confusion
Twitch	sudden quick movement or a muscle

CHAPTER 5
LEARNING: HOW WE'RE CHANGED BY EXPERIENCE

INTEGRATED CHAPTER OUTLINE: Survey and Question

This section presents the major topics and ideas from the chapter. Use it as a tool for seeing how the components of the chapter fit together. At the end of each major topic, we have asked you a question that relates to the major learning objectives. If you can answer these questions, you have taken a major step toward mastering this material.

I. Classical Conditioning: Learning That Some Stimuli Signal Others

Any relatively permanent change in behavior or behavior potential produced by experience is called learning. This experience can be direct as well as indirect through observation.

Classical, operant and observational learning are three forms of learning. In classical conditioning, a stimulus can acquire the ability to elicit a response by pairing it with another stimulus that already elicits this response. This first section deals with this form of learning.

A. Pavlov's Early Work on Classical Conditioning: Does This Ring a Bell?

Classical conditioning was first studied by Pavlov, who studied salivation in dogs. He used an unconditioned stimulus (UCS), such as meat powder, that already elicited salivation. He preceded this by a neutral stimulus, such as a bell, that did not elicit salivation. After repeated pairing(s) or conditioning trials, the bell elicited salivation. The salivation produced by the bell was termed the conditioned response (CR) and the bell was termed the conditioned stimulus (CS). The salivation produced by the meat powder was termed the unconditioned response (UCR).

B. Classical Conditioning: Some Basic Principles

Acquisition is the process in which a conditioned stimulus gradually acquires the capacity to elicit a conditioned response. At first, conditioning proceeds rapidly. Later, it slows down and finally levels off.

Conditioning is determined by the number of conditioned-unconditioned stimulus pairings. It is also influenced by timing. Forward conditioning refers to situations in which the conditioned stimulus always precedes the unconditioned stimulus. Delayed and trace conditioning are examples of forward conditioning. The conditioned and unconditioned stimulus overlap to some degree in delayed but not in trace conditioning. Delayed conditioning is generally the most effective conditioning method, possibly because in delayed conditioning the conditioned stimulus predicts the occurrence of the unconditioned stimulus. In backward conditioning the unconditioned stimulus precedes the conditioned stimulus whereas in simultaneous conditioning they begin and end at the same time.

In addition to number and timing, conditioning also depends on the time interval between the conditioned and unconditioned stimulus, on the intensity of either the conditioned or unconditioned stimulus and on familiarity. The optimal time interval is .2 to 2 seconds in most situations. Conditioning improves as the intensity of either the conditioned or unconditioned stimulus increases. It is not, however, the absolute intensity that is important to the conditioning process. At least for the conditioned stimulus, it is the intensity of the CS relative to other background stimuli that is important for the process.

Finally, familiarity may influence conditioning by influencing the predictive power of a conditioned stimulus. The eventual decline and disappearance of a conditioned response in the absence of an unconditioned stimulus is known as extinction. The conditioned response to the conditioned stimulus can return very quickly if the CR is again paired with the conditioned stimulus. This is termed reconditioning. Once extinction occurs, the conditioned response to the conditioned stimulus can recover if there is a time delay between the last extinction trial and the presentation of the conditioned stimulus. This is called spontaneous recovery.

The tendency of stimuli that are similar to the conditioned stimulus to produce conditioned reactions is called stimulus generalization. This process allows us to apply what we have learned to other situations. Stimulus discrimination occurs when stimuli similar to the conditioned stimulus do not produce reactions that are similar to those produced by the conditioned stimulus.

C.   Classical Conditioning: The Neural Basis of Learning

The cerebellum appears to play a significant role in learning. First, the rate of neural firing of cells in the cerebellum predicts the onset of a conditioned response. Second, conditioned and unconditioned responses can be elicited by electrically stimulating specific pathways in the cerebellum. Third, previous learning can be severely disrupted when structures in the cerebellum of animals are surgically destroyed. Fourth, it is extremely difficult to establish conditioned responses in persons who have sustained damage to structures in their cerebellum.

D.   Classical Conditioning: Exceptions to the Rules

It appears that all responses or associations are not learned with equal ease. Studies by Garcia and Koelling found that learned aversion to taste was less easily learned by using shock as an unconditioned stimulus than a nausea producing injection. This work also contradicted the belief that conditioning can occur only if the time interval between the conditioned and unconditioned stimulus is very short.

Species differ in the relative ease with which various types of conditioning occur. These are called biological constraints. Most instances of conditioning require a conditioned stimulus-unconditioned stimulus interval of a few seconds. Conditioned taste aversions can occur with a conditioned-unconditioned stimulus interval of a few hours. They can also be acquired in a single CS-UCS pairing and are difficult to extinguish.

E.   Classical Conditioning: A Cognitive Perspective

The cognitive perspective suggests that classical conditioning is based on the development of an expectation that the conditioned stimulus will be followed by the unconditioned stimulus. This view is supported by the fact that conditioning will not occur if the pairing of the conditioned and unconditioned stimuli occurs in a random manner. Also, once a conditioned stimulus has been learned, it is difficult to condition another stimulus since it provides no new information. This phenomenon is known as blocking.

Stimulus generalization may also involve cognitive processes. According to one theory, memory and active comparison processes play an important role in stimulus generalization -- a phenomenon that was once thought to be automatic.

F.   Classical Conditioning: Turning Principles Into Action

Knowledge about classical conditioning has been put to practical use. One of the most practical uses has been in reducing phobias (strong fears of objects or events). When fear-provoking thoughts are not too painful to deal with, techniques like flooding have been used to reduce fear. In flooding, a person is forced to confront the fear-eliciting stimulus, without an avenue of escape. Systematic desensitization is a progressive technique designed to replace anxiety with a relaxation response. It has also been found to reduce fear. First, a person is asked to describe the least aversive situation; then when the person learns to relax in this situation and the person is asked to describe another situation which is the next most aversive. This sequence continues until the person learns to relax to the most aversive situation.

Conditioning may also be involved in instances of drug overdose. This is because for certain addictive drugs, the conditioned response can be just the opposite of the unconditioned response. For example, conditioned stimuli may signal the body to prepare for morphine by suppressing the response to it. When these conditioned stimuli are present, the influence of the drug may be less severe than when they are not present. Conditioning can exert powerful effects on the immune system. A CS was originally paired with a substance that was beneficial to the immune system. Subsequently, even though the CS was presented in the absence of the substance that benefited the immune system, the CS had a positive influence on the immune system.

- **Beyond the Headlines: As Psychologists See It**

  Psychotherapists Successfully Treats Stage Fright: Exotic New Cue, or Window Dressing on Tried and True Techniques:

  A recent newsprogram presented a psychotherapist who claimed to have an effective treatment for stage fright. Her approach involved having persons identify childhood incidents in which they felt humiliated and then asking them to relax while hanging on to the image. She then proceeds to ask them to act out such a scene. This technique appears to work. Baron points out that you should recognize this treatment resembles systematic desensitization and flooding.

Questions:

5-1.   How is learning defined and what are the three basic forms of learning? _____

_____

_____

_____

5-2.   What are the general characteristics of classical conditioning? _____

_____

_____

_____

5-3.   How did Pavlov research classical conditioning?_____

_____

_____

_____

5-4.   What are the basic components of the classical conditioning procedure? _____

_____

_____

_____

5-5.   What are the basic principles of classical conditioning? _____

_____

_____

_____

5-6.   How can a conditioned stimulus gradually cease to elicit a conditioned response through extinction
        and how can it regain this ability? _____

_____

_____

_____

5-7.   How does stimulus generalization differ from stimulus discrimination? _____

_____

_____

_____

5-8.   What is the neural basis of learning? _____

_____

_____

_____

5-9.   Why is the work of Garcia and his colleagues important for an understanding of classical
        conditioning? _____

_____

_____

_____

5-10.   What does the research on acquired taste aversion tell us about the traditional principles of classical
        conditioning? _____

_____

_____

5-11. How does the cognitive approach to classical conditioning differ from the more traditional approach? _____

_____

_____

_____

5-12. What are the practical implications of classical conditioning? _____

_____

_____

_____

II.   Operant Conditioning: Learning Based on Consequences

A.   The Nature of Operant Conditioning: Consequential Operations

In operant conditioning, organisms learn the relationships between certain behaviors and the consequences they produce. In this form of learning, the probability that a given response will occur changes depending upon the consequences that follow it. Stimuli that strengthen responses that precede them are positive reinforcers. Ones that are related to biological needs are primary reinforcers (e.g., food). Those objects or events that acquire their reinforcing quality by association with primary reinforcers are conditioned reinforcers (e.g., money). Those stimuli that strengthen responses related to escape or avoidance are negative reinforcers. When preferred activities reinforce behavior, the Premack Principle is in effect. This principle suggests that preferred activities can be used to reinforce less preferred activities.

In contrast to reinforcement, punishment refers to procedures that weaken or decrease the rate of behavior. Thus, positive and negative reinforcers increase the likelihood that a behavior will occur, but punishment decreases the likelihood that a behavior will occur. In positive punishment, behaviors are followed by aversive stimuli or punishers; in negative punishment, behavior is weakened by the loss of potential reinforcers.

B.   Operant Conditioning: Some Basic Principles

There are two primary differences between classical and operant conditioning: (1) in classical conditioning, organisms learn associations between stimuli whereas in operant conditioning, organisms learn associations between particular behaviors and the consequences that follow them; (2) in classical conditioning, responses performed are generally involuntary and are elicited by a specific UCS whereas in operant conditioning, responses are more voluntary and are emitted by organisms in a given environment. To understand operant conditioning, we need to find out why certain behaviors are emitted in the first place and what determines the frequency with which these behaviors are repeated. The following sections address these issues.

Shaping involves reinforcing subjects for behaviors that resemble the desired behavior. Gradually, greater and greater resemblance is required to receive reinforcement. Chaining usually begins by shaping the final response in a sequence of behaviors. It is used to teach complex sequences of behavior.

Operant conditioning is subject to biological constraints. For example, animals that have been shaped to do unusual behaviors may return to more natural behaviors. This is called instinctual drift.

Operant conditioning is influenced by perceptions of reward magnitude and reward delay. In most instances, operant conditioning proceeds faster with increments in reward magnitude and decrements in the delay of reinforcement.

Children will often choose smaller, immediate rewards over rewards of greater value that they most wait to receive. This is sometimes called impulsiveness. In one study children were more impulsive than adults. The effects of reward delay may be reduced when both reward options are relatively distant events. Persons who perform a smaller, less effortful task now (versus tackling a larger, more effortful task later) can be called procrastinators.

Rules for the delivery of reinforcements are called schedules. With a continuous reinforcement schedule (CRF), a reward is given after every response. When a reward is given only after a specific period of time, a fixed interval (FI) schedule is being used. This schedule leads to low rates of responding immediately after the presentation of the reward. When the time for reward is near, high rates of responding are observed. In variable-interval schedules (VI), the period of time which must elapse before the reward is presented varies around some average value. This leads to a fairly steady level of responding. If reinforcement is provided only after a number of responses have been performed, a fixed-ratio schedule (FR) is being used. This leads to a high rate of responding with a brief pause after each reinforcement.

With variable-ratio schedules, (VR) the reinforcement occurs after completion of a variable number of responses. This typically leads to consistently high response rates. Behaviors acquired by this schedule are usually very resistant to extinction. This is known as the partial reinforcement effect.

A person is exposed to a concurrent schedule of reinforcement when he/she is free to determine continuously between two or more responses, each having its own schedule of reinforcement. For example, you may now be deciding whether to continue to do homework or to go out with your friends. This describes a concurrent schedule of reinforcement. The matching law describes the situation in which a rat distributes its behavior in a way that maximizes the reinforcement received for its effort. The matching law has been applied to situations involving more than two alternatives — for example, doing homework and all other activities. This law has several important implications. First, behavior can be viewed as a choice. Second, it helps describe why an event is attractive at certain times, but not at others; for example, watching a relatively poor movie may be attractive when you have nothing else to do but not when you have better alternatives. Third, it may lead to more effective behavioral interventions.

Stimuli that have been associated with reinforcement come to serve as signals of whether operant behaviors should be performed. This is known as stimulus control. When an event signals the availability of rewards, the stimulus is called a discriminative stimulus.

C.   Operant Conditioning: A Cognitive Perspective

Cognitive factors seem to play a role in operant conditioning, as they do in classical conditioning. When subjects are exposed to situations in which it is not possible to attain reinforcement or avoid negative events, learned helplessness may occur. In these situations, people may become helpless and may not respond even when the situation changes so that some responses will work. Cognitive factors such as expectations may be involved in learned helplessness. Organisms may learn a general expectation of helplessness that transfers across situations. Research suggests that the onset of learned helplessness may depend upon perceptions of control. Persons who believe that they have no control may be more susceptible to learned helplessness than those who perceive that they have control. The trait neophobia refers to a tendency to withdraw from the unfamiliar. Scores on this trait measure predicted learned helplessness among rats.

Belief is another cognitive factor. Several studies have found that beliefs about schedules may be more influential than the actual schedules. Another cognitive factor is the evaluation of the reward. A positive contrast effect occurs when subjects are shifted from a small to a large reward. In this situation, there is an increase in performance to a level greater than that of subjects receiving the large reward only. Positive and negative contrast effects provide evidence that behavior is influenced not by the absolute level of obtained (or expected) reward but also by the relative level of reward. Thus, our evaluation of rewards is important. Finally, animals may form mental representations or cognitive maps that aid learning.

- **Research Methods: How Psychologists Study Applications of Operant Conditioning**

Applied behavior analysts use a four step process to study behavior. They <u>define</u> the target behaviors to be changed, develop procedures to <u>observe</u> the frequency of the behaviors under existing (or baseline) conditions. Next, they <u>intervene</u> to change the target behaviors and then they <u>test</u> the impact of their intervention. These four steps can be summarized by the acronym "DO IT."

D.   Applying Operant Conditioning: Can We Make a Difference?

There are many practical applications of operant conditioning. It is used in biofeedback — a technique in which equipment allows people to monitor and then alter bodily responses not usually available to them, such as blood pressure. It is used in computer assisted instruction, the workplace, and has been applied to solve socially significant problems such as crime, recycling, and safety promotion.

Questions:

5-13.   What is the basic nature of operant conditioning? _____

_____

_____

_____

5-14.   How do punishment and reinforcement differ? How does operant conditioning differ from classical conditioning? _____

_____

_____

_____

5-15.   What is the Premack Principle? _____

_____

_____

_____

5.16   What are the procedures involved in shaping and chaining? _____

_____

_____

_____

5.17.   How is delay of reinforcement involved in a description of impulsivity and procrastination? __

_____

_____

_____

5-18.   What is the connection between instinctual drift and biological constraints on learning? _____

_____

_____

_____

5-19.   What role does the size and timing of reinforcement play in operant or instrumental conditioning?

_____

_____

_____

5-20.   What are the different schedules of reinforcement and what are their defining characteristics?

_____

_____

_____

5-21.   What is stimulus control and why is it important? _____

_____

_____

_____

5-22. What are the cognitive factors that seem to be involved in operant conditioning? What findings support the belief that cognitive factors are involved in operant conditioning? _____

_____

_____

_____

_____

5-23. What is the matching law and why is it important? _____

_____

_____

_____

5-24. How has operant conditioning been applied to practical problems? _____

_____

_____

_____

III.   Observational Learning: Learning From the Behavior and Outcomes of Others

A.   Observational Learning: Some Basic Principles

Acquiring new forms of behavior or information from exposure to others (models) is observational learning. This can occur by merely watching others. According to Bandura, observational learning requires that we attend to models (other persons performing an activity). We tend to focus on attractive and knowledgeable models. We also need to remember what the models have done. It is necessary to transform the observations into behavior. This is affected by our physical abilities and our capacity to match our performance with that of the model. This is called the production process. The fourth factor is motivation. One must be motivated to reproduce the behavior.

B.   Observational Learning and Aggression

There is evidence that children and adults exposed to media violence tend to acquire aggressive behaviors. Media violence may also convey the message that violence is acceptable. It may also make violence less upsetting to an observer. The overall impact may contribute to an increased tendency among many persons to engage in acts of violence. However, not all findings support such conclusions. The effects of exposure to media violence, when they occur, seem to be modest in scope.

C.   Observational Learning: Some Interesting Applications

Observational learning among peers may contribute to the development of smoking. Peer influence, however, may also be used to promote more productive behaviors. For example, it has been used to teach spelling and other skills to mildly retarded children.

- **Exploring Gender and Diversity: Learning to Avoid "Culture-Shock"**

Observational learning has been used in an attempt to prepare employees for cross cultural assignments. One approach is the experiential approach; it involves behavioral modeling in which trainees first watch a model perform the correct behaviors. Then, they are put in a roleplay setting and act out the modeled behavior. Finally, they receive constructive feedback. The results of several studies indicate that the experiential approach as well as others based on observational learning seem effective in cross-cultural training.

- **Making Psychology Part of Your Life**

Getting in Shape: Applying Psychology to Get Fit and Stay Fit

You can use the basic principles you have learned in this chapter to establish your personal fitness program. Baron offers you five suggestions.

1)   Set your sights realistically.
2)   Take advantage of shaping techniques by setting yourself up for small wins.
3)   Specify and write down the amount and intensity of the exercise you will do -- and write it down.
4)   Use the principles of stimulus control to set the stage for healthy responses.
5)   Take advantage of observational learning by identifying people with desirable skills and traits.

Questions:

5-25.   What is observational learning and what are some instances of observational learning? _____

_____

_____

_____

5-26.   According to Bandura, what are the four factors that influence observational learning? _____

_____

_____

_____

5-27. What are the effects of exposure to media on aggression and other kinds of behavior? _____

_____

_____

_____

5-28. How has observational learning been used to prepare employees for cross-cultural assignments?

_____

_____

_____

5-29. Discuss how you might use these suggestions to develop your own fitness program. What other ideas can you apply from this chapter to your program? _____

_____

_____

_____

MAKING PSYCHOLOGY PART OF YOUR LIFE: Key Terms and Concepts

Knowing the important concepts and key terms contained in this chapter is a very important part of mastering the material. We have presented a sample of these concepts below. Define each concept and check your definition with that presented in the chapter. It will also be beneficial for you to think of an example of each concept. Use your own personal experience to provide an example of each term below.

5-1.   **Acquisition**: _____

        Example: _____

5-2.   **Applied Behavior Analysis**: _____

        Example: _____

5-3.   **Backward Conditioning**: _____

        Example: _____

5-4.   **Biofeedback**: _____

        Example: _____

5-5.   **Biological Constraints on Learning**: _____

        Example: _____

5-6.   **Chaining**: _____

        Example: _____

5-7.   **Classical Conditioning**: _____

        Example: _____

5-8.   **Concurrent Schedule of Reinforcement**: _____

        Example: _____

5-9.   **Conditioned Response (CR)**: _____

        Example: _____

5-10.   **Conditioned Stimulus (CS)**: _____

Example: _____

5-11.   **Conditioned Taste Aversion**: _____

Example: _____

5-12.   **Continuous Reinforcement Schedule**: _____

Example: _____

5-13.   **Delayed Conditioning**: _____

Example: _____

5-14.   **Discriminative Stimulus**: _____

Example: _____

5-15.   **Extinction**: _____

Example: _____

5-16.   **Fixed-Interval Schedule**: _____

Example: _____

5-17.   **Fixed-Ratio Schedule**: _____

Example: _____

5-18.   **Flooding**: _____

Example: _____

5-19.   **Learning**: _____

Example: _____

5-20.   **Negative Reinforcers**: _____

Example: _____

5-21. **Observational Learning**: _____

Example: _____

5-22. **Operant Conditioning**: _____

Example: _____

5-23. **Phobia**: _____

Example: _____

5-24. **Positive Reinforcers**: _____

Example: _____

5-25. **Premack Principle**: _____

Example: _____

5-26. **Punishment**: _____

Example: _____

5-27. **Reconditioning**: _____

Example: _____

5-28. **Reinforcement**: _____

Example: _____

5-29. **Schedules of Reinforcement**: _____

Example: _____

5-30. **Shaping**: _____

Example: _____

5-31. **Simultaneous Conditioning**: _____

Example: _____

5-32.   **Stimulus**: _____

      Example: _____

5-33.   **Spontaneous Recovery**: _____

      Example: _____

5-34.   **Stimulus Control**: _____

      Example: _____

5-35.   **Stimulus Discrimination**: _____

      Example: _____

5-36.   **Stimulus Generalization**: _____

      Example: _____

5-37.   **Trace Conditioning**: _____

      Example: _____

5-38.   **Unconditioned Response (UCR)**: _____

      Example: _____

5-39.   **Unconditioned Stimulus (UCS)**: _____

      Example: _____

5-40.   **Variable-Interval Schedule**: _____

      Example: _____

5-41.   **Variable-Ratio Schedule**: _____

      Example: _____

CHALLENGE: Develop Your Critical Thinking Skills

Critical thinking is an important skill in our complex world. Practice expanding your critical thinking skills by analyzing the following learning situations. Your task is to identify the principle of learning that may be involved. [Please refer to the answers at the end after you complete the exercise.]

5-1. Mary's boss yells at her every time she returns late from lunch. Now she is always prompt...she returns on time.

Learning principle: _____

5-2. After seeing the joy that his parents feel when they give to charity, Johnny is more likely to share his toys with his friends.

Learning principle: _____

5-3. A salesperson is paid a commission for every car sold.

What kind of reinforcement schedule is this? _____

5-4. A worker is paid a weekly salary.

What kind of reinforcement schedule is this? _____

5-5. Susan had a bad case of the stomach flu the first night she ate feta-cheese pizza. Now she feels nauseated every time she sees feta cheese.

What type of learning is involved? _____

5-6. Carol was attacked by a bluebird when she was very young and she became afraid of bluebirds. Now, she feels afraid when she sees any bird.

What type of learning is involved? _____

5-7. Referring to the situation above, assume that Carol is now 30 years old and she finds that she is no longer afraid of birds at all.

What principle of learning is involved here? _____

Answers to Critical Thinking Exercises

5-1. Negative reinforcement
       Explanation: The probability of the response "returning from lunch on time" is increased because it avoids the
       negative consequence of her "boss yelling."

5-2. Observational learning
       Explanation: Exposure to his parents' behavior, and the consequences that follow, has taught Johnny to engage
       in a conceptually similar kind of behavior (sharing with others).

5-3. Fixed-ratio schedule
       Explanation: Fixed-ratio schedules involve giving reinforcement after a set number of responses have been
       emitted. Paying this salesperson on the basis of the response of "selling a car" involves giving
       reinforcement based upon the emission of a response.

5-4. Fixed-interval schedule
       Explanation: Fixed-interval schedules involve giving reinforcement after a specific interval of time has passed.
       Paying a worker a salary at the end of a week fits this requirement.

5-5. Conditioned taste aversion
       Explanation: The internal cues (UCS) associated with the flu (e.g., nausea) occurred after Susan ate a novel food
       (the CS). This led to a strong CS-UCS pairing in a single trial.

5-6. Stimulus generalization
       Explanation: Stimulus generalization refers to the tendency for stimuli similar to a conditioned stimulus to elicit
       similar conditioned responses. Carol's initial fear of bluebirds was acquired by classical
       conditioning in her early years. Now, it has spread to all members of the bird category.

5-7. Extinction
       Explanation: Extinction is the process through which a conditioned stimulus gradually loses its ability to evoke
       conditioned responses when it is no longer followed by the unconditioned stimulus. If Carol has
       been in the presence of birds and has not been attacked for a number of years, she may lose her
       fear through this process.

CHALLENGE: Taking Psychology With You

Doing well on tests is great! But in order for this material to be really useful, you should be able to apply psychology to your life. Try applying what you've learned to the following situation:

Situation

Many of us have experienced both the pleasure and pain of getting a new puppy. The pleasure of a puppy includes the "tail-wagging" joy that greets you when your charge sees you walk in the door...and the fun of teaching him or her new tricks. And the "pain" often includes house-breaking. Imagine that you just got a new puppy...named Bruno. See if you can apply what you've learned to his training.

Application Question

5-1.   What operant conditioning principles might you use in his training? (Hint: How would you arrange rewards such as dog-treats, in order to increase the probability of desired responses?)

5-2.   Could you use observational learning to increase the speed of training? (Hint: Would it help if you had an older dog to teach him how to behave?)

5-3.   Do you think it might be more difficult to teach your new puppy new skills at 2 or 3 weeks of age vs. 10 to 12 weeks? Why or why not? (Hint: Refer to the research on biological constraints on learning.)

5-4.   Could you make use of classical conditioning procedures? (Hint: Are there some reflexes that you might build upon to elicit desirable responses?)

CHALLENGE: Review Your Comprehensive Knowledge

SAMPLE TEST QUESTIONS

Once you have worked through the preceding sections, you should be ready for a comprehensive self-test. You can check
your answers with those at the end of this section. An additional practice test is given in the supplementary section at the
end of this study guide.

5-1.   Classical conditioning was first examined by:
      a. Freud.   c. Pavlov.
      b. Watson.   d. Bandura.

5-2.   A stimulus that is paired with another stimulus that already elicits a response is called a(n):
      a. stimulus intensity.   c. conditioned stimulus.
      b. unconditioned stimulus.   d. evoking stimulus.

5-3.   When the unconditioned stimulus no longer follows the conditioned stimulus, _____ occurs.
      a. spontaneous recovery   c. classical conditioning
      b. extinction   d. operant conditioning

5-4.   The salivation produced by meat powder is termed a(n):
      a. learned response.   c. conditioned response.
      b. reinforcer.   d. unconditioned response.

5-5.   The _____ appears to play a significant role in learning.
      a. occipital lobe   c. brain stem
      b. medulla   d. cerebellum

5-6.   The therapeutic technique that involves the extinction of classically conditioned fears is called:
      a. operationalization.   c. flooding.
      b. defusing.   d. psychoanalysis.

5-7.   Stimuli that strengthen responses related to their escape and avoidance are:
      a. negative reinforcers.   c. primary reinforcers.
      b. positive reinforcers.   d. secondary reinforcers.

5-8.   The process of acquiring new behaviors or information from others is called _____ learning.
      a. conformity   c. empathy
      b. instigation   d. observational

5-9.   Negative reinforcement is to punishment as:
      a. response decrease is to response increase.   c. response decrease is to response decrease.
      b. response increase is to response decrease.   d. response increase is to response increase.

5-10.   Individuals who are paid on a piecework basis are operating on a _____ schedule.
      a. fixed-interval   c. variable-ratio
      b. variable-interval   d. fixed-ratio

5-11.   Behaviors acquired by the _____ schedule are the most resistant to extinction.
      a. fixed-interval   c. variable-interval
      b. fixed-ratio   d. variable-ratio

5-12.   Which of the following is false?
a. Conditioning improves as the intensity of either the conditioned or unconditioned stimulus increases.
b. All responses or associations are learned with equal ease.
c. Taste aversion research shows that classical conditioning can occur with a relatively long interval between the conditioned stimulus and the unconditioned stimulus.
d. Chaining usually begins by shaping the final response in a sequence of behaviors.

5-13.   Exposure to conditions in which it is not possible to attain reinforcement or avoid negative events may result in:
a. enhanced avoidance.   c. learned helplessness.
b. extinction of avoidance.   d. enhanced escape.

5-14.   The process by which organisms learn to respond to certain stimuli and to not respond to others is called:
a. stimulus generalization.   c. punishment.
b. flooding.   d. stimulus discrimination.

5-15.   Stimulus generalization:
a. is the tendency of stimuli dissimilar to the conditioned stimulus to produce conditioned responses.
b. is identical to stimulus discrimination.
c. is the tendency of stimuli similar to the conditioned stimulus to produce conditioned reactions.
d. occurs when the UCS and CS are no longer paired.

5-16.   The schedule of reinforcement that leads to low rates of responding immediately after the presentation of the reward but a high rate of responding when the time for reward is near is called:
a. fixed-ratio.   c. variable-ratio.
b. fixed-interval.   d. variable-interval.

5-17.   Animals that have been shaped to do unusual behavior may return to more natural behavior. This is called:
a. extinction.   c. instinctual drift.
b. acquisition.   d. shaping.

5-18.   The _____ _____ predicts that an organism will distribute behavior in a way that maximizes the reinforcement received for the amount of expended effort.
a. Premack Principle   c. Contrast Principle
b. Matching Law   d. Opponent Principle

5-19.   Conditioned taste aversions:
a. are easy to extinguish.
b. require many conditioned stimulus-unconditioned stimulus pairings.
c. are difficult to extinguish.
d. occur with animals, but not with people.

5-20.   A positive contrast effect occurs when subjects are shifted from a _____ to a _____ reward.
a. small, large   c. large, large
b. large, small   d. small, small

Answers and Feedback to Sample Test Questions:

5-1.   C Pavlov was the Russian psychologist who first examined classical conditioning. (p. 172)

5-2.   C A previously neutral stimulus that acquires the ability to evoke a response after its repeated pairing with another stimulus (unconditioned stimulus) that already elicits a response is called a conditioned stimulus. (p. 172)

5-3.   B Extinction (the gradual decline and disappearance of a conditioned response) occurs when the unconditioned stimulus no longer is paired with the conditioned stimulus. (p. 174-175)

5-4.   D Salivation is an example of a reflex or UCR that naturally occurs when meat powder is placed in the mouth. (p. 172)

5-5.   D The cerebellum appears to play this role. (p. 176)

5-6.   C Flooding is a therapeutic technique involving confronting the fear-eliciting stimulus. (p. 182)

5-7.   A Negative reinforcers strengthen responses that lead to the avoidance or escape of aversive stimuli. (p. 187)

5-8.   D Acquiring new behaviors by observing models is observational learning. (p. 202)

5-9.   B Negative reinforcers increase responses; punishment decreases response rates. (p. 186-187)

5-10.   D Piece-work involves being paid per unit produced and is an example of a fixed ratio schedule of reinforcement. (p. 191)

5-11.   D Variable-ratio schedules produce behaviors that are very resistant to extinction. (p. 192)

5-12.   B Acquisition of a conditioned response does not occur with equal ease for different stimuli. (p. 177)

5-13.   C Learned helplessness can occur when it is not possible to obtain reinforcement or avoid negative events. (p. 194-195)

5-14.   D Stimulus discrimination is the process by which organisms learn to respond to certain stimuli and not to respond to others. (p. 175)

5-15.   C The tendency of stimuli similar to the conditioned stimulus to produce conditioned responses is called stimulus generalization. (p. 175)

5-16.   B Fixed interval schedules lead to low rates of responding immediately after reward presentation and high rates just prior to reward. (p. 191)

5-17.   C The tendency for animals that have been trained to do unusual behaviors to return to more natural patterns of behavior is called instinctive drift. (p. 189)

5-18.   B The Matching Law makes this prediction. (p. 192)

5-19.   C Conditioned taste aversions are hard to extinguish. (p. 179)

5-20.   A Positive contrast effects occur when subjects are shifted from small to large rewards. (p. 196)

GLOSSARY OF DIFFICULT WORDS AND EXPRESSIONS

These terms from your text and this study guide were identified by students as potentially hard to understand. We have defined these terms and expressions.

Term or expression	Definition
A food pellet	a little bit of food
Antics	perform; relive
Antics	devices used to procure a desired response
Avenue of escape	a method of getting away from something
Begin to feel dreadful	start to be afraid
Bland foods	foods that have little taste
Blurts out	says something spontaneously
Contradicted	was opposed to; went against
Cozy	secure, relaxed
Cram for tests	study at the last minute
Decrements	decreases in something
Dingy	unclean
Forthcoming	something that will happen in the future
Frequency	how often something occurs
…has chewed you out	has verbally scolded you
Hectic	very busy
Humiliated	feeling ashamed or embarassed
Levels off	no further change occurs
Losing a bundle	losing a large amount
Media blitz	multiple reports on tv, news, and radio
Metronome	instrument that keep time with clicking noises
"Modest in scope"	something that doesn't have a very large effect
Noteworthy	worth remembering
Random	no pattern or plan
Stings	injury from a bee
Tackling	agreeing to perform; taking on a task

Term or expression	Definition
Tantrums	outburst of anger
The breed of the dog	the type of dog
Unsettling	disturbing
Urban slums	poor neighborhood in a big city
Uttered	spoke
"With equal ease"	as it is used here, this refers to the fact that all responses are not learned as easily or quickly

CHAPTER 6
MEMORY: OF THINGS REMEMBERED AND FORGOTTEN

INTEGRATED CHAPTER OUTLINE: Survey and Question

This section presents the major topics and ideas from the chapter. Use it as a tool for seeing how the components of the chapter fit together. At the end of each major topic, we have asked you a question that relates to the major learning objectives. If you can answer these questions, you have taken a major step toward mastering this material.

I. Human Memory: The Information-Processing Approach

L.O. 6.1: Be able to describe the information-processing approach to the study of human memory.

Today, memory is understood from an information processing perspective. This view uses the computer as a model to understand human memory. Like people, computers have temporary working memories (known as random access memory) and more permanent memory. Note, however, that although human memory and computer memory share similarities, they are definitely not identical. The way information is entered into memory is termed encoding. The way it is retained in memory is called storage. The procedure involved in locating and using information in memory is termed retrieval.

A. Human Memory: A Basic Model

According to the information-processing model of memory, memory consists of three different systems. The information from our senses is held by sensory memory. It can hold much information, but it retains information for a brief time. The part of memory that holds information we are currently using for a brief period is called short-term memory. The part of memory that holds large quantities of information for long periods of time is long-term memory.

Information moves from one system to another by means of active control processes. Information goes from sensory memory to short-term memory when we attend to it. It moves from short-term memory to long-term by means of elaborative rehearsal.

B. Types of Information In Memory

There are several types of information stored in memory. Our general abstract knowledge about the world is known as semantic memory. Our memory for the specific events we have experienced in our lives is known as episodic memory. Our knowledge of how to perform various tasks, such as driving a car, is known as procedural memory.

Questions:

6-1.   Why does the information-processing approach use the computer as a model for human memory?

_____

_____

_____

_____

6-2.   What are the basic components of the information-processing model of memory? _____

_____

_____

_____

6-3.   How does information move from one memory system to another? _____

_____

_____

_____

6-4.   What are the three types of information stored in memory? _____

_____

_____

_____

II.   Sensory Memory, Short-term Memory, and Long-term Memory: Our Basic Memory Systems

L.O. 6.2:   Know the functions of sensory memory.

L.O. 6.3:   Know the functions of short-term memory and be able to describe how it is studied.

L.O. 6.4:   Describe the nature of long-term memory.

L.O. 6.5:   Be able to describe the recent research on the effects of odor on arousal.

A. Sensory Memory: The Gateway to Consciousness

The capacity of sensory memory appears to be quite large. It holds fleeting representations of everything we see, hear, taste, smell or feel. However, it can only hold information for a very brief period of time. Visual sensory memory lasts for less than a second. Acoustic sensory memory lasts for no more than a few seconds. Thus, representations in sensory memory are broad in scope but last a very short period of time.

B. Short-term Memory: The Workbench of Consciousness

Experiences such as forgetting numbers immediately after dialing directory assistance suggest the existence of a short-term memory system. Because this system is also thought to hold information we are actively processing at the moment, this system is also known as working memory.

Formal evidence exists suggesting the presence of short-term memory (STM). One source of evidence is found in the pattern of ordered memory shown for unrelated words. Individuals are more likely to remember words at the beginning and end of a word list. This effect is known as the serial position curve. You are presumed to remember the words at the end of the list well because they are in short-term memory. Words at the beginning of the test are presumed to be retrieved from long-term memory.

The word-length and word similarity effects also provide evidence for the existence of STM. Our memory span for immediate recall is greater for lists of short words than for lists of longer words (the word length effect). It is thought that longer words take longer to pronounce and thus interfere with the rehearsal needed to maintain them in STM.

The word-similarity effect refers to the finding that our memory span for immediate recall is greater for words that do not sound alike. Similar-sounding words are thought to produce confusions in STM that interfere with memory.

One feature that distinguishes the different memory systems is the way information is represented in each system. Sensory memory represents information in a form similar to that reported by our senses. It is suggested that STM stores information acoustically whereas information is entered into long-term memory primarily in terms of its meaning.

Short-term memory can hold about 5 to 9 separate items. Each of these items can represent several other pieces of information. This is called chunking. Information is retained in short-term memory by means of rehearsal and there is a phonological store which represents words in terms of how they sound. When rehearsal is prevented, information is almost totally gone within twenty seconds. STM is thought to be the workbench of consciousness -- it temporarily stores the information you are using at the present.

- **Research Methods: How Psychologists Study the Nature of Short-Term Memory**

    It is difficult to study STM because it holds information for only a few seconds. One way of studying this system is to use positron emission tomography (PET) to scan activity in the brain. Using this technique, researchers give participants tasks that should separate storage and rehearsal mechanisms and measure brain activity. The logic of the tasks involves requiring participants to retrieve from STM and rehearse. One task (two-back) requires both components of short-term memory: storage and rehearsal. Another task (rehearsal control) requires only rehearsal. Subtracting brain activation during the rehearsal control task from brain activation during the two-back task provides information on regions of the brain required by the storage components. This is what's left after activation required for rehearsal is removed. A third task (search control) requires neither component. Subtracting activation during this task from activation during the task requiring both components, and comparing the result with activation during the rehearsal control task, indicates which brain regions are required during rehearsal.

C. Long-Term Memory: The Storehouse of Consciousness

LTM can store huge quantities of information for long periods of time. But the information in LTM can be difficult to locate (i.e., there can be retrieval problems).

The tip-of-the-tongue phenomenon is an example of this location difficulty — sometimes we feel we know the information we want to recall but just can't locate it in our memory.

Information enters long-term memory from short-term memory by means of rehearsal. The type of rehearsal required is called elaborative rehearsal. This involves thinking about the meaning of new information and relating it to information in memory. Factors, such as alcohol consumption and depression, that interfere with rehearsal interfere with long-term memory.

According to a levels of processing view, information can be processed at different levels. This can range from shallow processing to deep processing. Apparently, the deeper the processing during the exposure to materials, the better the memory. For example, in one study it was found that thinking about the meaning of words (deep processing) aided memory more than thinking about how they looked or rhymed (shallow or moderate processing). This view is known as the levels of processing approach. It has been suggested that deeper or more effortful processing promotes the encoding of more features of the item, making it easier to locate in the memory system later. There are problems, however, associated with this view. First, it is difficult to determine what constitutes deep and shallow processing. Second, it is difficult to speak about discrete levels of processing when several forms of processing may occur at once.

The process of getting information out of long-term memory is called retrieval. Retrieval is related to the form in which information is entered into memory or storage. The more organized this information, the easier the retrieval. Sometimes information is represented in terms of categories and sometimes it is represented in terms of hierarchies.

Stimuli that are associated with information stored in memory and that help us retrieve it are called retrieval cues. Research indicates that words learned in a particular environment were remembered better in the same than in a different environment. This is known as context dependent memory. Several studies have found that internal states can serve as retrieval cues. This is known as state-dependent retrieval. Mood - dependent memory is related to this in that it refers to the fact that it is often easier to recall information when we are in the same mood at the time of encoding and retrieval. You should not confuse this effect with mood-congruence effects, which refer to the finding that we are likely to notice and remember information that matches our current mood. In mood-dependent memory, what matters is the mood we're in when we learned the information and our current mood; what matters in mood-congruence is the affective nature of the information and whether it matches our current mood.

- **Beyond the Headlines: As Psychologists See It -- The Scent of Romantic Ardor?**

    Baron discusses a report of research that seems to indicate that food-related odors stimulate sexual arousal in males. He points out that the procedures used in this study are unusual (e.g., having men inhale various fragrances through face masks while measuring blood flow to their sexual organs). So, while this research is interesting, it raises more questions than it answers. This report should induce you to think critically about these issues.

Questions:

6-5.   What are the characteristics and functions of sensory memory? _____

_____

_____

_____

6-6.   What is the evidence for the existence of a short-term memory system and how is STM studied?

_____

_____

_____

6-7.   What are the basic features of short-term memory? _____

_____

_____

_____

6-8   What is the basic operation of long-term memory? _____

_____

_____

_____

6-9.   How does the levels of processing perspective view encoding? _____

_____

_____

_____

6-10.   What are the factors that influence retrieval information from long-term memory? _____

_____

_____

_____

III. Forgetting From Long-Term Memory

L.O. 6.6: Compare and contrast the trace decay and interference accounts of forgetting.

L.O. 6.7: Discuss how repression and intentional forgetting processes operate.

L.O. 6.8: Describe the nature of prospective memory.

We are most typically aware of memory when it fails. The classic research by Ebbinghaus studied the rate of forgetting; he found that forgetting is rapid at first and then slows down with the passage of time. Recent research confirms his findings. Research has also found that discrete skills are subject to a great amount of forgetting. Discrete skills involve associations between specific stimuli and responses (e.g., procedures for programming a VCR).

A. The Trace Decay Hypothesis: Forgetting With the Passage of Time

The simplest view of forgetting suggests that information is lost from LTM because of the mere passage of time; this is the trace decay hypothesis. This view is not supported by research.

B. Forgetting As a Result of Interference

Forgetting appears to result from interference among information stored in memory. This can take two forms: retroactive and proactive interference. For example, if learning the rules of a new game causes you to forget the rules of an old game, this is termed retroactive interference. If information you know about the board game causes you to have problems learning the information about the new board game, this is termed proactive interference. You can remember this distinction by recognizing that the label refers to whether interference is acting forward in time, which would be proactive interference, or is having an influence on material that has already been learned. The latter would be called retroactive interference.

C. Repression: "What's Too Painful to Remember, We Simply Choose to Forget"

Repression refers to the idea that we forget some information and experiences because we find them too frightening or threatening to bear. Although repression may occur, there is little scientific evidence for its existence. Most support comes from case studies. Accounts of repression may be "invented" in that, in some cases, therapists or the media may lead some persons into reporting memories that do not exist.

D. Intentional Forgetting: Removing Inaccurate or Useless Information from Memory

In some circumstances, we want to forget information because it is painful or frightening or because it is inaccurate or no longer useful. This is called intentional forgetting. There are several ways we "intentionally forget." We can initially encode the information in a way that we tag or label it as "soon-to-be-forgotten" material. When we don't know in advance that we'll want to forget it, we can focus on inhibiting the information; when information is not used or rehearsed, it is forgotten. Often, our attempts to intentionally forget are successful but, in some cases (for example, in person perception), we cannot totally ignore information we want to forget.

E. Prospective Memory: Forgetting to Do What We're Supposed to Do

Prospective memory involves remembering things that we are supposed to do at a certain time. Forgetting of this type appears to be closely related to motivation. In addition, like other forms of memory, it is influenced by retrieval cues. For example, the structure of our day (such as the route we take to work) can serve as retrieval cues for tasks we need to accomplish (e.g., going to the cleaners). Other cues are internal, such as our perception of time passing.

Questions:

6-11.   What is the trace delay hypothesis, the interference view, and the repression view of forgetting?

_____

_____

_____

6-12.   What factors influence prospective memory and intentional forgetting? _____

_____

_____

_____

IV. Memory in Natural Contexts

L.O. 6.9: Discuss how memory operates in natural contexts.

A. Autobiographical Memory: Remembering the Events of Our Own Lives

Our memory for the events of our lives is called autobiographical memory. A useful technique to study this form of memory is the autobiographical memory schedule in which individuals are systematically questioned about different periods of their lives.

Another technique is the diary method in which individuals attempt to keep detailed diaries of events in their own lives. An extensive diary study has found that autobiographical memory is affected by many of the same variables that affect memory for abstract information under controlled conditions. However, because this research is observational in nature, it cannot establish cause-and-effect relationships.

B. Infantile Amnesia: Forgetting the Events of Our Earliest Years

Few individuals have accurate memories for events occurring before their third or fourth birthday. This is known as infantile amnesia. Until recently, there have been two accepted explanations for infantile amnesia. According to one explanation, brain structures are not sufficiently developed before this time, and this fact may account for a lack of early memories. According to the second explanation, the absence of language skills prior to this time accounts for infantile amnesia. Both of these accounts assume that children do not have well-developed memory abilities.

Recent findings, however, suggest that neither of these explanations is entirely accurate -- infants do appear to have well-developed memory abilities. According to a new interpretation, we cannot remember events from our first few years of life because we have not yet developed a clear self-concept.

C. Flashbulb Memories: Memories That don't Fade — Or Do They?

Our memories for highly unusual events that are accompanied with the subjective impression that we can remember exactly what we were doing at the time the event occurred are called flashbulb memories. Research on this topic indicates that this form of memory is inaccurate. These findings may be due to the role that emotion plays in encoding unusual events.

Questions:

6-13.   How does autobiographical memory operate, and how is it studied? _____

_____

_____

_____

6-14.   What is the nature of infantile amnesia? _____

_____

_____

_____

6-15.   What is the evidence for and against the existence of flashbulb memories? _____

_____

_____

_____

V. Memory Distortion and Memory Construction

L.O. 6.10: Describe how memories are distorted and constructed.

A. Distortion and the Influence of Schemas

Schemas are cognitive frameworks developed through experience which help structure the processing and storing of new information. Schemas may lead to distortions of memory. Research suggests that we are likely to notice and remember information that is consistent with well-formed schemas. However, when a schema is initially being formed, we are likely to notice and remember inconsistent information. Motivational factors also play a role in memory distortions. For example, our feelings about people affect what we remember about them. For example, we remember good things about people we like.

B. Memory Construction: Remembering What Didn't Happen

We may "fill in details" of natural events, or remember experiences we never had to make our memories more complete or sensible. This is called construction. When we enter information into memory, we may store the information itself, but not the details about the context in which it occurred. This contributes to construction.

False memories are difficult to change and can have devastating effects, such as in eyewitness testimony based on constructed memories.

While child sexual abuse is all too real and frequent, some charges seem to be false. Research on constructed memories are relevant because it demonstrates that both children and adults can report "memories" of events that never occurred. In one study, the researchers knew the events did not happen because they made up completely false stories and presented them to the participants, who then reported these events as their "memories."

The use of anatomically detailed dolls that show male and female genitals is common in evaluating child abuse. Although they are useful in helping children describe what has happened to them, they are potentially dangerous because they may lead young children to report false memories in response to questions about where they have been touched.

Contrary to popular belief, research indicates that eyewitnesses to crimes are often not nearly as accurate as the legal system generally assumes. It appears that the accuracy of eyewitness testimony can be enhanced by using techniques that are based on current information of how our memory operates. Several techniques have been developed. One asks witnesses to report everything they can remember. A second involves asking them to describe the events from several different perspectives. A third involves asking them to imagine themselves back at the scene and to reconstruct as many details as possible. In addition, giving eyewitnesses repeated opportunities to recall the events sometimes helps. It appears that hypnosis is not an effective eyewitness testimony technique.

- **Exploring Gender and Diversity: Does Culture Influence Memory?**

    The basic operation of the memory system is the same across cultures. But culture does affect memory. It affects the kinds of information people remember. And cultures influence the kinds of memory skills children are taught, such as memorization. Third, formal education practices in industrialized societies influence persons' familiarity with styles of asking questions about information they have committed to memory. Thus we must be careful in conclusions we draw based on the results of standard memory tests from people from different cultures.

Questions:

6-16.   How do schemas influence memory distortions and constructions? _____

_____

_____

_____

6-17.   How accurate is eyewitness testimony? What factors affect the accuracy of eyewitness testimony?

_____

_____

_____

VI.   The Biological Bases of Memory: How the Brain Stores Knowledge

L.O. 6.11: Be able to discuss the biological bases of memory.

L.O. 6.12: Know how you can use what you have learned to improve your memory.

A. Amnesia and Other Memory Disorders: Keys For Unlocking the Biology of Memory

The study of amnesia has provided important insights into the biological bases of memory. Loss of memory as a result of injuries or illness is called amnesia. Loss of memory for events after an accident is anterograde amnesia. Loss of memory for events prior to an accident is called retrograde amnesia. The case study of H. M. suggests that portions of the temporal lobes play a crucial role in memory. Specifically, these structures appear to be crucial in the consolidation of memories or shifting new information from STM to LTM. Subsequent research has confirmed this conclusion and suggests that it is the hippocampus, a portion of the temporal lobes, that plays a key role in our memory systems.

Research indicates that we possess at least two distinct memory systems and that different portions of the brain play a key role in each. An explicit memory system brings information that we know into consciousness and, if necessary, describes it. An implicit memory system may retain information that is not directly accessible to consciousness. The hippocampus appears to play a key role in the explicit memory system, but not the implicit memory system. The occipital lobe appears to relate to implicit memory.

When individuals abuse alcohol for many years, they sometimes develop Korsakoff's syndrome. These persons report that they cannot remember many of the events that took place before the onset of their illness. Medical examinations reveal that these individuals experienced extensive damage to portions of the diencephalon, especially to the thalamus and hypothalamus. This suggests that these portions of the brain play a key role in LTM.

Alzheimer's disease is an illness that afflicts about 5% of all people over the age of 65 and progresses to the point that there is almost a total loss of memory. Careful study of the brains of deceased patients reveal that, in most cases, they contain bundles of amyloid beta protein which may cause damage to neurons that transmit information through the neurotransmitter acetylcholine. Individuals who suffer from Alzheimer's disease show a decrease in acetylcholine in their brains.

B. Memory and the Brain: A Modern View

Modern views of the relationship between brain and memory suggests that memories are stored in different locations in the brain and that our brains process and store information simultaneously at several different locations. It appears that the formation of long-term memories involves alterations in the rate of production or release of specific neurotransmitters. It may also involve changes in the actual structure of neurons.

- **Making Psychology Part of Your Life**

Improving Your Memory: Some Useful Steps

Memory research offers several practical suggestions for improving our memory. These include the following:

1)   Really think about what you want to remember.
2)   Pay attention.
3)   Minimize interference.
4)   Use visual imagery and other mnemonics.
5)   Give yourself extra retrieval cues.
6)   Develop your own shorthand codes.

Questions:

6-18. What are the two distinct memory systems discuss in this section and what evidence suggests that they are really different systems?_____

_____

_____

_____

6-19. What do memory disorders tell us about the relationship between the brain and memory. (Be able to discuss this as it relates to Korsakoff's syndrome and Alzheimer's disease.) _____

_____

_____

_____

6-20. What is the modern view on the storage and processing of information within the brain? _____

_____

_____

_____

6-21. How can you use what you have learned about memory to improve your memory? _____

_____

_____

_____

6-22. Describe how you might use what you have learned about memory to improve your own memory.

_____

_____

_____

6-23. Now might be a good time to review your study strategy for this class. How can you incorporate the steps listed in your textbook into your study habits? _____

_____

_____

_____

MAKING PSYCHOLOGY PART OF YOUR LIFE: Key Terms and Concepts

Knowing the important concepts and key terms contained in this chapter is a very important part of mastering the material. We have presented a sample of these concepts below. Define each concept and check your definition with that presented in the chapter. It will also be beneficial for you to think of an example of each concept. Whenever possible, use your own personal experience to provide an example of each term below.

6-1.   **Alzheimer's Disease:** _____

Example: _____

6-2.   **Amnesia:** _____

Example: _____

6-3.   **Anterograde Amnesia:** _____

Example: _____

6-4.   **Autobiographical Memory:** _____

Example: _____

6-5.   **Context-Dependent Memory:** _____

Example: _____

6-6.   **Elaborative Rehearsal:** _____

Example: _____

6-7.   **Encoding:** _____

Example: _____

6-8.   **Episodic Memory:** _____

Example: _____

6-9.   **Explicit Memory:** _____

Example: _____

6-10. **Eyewitness Testimony:** _____

Example: _____

6-11. **Flashbulb Memories:** _____

Example: _____

6-12. **Implicit Memory:** _____

Example: _____

6-13. **Infantile Amnesia:** _____

Example: _____

6-14. **Information-Processing Approach:** _____

Example: _____

6-15. **Intentional Forgetting:** _____

6-16. **Korsakoff's Syndrome:** _____

Example: _____

6-17. **Levels of Processing View:** _____

Example: _____

6-18. **Long-Term Memory:** _____

Example: _____

6-19. **Memory:** _____

Example: _____

6-20. **Mood Dependent Memory:** _____

Example: _____

6-21. **Mood Congruence Effects**: _____

   Example: _____

6-22. **Proactive Interference**: _____

   Example: _____

6-23. **Procedural Memory**: _____

   Example: _____

6-24. **Prospective Memory**: _____

   Example: _____

6-25. **Repression**: _____

   Example: _____

6-26. **Retrieval**: _____

   Example: _____

6-27. **Retrieval Cues**: _____

   Example: _____

6-28. **Retroactive Interference**: _____

   Example: _____

6-29. **Schemas**: _____

   Example: _____

6-30. **Selective Attention**: _____

   Example: _____

6-31. **Semantic Memory**: _____

   Example: _____

6-32.   **Sensory Memory**: _____

   Example: _____

6-33.   **Serial Position Curve**: _____

   Example: _____

6-34.   **Short-Term Memory**: _____

   Example: _____

6-35.   **State-Dependent Retrieval**: _____

   Example: _____

6-36.   **Storage**: _____

   Example: _____

6-37.   **Tip-of-the-Tongue-Phenomenon**: _____

   Example: _____

CHALLENGE: Develop Your Critical Thinking Skills

Metacognition: Improving Your Study Skills

Critical thinking requires knowledge about what types of strategies to use for different types of situations. One practical benefit of developing these skills is that it increases your ability to plan and improve your study skills. Below, we provide you examples of typical problems students have with their studies. The material in this chapter should help you identify the problem and formulate a strategy for dealing with the problem. Check your answers with those provided at the end of this section.

6-1. Cathy is taking a French class. She tries to memorize the vocabulary by repeating the words over and over again. She isn't doing well in the class.

Problem: _____

_____

Solution: _____

_____

6-2. John has an American literature class right before his English literature class. He finds that he confuses American authors with British authors on his exams in English literature.

Problem: _____

_____

Solution: _____

_____

6-3. Sherry is taking a class in biology. She is unfamiliar with the material and tries to write down everything the professor says. She isn't understanding the material.

Problem: _____

_____

Solution: _____

_____

<u>Answers to Critical Thinking Exercises</u>:

6-1. Cathy is trying to learn French by using **rote rehearsal** strategies. She should use **elaborative rehearsal**, such as thinking about the meaning of the words.

6-2. John is experiencing **proactive interference**. He should try to schedule his classes so that classes with different content follow another.

6-3. Sherry is straining her attentional capacity. She should attend to her professor, think about what she says, and summarize the relevant material in her notes. She needs to develop a framework for assimilating the information.

YOUR NOTES:

CHALLENGE: Taking Psychology With You

<u>Eye-Witness Memory</u>

We rely on our memory systems in thousands of ways. But, just like our cars, we don't notice its importance until it fails us. The material in this chapter should provide you with a greater appreciation of how your memory system operates. Practice applying this knowledge to an important domain -- eye-witness memory.

<u>Situation</u>

Assume that as you were driving home from school one day, you saw a car run through a red light and hit a pedestrian. Being a "good citizen," you left your name with the police at the scene and told him/her that you saw what happened. Now, a year has passed, and the driver is appearing in court to face charges. The driver claims that the pedestrian walked in front of his/her car and was crossing against the light.

Given the knowledge you have acquired concerning the factors that are important for accurate eyewitness testimony:

<u>Analysis</u>

6-1.   How would you prepare yourself for your account of what happened?

6-2.   What factors would you look for in the manner of questioning that might influence your memory?

6-3.   What kinds of events are you likely to forget?

6-4.   What kinds of events are you likely to remember?

6-5.   How might your past experiences influence your memory for these events?

6-6.   Speculate on the kinds of distortions and constructions that are likely to affect your memory.

CHALLENGE: Review Your Comprehensive Knowledge

SAMPLE TEST QUESTIONS

Once you have worked through the preceding sections, you should be ready for a comprehensive self-test. You can check your answers with those at the end of this section. An additional practice test is given in the supplementary section at the end of this study guide.

6-1.   The way information is entered into memory is called:
    a.   retrieval.   c.   storage.
    b.   encoding.   d.   programming.

6-2.   Sensory memory can hold:
    a.   little information.   c.   5-9 chunks.
    b.   much information.   d.   7-10 chunks.

6-3.   According to the information-processing model, there is(are) _____ kind(s) of memory systems.
    a.   2   c.   1
    b.   3   d.   5

6-4.   Information goes from sensory memory to short-term memory when we:
    a.   attend to it.   c.   ignore it.
    b.   rehearse it.   d.   retrieve it.

6-5.   The first memory structure involved in the encoding of information is:
    a.   sensory memory.   c.   LTM.
    b.   STM.   d.   procedural memory.

6-6.   Short-term memory can hold _____ separate items.
    a.   2 to 3   c.   5 to 9
    b.   4 to 5   d.   8 to 10

6-7.   Few individuals have accurate memories for events occurring before their third or fourth birthdays. This is called:
    a.   retroactive interference.   c.   repression.
    b.   proactive interference.   d.   infantile amnesia.

6-8.   Research on the influence of alcohol on long-term memory indicates that it:
    a.   enhances memory.   c.   interferes only with acoustic memory.
    b.   interferes with memory.   d.   interferences only with semantic memory.

6-9.   Memory for the events of our lives is called _____ memory.
    a.   semantic   c.   personal
    b.   procedural   d.   autobiographical

6-10.   The view that suggests that words learned in a particular environment will be remember better in the same vs. a different environment is called:
    a.   encoding specificity.   c.   context-dependent memory.
    b.   state-dependent retrieval.   d.   levels of processing.

6-11.   When we fill in details of events to make memories more complete, we are using:
    a. association.
    b. shallow processing.
    c. construction.
    d. distortion.

6-12.   Which of the following kinds of memory is very accurate?
    a. reports of child sexual abuse
    b. flashbulb memories
    c. memories about people we like
    d. none of the above

6-13.   Research on the levels of processing indicates that memory is better with _____ processing.
    a. deep
    b. shallow
    c. moderate
    d. rote

6-14.   Stimuli that are associated with information stored in memory and aid retrieval are called:
    a. loci.
    b. state-dependents.
    c. cues.
    d. phonological loops.

6-15.   Susan cannot remember what happened the week before she was in a serious car accident. This is an example of:
    a. anterograde amnesia.
    b. retrograde amnesia.
    c. phobic amnesia.
    d. Korsakoff's syndrome.

6-16.   The most important factor in forgetting appears to be:
    a. attention.
    b. emotion.
    c. interference.
    d. decay.

6-17.   Our memory of our first date is an example of:
    a. episodic.
    b. semantic.
    c. univariate.
    d. associationistic.

6-18.   You are having problems learning the rules of a new board game. The problem seems to be in confusing the rules of chess with this new game. You are experiencing:
    a. reactive interference.
    b. retroactive interference.
    c. proactive interference.
    d. anticipatory interference.

6-19.   Our memory for things we are supposed to do in the future is:
    a. retrospective memory.
    b. futuristic memory.
    c. procedural memory.
    d. prospective memory.

6-20.   Research on flashbulb memory indicates that:
    a. it increases over time.
    b. it decreases over time.
    c. it is accurate.
    d. it is not accurate.

Answers and Feedback to Sample Test Questions:

6-1.   B   Encoding is the process responsible for entering information into memory. (p. 215)

6-2.   B   In contrast with STM, sensory memory is unlimited and holds a great deal of information for a very brief period of time. (p. 215)

6-3.   B   The information procession model of memory proposes three kinds of memory systems: sensory memory, STM, and LTM. (p. 215-216)

6-4.   A   Attending to information transfers it from sensory memory to STM. (p. 216)

6-5.   A   Sensory memory is the first memory structure in the information processing sequence. (p. 218-219)

6-6.   C   STM holds between seven to nine chunks of information. (p. 221)

6-7.   D   This loss of autobiographical memory for early life events is called infantile amnesia. (p. 236)

6-8.   B   Alcohol interferes with memory. (p. 224)

6-9.   D   Autobiographical memory is the term used for our memory of our own life events. (p. 235)

6-10.   C   Context-dependent memory describes this effect. (p. 227)

6-11.   C   Construction refers to filling in details of an event to make our memories more complete. (p. 239)

6-12.   D   None of the described memories are accurate; they're all affected by memory construction distortions. (p. 239-242)

6-13.   A   Deeper levels of processing (e.g., semantic processing) leads to good memory, according to the levels of processing approach. (p. 224)

6-14.   C   "Cues" fit this definition. (p. 226)

6-15.   B   Loss of memory for events that happened before an accident is called retrograde amnesia. (p. 244)

6-16.   C   Interference among information stored in memory is thought to produce forgetting. (p. 231-232)

6-17.   A   Memory for specific times or places is called episodic memory. (p. 217)

6-18.   C   Proactive interference refers to problems in acquiring new information due to the influence of previously learned material. (p. 244)

6-19.   D   Prospective memory refers to our memory for things we are suppose to do in the future. (p. 234-235)

6-20.   D   Despite our impressions, research indicates that flashbulb memories are not accurate. (p. 243)

GLOSSARY OF DIFFICULT WORDS AND EXPRESSIONS

These terms from your text and this study guide were identified by students as potentially hard to understand. We have defined these terms and expressions.

Term or expression	Definition
Acoustic	related to sound; for example, how a word is pronounced
Acronyms	words formed from the initial letters of the name
Adopting	taking as one's own; applying
Array of	variety of
Associated	connected to
Blazingly hot	extremely hot
Broad in scope	covering a great deal of information
Converging	coming towards each other and meeting at a point
Codes	symbols that stand for something else
Culprits	guilty party
Detrimental	harmful
Discrete	separate and individual
Effortful	involving a lot of effort
Errands	short journeys to take or get something
Evoke	call up; bring out
Fleeting	lasting for a short time
Flooding back	coming back rapidly
Fruitful	producing good results
Gaze	to look at something intensively
Groaning	making a deep sound forced out by pain
Hazardous	dangerous, not beneficial
Hierarchies	classification systems that move from inclusive to increasingly specific levels (e.g., animals -- mammals -- dogs)
Infallible	incapable of making a mistake or doing wrong
Jumble	things mixed in a confusing way
"Mental scaffolds"	mental frameworks
Mnemonics	tactics for improving memory
Molested	intentionally hurt

Term or expression	Definition
Omitted	disregarded; not included
Onset	beginning; starting point
Ostensible	apparent; revealing
Presumed	thought to be the case; assumed
Probings	procedures or methods of
Refrain	stop yourself
Rehearsing	practicing
Retrieving	getting back
Saliency	standing out
Seizure	physical attack
Shorthand	a brief version of something
Startling	amazing
Thrusts	push suddenly or violently
Trivial	unimportant
Unravel	separate; figure out
Unsettling	troubled, anxious or uncertain
Vanished	disappeared
Wander	to move about without a definite purpose
"What had become of"	what happened to

CHAPTER 7
COGNITION: THINKING, DECIDING, COMMUNICATING

INTEGRATED CHAPTER OUTLINE: Survey and Question

This section presents the major topics and ideas from the chapter. Use it as a tool for seeing how the components of the chapter fit together. At the end of each major topic, we have asked you questions that relate to the major learning objectives. If you can answer these questions, you have taken a major step toward mastering this material.

I. Thinking: Forming Concepts and Reasoning to Conclusions

L.O. 7.1:   Define the basic elements of thought.

L.O. 7.2:   Be sure you can describe how psychologists study cognitive processes.

L.O. 7.3:   Describe the reasoning process.

Two strategies have been used to understand the nature of thought. One strategy is to focus on the basic elements of thought. A second strategy is to determine the way in which we reason. These strategies are discussed in the following sections.

A. Basic Elements of Thought: Concepts, Propositions, Images

Our thought consists of 3 basic components: concepts, propositions, and images. Mental frameworks for categorizing diverse items as belonging together are concepts. Artificial concepts can be clearly defined by a set of rules or properties. Concepts that we use in everyday life and that have "fuzzy" boundaries are called natural concepts. These are based on the best examples of concepts or prototypes. The more similar a stimulus is to the prototype, the more likely it is placed in the category. This is a probabilistic strategy. Several possibilities exist concerning how concepts are represented. One possibility is that they may be represented in terms of the features or attributes they possess. A second possibility is that they're presented in terms of mental pictures or visual images of the external world. Concepts are closely related to schemas, which are cognitive frameworks that represent our knowledge of and assumptions about the world. Schemas are more complex than concepts.

Thinking involves the active manipulation of internal representations of the external world. Because we possess highly developed language skills, these cognitive actions often take the form of propositions or sentences that can stand as separate assertions. Propositions are useful for relating one concept to another, or for relating one feature to the entire concept. Controversy exists as to whether our use of visual images in thinking is precisely that of actual vision.

- **Research Methods: How Psychologists Study Cognitive Processes**

    Cognitive psychologists use a variety of methods to study cognitive processes. These include reaction time and verbal protocol analysis. Reaction time is the amount of time it takes a person to react to a particular stimulus. When the verbal protocol analysis is used, participants are asked to give continuous verbal reports, or to "think aloud," while making a decision or solving a problem. Results obtained by the verbal protocol or "think aloud" procedure is typically consistent with those obtained with other cognitive assessment techniques. There are some problems with the verbal protocol analysis. It can be time-consuming, the data obtained might reflect what participants believe they should say and not their underlying cognitive processes, and in verbalizing their thoughts, participants may use different mental processes than those used when they are not verbalizing.

Some evidence suggests that experts concentrate on deep structure and do not concentrate on surface structure whereas novices concentrate on surface and not on deep structure. Deep structure refers to the underlying principles or mathematical equations needed to solve problems whereas surface structure refers to the specific descriptions used to convey the problem. Baron reports on a study that used the verbal protocol procedure. This study found data suggesting that experts do not ignore surface structure when it is a relevant clue to the type of problem under investigation and to the problem's solution.

B. Reasoning: Transforming Information to Reach Conclusions

Drawing accurate conclusions from available information is called reasoning. In formal reasoning, all the required information is supplied, the problem to be solved is straight-forward, and there is typically only one correct answer. Syllogistic reasoning is one example of this type of reasoning. It involves situations in which conclusions are based on two propositions. In contrast, everyday reasoning involves planning, making commitments, and evaluating arguments in our daily lives.

Reasoning is subject to error and can be influenced by social factors and beliefs. We also tend to test conclusions for hypotheses by examining only evidence that we expect will confirm them. This is called confirmation bias. Learning that an event actually happened can cause individuals to assume that they knew it all along. This is the hindsight effect. This hindsight effect may be reduced if individuals are asked to explain a reported outcome along with other possible outcomes that did not occur.

C. Animal Cognition: Do Animals Really Think?

A growing body of researchers suggests that animals do possess cognitive abilities. First, many instances of animal learning cannot be explained through conditioning alone. Second, evidence suggests that animals form complex mental representations of their environment. Recent work on this question uses the ecological approach, which tests for cognitive processes appropriate to a particular species.

Research indicates that there are some similarities between the cognitive processes of animals and human beings. Baboons appear to be able to mentally rotate visual forms. This is a cognitive ability that is well established in human beings.

Questions:

7-1.   What are the two strategies adopted for studying the nature of thought? _____

_____

_____

_____

7-2.   What are the basic characteristics of concepts? _____

_____

_____

_____

7-3.   How are propositions and concepts related? _____

_____

_____

_____

7-4.   How does formal reasoning differ from everyday reasoning? _____

_____

_____

_____

7-5.   What are the basic sources of bias in reasoning? _____

_____

_____

_____

7-6.   What are the research findings concerning animal cognition? _____

_____

_____

_____

II. Making Decisions: Choosing Among Alternatives

L.O. 7.4:   Know the various heuristics that we use in decision-making.

L.O. 7.5:   Know how framing and decision strategies affect decision-making.

L.O. 7.6:   Know how escalation and commitment factors can lead to poor decisions.

L.O. 7.7:   Understand the factors that influence decision-making in real world contexts.

Decision making is a process of choosing among various courses of action or alternatives. One description of a rational decision maker is expected utility -- the product of the probability and value of each possible outcome. Usually, we don't take the time to reason in such a systematic way. The following material describes other decision-making strategies.

A.   Heuristics: Using Quick -- But Fallible -- Rules of Thumb to Make Decisions

When we have to make decisions quickly, we may use guidelines from our past experience (heuristics).

The more easily we can think of instances of something, the more frequent we judge it to be. This is the availability heuristic.

When we judge the likelihood of something based on how much an item resembles the prototype, we are using the representativeness heuristic. This heuristic may lead us to ignore the relative frequency of objects or events in the world (base rates).

Our tendency to make decisions by using a reference point as an initial starting point is the anchoring and adjustment heuristic. In this heuristic, the reference point is known as the anchor.

B.   Framing and Decision Strategy

Decisions can be affected by the way in which decisions are framed. Framing involves the presentation of information about potential outcomes in terms of gains or in terms of losses. Research indicates that when emphasis is on potential gains, people are risk averse -- they prefer to avoid unnecessary risks. When the emphasis is on potential losses, people are risk prone -- they prefer to take risks rather than accept certain losses.

Framing effects do not occur when a rationale for the relationship between the potential gains and losses are given to participants. Therefore, although the effects of framing are powerful, they can be offset when people are given a more complete picture of the choices to be made. In addition, people's attitudes can also offset framing effects.

C.   Escalation of Commitment: Getting Trapped in Bad Decisions

Entrapment occurs when decision-makers feel they must stay with their original decisions and they feel a need to justify their decisions. There can be several phases in the escalation of commitment process. In the initial phase, decisions are based on rational considerations. Later, psychological factors, such as the desire for self-justification comes into play when there are early losses. External factors, such as political pressure comes into play with continued losses.

Research suggests that escalation can be reduced if available resources to commit to further action are limited and the evidence of failure is overwhelming. If responsibility can be diffused for taking part in a bad decision, escalation can be prevented.

D.   Naturalistic Decision Making: Making Choices in the Real World

Studying decision making in the real world is known as naturalistic decision making. With this type of decision making, people's experiences, the decision context, and the dynamic nature of decision making are brought to bear on decisions. This is in contrast to laboratory research in which the stories are often contrived and without context and, therefore, have little real meaning to participants.

Questions:

7-7.   How do people make decisions based on expected utility? _____

_____

_____

_____

7-8.   How do we use heuristics in decision making? _____

_____

_____

_____

7-9.   How can framing influence decision making? _____

_____

_____

_____

7-10.   How can framing effects be reduced? _____

_____

_____

_____

7-11.   How do we become committed to bad decisions? _____

_____

_____

_____

7-12.   How can we overcome escalations of commitment? _____

_____

_____

_____

7-13.   What is naturalistic decision making? _____

_____

_____

_____

III.   Problem Solving: Finding Paths to Desired Goals

L.O. 7.8:   Discuss the nature of problem-solving and describe methods used in solving problems.

L.O. 7.9:   Understand the factors that interfere with effective problem-solving.

L.O. 7.10:   Discuss the controversies involved in artificial intelligence.

A.   Problem Solving: An Overview

Problem solving involves efforts to develop responses in order to attain desired goals. The first part of problem-solving is understanding the problem. The second step in problem-solving is formulating potential solutions. Third, we evaluate alternatives and outcomes. In the fourth stage, solutions are tried and results are evaluated.

B.   Methods For Solving Problems: From Trial and Error to Heuristics

Trial and error is the problem-solving technique that involves trying a variety of different responses. Rules for solving problems that eventually will lead to the solution are algorithms. Problem-solving strategies suggested by prior experience are heuristics.

One heuristic we often employ is to divided a problem into a series of smaller subproblems. This is a means-end analysis or subgoals analysis. It involves deciding on the ends we want to attain and the means used to get there. Assuming that a problem is similar to a past one and applying solutions that worked on it is the analogy strategy.

C.   Facilitating Effective Problem Solving: The Role of Metacognitive Processing

Metacognitive processing involves an awareness of ourselves engaged in the problem-solving process. This type of processing appears to improve performance on problem-solving tasks. Talking through a problem can facilitate problem-solving when it leads to metacognitive processing and focus on the problem-solving process.

D.   Factors that Interfere with Effective Problem Solving

Functional fixedness is our tendency to think of using objects only in the way that they were used before. This tendency has been shown to interfere with problem solving.

Once we have solved a problem in a particular way, we tend to stay with it. We develop a mental set based on our past experience that interferes with our ability to see better alternatives.

E.   Artificial Intelligence: Can Machines Really Think?

The field of artificial intelligence studies the capacity of computers to demonstrate performance that, if produced by humans, would be described as intelligent. Computers carry out complex computations at a very fast pace. Computers can be efficient problem solvers and also have some language abilities. They are also useful in situations deemed too dangerous for humans.

Older computers process information in a sequential way. Humans do not. Recently, computers have been designed with neural networks -- structures consisting of highly interconnected elementary computational units that work together in parallel. There are two major advantages to neural networks. First, the units can work together. Second, they have the capacity to learn from experience by adjusting output strength. However, most psychologists believe that the early predictions about the capacities of computers to show characteristics such as intention, understanding, and consciousness were greatly overstated.

•   **Beyond the Headlines: As Psychologists See It -- Machine Bests Human -- Experts Say It Was Only a Matter of Time**

In a recent match between a chess master (Kasparov) and a computer called Deep Blue, the computer was victorious. At least in this match, Deep Blue's advantage was one of "power" -- it could evaluate the consequences of about 200 moves per second. In contrast, human beings can only evaluate about 1 move per second. But, Kasparov had two major advantages. He was able to predict what the general shape of a game would be many moves into the future and he could learn both as a game progressed and between games.

Questions:

7-14. What are the characteristics of problem solving? _____

_____

_____

_____

7-15. What are the different methods of problem solving? _____

_____

_____

_____

7-16. How can functional fixedness and mental set interfere with effective problem solving? _____

_____

_____

_____

7-17. What is the current consensus on the question of whether machines really think? _____

_____

_____

_____

7-18. What cognitive skills allowed Kasparov to outwit a computer (Deep Blue)? _____

_____

_____

_____

IV. Language: The Communication of Information

L.O. 7.11: Describe the basic nature of language.

L.O. 7.12: Describe language development.

L.O. 7.13: Discuss the relationship between language and thought.

L.O. 7.14: Describe how research on bi-lingualism gives us insight into the relationship between language and culture.

L.O. 7.15: Know how you can use what you have learned to improve your decision-making.

A. Language: Its Basic Nature

Communication through sounds, written symbols, and gestures is language. For a set of symbols to be a language, three criteria must be met. They must transmit information or carry meaning. It must be possible to combine the symbols into an essentially infinite number of sentences. The meaning of these sentences must be independent of the settings in which they are used.

Language consists of two components: Comprehension and the production of speech. The basic sounds of language are phonemes. The smallest units of speech that convey meaning are morphemes. English has about 10,000 morphemes. Rules about how the sounds can be combined into sentences are syntax. English has forty-six separate phonemes. These include vowels, consonants, and blends of the two.

Not all speech is equally easy to interpret. Sentences that contain negatives are more difficult to understand. Ambiguous sentences (those with two or more possible meanings) are hard to understand.

Chomsky distinguished between two kinds of linguistic components. Surface structure refers to the actual words people use. Deep structure refers to the underlying meaning contained in a sentence.

B. The Development of Language

Babies make vowel and consonant sounds are made while cooing at 20 weeks. Understanding of some words occurs around 12 months. At 18 months about fifty words can be produced. A 1000-word vocabulary may be reached at 36 months. At 48 months most aspects of language are well established. Table 7-3 (p. 284) summarizes some milestones of language development. This section focuses on the mechanisms responsible for language development as well as the ages children acquire these skills.

The social learning view suggests that speech is acquired through operant conditioning and imitation. According to Chomsky and the innate mechanism view, we have a built-in neural system which provides an intuitive grasp of grammar. That is, humans are prepared to acquire language skills.

A third view is that both innate mechanisms and learning are important. This cognitive view assumes children have certain information-processing abilities that they use in acquiring language. These operating principles are assumed to be present, or develop, very early in life. Each view has some empirical support, but none seems able to account for all aspects of language development.

Learning seems to play a role in language development; parents provide differentiating feedback to their children and children's speech resembles that of their parents. However, parental feedback may be too infrequent to account fully for the quickness of language development.

Evidence for an innate language acquisition device is supported by the fact that these may be a critical period for language development during which time children find it easiest to acquire language. However, details regarding the neural structure and precise function of the language acquisition device remain somewhat vague.

Given the mixed pattern of evidence, Baron concludes that language development is the result of a complex process involving several aspects of learning, many cognitive processes, and perhaps various genetically determined mechanisms as well.

There are three basic milestones of language development. The development of the ability to pronounce the sounds and words of one or more languages is phonological development. Many children use phonological strategies or techniques to simplify the pronunciation of many words.

The second milestone is semantic development -- learning to understand the meaning of words. Some psychologists believe that children are able to build a vocabulary of more than 14,000 words by age six because they engage in fast mapping -- a process of "mapping" a new word to an underlying concept in a single exposure.

The first words acquired by children are object words which apply to concrete objects followed by action words, which describe specific activities. Children often make several errors. They demonstrate mismatches which are instances in which a new word is attached to an inappropriate concept.

In addition, they often apply a term to either a smaller or larger range of objects or events than its true meaning. Underextension is the label for applying a term to a smaller range and overextension is the label for applying a term to a larger range.

The third milestone is grammatical development. Grammar refers to a set of rules dictating how words can be combined into sentences. Before the age of two, grammar poses little problems in that speech is holophrastic. In holophrastic speech, single words are used to express complex meanings. Around age two, speech is telegraphic in that less important words are omitted. Between two and three years of age, most children use simple sentences. Between three and six years of age, more complex grammatical forms appear, including the use of conjunctions. Complexity continues to develop and is not complete until early adolescence.

The development of spoken language may arise, in part, from basic forms of nonverbal interactions that occur between children.

C.   Language and Thought: Do We Think What We Say or Say What We Think?

The idea that language shapes or determines our thought is the linguistic relativity hypothesis. The other view is that thought shapes language. The evidence best supports the second view. For example, evidence suggests that having more words for color does not affect one's recognition of differences in color.

- **Exploring Gender and Diversity: Language and Culture: Revelations Based on Studies of Bilingualism**

  The tendency of immigrant bilinguals to think and behave in accordance with the expectations of the culture that is associated with the language they are currently speaking is known as the culture-affiliation hypothesis. Several lines of research support this hypothesis.

D.   Language In Other Species

Primates (and other animals) lack the vocal control necessary to produce words. However, animals can learn to use some forms of language. For example, chimps and gorillas are able to learn sign language and parrots have used speech in highly complex ways.

Some feel that research with animals, like chimps and parrots, provides evidence for true language ability. However, others feel that the animals may simply be responding to cues of their trainers or that the trainers are over-interpreting the animals' responses. Further, they feel that the animals do not demonstrate syntax and generativity. Work with bonobos and dolphins seem to rule out criticisms like cues and over interpretation. This research suggests that animals may be able to grasp syntax and show generativity. However, the capacity of the animals may be limited, as evidenced by the fact that the ability of the bonobo named Kanzi topped out at the level of a 2 ½ year old child.

Questions:

7-19.   What are the characteristics of language and speech? _____

_____

_____

_____

7-20.   What are the different views of language development and what are the general findings concerning these views? _____

_____

_____

_____

7-21.   What are the basic milestones of development? _____

_____

_____

_____

7-22. What are the contrasting views and research findings on the relationship between language and thought? _____

_____

_____

_____

7-23. What is the evidence concerning the use of language by animals? _____

_____

_____

_____

- **Making Psychology Part of Your Life: Making Better Decisions**

    The information in this chapter can help you make better decisions. Here are a few guidelines.

    1)   Don't trust your own memory (beware of availability).
    2)   Don't take situations at face value (question all anchors).
    3)   Remain flexible (don't fall in love with your own decisions).
    4)   Consider all options (or is half an orange better than none)?

YOUR NOTES:

MAKING PSYCHOLOGY PART OF YOUR LIFE: Key Terms and Concepts

Knowing the important concepts and key terms contained in this chapter is a very important part of mastering the material. We have presented a sample of these concepts below. Define each concept and check your definition with that presented in your textbook. It will also be beneficial for you to think of an example of each concept. Whenever possible, use your own personal experience to provide an example of each term below.

7-1. **Algorithm**: _____

Example: _____

7-2. **Analogy**: _____

Example: _____

7-3. **Anchoring-and-Adjustment Heuristic**: _____

Example: _____

7-4. **Artificial Concepts**: _____

Example: _____

7-5. **Artificial Intelligence**: _____

Example: _____

7-6. **Availability Heuristic**: _____

Example: _____

7-7. **Babbling**: _____

7-8. **Cognition**: _____

Example: _____

7-9. **Concepts**: _____

Example: _____

7-10. **Confirmation Bias**: _____

   Example: _____

7-11. **Decision Making**: _____

   Example: _____

7-12. **Deep Structure**: _____

   Example: _____

7-13. **Escalation of Commitment**: _____

   Example: _____

7-14. **Expected Utility**: _____

   Example: _____

7-15. **Fast Mapping**: _____

   Example: _____

7-16. **Framing**: _____

   Example: _____

7-17. **Functional Fixedness**: _____

   Example: _____

7-18. **Grammar**: _____

7-19. **Heuristics**: _____

   Example: _____

7-20. **Hindsight Effect**: _____

   Example: _____

7-21. **Language**: _____

      Example: _____

7-22. **Linguistic Relativity Hypothesis**: _____

7-23. **Means-End Analysis**: _____

      Example: _____

7-24. **Mental Set**: _____

      Example: _____

7-25. **Metacognitive Processing**: _____

7-26. **Morphemes**: _____

      Example: _____

7-27. **Natural Concepts**: _____

      Example: _____

7-28. **Naturalistic Decision Making**: _____

7-29. **Neural Networks**: _____

7-30. **Phonemes**: _____

      Example: _____

7-31. **Phonological Development**: _____

7-32. **Phonological Strategies**: _____

      Example: _____

7-33. **Problem Solving**: _____

      Example: _____

7-34. **Propositions**: _____

Example: _____

7-35. **Prototypes**: _____

Example: _____

7-36. **Reasoning**: _____

Example: _____

7-37. **Representativeness Heuristic**: _____

Example: _____

7-38. **Semantic Development**: _____

7-39. **Surface Structure**: _____

Example: _____

7-40. **Syllogistic Reasoning**: _____

Example: _____

7-41. **Syntax**: _____

7-42. **Trial and Error**: _____

Example: _____

7-43. **Verbal Protocol Analysis**: _____

7-44. **Visual Images**: _____

CHALLENGE: Develop Your Critical Thinking Skills

A.   Creative Problem Solving

Effective critical thinking involves the ability the recognize established facts and to propose testable hypotheses. It also relies on the use of logical deduction. This problem stretches your ability to use these skills. Check your analysis with the discussion at the end of this section.

Problem: You are a space traveler and in your travels, you land on a planet in which there are two species -- Morks and Murds. Morks communicate by only telling the truth. Murds communicate by saying the opposite of what is the truth. Using your universal communicator, you ask the first alien you meet, "Are you a Mork or a Murd?" Your communicator didn't translate what the first alien said so you ask a second alien. He says, "He's a Mork and so am I." Can you believe what he says?

Your Analysis:

B.   Making Better Decisions

Decision-making is an important part of our day-to-day lives. We make decisions that vary in importance all the time -- from what to have for lunch to where to go to college. The material in this chapter can help you make better decisions. And it can help you become aware of the pitfalls that may interfere with effective decision-making. Complete the following exercises and provide an analysis of each. An analysis of these exercises can be found at the end of this section.

7-1.   Your cousin, Susan, just moved to New York City. You hear that she is in the hospital.

    A.   What is the probability that she was mugged? _____

    B.   What is the probability that she was in an automobile accident? _____

    Analysis: _____

    _____

    _____

    _____

    _____

    _____

    _____

7-2.   Prospect 1: Imagine that the U.S. is preparing for a disaster that could kill up to 600 people. Please decide which option you would choose:

    If Option A is taken, 200 lives will be saved
    If Option B is taken, there is a 1/3 probability that 600 people will be saved and a 2/3 probability that 600 people will die

    Which option would you choose? _____

    Analysis: _____

    _____

    _____

    _____

    _____

    _____

    [Note #2 and #3 based on: Kahneman, D., & Tversky, A. (1979). An analysis of decision under risk. Econometrica, 47, 263-291.]

7-3.   Prospect 2: Imagine that the U.S. is preparing for a disaster that could kill up to 600 people. Please decide which option you would choose:

If Option A is taken, 400 people will die

If Option B is taken, there is a 1/3 probability that no one will die and a 2/3 probability that 600 people will die

Which option would you choose? _____

Analysis: _____

_____

_____

_____

_____

_____

_____

YOUR NOTES:

Problem Analyses

A. Creative Problem Solving

Yes, you can believe him. The key to solving this problem is to realize that everyone claims to tell the truth. The Morks claim this honestly and the Murds claim this dishonestly. Thus, we know that the first alien stated that he was a Mork. Knowing this, we can test our hypothesis concerning the nature of the second alien. What would he say if he was a Murd?

He would have said that the first man was a Murd -- a liar. Since he did not say this, what can we infer? We can infer that the second man is not a Murd; thus, we can trust these aliens.

[Based on Hayes, J. R. (1981). The complete problem solver. Philadelphia: Franklin Institute Press.]

B. Making Better Decisions

7-1.   If you chose Option A, your decision was probably influenced by the **availability heuristic** -- the tendency to make judgments about the likelihood of events in terms of how readily examples of them can be brought to mind. The extensive publicity about violent crimes in New York City leads us to bring this information to mind and overestimate the probability of our cousin being a victim.

7-2.   The prospects presented in these two problems are identical except that, in Prospect 1, the options are
&   framed in terms of lives saved, and in Prospect 2 this framing is in terms of lives lost. This framing
7-3.   significantly affects the choices people make between options. If you chose Option A with Prospect 1 and Option B with Prospect 2, you demonstrated the typical pattern of choices.

CHALLENGE: Taking Psychology With You

In this chapter, you've learned a great deal about how people can get caught=up in bad decisions. Try applying what you've learned to the following situation:

Situation

As her wedding day approached, Patsy felt increasingly depressed. Why had she agreed to marry Jeff when she knew it wouldn't work? At first it seemed the right thing to do, since they had been dating for years. Marriage seemed to be the logical next step. But now it seemed like a bad idea. "Well, what's done is done," she thought to herself. "I can't get out of this now. The invitations have been mailed, the dress is paid for; and the food and flowers have been ordered. And what will people think if I back out now?"

The only person she confided her feelings to was her best friend -- Carol. Carol suggested that she have a heart-to-heart talk with Jeff and her parents.

"Maybe Jeff feels the same way," Carol observed. "You know, your parents really pushed both of you into this step. But they're not the ones that have to live with this decision."

Application Questions

7- 1.   Do you think Patsy is caught up in an "escalation of commitment" spiral?

_____

_____

7- 2.   Can you describe the factors that may be affecting Patsy's decision to marry Jeff?

_____

_____

7- 3.   How might the unpleasant consequences of backing out of her engagement affect her decision to get married?

_____

_____

7- 4.   What role, if any, might external pressures from others play in her decision process?

_____

_____

7- 5. Can you relate the various phases of her thoughts to the course of escalation processes (see Figure 7-5, p. 272, in your textbook)?

_____

_____

7- 6. Can you relate Carol's advice to strategies that have been found to counter pressures to escalate their commitment?

_____

_____

7- 7. What would you do in these circumstances?

_____

_____

YOUR NOTES:

CHALLENGE: Review Your Comprehensive Knowledge

SAMPLE TEST QUESTIONS

Once you have worked through the preceding sections, you should be ready for a comprehensive self-test. You can check your answers with those at the end of this section. An additional practice test is given in the supplementary section at the end of this study guide.

7-1.   Mental frameworks for categorizing diverse items as belonging together are:
    a.   hypotheses.
    b.   ideas.
    c.   prototypes.
    d.   concepts.

7-2.   Concepts can be represented as:
    a.   images.
    b.   features.
    c.   schemas.
    d.   all of the above

7-3.   Natural concepts are often based on:
    a.   prototypes.
    b.   logic.
    c.   induction.
    d.   imitation.

7-4.   External factors stemming from group pressure begin to play a role in the escalation of commitment process:
    a.   during its initial phase.
    b.   when there are early losses.
    c.   when there are continuing losses.
    d.   during all of its phases.

7-5.   When this analysis is used, participants are asked to give continuous verbal reports or to "think ahead" while making a decision:
    a.   semantic priming
    b.   verbal priming
    c.   verbal protocol
    d.   reaction time

7-6.   According to the availability heuristic, the more easily we think of something, the more:
    a.   common we judge it to be.
    b.   we like it.
    c.   we dislike it.
    d.   we understand it.

7-7.   This process involves an awareness of ourselves engaged in the problem-solving process:
    a.   illumination
    b.   means-end
    c.   semantic
    d.   metacognitive

7-8.   The anchoring and adjustment heuristic is strongly influenced by:
    a.   expected utility.
    b.   base rates.
    c.   a reference point.
    d.   ambiguous information.

7-9.   Rules for solving problems that eventually will lead to solutions are:
    a.   trial-and-error rules.
    b.   heuristics.
    c.   algorithms.
    d.   inducers.

7-10.   Dividing a problem into a series of subproblems is the technique of:
    a.   means-end-analysis.
    b.   analogies.
    c.   anchoring and adjustment.
    d.   schematizing.

7-11.   Research on framing decisions indicates when the emphasis is on potential gains of outcomes, people are _____ and when the emphasis is on potential losses people are _____.
   a. risk averse, gain averse   c. gain prone, gain averse
   b. risk averse, risk prone   d. risk prone, risk averse

7-12.   The smallest unit of speech that conveys meaning is called a:
   a. phoneme.   c. deep structure.
   b. morpheme.   d. surface structure.

7-13.   Rules about how units of speech can be combined into sentences are called:
   a. phonemes.   c. syntax.
   b. morphemes.   d. semantics.

7-14.   The type of knowledge that involves understanding of the meaning of words is known as:
   a. semantic.   c. syntactical.
   b. phonological.   d. morphological.

7-15.   At about _____ months, most children have mastered most of the basic aspects of language.
   a. 12   c. 36
   b. 24   d. 48

7-16.   According to Chomsky, the underlying meaning contained in a sentence is known as:
   a. phoneme.   c. deep structure.
   b. morpheme.   d. surface structure.

7-17.   The basic sounds of languages are:
   a. phonemes.   c. syntax.
   b. morphemes.   d. algorithms.

7-18.   The social learning view of language development suggests that:
   a. language is innate.
   b. language is acquired through operant conditioning and imitation.
   c. language is acquired through the application of operating principles.
   d. language is based on deep structure.

7-19.   The view that language determines thought is known as:
   a. the linguistic relativity hypothesis.   c. Chomsky's hypothesis.
   b. the social learning approach.   d. the artificial intelligence approach.

7-20.   What are the three basic milestones of language development?
   a. holophrastic, telegraphic, semantic   c. intuitive, semantic, phonological
   b. phonological, semantic, grammatical   d. deep structure, surface structure, fast mapping

Answers and Feedback for Sample Test Questions

7-1.   D   Concepts are mental frameworks for categorizing diverse items as belonging together. (p. 257)

7-2.   D   Concepts can be represented in terms of images, features, or schemas. (p. 258-259)

7-3.   A   Natural concepts are often based on prototypes, which are idealized images of stimuli. (p. 258)

7-4.   C   Continuing losses increase escalation of commitment. (p. 271-272)

7-5.   C   When the verbal protocol analysis is used, participants are asked to give continuous verbal reports. (p. 260-261)

7-6.   A   The availability heuristic leads us to overestimate the frequency or base rates of events. (p. 268)

7-7.   D   Metacognitive processing involves an awareness of ourselves engaged in the problem-solving process. (p. 276-277)

7-8.   C   Our tendency to make decisions by using a reference point is known as the anchoring and adjustment heuristic. (p. 269)

7-9.   C   Algorithms are rules that, when followed, will eventually lead to a solution. (p. 276)

7-10.   A   Means-end analysis consists of dividing a problem into a series of subproblems and deciding on the ends we want to attain and the means used to get there. (p. 276)

7-11.   B   Research indicates that when decisions are framed in terms of potential gains, people are risk averse -- they prefer to avoid unnecessary risks. When the emphasis is on potential losses, they are risk prone -- they prefer to take risks vs. accept certain losses. (p. 270-271)

7-12.   B   Morphemes are the smallest units of speech that convey meaning. (p. 282)

7-13.   C   Syntax defines rules about how units of speech can be combined into sentences. (p. 282)

7-14.   A   Semantic knowledge involves understanding the meaning of words. (p. 286)

7-15.   D   At 48 months, most children have mastered the basic aspects of language. (p. 284, see Table 7.3)

7-16.   C   In Chomsky's theory, the underlying meaning of a sentence is contained in deep structure. (p. 283)

7-17.   A   Phonemes are the basic sounds of language. (p. 282)

7-18.   B   Social learning theory suggests that both operant conditioning and imitation contribute to language development. (p. 284)

7-19.   A   The idea that language shapes or determines our thought is the linguistic relativity hypothesis. (p. 288-289)

7-20.   B   The three milestones of language development are: phonological development (the ability to pronounce the sounds and words of language), semantic development (the ability to understand the meaning of words), and grammatical development (the ability to correctly combine words into sentences). (p. 285)

GLOSSARY OF DIFFICULT WORDS AND EXPRESSIONS

These terms from your text and this study guide were identified by students as potentially hard to understand. We have defined these terms and expressions.

Term or expression	Definition
Agonized over	spent a lot of effort or worry about something
"All-or-nothing decision"	a choice that something is very important and excludes other possibilities
Aloof	distant, beyond approach
Arranged counterparts	put in a certain order persons that are matched on some dimensions such as age
Assertions	strong statements
Assessing	evaluating, attempting to understand
Boundaries	limits
Concessions	giving in
Conjure	create as an image
Convey	give information
Feat	task; accomplishment
Fetch	bring, take from one point to another
Flawed	not perfect, having a defect
Fluttering	quick movements, going back and forth
Frozen yogurt	A less fattening alternative to ice cream
Fuzzy	blurred, not clear
Graded	to a greater or less degree; small increments
Grasp	understand
Hunches	vague feeling or ideas
Infinite	having no end; going on forever
Milestones	important marker
Neat	clean cut
Obstacle	something that blocks or stands in the way
Plausible	seeming to be right or reasonable
Progress	moving forward; advancing
Prone to	have a tendency to

Term or expression	Definition
Refrain	not to do something; stop from doing
Relentless	not giving up; continuing to act
Rudder	a piece of a boat
solely	only; the single element
Sought to	tried to, attempted
The launch of	to begin or propel
Topped out	reached the highest level
Tradeoffs	exchanges, one event balances another
Trustworthy	dependable
Vacillate	doubt or to see two sides
"Wandering about"	going from place to place without any special purpose or destination
Widespread	popular or common

Chapter 8
HUMAN DEVELOPMENT I: THE CHILDHOOD YEARS

INTEGRATED CHAPTER OUTLINE: Survey and Question

This section presents the major topics and ideas from the chapter. Use it as a tool for seeing how the components of the chapter fit together. At the end of each major topic, we have asked you a question that relates to the major learning objectives. If you can answer these questions, you have taken a major step toward mastering this material.

I.   Physical Growth and Development

L.O. 8.1:   Trace the course of development in the prenatal period.

L.O. 8.2:   Discuss the potential impact of synthetic chemicals on the endocrine system.

L.O. 8.3:   Trace the course of physical and perceptual development during childhood.

L.O. 8.4:   Know the research methods used to study human development.

The area of psychology concerned with physical, social, and mental change during the lifespan is developmental psychology. Our survey begins with an exploration of physical growth and development.

A.   The Prenatal Period

Development begins when the sperm fertilizes the ovum. The ovum travels to the uterus. Ten to fourteen days after fertilization, the ovum becomes implanted in the uterus and is known as the embryo for the next six weeks. It develops rapidly, and by the third week, the heart begins to beat. By the eighth week the face, arms, and legs are developed. The major internal organs have begun to form, the sex glands begin to function, and the nervous system is developing rapidly.

During the next seven months, the developing child is now called a fetus. During this time the hair, nails, and eyes develop and physical growth is rapid. By the seventh or eighth month, the fetus appears to be virtually fully formed. However, if born prematurely, the baby may still experience difficulties. Tiny air sacs (alveoli) in the lungs are not fully formed.

There is evidence that cognitive abilities develop during the prenatal period. In one study, the fetus could distinguish familiar and unfamiliar stories. Familiar stories were associated with decreased heart rate, which is thought to indicate increased attention. Follow-up research conducted after the birth of the child indicated that the babies quickly learned to suck in a way that produced the familiar story.

B.   Prenatal Influences on Development

Many environmental factors can interfere with prenatal growth. Such factors are known as teratogens. Since the blood supply of the mother and fetus come close together in the placenta, disease from the mother's blood can infect the child. For example, rubella or German measles can cause blindness, deafness or heart disease if contracted during the first four weeks of pregnancy. Other diseases that can affect prenatal development include chicken pox, mumps, tuberculosis, malaria, syphilis, herpes, and

AIDS. Drugs can also have an effect. For example, excessive use of aspirin can harm the circulatory system of the developing child. Fetal alcohol syndrome results from alcohol consumption during pregnancy and smoking also has a negative affect on the developing fetus. Research also suggests that synthetic chemicals in the environment may harm the endocrine system.

- **Beyond the Headlines: As Psychologists See It -- Hormonal Sabotage?**

Scientists are finding evidence that synthetic compounds found in pesticides and industrial chemicals may be harming our immune systems. The chemical DES, which is a growth hormone used in animal feed may be dangerous because it circumvents mechanisms that absorb excess estrogen int he fetal blood supply. Preliminary evidence suggests this can lead to various forms of cancer. This issue will be a "hot one" in future years.

C. . Physical and Perceptual Development During Our Early Years

Physical growth is rapid during infancy. And newborns possess a number of simple reflexes, such as sucking. Newborns can learn through classical conditioning. However, for young infants, conditioning occurs most readily for stimuli that have survival value. A considerable body of evidence indicates that newborns demonstrate operant conditioning. Evidence also suggests that infants are capable of imitating the facial gestures of adults.

Because infants can't talk, it is necessary to use indirect methods to study their perceptual abilities. These methods include observing changes in heart rate, sucking responses, or the amount of time they spend gazing at stimuli. The rationale of this method is that if infants can detect differences between two stimuli, we may observe changes in their responses to the stimuli. The use of these methods has demonstrated that infants can distinguish between different colors, odors, and auditory stimuli. Classic research by Fantz has shown that six-month-old babies prefer patterned stimuli. This research also suggested that babies prefer the human face as opposed to all other tested stimuli.

Studies using the visual cliff show that infants as young as six months perceive depth. This test is limited by infants' ability to crawl. Studies using tests without this limitation have shown that three-month-old infants can perceive depth.

- **Research Methods: How Psychologists Study Development**

The method that involves testing individuals on several occasions over a period of time is longitudinal research. There are advantages to this method. First, individual variations can be studied. Second, because the same persons are tested, it may be possible to draw conclusions about how specific events influence development. However, there are also disadvantages. There may be a loss of participants and this research is subject to practice effects. The method that involves testing different age groups only once is called cross-sectional research. There are several advantages to this method. It can be conducted more quickly than longitudinal research and it minimizes practice effects in that participants are tested only once. However, this method has disadvantages. For example, it is subject to cohort effects. This refers to the fact that differences correlated to age could influence the results, such as being born at different times, different life experiences and different cultural conditions.

An approach that maximizes the advantages of both of the above while minimizing their disadvantages is known as the longitudinal-sequential design. It involves studying several samples of people of different ages for a number of years. It allows for both longitudinal and cross-sectional comparisons in that it tests for each participant across time and also tests different age groups. For example, it can test for cohort effects by comparing persons born in different years with one another when they reach the same age.

Questions:

8-1. What is the scope of developmental psychology? _____

_____

_____

_____

8-2. What are the characteristics of the prenatal period? _____

_____

_____

_____

8-3. What are the influences of environmental factors on prenatal development? _____

_____

_____

_____

8-4. What is the course of physical development in infancy and childhood? _____

_____

_____

_____

8-5. What kind of learning abilities do newborns have? _____

_____

_____

_____

8-6. What is the course of infant's perceptual development? _____

_____

_____

_____

8-7.   What are the advantages and disadvantages of the three basic methods for studying human development? _____

_____

_____

_____

II. Cognitive Development: Changes in Our Ability to Understand the World Around Us

L.O. 8.5:   Be able to describe Piaget's theory of development and provide a critical assessment of its assumptions.

L.O. 8.6:   Describe the information processing approach to development and be able to compare and contrast it with Piaget's view of cognitive development.

L.O. 8.7:   Be able to discuss cross-national differences in mathematical competence.

L.O. 8.8:   Understand the nature of moral development.

A.   Piaget's Theory: An Overview

Piaget believed that children begin life with limited cognitive skills. He believed that cognitive development occurs in a series of stages that represent different ways of thinking and reasoning. Stage theorists assume that all persons move through a set series of stages, that they do so at certain ages, and that the order of progress is fixed. Many psychologists question this assumption.

Piaget believed that the mechanism responsible for cognitive development is adaptation. This process results in the development of mental representations of the world through interaction. Interactions with the world have two consequences. First, our experiences can be fit into existing schemes; this tendency is called assimilation. Second, interactions with the world can alter existing schemes; this tendency is called accommodation. The interplay between these two components of adaptation fosters cognitive development. Cognitive development results in progress through ever-more complex conceptions of the world around us.

According to Piaget, young children do not think or reason like adults. He proposes that children go through an orderly sequence of four major stages toward cognitive maturity. The first stage is the sensorimotor stage. In this stage, the infant knows the world only through motor activities and sensory impressions. They acquire the basic concept of cause and effect. But they have not learned to use symbols to represent objects, so they will act as if an object hidden from view no longer exists. Understanding that such objects do exist is called object permanence.

Between the ages of 18 to 24 months, children acquire the ability to form mental images of the world around them and begin to think in verbal symbols. This marks the beginning of the preoperational stage. Their thought is still immature in many ways. They are egocentric in that they have difficulty understanding that others may see the world differently from them. [However, this effect depends on how the question is asked.] They can also be fooled by appearance and believe, for example, that a dog mask on a cat makes it a dog. Their thought is also animistic in that they often attribute human feelings to inanimate objects. They also lack understanding of relational terms (e.g., "larger") and cannot arrange objects in order along some dimension (serialization). They lack the principle of conservation, which is the knowledge that an underlying dimension remains unchanged by minor shifts in appearance.

By age seven, most children can solve the problems of the previous stage and enter the period of concrete operations. During this stage, they understand that many physical changes can be undone by reversing the original actions or reversibility. They begin to make greater use of conceptual categories and begin to engage in logical thought.

At about age 12, most children enter the final stage of cognitive development known as formal operations. In this stage, the major features of adult thought emerge. In contrast to the concrete operational child who can think logically, the formal operational child can think abstractly. The formal operational child is capable of hypothetic-deductive reasoning in which a general theory is formulated and tested in problem-solving. A person in this stage can also assess the logical validity of verbal assertions even when these refer to possibilities rather than to events in the real world (i.e., propositional reasoning). It should be noted that although individuals in this stage have the capacity or ability for logical thought, there is no guarantee that such systematic reasoning will occur.

B.   Piaget's Theory: A Modern Assessment

Research focusing on Piaget's theory suggest that Piaget's theory is incorrect or in need of revision for three reasons. First, it suggests that he underestimated the cognitive abilities of infants and young children. For example, infants of 4.5 months appear to possess a rudimentary understanding of object permanence and three year olds show some understanding of the concept of conservation. Second, research suggests that development may not proceed through discrete stages and that these stages may not be discontinuous in nature. Rather, cognitive changes may be gradual. Finally, research suggests that Piaget downplayed the importance of language and social interactions.

C.   Cognitive Development: An Information-Processing Perspective

During the past 20 years, an information-processing perspective to cognitive development has been developed by psychologists who seek to understand how, and in what ways, children's capacity to process, store, retrieve, and actively manipulate information increases with age. According to this approach, children show increasing ability to notice subtle features of the external world and develop increasingly sophisticated cognitive frameworks or schemas. Children show an increasing ability to focus their attention and block out distractions. They also show an increasing ability to plan. For example, in one study, most three year olds did not show evidence of planning whereas most five year olds did show evidence of planning. Three to five percent of all children suffer from attention-deficit hyperactivity disorder (ADHD). Children who suffer from this disorder have normal intelligence but find it difficult to ignore irrelevant information and are unable to concentrate their attention on any task for more than a few minutes. Heredity, high levels of stress, and exposure to prenatal teratogens have all been implicated as possible causes of this disorder. It can be effectively treated with medication and therapy.

With maturity, children's memory improves in many ways. Improvements occur with respect to short-term and long-term memory. A key change associated with short-term memory is the increasing use of strategies for retaining information. Rehearsal and organizational strategies both improve as children mature. Children as young as three years appear to engage in efforts to improve their memories; and by eight years of age, they engage in simple forms of rehearsal. One key change associated with long-term memory involves expression of knowledge that pertains to specific areas of life and activity. This knowledge is called domain-specific knowledge. But their memory is still very susceptible to distortions.

Metacognition refers to an awareness and understanding of our own cognitive processes. With maturity, children develop an increasing awareness and understanding of their cognitive processes, which allows them to become increasingly capable of self-regulation. They can develop more sophisticated strategies for maximizing their own efficiency and for enhancing attention and memory. Further, they can monitor their own progress toward goals as well as remember and evaluate their own understanding.

- **Exploring Gender and Diversity: Cross-National Differences in Mathematical Competence**

There are differences among groups in mathematical abilities. For example, Asian children generally outscore U.S. children. These differences emerge quite early in life and may be related to differences between languages in these nations. In Asian languages, such as Chinese, number names follow a consistent rule (e.g., "eleven" is literally "ten one"); this isn't true in English. Research shows that group differences in counting emerge between the numbers 11 and 20, not in smaller sets. These findings underscore the important contribution of language and other cultural factors on cognitive development.

D.   Moral Development: Reasoning About "Right" and "Wrong"

The issue of whether children and adults reason about moral issues in similar ways is a key question addressed by research on moral development. The most influential theory in this area was proposed by Kohlberg. He proposed that human beings move through three distinct levels of moral reasoning. Each level is divided into two separate stages. The method he uses to assess moral reasoning involves asking subjects to imagine moral dilemmas in which competing causes of action are possible. The subjects' explanations are the critical key to their stage of moral development.

In the preconventional level of moral development, morality is judged in terms of the consequences of actions. For example, actions that lead to punishment are viewed as unacceptable. Within Stage 1 of this level, known as the punishment and obedience orientation, children cannot grasp the existence of two points of view in a moral dilemma. As a result, they unquestioningly accept an authority's perspective as their own. In Stage 2 of this level of moral development, known as the naive hedonistic orientation, children judge morality in terms of what satisfies their own or others needs.

The second level is known as the conventional level. At this level, children judge morality in terms of what supports and preserves the social order. Stage 3 of moral development occurs within this level, known as the good boy - good girl orientation, and reflects moral judgments based on a desire to seek approval from the people they know by adhering to social norms. In Stage 4, known as the social-order-maintaining orientation, children extend judgments of morality to include the perspective of people they do not know. Thus they believe that the law applies to everyone.

In adolescence or early adulthood, some people enter the postconventional or principles level. At this level, morality is judged by abstract principles or values. Stage 5 represents a values orientation in which individuals realize that laws can be inconsistent with the rights of individuals and can envision alternative laws. This stage is termed the social contract, legalistic orientation stage. In Stage 6, known as the universal ethical principle orientation, individuals believe that certain obligations and values transcend the laws of society at points in time. Morality is judged in terms of self-chosen ethical principles.

Evidence supports the suggestion that moral reasoning increases in complexity with age and that individuals pass through these stages. However, Kohlberg's theory needs revision in several respects.

Some early studies suggested that men scored higher than females in moral reasoning. In response to this work, Gilligan proposed that Kohlberg's theory was sex-biased. According to Gilligan, Kohlberg overlooked concern for others or care-based principles of morality as is a key factor for women. Research suggests that males and females do not focus on different aspects of moral dilemmas, as postulated by Gilligan. Further, females score as high as males in moral reasoning on both hypothetical dilemmas and everyday moral problems. If anything, females tend to score higher in moral reasoning than males. These findings are counter to the early studies that suggested that females lag behind males in moral reasoning. Thus, contrary to initial findings, there is no evidence that men and women attain different levels of moral development.

Kohlberg's theory is a stage theory. Given this framework, it would be expected that individuals' moral reasoning would be consistent within each level. However, people do not show such consistency. Their responses to moral dilemmas change depending upon the kind of dilemma that is presented to them.

The stages described by Kohlberg and the movement through them do not appear in all cultures. Therefore, culture plays a role in shaping moral development. Kohlberg's theory does not take this into account.

Questions:

8-8. What are the general assumptions of Piaget's theory of cognitive development? _____

_____

_____

_____

8-9. What are the characteristics of the sensorimotor stage? _____

_____

_____

_____

8-10. What is the nature of a child's thought during the preoperational stage? _____

_____

_____

_____

8-11. Why does the stage of concrete operations mark a major turning point in cognitive development?

_____

_____

_____

8-12. What are the competencies of adolescents during the formal operational stage? _____

_____

_____

_____

8-13. Why do many psychologists believe that Piaget's theory is inaccurate or in need of revision?

_____

_____

_____

8-14. What are the major assumptions and major goals of the information-processing perspective of cognitive development? _____

_____

_____

_____

8-15. Do infants form mental representations of the external world? _____

_____

_____

_____

8-16. How does the attentional focus of younger children compare to that of older children? _____

_____

_____

_____

8-17. What are the consequences, possible causes, and treatment of ADHD? _____

_____

_____

_____

8-18. What are the ways in which memory improves with age? _____

_____

_____

_____

8-19. What is metacognition and why is it important? _____

_____

_____

_____

8-20. What are the major characteristics of Kohlberg's stages of moral development? _____

_____

_____

_____

8-21. What is the status of the controversy concerning whether Kohlberg's theory is sex-biased?

_____

_____

_____

8-22. What is the evidence that does not support Kohlberg's theory? _____

_____

_____

III. Social and Emotional Development: Forming Relationships With Others

L.O. 8.9:   Describe how we develop emotionally throughout childhood.

L.O. 8.10:   Understand how we develop attachments to other persons.

L.O. 8.11:   Be able to discuss the role of school and friendships in social development.

A.   Emotional Development and Temperament

A crucial question in the area of emotional development concerns when infants begin to experience and demonstrate discrete emotions. Because infants cannot describe their feelings, efforts to answer this question focus on discrete facial expressions. Infants as young as two months old demonstrate social smiling in response to human faces and show laughter by three or four months. Many other emotions such as sadness, surprise, and anger appear quite early and are readily recognized by adults. Research indicates that emotional development and cognitive development occur simultaneously. Children also acquire increasing abilities to determine the emotional expressions of others and to regulate their own emotional reactions. By eight months they demonstrate social referencing -- using another's reactions to appraise an uncertain situation. Although infants have very limited ability to regulate their own emotions, preschoolers are actively involved in efforts to understand and control their internal states.

Stable individual differences in the quality or intensity of emotional responding is known as temperament. Infants do differ in their emotional style at birth. These differences have a powerful influence on infants' interactions with caregivers and can influence the course of social development. Children can be divided into three categories: easy, difficult, and slow-to-warm-up. During the first three years of life, boys and girls don't differ in temperament. But by school-age, boys show higher rates of externalizing disorders and problems relating to overt behavior such as hyperactivity. Some aspects of temperament, like attentiveness, activity level, and irritability appear to be quite stable. In one study, the reactivity of a population of infants remained relatively stable into middle childhood. However, other studies suggest that extended stability in various aspects of temperament may only occur for persons who have relatively extreme scores on these measures. Differences in temperament appear to be influenced by both biological and environmental factors.

B.   Attachment: The Beginnings of Love

By age of six or seven months most infants show a strong bond or attachment to their caregivers. The strange situation test is used to study attachment in young children. Children are placed in a distressing environment and their reactions when their mother leaves and returns are monitored. About two-thirds of American middle-class infants show secure attachment. They take little comfort from the presence of a stranger and actively seek contact with their mother when she returns. About twenty percent of this population shows avoidant attachment. These children react to their mother and stranger in much the same way and either avoid or are slow to make contact with their mother when she returns. About ten percent of this population show a resistant attachment. Prior to separation, these infants seek contact with their mother; but after separation they are angry and push her away. About five percent show disorganized or disoriented attachment. After separation, these infants show disorganized responses when reunited with their mothers.

Securely attached children are more sociable, more flexible, better at solving certain problems, and have fewer behavioral problems than avoidant and unsecurely attached children. The quality of caregiving and maternal deprivation are two factors that may determine the pattern of attachment. For example, when caregivers are sensitive to their children's needs and signals, their children are more likely to be securely attached than when caregivers are not sensitive. Avoidant children tend to have caregivers who are either insensitive or overstimulating. Finally, children who experience long-term separation from their mother do not appear to evidence secure attachment.

Close physical contact with soft objects is an additional factor that plays an important role in attachment. Studies with monkeys have shown that the satisfaction of physical needs is not a sufficient condition for attachment. Harlow found that the need for contact comfort seems to be the important factor. Provisions of milk by a mother does not increase attachment. In other studies, he found that the presence of soft cloth mothers, but not wire mothers, was able to reduce fear of monkeys in the presence of strange objects. Having cloth mothers reject the baby monkeys by presenting various noxious stimuli did not alter the degree of attachment. There is some evidence that human babies also have a need for contact comfort.

C.   School and Friendships: Key Factors in Social Development

School and friendships play an important role in social development. Schools provide an opportunity to learn many social skills, such as cooperation: "Friendship" is a special type of social relationship that is important to children. Friends have strong emotional ties, cooperate with one another, see themselves as equals and are more similar to one another than other peer relationships.

Questions:

8-23. What is the course of children's emotional development? _____

_____

_____

_____

8-24. What are the individual differences that exist in temperament? _____

_____

_____

_____

8-25. How is attachment measured? _____

_____

_____

_____

8-26. What are the characteristics of the four different patterns of attachments? _____

_____

_____

_____

8-27. What factors affect attachment between infants and their caregivers? _____

_____

_____

_____

8-28. What did Harlow's research teach us about the role of contact comfort in attachment? _____

_____

_____

_____

8-29. How do schools and friendship relationships contribute to social and emotional development?

_____

_____

_____

IV. Gender: Gender Identity and Gender Differences

L.O. 8.12:   Compare and contrast the views on the development of gender identity.

L.O. 8.13:   Know what differences exist between males and females and be able to discuss the possible origins of these differences.

L.O. 8.14:   Know how you can use what you've learned to avoid common mistakes in disciplining children.

A.   Gender Identity: Some Contrasting Views

The knowledge that a child belongs to a specific sex is called gender identity. Evidence exists that this process beings early in life. By the age of two years, many children use gender labels appropriately. Between three and ½ and four and ½ years, children begin to understand that gender is stable over time.

According to the social learning view, gender identity is acquired through operant conditioning and observational learning. Through observational learning, children gradually come to match their behaviors to the behaviors of same-sex individuals. This imitation is actively reinforced by adults. The gender schema theory suggests that children develop cognitive frameworks reflecting their society's beliefs about gender. Once established, gender schemas influence the processing of social information.

B.   Gender Differences: Do Males and Females Really Differ, and If So, How?

All societies have gender stereotypes (preconceived notions of the traits thought to be possessed by males and females) and gender roles (expectations concerning the roles each sex should fill and how they are supposed to behave).

Research indicates that there are several differences in the social behavior of males and females. For the most part, they are subtle and small. They differ in emotional expression. Females are better than males at both transmitting their own feeling via nonverbal cues and understanding the nonverbal cues of others. Possibly, because of gender stereotypes, females are more likely to express positive emotions toward others whereas males are more likely to express positive emotions about their own accomplishments.

Males appear to be more likely than females to engage in direct forms of aggression whereas females appear to be more likely to engage in indirect forms of aggression. These differences may be due, in part, to gender stereotypes. There are no gender differences in susceptibility to social influence.

Although differences between males and females in cognitive abilities do exist, they are generally smaller than gender stereotypes would suggest. In addition, there is a tendency for these differences to decrease in magnitude, especially in recent years.

Contrary to popular belief, females are not more emotional than males. However, females are more likely to suffer from depression and to have eating disorders. Psychological and cultural factors may play a strong role in causing depression in women. Because of cultural factors, females may feel helpless and may feel pressures to conform to standards of attractiveness, such as slimness.

C.   Gender Differences: A Note on Their Possible Origins

Gender differences arise because of (a) contrasting socialization practices for girls and boys, (b) from the powerful influence of gender stereotypes and gender roles and, (c) from biological factors. Evidence for biological factors includes the fact that the structure of the corpus callosum is different for males and females. Other findings indicate that the gonadal hormones (hormones produced by the ovaries and testes) influence gender differences.

Questions:

8-30. What are the two different views on the development of gender identity? _____

_____

_____

_____

8-31. What is the nature of sex stereotyped beliefs and behavior? _____

_____

_____

_____

8-32. What gender differences have been found to exist and what are their possible origins? _____

_____

_____

_____

• **Making Psychology Part of Your Life: Being a Successful Parent**

Baron points out ways that you can apply information about psychology to being a successful parent. These principles are as follows: (1) Don't expect too much too early, (2) Don't assume that children can reason like adults, (3) Never let your child "divide and conquer," (4) Remember that you are always a model for your child, (5) Choose a daycare center carefully, and (6) Be consistent.

MAKING PSYCHOLOGY PART OF YOUR LIFE: Key Terms and Concepts

Knowing the important concepts and key terms contained in this chapter is a very important part of mastering the material. We have presented a sample of these concepts below. Define each concept and check your definition with that presented at the end of this chapter. It will also be beneficial for you to think of an example of each concept. Whenever possible, use your own personal experience to provide an example of each term below.

8-1.   **Accommodation**: _____

       Example: _____

8-2.   **Adaptation**: _____

       Example: _____

8-3.   **Assimilation**: _____

       Example: _____

8-4.   **Attachment**: _____

       Example: _____

8-5.   **Attention-Deficit Hyperactivity Disorder**: _____

8-6.   **Avoidant Attachment**: _____

       Example: _____

8-7.   **Cognitive Development**: _____

8-8.   **Cohort Effects**: _____

       Example: _____

8-9.   **Concrete Operations**: _____

       Example: _____

8-10.   **Conservation**: _____

       Example: _____

8-11.   **Conventional Level (of Morality)**: _____

       Example: _____

8-12.   **Cross-Sectional Research**: _____

       Example: _____

8-13.   **Developmental Psychology**: _____

8-14.   **Disorganized or Disoriented Attachment**: _____

       Example: _____

8-15.   **Egocentrism**: _____

       Example: _____

8-16.   **Embryo**: _____

8-17.   **Emotional Development**: _____

       Example: _____

8-18.   **Fetus**: _____

8-19.   **Formal Operations (Stage of)**: _____

       Example: _____

8-20.   **Friendships**: _____

       Example: _____

8-21.   **Gender**: _____

8-22.   **Gender Constancy**: _____

       Example: _____

8-23.   **Gender Differences**: _____

8-24.   **Gender Identity**: _____

Example: _____

8-25.   **Gender Roles**: _____

Example: _____

8-26.   **Gender Schema Theory**: _____

8-27.   **Gender Stereotypes**: _____

8-28.   **Hypothetico-Deductive Reasoning**: _____

Example: _____

8-29.   **Information-Processing Perspective**: _____

8-30.   **Longitudinal Research**: _____

Example: _____

8-31.   **Longitudinal-Sequential Design**: _____

Example: _____

8-32.   **Make-Believe Play**: _____

Example: _____

8-33.   **Metacognition**: _____

Example: _____

8-34.   **Moral Development**: _____

Example: _____

8-35.   **Object Permanence**: _____

Example: _____

8-36.   **<u>Physical Growth and Development</u>**: _____

8-37.   **<u>Placenta</u>**: _____

8-38.   **<u>Postconventional Level</u>**: _____

Example: _____

8-39.   **<u>Preconventional Level</u>**: _____

Example: _____

8-40.   **<u>Preoperational Stage</u>**: _____

Example: _____

8-41.   **<u>Propositional Reasoning</u>**: _____

Example: _____

8-42.   **<u>Resistant Attachment</u>**: _____

Example: _____

8-43.   **<u>Scripts</u>**: _____

Example: _____

8-44.   **<u>Secure Attachment</u>**: _____

Example: _____

8-45.   **<u>Sensorimotor Stage</u>**: _____

Example: _____

8-46.   **<u>Social Development</u>**: _____

8-47.   **<u>Social Referencing</u>**: _____

Example: _____

8-48. **Socialization**: _____

8-49. **Stage Theory**: _____

      Example: _____

8-50. **Strange Situation**: _____

      Example: _____

8-51. **Temperament**: _____

8-52. **Teratogens**: _____

      Example: _____

YOUR NOTES:

CHALLENGE: Develop Your Critical Thinking Skills

<u>Going Beyond Definitions</u>

A critical thinker is able to go beyond definition terms and is able to recognize situations where a concept is applicable. The ability to extend basic definitions to more complex applications is a sign of true understanding. Stretch your skills in "going beyond definitions" in the following exercises. Check your answers with those that we suggested at the end of this section.

8-1.   Carrie is babysitting Johnny for the very first time. She is nervous because he is 4-months-old. He begins to cry and she attempts to distract him by playing a game. She holds a stuffed bunny in front of him and then hides it beneath a blanket. Johnny shows no interest in this game. According to Piaget, why would this be the case?

_____

_____

8-2.   Given the information that Sam has read about the amount of sugar children consume, he is trying to restrict the sugar in his 4-year-old's diet. But Gary is unhappy about this and insists on having two cookies. Given Sam's knowledge about Piaget's stages of development, he breaks a cookie in half and gives the two halves to Gary. Gary is now content. Why?

_____

_____

8-3.   Susie does poorly on her biology exam. Of course, she is disappointed, but thinks to herself, "Next time, I need to concentrate on examples of concepts." What cognitive skill has Susie acquired?

_____

_____

8-4.   Jessica is involved in the anti-nuclear power movement. She argues with her parents that blocking the entrance to a nuclear power plant is justified by saying, "I know it is against the law to trespass -- but it is justified. Doing this will help save our planet and life is more important than property." What stage of moral development is she in, according to Kohlberg?

_____

_____

Discussion of Critical Thinking Challenge

8-1.   Johnny shows no interest in this game because he is in the early part of the sensorimotor stage of development. In this stage, he lacks the concept of object permanence. When the bunny disappears...it is truly "out of sight -- out of mind."

8-2.   Gary is in the preoperational stage of development and lacks, according to Piaget, the ability to <u>conserve</u>. Changing the outward appearance of the cookie (from 1 cookie to 2) is interpreted as obtaining more cookies; he does not realize that the physical attributes of the cookie remains unchanged in spite of its outward appearance.

8-3.   Metacognition: Awareness and understanding of our own cognitive processes.

8-4.   The postconventional stage. In this stage, morality judged in terms of abstract principles and values, rather than existing law or rules of society. Specifically, she would be at Stage 5 within this level, known as the social contract, legalistic orientation.

YOUR NOTES:

CHALLENGE: Taking Psychology With You

Childrearing: Past, Present, and Future

In these fast-paced times, when there are more working couples and an increased amount of time spent at work, childrearing is quite different than it was in the recent past. It is important to consider the implications of these changes for our children's development. Given the knowledge that you have acquired about early development, please consider the following issues:

8-1.   Television is now a socialization agent. Most of you were exposed to this source of socialization throughout your development. What effects do you think TV has had on you?

_____

_____

_____

_____

_____

_____

8-2.   How would you use what you have learned in this chapter to regulate your child's TV viewing?

_____

_____

_____

_____

_____

_____

8-3.   Are there both advantages and disadvantages to this source of socialization?

_____

_____

_____

_____

8-4.   If you were in daycare as a child, retrospect on your experiences and speculate on how these experiences may
have affected your development. Or, if you have children, speculate on how daycare may affect their
development.

_____

_____

_____

_____

_____

8-5.   If you found it necessary to place your child in daycare, what features would you look for in a daycare
environment?

_____

_____

_____

_____

_____

_____

8-6.   Can you think of any positive influences that daycare may have on a child's development?

_____

_____

_____

_____

8-7.   What other changes in childrearing practices have occurred in recent years?

_____

_____

_____

_____

8-8.   What effects do you think these changes might have on development?

_____

_____

_____

_____

8-9.   What changes do you think may occur in future years?

_____

_____

_____

_____

8-10.   Can you anticipate what the effects of such changes might be?

_____

_____

_____

_____

CHALLENGE: Review Your Comprehensive Knowledge

SAMPLE TEST QUESTIONS

Once you have worked through the preceding sections, you should be ready for a comprehensive self-test. You can check your answers with those at the end of this section. An additional practice test is given in the supplementary section at the end of this study guide.

8-1.   The face, arms, and legs are present by the _____ week of prenatal development.
a.   third
b.   fourth
c.   sixth
d.   eighth

8-2.   In one study, mothers read stories to the fetus during pregnancy. It was found that reading _____ stories _____ heart rate.
a.   familiar, decreased
b.   familiar, increased
c.   unfamiliar, decreased
d.   unfamiliar, increased

8-3.   The fetal disorder that may involve retarded growth, damaged nervous system, and facial distortions is associated with maternal:
a.   alcohol consumption.
b.   caffeine intake.
c.   illegal drug use.
d.   smoking.

8-4.   Which of the following is not a reflex that is present at birth?
a.   sucking
b.   crawling
c.   following a moving light with eyes
d.   grasping

8-5.   The method of studying development that provides the clearest picture of the course of human development is the:
a.   cross-sectional approach.
b.   longitudinal approach.
c.   longitudinal-sequential design.
d.   experimental design.

8-6.   According to Piaget, cognitive development involves interplay between _____ and _____.
a.   sensation and cognition
b.   the id and the ego
c.   assimilation and accommodation
d.   emotion and motivation

8-7.   The stage in which logical thought first occurs is:
a.   preoperational.
b.   sensory-motor.
c.   formal operations.
d.   concrete operations.

8-8.   Research with children on the development of cognitive abilities has found that Piaget:
a.   was essentially correct.
b.   underestimated cognitive abilities.
c.   overestimated cognitive abilities.
d.   overemphasized the role of sensory process.

8-9.   The morality of behavior is judged in terms of consequences at the _____ level of morality.
a.   preconventional
b.   conventional
c.   postconventional
d.   abstract

8-10.   At the _____ level of moral development, we tend to judge morality in terms of what supports and preserves the social order.
a.   preconventional
b.   conventional
c.   postconventional
d.   abstract

8-11.   Harlow's research with monkeys showed that:
a.   baby monkey's attachments to their cloth mother could be reversed by rejection.
b.   the satisfaction provided by feeding is sufficient for attachment.
c.   the satisfaction provided by feeding is not sufficient for attachment.
d.   attachment in human infants is not the same as attachment in monkeys.

8-12.   What are psychologists measuring when they use the strange situation test?
a.   cognitive development   c.   the appearance-reality distinction
b.   conservation   d.   attachment to the mother

8-13.   Beliefs about the supposed characteristics of males and females are called:
a.   sex-role stereotypes.   c.   sex differences.
b.   gender roles.   d.   gender schemas.

8-14.   At what age do children acquire gender constancy?
a.   around 2 years of age   c.   between 4 and 7 years of age
b.   between 3 ½ and 4 ½ years of age   d.   between 7 and 9 years of age

8-15.   Fitting experience into existing schema is known as:
a.   preoperation.   c.   accommodation.
b.   adaptation.   d.   assimilation.

8-16.   Environmental factors that interfere with prenatal growth are called:
a.   teratogens.   c.   cohort effects.
b.   health hazards.   d.   poisons.

8-17.   The information-processing perspective of cognitive development:
a.   seeks to map out the stages of development.
b.   seeks to understand how, and in what ways, children's capacity to process, store, retrieve, and actively manipulate information changes with age.
c.   proposes that private speech is egocentric.
d.   proposes that private speech represents attempts in social communication.

8-18.   The proposal that changes in the ability of children to perform cognitive tasks result from changes in their ability to block out distractors and focus attention is most consistent with _____ view of development.
a.   Piaget's   c.   the psychodynamic
b.   Vygotsky's   d.   the information processing

8-19.   The proposal that changes in the ability of children to perform cognitive tasks represent different stages of cognitive development is most consistent with _____ view of development.
a.   Piaget's   c.   Kohlberg's
b.   Vygotsky's   d.   the information processing

8-20.   Which of the following is not a true statement about gender differences?
a.   There are differences in emotional expression.
b.   There are differences in forms of aggression.
c.   There are differences in understanding nonverbal cues.
d.   There are differences in susceptibility to social influence.

Answers and Feedback for Sample Test Questions:

8-1.   D   By the 8th week of prenatal development, the face, arms, and legs are developed. (p. 299)

8-2.   A   The fetus can distinguish between familiar (stories the mother has read aloud during the prenatal period) and unfamiliar stories. Familiar stories were associated with decreased heart-rate, which is thought to indicate increased attention. (p. 299)

8-3.   A   The fetal alcohol syndrome is related to maternal alcohol consumption. (p. 301)

8-4.   B   Newborns are not able to crawl. The remaining options are reflexes present at birth. (p. 301-303)

8-5.   C   The longitudinal-sequential research design provides the clearest view of development because it allows us to sample people of different ages and track their development over a number of years. (p. 306-307)

8-6.   C   Piaget believed that development results from the interplay between assimilation (fitting experience into existing schemas) and accommodation (altering existing schemas as a result of experience). These two processes are part of the adaptation mechanism. (p. 309)

8-7.   D   In Piaget's theory, logical thought first appears during the concrete operations stage, although it is not developed fully until the formal operations stage. (p. 310)

8-8.   B   Recent research indicates that Piaget may have underestimated children's cognitive abilities. (p. 312)

8-9.   A   In Kohlberg's theory, the preconventional stage of moral development is characterized by judging the morality of a behavior in terms of its consequences. (p. 318)

8-10.   B   The conventional stage of moral development is characterized by considerations concerning the social order. (p. 318)

8-11.   C   Harlow's research demonstrated that the need for attachment is satisfied, in part, by contact comfort. Merely providing nourishment is not sufficient for attachment. (p. 327)

8-12.   D   The strange situation test is used to study attachment. It involves placing children in a distressing environment and monitoring their reactions to their mother leaving and returning. (p. 325)

8-13.   A   Beliefs about the supposed characteristics of males and females are called sex role stereotypes. In contrast, gender roles are beliefs about how males and females are expected to behave. (p. 330)

8-14.   B   Children are thought to acquire gender constancy between 3 ½ and 4 ½ years of age. (p. 330)

8-15.   D   Assimilation is the process in which we fit experience into existing schemas. (p. 309)

8-16.   A   Teratogens are environmental factors that interfere with prenatal development. (p. 299)

8-17.   B   The information processing view of development seeks to understand how children's information processing abilities change with age. (p. 313)

8-18.   D   Information processing views of development explain change by analyzing how cognitive processes, such as attention, vary as a function of age. See also 8-17 above. (p. 313)

8-19.   A   Piaget proposed a stage view of cognitive development. (p. 308)

8-20.   D   Despite earlier conclusions, there appears to be no differences in males and females' susceptibility to social influence. (p. 332)

YOUR NOTES:

GLOSSARY OF DIFFICULT WORDS AND EXPRESSIONS

These terms from your text and this study guide were identified by students as potentially hard to understand. We have defined these terms and expressions.

Term or expression	Definition
Bitterly	in an intense or harsh way
Bleak	not good
Chatted	informal talk
Circumvent	to prevent
Cliff	high, steep face of rock
Countless	numerous; many
Cuddling	hugging tenderly
Deeds	an act or action that is carried out
Deferring to	give in to the opinion of another
Discrete	individual; separate from something else
Distressed	suffering
Fixated	to focus one's eyes or attention on
Foster	encourage
Frazzled	become exhausted physically or emotionally
Fretting	to cause to be uneasy
Gazing	looking steadily, intently
Hinge on	depend on
Hinder	prevent, make more difficult
"Hobgoblin of little minds"	something that should not be attended to
Hyperactive	very active
Insightful	perceptive
Intrusive	to put or force inappropriately
It merits...	it deserves
Manipulate	control
Medical inoculations	vaccinations against disease

Term or expression	Definition
Milestones	important breakthrough
Mystified	puzzled mentally; bewildered
Newborn	recently born
Naive	not sophisticated; unknowledgeable
Out-of-wedlock	outside marriage
Outside the realm	outside the limits; not applicable
Pour	to make a liquid stream or flow
Prognosis	prediction of the probable cause and outcome of a disease
Protrusions	sticking out
Preach	to proclaim or advocate
Ranging in	varying in
Readily	available for immediate use
Rehearse	practice; repeat over and over
Rudimentary	elementary
Scraps of	pieces of
Scrutiny	a close, careful examination
Shallow	lacking physical depth; not deep
Simultaneously	at the same time
Solely	only
Struck by	impressed by
Sweeping	having wide-ranging influence or effect
They are acquainted	they know each other
Tiny speck	small spot or mark
Toddlers	young child learning to walk
Transcend	pass beyond the limits of
Tricky	difficult; complicated
Unruly	difficult to control
Upbeat	happy; cheerful
Vow	assert
Wreaking havoc	disrupting or causing problems

CHAPTER 9
HUMAN DEVELOPMENT II:
ADOLESCENCE, ADULTHOOD, AND AGING

INTEGRATED CHAPTER OUTLINE: Survey and Question

This section presents the major topics and ideas from the chapter. Use it as a tool for seeing how the components of the chapter fit together. At the end of each major topic, we have asked you a question that relates to the major learning objectives. If you can answer these questions, you have taken a major step toward mastering this material.

I. Adolescence: Between Child and Adult

L.O. 9.1:   Describe physical development during adolescence.

L.O. 9.2:   Describe cognitive development during adolescence.

L.O. 9.3:   Describe the nature of social and emotional development during adolescence.

L.O. 9.4:   Know how psychologists study the social behavior of children and adolescents.

L.O. 9.5:   Be able to discuss the problems of adolescents in the late 1990s.

Adolescence traditionally is thought to begin with the onset of puberty and end when individuals assume the responsibilities of adulthood. Adolescence is not a clearly defined developmental period in that it is culturally defined. Social factors play an important role in determining when adolescence begins.

A.   Physical Development During Adolescence

The beginning of adolescence is signaled by a sudden growth spurt. This occurs sooner for females than males. During puberty, the gonads or sex glands produce increased levels of sex hormones and the external sex organs assume their adult form. Females begin to menstruate and males begin to produce sperm.

Early-maturing boys seem to have an advantage over those who mature later. But early sexual maturation appears to be associated with fewer benefits for girls than for boys.

B.   Cognitive Development During Adolescence

According to Piaget, adolescents are in the stage of formal operations. Therefore, they can assess the logical validity of verbal statements and test theories they have generated (reason deductivity). However, their theories may be naive because of lack of experience and they tend to be egocentric -- assume that no other view but their own is correct. In addition, they tend to feel they are the focus of others' attention -- the imaginary audience. At the same time, they often feel that their feelings and thoughts are totally unique. This is referred to as the personal fable.

Adolescents engage in many high risk behaviors, such as reckless driving. They are high in a characteristic called sensation-seeking -- the desire to seek out novel and intense experiences. Egocentric thinking leads them to believe they are "special" and invulnerable. And male adolescents tend to be more aggressive than adults, which shows up in dangerous driving and criminal behavior which puts them at risk. When these tendencies are combined with what is called broad socialization (social practices that encourage individuality and autonomy with a minimum of personal restraint) reckless and risky behavior emerges. A common explanation for this is that they do not perceive risks the same way adults do.

C.   Social and Emotional Development During Adolescence

Research confirms the common folklore that adolescents experience frequent and large swings in mood. Other widely accepted views about adolescent emotionality are not supported. For example, it is often assumed that adolescents experience great stress and unhappiness; rather, most teenagers report feeling quite happy and self-confident. Teenagers also report that they have good relationships with their parents. Being part of a social group is essential to the self-esteem and self-confidence of most adolescents. Friendship plays an important role in the personal identity of adolescents. They are usually members of a large social network of friends. During adolescence, social goals involving social relationship are formed, and strategies to meet these goals are formulated.

In contrast to Piaget's stage theory, Erikson's theory is primarily concerned with social development across the life-span. He contends that each stage of life is marked by a specific conflict or crisis. The first four occur during childhood. One takes place during adolescence. The final three take place during adulthood.

The first phase in Erikson's theory determines the development of trust in one's environment. The second centers around the development of self-confidence and involves resolving a crisis between autonomy vs. shame and doubt. The third, occurring in preschool years, involves the crisis of initiative vs. guilt. The fourth involves the crisis of competence versus inferiority.

Adolescents must integrate various roles into a consistent self-identity. Failure to do so results in role confusion. The social conflict associated with young adulthood involves the development of a sense of intimacy versus isolation. During middle adulthood, individuals are faced with a conflict that leads to either generativity or self-absorption. In the closing years of life, individuals ask whether their lives have had meaning and develop either a sense of integrity or despair.

To summarize, Erikson's eight stages of psychosocial development are:

1)   trust vs. mistrust
2)   autonomy vs. shame and doubt
3)   initiative vs. guilt
4)   industry vs. inferiority
5)   identity vs. role confusion
6)   intimacy vs. isolation
7)   generativity vs. self-absorption
8)   integrity vs. despair

•   **Research Methods: How Psychologists Study the Social Behavior of Children and Adolescents**

Because social behavior involves interactions between two or more persons, it is often difficult to observe in the laboratory. Naturalistic observation methods, in which psychologists observe behavior in the setting in which it normally occurs, are often used in the study of social behavior. Psychologists study aggression in this way — they use videocameras and wireless microphones to record children's behavior as they play in natural settings.

Although useful, these methods have problems. Ethical issues are raised. Is it appropriate to listen in on conversations, even if consent is obtained? Should the researcher intervene if aggression is observed?

D.   Adolescence in the Late 1990s: A Generation at Risk?

There are many risks that face an adolescent in the late 1990s. For example, many adolescents will live in a one-parent family since more than half of all marriages end in divorce. And the number of children born to teenage mothers is increasing. Many children live in dysfunctional families -- families that do not meet the needs of children and may do them serious harm. They can, for example, be harmed by exposure to drugs or by sexual abuse. Some experts feel that children are at greater risk for sexual abuse than was true in the past.

To minimize the risks associated with high risk environments, several steps can be taken. For example, families can use protective factors -- factors that serve to buffer resilient individuals from aversive conditions. Parents can work with teachers to establish support in the classroom and ties between home and school. Establishing a close bond with at least one stable person can give the sense of trust that is crucial for healthy growth. It is also the case that resilience in development arises from protective factors within individuals. Resilient person's possess traits and temperament that elicit positive responses from many caregivers. When children and adolescents benefit from protective factors, they can "beat the odds" and develop in a healthy way.

Questions:

9-1.   Why is it difficult to define the dividing line between childhood and adolescence? _____

_____

_____

_____

9-2.   What are the characteristics of physical development during adolescence? _____

_____

_____

_____

9-3.   What are the different views concerning whether adolescents do or do not think like adults?

_____

_____

_____

9-4.   What are the emotional changes and social development of the adolescent? _____

_____

_____

_____

9-5.   What are Erikson's eight stages? _____

_____

_____

_____

9-6.   What are the potential risks that face an adolescent? What are some of the steps that can be taken
        to minimize the risks associated with high-risk environments? _____

_____

_____

_____

II.   Adulthood and Aging

L.O. 9.6:   Compare and contrast different views of adult development.

L.O. 9.7:   Discuss the evidence that suggests that we are shaped by the events of our youth.

L.O. 9.8:   Know the physical changes that occur in adulthood.

L.O. 9.9:   Describe the cognitive changes that occur in adulthood.

L.O. 9.10:   Be able to describe the social changes that occur in adulthood.

L.O. 9.11:   Discuss the crises that are common in adulthood.

A.   Contrasting Views of Adult Development: Internal Crisis, External Life Events or Active Development Regulation?

Assuming an average life length, you will spend more than 70 percent of your life as an adult. Recent
research has focused on the changes that occur during adulthood. The driving mechanism behind such
change is a source of debate. Erikson's theory is an example of the crisis approach. As individuals grow
older, individuals are assumed to confront new combinations of biological drives and societal demands.
The drives reflect growth and physical change, while the societal demands reflect the expectations and
requirements of society for individuals at different stages of life. The three crises that face individuals
during adulthood are: intimacy vs. isolation, generativity vs. self-absorption, integrity vs. despair. The
way in which we deal with these crises determine the course of our adult lives. All human beings are
assumed to pass through these sequences in a fixed manner.

In contrast to the internal crises approach, the life events model assumes that development does not occur in accordance with a built-in biological clock. Rather, development is tied to a social clock. This model divides the social events that shape development into two categories. Normative events are expected life events and include events such as graduation, marriage, and parenthood. Non-normative events are unexpected life events and include such events as divorce, accidents, and death. The timing of such events is important.

A third approach focuses on the ways we regulate our lives; it focuses on the ways our personal goals change over time. For example, as we grow older, we recognize that some goals may be unrealistic and we set new goals for ourselves. Research also suggests that we shift from goals concerning gains in various areas to goals focusing on avoiding losses.

Psychologists question the idea that people pass through stages. Most prefer either the life-event or the developmental regulation approach.

- **Exploring Gender and Diversity: Life Stages and Societal Events**

    Research that asked women of different ages to describe the societal events that were most important in their lives found that women mentioned events that occurred when they were adolescents or young adults as most influential. And research also finds that these events were influential in shaping their lives. For example, women who rated the women's movement as very influential were more confident and successful in mid-life. Thus it appears that societal events do shape our later development.

B.   Physical Change During Our Adult Years

Physical changes that occur during adulthood are a reflection of the lifestyles individuals adopt as well as genetically-determined biological clocks. Aging, like physical growth, is a continuous process that begins early in life. This process proceeds slowly at first, but then proceeds rapidly in later decades. Muscular strength, sensory acuity, heart action and output are at the peak during the mid-twenties. These biological systems decline very slowly through the mid-thirties.

Most people are aware of physical changes in the strength and vigor of several organ systems and changes in their body shape and skin by the time they are in their 40s. The climacteric is a period of several years during which the functioning of the reproductive system and aspects of sexual activity change greatly. Sexual activity tends to decrease for both sexes in their late 40s or early 50s. Women experience menopause, which involves hormonal changes, cessation of menstruation and infertility. In the past, this was considered to be a stressful period for women; now research suggests that many women feel better after menopause. Males do not experience a process that corresponds to menopause. However, levels of testosterone, prostate gland functioning, and sperm counts do decline with age.

While some physical decline is inevitable during middle adulthood, the rate and magnitude of decline is strongly influenced by individuals' lifestyles. Evidence suggests that factors such as exercise, nutrition, and stress management may be better predictors of health and vigor than age. Average age in many countries is rising. Contrary to stereotypes, people between 60-80 years old generally are in good health and aren't more likely than middle-aged people to suffer from chronic disease.

It is important to distinguish between two kinds of aging. Changes produced by increasing age per se are part of primary aging. Changes that can be traced to disease, disuse, or abuse of our bodies are part of secondary aging. Our physical state during later life is more under our own control than many have thought. However, aging does produce important physical changes. Sensory abilities such as visual acuity decline with age. Although there are large individual differences, there is also a slowing in reflexes.

C.   Cognitive Change During Adulthood

There is reason to expect that cognitive abilities might increase with age. Practice and a greater knowledge base might be expected to enhance cognitive performance. Research suggests that the short-term memory of older adults is as good as that of younger adults, as long as the information does not need to be processed extensively. For example, anagram-solving abilities appear to decline with age. Young adults seem to have better long-term memories, but not better recognition memory. The long-term memory advantage of younger adults disappear when older adults are expert in the area under investigation. With respect to meaningful information, older adults often perform as well as younger adults. And declines in memory are not seen in older people that engage in mental exercise — those who stretch their minds and memories on a day-to-day basis. Thus declines in our mental abilities are not inevitable.

Psychologists believed that intelligence increases into early adulthood, remains stable through the 30s, and then begins to decline as early as the 40s. However, this belief was based on cross-sectional research. Recent longitudinal research on standardized intelligence tests indicate that many intellectual abilities seem to remain stable across the entire lifespan (see Chapter 8 for a discussion of longitudinal and cross-sectional research methods). However, these tests did not capture the difference between crystallized and fluid intelligence. Fluid intelligence appears to increase into the early twenties and then gradually decline whereas crystallized intelligence tends to increase across the lifespan. Fluid intelligence involves the ability to form concepts, reason, and identify similarities, whereas crystallized intelligence involves drawing from previously learned information. There is little or no decline in practical intelligence.

Research using standard tasks indicates that creativity declines with age. But the age at which peak creativity occurs in a career varies greatly from one field to another. In some fields, peak creativity tends to occur when persons are in their 40s or 50s. While the number of creative accomplishments declines with age, their quality does not.

D.   Social Change in Adulthood: Tasks and Stages of Adult Life

Levinson suggests that there are four major eras of life, each separated by a transition period lasting about 5 years. The first transition occurs between the preadult era and early adulthood. This transition involves establishing one's independence. Once this transition is complete, individuals enter early adulthood. The two key components of their life structure are the dream and mentor. At about age 30, Levinson suggests people experience the "age 30 transition." At this point, people realize they are nearing the time at which they will have too much invested in their present life course to change and they reappraise their initial choices. This is followed by a period in which individuals stick to their existing life structures.

After the closing years of early adulthood (around 40-45), individuals move into a potentially turbulent transitional period called the mid-life transition. At this time, individuals must come to terms with their mortality and come to view themselves as part of the older generation. This realization leads to a period of emotional turmoil and leads people to review their lives up to this point and reexamine their possibilities. A new life structure is formed which takes account of the individual's new position in life as a middle-aged person. Life structures are often modified again between the ages of 50 and 55. A more dramatic transition occurs between the ages of 60 and 65 -- at the close of the middle years and the start of late adulthood. During this late adult transition, individuals come to terms with their impending retirement and the leisure activities this will bring. All of these transitions involve a series of changes in the individual's life structure or cognitive framework concerning the nature and meaning of his/her life.

Critics of Levinson's theory argue that it was based on a small and restricted sample. There is also debate about whether it applies to women as well as men. Therefore, it should be viewed as an interesting but unverified theory.

E.   Crisis of Adult Life and a Little About Personal Happiness

In contrast to Levinson's stage model, other psychologists focus on the impact of major life events. For example, divorce and unemployment can be viewed as two major crises of adult life. This approach focuses on how major crises affect our development. Baron discusses three events that can be viewed as major crisis of adult life that affects our happiness.

Divorced persons experience anger, depression, and disequilibrium. Research has identified many factors associated with couples who remain happily married. For example, happily married couples agree with their spouse on many important issues, are committed to the relationship, and engage in a high level of positive communication. In contrast, unhappy married couples often engage in a negative pattern of communication. Divorced couples are bored in the relationship and report that their spouse no longer satisfies their needs. Additional factors associated with divorce include low income, unrealistic expectations, a brief courtship, sexual jealousy, and pregnancy at the time of marriage. Recent work indicates that genetic factors may also play a role in divorce. This unexpected finding suggests that individuals from divorced families may inherit characteristics that make it hard for them to maintain long-term relationships.

The baby-boom generation is now facing the crisis of caring for their aging parents. This can create serious emotional turmoil and financial strain. This can be a key crisis of adult life.

Unemployment is an increasingly common experience. Unemployed individuals reported lower self-esteem, greater depression, more negative affect and poorer personal health than those who are employed. This is a crisis in life that can threaten both physical and psychological health.

Most people report relatively high levels of subjective well-being or personal happiness. Research on why people are satisfied with their lives is just beginning; but it appears that two factors are involved. First, people are in relatively good moods most of the time, which may be adaptive from the point of view of survival. Second, feeling happy may motivate people to approach new situations and stimuli.

Questions:

9-7.   What are the internal crisis and life-event models of adult development? _____

_____

_____

_____

9-8.   According to the crisis approach, what are the three major crises that are faced during adulthood?

_____

_____

_____

9-9.   What are the major life events that are thought to affect the course of adult development?

_____

_____

_____

9-10.   What are the physical changes that occur during early adulthood? _____

_____

_____

_____

9-11.   What are the physical changes that occur during mid-life? _____

_____

_____

_____

9-12.   What are the physical changes that occur in later life, and what are primary and secondary aging
        factors? _____

_____

_____

_____

9-13.   What is the influence of aging on memory? _____

_____

_____

_____

9-14.   How can declines in memory with aging be avoided? _____

_____

_____

_____

9-15.   How is intelligence influenced by age? _____

_____

_____

_____

9-16. How is creativity influenced by age? _____

_____

_____

_____

9-17. How does Levinson's stage theory address adult change? _____

_____

_____

_____

9-18. What are three major crises of adult life? _____

_____

_____

_____

9-19. What are two reasons that people may report high levels of subjective well-being? _____

_____

_____

_____

III. Aging and Death and Bereavement

L.O. 9.12: Discuss theories of aging.

L.O. 9.13: Discuss the challenges of meeting death and bereavement.

L.O. 9.14: Know how you can use what you have learned to prepare for the job market.

A.   Theories of Aging: Contrasting Views About Why We Grow Old

One question concerning the end of life centers around the causes of aging. The wear-and-tear view suggests that we grow old because of the small highly charged atoms. These atoms are called free radicals and are very unstable. They react violently with other chemical compounds producing damage. When the damage affects DNA, they interfere with cell maintenance and repair. Indirect evidence for this view comes from persons who expose their bodies to harmful environmental conditions. These persons often show premature signs of aging.

According to genetic programming theories, built-in biological clocks regulate the aging process by regulating the number of times cells can reproduce. Once reached, no further cell divisions can occur. This produces biological decline. Recent evidence suggests that this biological clock may be related to strips of DNA that caps the end of chromosomes. These caps are called teleomeres and become shorter every time a cell divides. Once they reach a critical length the cell can no longer divide. Another genetic theory, gene mutation theory, suggests that when genetic mutations reach high enough levels, death results. Support comes from evidence suggesting that certain cells only divide a certain number of times and environmental conditions seem unable to alter this number. It is also the case that members of all species do not live more than a specified period of time under optimal conditions.

The best conclusion concerning the aging process is that aging is the result of several different mechanisms and results from a complex interplay between environmental and genetic factors.

B.   Meeting Death: Facing the End of Life

Defining death is complex. There are several different kinds of death: physiological death, brain death, cerebral death, and social death. Physiological death occurs when all life sustaining physical processes cease. A total absence of brain activity for at least 10 minutes defines brain death. Cerebral death is defined by the lack of activity in the cerebral cortex. Social death refers to the process of giving-up our relationships with the deceased. There are a number of complex ethical issues that stem from the question of whether individuals have the right to die when they choose.

Kübler-Ross conducted detailed interviews with terminally ill persons and concluded that they pass through a series of five distinct stages in their reactions to impending death. The first is denial. The second is anger over being singled out. The third is bargaining followed by a stage of depression. Many persons move from this to a final reaction of acceptance in which they face death with calm and dignity. Evidence suggests that all people do not move through these stages.

- •   **Beyond the Headlines: As Psychologists See It — Personality and the Human Lifespan**

    A 60 year study of more than 1,000 persons finds that those who were conscientious as children were less likely to die in any given year of adulthood than others. This link between personality and longevity may be due to the fact that conscientiousness people are less likely to engage in high risk behaviors. It has also been found that people from divorced families tend to die younger. Thus personality and social factors affect the length of our life.

C.   Bereavement: Coming to Terms With the Death of Loved Ones

A bereaved person mourns the loss of a loved one. The results of research on bereavement indicate that most persons experience shock followed by protest and yearning. A third stage is disorganization and despair. For most persons this is followed by detachment, reorganization, and recovery. After a prolonged period of mourning, most people recover and are able to go on with their lives.

Questions:

9-20. What are the contrasting views on why we grow old? _____

_____

_____

_____

9-21. What are the stages in Kübler-Ross's stages in the dying process? _____

_____

_____

_____

9-22. What are the stages that follow the loss of a loved one? _____

_____

_____

_____

- **Making Psychology Part of Your Life: Preparing for Tomorrow's Job Market Today**

  The job market is uncertain, and it is wise to take all the steps you can in order to prepare for your future. Baron offers several steps that may be helpful. These are:

  1)   choose a field with a future
  2)   focus on small and medium-sized companies
  3)   be ready to work for a foreign company
  4)   consider part-time or contract work as a way to get started
  5)   think of any job as a potential learning experience

YOUR NOTES:

CHALLENGE: Key Terms and Key Concepts

Knowing the important concepts and key terms contained in this chapter is a very important part of mastering the material. We have presented a sample of these concepts below. Define each concept and check your definition with that presented in the chapter. It will also be beneficial for you to think of an example of each concept. Whenever possible, use your own personal experience to provide an example of each term below.

9-1.   **Adolescence**: _____

9-2.   **Adolescent Recklessness**: _____

       Example: _____

9-3.   **Bereavement**: _____

       Example: _____

9-4.   **Climacteric**: _____

9-5.   **Crystallized Intelligence**: _____

9-6.   **Dream:** _____

       Example: _____

9-7.   **Dysfunctional Families**: _____

9-8.   **Fluid Intelligence**: _____

9-9.   **Genetic Theories of Aging**: _____

9-10.   **Late-Adult Transition**: _____

9-11.   **Life Structure**: _____

       Example: _____

9-12.   **Menopause**: _____

9-13.   **Mentor**: _____

         Example: _____

9-14.   **Mid-life Transition**: _____

9-15.   **Primary Aging**: _____

9-16.   **Puberty**: _____

9-17.   **Resilience in Development**: _____

9-18.   **Secondary Aging**: _____

9-19.   **Sensation Seeking**: _____

9-20.   **Sexual Abuse**: _____

9-21.   **Subjective Well Being**: _____

9-22.   **Teleomeres**: _____

9-23.   **Wear-and-Tear Theories**: _____

CHALLENGE: Develop Your Critical Thinking Skills

Metacognition, Retrospection, and Comparative Analysis: Thinking "Then and Now"

Awareness of the nature of our thought-processes (metacognition) is an important cognitive skill. The development of critical thinking requires this skill. It is also useful to recognize how the nature of our thought processes may have changed over time. As an exercise in becoming aware of changes in the nature of our thought processes, we invite you to retrospect on your adolescent period and compare the nature of your thinking "then and now." Although research suggests that differences between adolescent and adult thought may have been exaggerated, it is useful for you to analyze your own experiences.

9-1.   Compare and contrast your views of life in adolescence vs. your present view. Do you notice differences in how sophisticated your views are?

_____

_____

_____

_____

_____

9-2.   Do you see differences across time in your acceptance of other person's viewpoints?

_____

_____

_____

_____

9-3.   Compare and contrast your willingness to engage in high-risk behaviors in adolescence vs. now. If such differences exist, do you think they result from changes in your sense of invulnerability? To what do you attribute any such differences?

_____

_____

_____

_____

_____

9-4.   What is the most salient change you see in your thinking "past and present?"

_____

_____

_____

_____

9-5.   Note any improvements you see in your thinking skills.

_____

_____

_____

_____

9-6.   Note the domains in which you seek improvement and the ways you plan to facilitate these changes.

_____

_____

_____

_____

YOUR NOTES:

CHALLENGE: Taking Psychology With You

Stages of Life

Your text discusses one of the most famous theories of life span development -- that of Erik Erikson. As you recall, Erikson proposed that development proceeds through a series of distinct stages, each separated by a specific crisis. How does this view relate to your life experiences?

We have listed these stages below. For each stage that you have experienced, write a brief discussion of the societal demands and feelings you experienced during that time. Did you experience the type of crisis Erikson suggests? For those stages that you have not yet reached, speculate on your probable feelings and reactions. How will you respond to the challenges of this developmental period?

Crisis/Phase

Trust vs. Mistrust: _____

_____

_____

Autonomy vs. Shame and Doubt: _____

_____

_____

Initiative vs. Guilt: _____

_____

_____

Industry vs. Inferiority: _____

_____

_____

Identity vs. Role Confusion: _____

_____

_____

Intimacy vs. Isolation: _____

_____

_____

Generativity vs. Self-Absorption: _____

_____

_____

Integrity vs. Despair: _____

_____

_____

YOUR NOTES:

CHALLENGE: Review Your Comprehensive Knowledge

SAMPLE TEST QUESTIONS

Once you have worked through the preceding sections, you should be ready for a comprehensive self-test. You can check your answers with those given at the end of this section. An additional practice test is given in the supplementary section at the end of this study guide.

9-1.   Which of the following statements is not correct concerning physical changes in adolescence?
   a. Growth spurts occur sooner for males than females.
   b. The gonads produce increased levels of sex hormones.
   c. There is great variability in the onset of sexual maturity.
   d. Girls begin to menstruate, and boys begin to produce sperm.

9-2.   According to Erikson's theory, the most important internal crisis faced by adolescents concerns resolving:
   a. competence vs. inferiority.   c. sexuality vs. sexual confusion.
   b. initiative vs. guilt.   d. identity vs. role confusion.

9-3.   According to Erikson, the crisis of middle adulthood involves:
   a. intimacy vs. isolation.   c. generativity vs. self-absorption.
   b. identity vs. role confusion.   d. integrity vs. despair.

9-4.   In the terminology of life events models of adult development, graduation from school would be an example of:
   a. an internal crisis.   c. a non-normative event.
   b. a normative event.   d. a social clock.

9-5.   Crisis theories view adult development as:
   a. the resolution of a series of internal conflicts.
   b. the responses of individuals to important life events.
   c. the influence of social clocks.
   d. all of the above

9-6.   People usually become aware of declines in their physical systems:
   a. in their twenties.   c. in their forties.
   b. in their thirties.   d. in their fifties.

9-7.   Physical changes that are due to increased age per se are referred to as:
   a. primary aging.   c. sensory aging.
   b. secondary aging.   d. genetic aging.

9-8.   Erikson's theory emphasizes the importance of _____ development across the life span.
   a. social   c. sexual
   b. cognitive   d. emotional

9-9.   The importance of free radicals in aging is emphasized by which of the following theories of aging?
   a. wear-and-tear theories   c. crisis theories
   b. genetic programming theories   d. life events theories

9-10.   According to Kübler-Ross, the first stage of the dying process is:
   a. denial.   c. depression.
   b. anger.   d. bargaining.

9-11.   Which is not true of cognitive development during adolescence (according to Piaget)?
   a. Adolescents can assess the logical validity of verbal statements.
   b. Adolescents tend to be egocentric.
   c. Adolescents tend to feel they are the focus of others' attention.
   d. Adolescents think in the same way as adults.

9-12.   Research supports all but one of the following statements about social and emotional development during adolescence. Identify the incorrect statement.
   a. Adolescents generally experience large swings in mood.
   b. Adolescents generally report that they have poor relationships with their parents.
   c. Adolescents generally report feeling happy.
   d. Adolescents generally report feeling self-confident.

9-13.   Which of the following is not true of the life events model?
   a. Normative events are expected life events.
   b. The timing of life events is important.
   c. Development is tied to a social clock.
   d. Social events are divided into four categories.

9-14.   Muscular strength, sensory acuity, heart action, and output decline very slowly through:
   a. the mid twenties.
   b. the mid thirties.
   c. the mid forties.
   d. none of the above.

9-15.   The climacteric is associated with:
   a. menopause.
   b. a person's ability to withstand intense heat.
   c. a persons' ability to withstand intense cold.
   d. Erikson's third stage.

9-16.   Which of the following is not true of cognitive change during adulthood?
   a. Exercising our mental abilities helps reduce the effects of aging on mental decline.
   b. The memory of older adults was equal to that of younger adults in terms of recall memory.
   c. Older persons are less able to deal with the effects of proactive interference.
   d. With respect to meaningful information, older adults often perform as well as younger adults.

9-17.   Fluid intelligence appears to _____ after the early twenties. Crystallized intelligence appears to _____ across the lifespan.
   a. increase; remain constant
   b. increase; decrease
   c. decrease; remain constant
   d. decrease; increase

9-18.   The caps at the end of our chromosomes which are linked to our "biological clock" are called:
   a. DNA.
   b. teleomeres.
   c. nodes of Ranier.
   d. pheromones.

9-19.   Research suggesting that intelligence declines with age was based on the _____ research model.
   a. cross-sectional
   b. longitudinal
   c. longitudinal-sequential
   d. experimental

9-20.   Aging is a continuous process that begins _____ in life. This process proceeds _____ at first.
   a. late; slowly
   b. early; slowly
   c. late; rapidly
   d. early; rapidly

Answers and Feedback for Sample Test Questions:

9-1.   A   Growth spurts occur sooner for females vs. males. (p. 343)

9-2.   D   In Erikson's theory, adolescence involves a crisis in which we must resolve role confusion vs. identity. (p. 349)

9-3.   C   In Erikson's theory, middle age involves a crisis of generativity vs. self-absorption. (p. 355)

9-4.   B   Normative events are expected life events. Graduation fits in this category. (p. 356)

9-5.   A   Internal crisis models propose that the way we resolve a series of internal conflicts determines the course of our adult lives. (p. 355)

9-6.   C   We notice declines in our physical systems during our forties. (p. 359)

9-7.   A   Primary aging refers to physical changes due to age per se. (p. 360)

9-8.   A   Erikson's theory emphasizes the importance of social factors (societal demands) and biological drives in adult development. (p. 355)

9-9.   A   Free radicals are biological factors associated with aging in wear-and-tear theories. (p. 372)

9-10.   A   Denial is the first stage of dying in Kübler-Ross's theory. (p. 374)

9-11.   D   The nature of adolescent thought is similar but not identical to adults. (p. 344)

9-12.   B   In contrast to our pre-conceptions, most adolescents report good relationships with their parents. (p. 346)

9-13.   D   In the life-events model, there are two categories of social events: normative and non-normative events. (p. 356)

9-14.   B   We find slow declines in these abilities in our mid-thirties. These declines aren't noticed until our forties. (p. 359)

9-15.   A   The climacteric is a period of several years during which the functioning of the reproductive system changes greatly. Menopause is the most obvious effect for females. (p. 359-360)

9-16.   B   Younger adults perform better than older adults on recall memory tasks. (p. 361-362; also see p. 365)

9-17.   D   Fluid intelligence decreases after our early 20s; crystallized intelligence increases across the life span. (p. 363-364)

9-18.   B   Teleomeres are caps at the end of our chromosomes which are thought to limit the number of times a cell can divide. (p. 373

9-19.   A   Cross-sectional research suggested that intelligence declined with age. This conclusion is flawed by the fact that persons of different ages have different life experiences, which affects their measured IQs. (p. 362)

9-20.   B   Aging processes begin early and proceed slowly at first. Aging is rapid in later decades. (p. 359)

GLOSSARY OF DIFFICULT WORDS AND EXPRESSIONS

These terms from your text and this study guide were identified by students as potentially hard to understand. We have defined these terms and expressions.

Term or expression	Definition
A backdrop for life	the background or context of one's life
Adrift	not under control
Aggression	actions designed to harm others in some manner
Aloud	in a voice loud enough to be heard
Amicable	friendly; easy to get along with
Aversive	harmful
"Baby boom" generation	generation born between 1946 and 1964 which is now the largest single segment of the population
"Beat the odds"	win spite of negative circumstances
Bereavement	feeling sad or without hope
Buffer	something that protects or separates from harm
Cessation of	termination of; end of
"Chasm"	wide difference of feelings or interests; a gap that separates
Consent	agreeing to do something
"Couch potato"	an inactive person
Cumulate	increase in amount; adding up
Deterred	held back; not allowed to; stopped
Dim	not bright
Disconcerting	upsetting
Doomed	condemned
Drawback	disadvantage; negative part
Dutiful	showing respect and obedience
Ebullient	overflowing with enthusiasm
Elicit	draw from
Fist fight	fight with tightly closed hand
Frail	weak; fragile; easily damaged

Term or expression	Definition
Go astray	go out of or off the right path
Grasp of	having an understanding of
Harsh	rough and disagreeable
Hurdles	obstacles; things that block one's way
Indulge	give way to and satisfy
Intervene	become involved in
Longevity	the length of life
Negative affect	negative feelings
Niches for...	suitable or fitting position
Novel	new; never thought of previously
Oncoming	approaching
Onset	vigorous star; the beginning
Overt	done or shown openly
Painful bouts	painful period of something
Peak levels	highest point; the top
Perils	serious dangers
Protégé	person to whom another gives protection or help
"Pulling the plug"	disconnecting; unplugging; stopping
Realm of	boundaries of; applies to
Reckless	not thinking or caring about the consequences
Rut	a fixed and boring way of living so that it becomes difficult to change
Siblings	brother or sister
Spurring	edging on; promoting
Steady	regular
Sweeping theories	having wide-ranging influence or effects
Swings in mood	changes in mood that vary dramatically
Traits	characteristics of a person
Unruly	not easily controlled; naughty
Wary	in the habit of being careful about possible danger or trouble

Term or expression	Definition
Wide array	wide variety; a lot of choices
Widespread	popular; general; having a lot of influence
Women were veiled	faces were covered with a fine net or other material to protect or hide
Yearns	long for, with great, tender feeling, affection, etc.
Yield	give way to; give in

YOUR NOTES:

CHAPTER 10
MOTIVATION AND EMOTION

SURVEY AND QUESTION

This section presents the major topics and ideas from the chapter. Use it as a tool for seeing how the components of the chapter fit together. At the end of each major topic, we have asked you a question that relates to the major learning objectives. If you can answer these questions, you have taken a major step toward mastering this material.

I.   Motivation: The Activation and Persistence of Behavior

L.O. 10.1:   Know the various theories of motivation.

L.O. 10.2:   Describe the basic nature of hunger.

L.O. 10.3:   Describe the basic nature of sexual motivation.

L.O. 10.4:   Describe the research concerning pheromones.

L.O. 10.5:   Describe the basic nature of aggression and how it is studied.

L.O. 10.6:   Be able to discuss the relationship between achievement motivation and economic growth.

L.O. 10.7:   Describe the basic nature of intrinsic motivation.

Motivation refers to internal processes. These serve to activate, guide, and maintain our behavior. Motives are internal processes that cannot be readily observed. Motives are often assumed to be a cause for behavior, especially when the cause of a particular behavior cannot be readily discerned in the immediate context.

A.   Theories of Motivation: Some Major Perspectives

Before using motivation as an explanation for many kinds of behavior, psychologists used instincts as explanatory concepts. Instincts are innate patterns of behavior that are universal in a species. They are independent of experience and are elicited by specific stimuli. A problem with the use of instincts is that they are often used in a circular way. That is, they are inferred from observations of behavior and then used to explain the occurrence of the same behavior.

Drive theory is a motivational account of behavior. It assumes that when our biological needs are not satisfied, a state of deprivation exists. This state is unpleasant. People are pushed to restore a balanced state (homeostasis) and reduce unpleasant states of arousal. Actions that satisfy these drives tend to be repeated. Actions that do not satisfy drives tend not to be repeated. One problem with this theory is that people often tend to increase rather than decrease various drives.

Arousal theory suggests that people seek an optimal level of arousal -- a level that is best suited to personal characteristics and the activity being performed. Although there is at least indirect support for arousal theory, there are limitations associated with this view. It is difficult to determine in advance what level of arousal will be optimal for a given task and for a given individual.

Expectancy theory assumes that our expectation of obtaining important outcomes or goals is the major factor underlying our motivation. For this approach, people are not pushed by inner urges. Rather, they are pulled by expectations of obtaining desired outcomes or incentives. Its most important application has been to understand work motivation. Research finds that people will work hard when they believe that doing so will improve their performance (expectancy) and when good performance will be rewarded (instrumentality).

Maslow proposes that motives exist in a hierarchy. The ones at the bottom must be satisfied first. Deficiency needs include physiological, safety, and social needs. Growth needs include self-actualization and esteem needs. Research on this view is mixed. Some studies suggest that growth needs come into play only after deficiency needs have been satisfied. However, other studies indicate that people sometimes seek higher-order needs, even when deficiency needs have not been satisfied. Furthermore, several needs may be active at once. Maslow's needs hierarchy theory may be best viewed as an interesting, but largely unverified framework.

B.   Hunger: Regulating Our Caloric Intake

Hunger motivation is the urge to obtain and consume food. It tends to take precedence over all other things. Mechanisms that regulate body weight and hunger contain special detectors that respond to levels of glucose, protein, and liquids. Hunger is also influenced by the sight, smell, and taste of food. In addition, it is affected by the feedback produced by chewing and swallowing. Further, hunger is influenced by learning and experience, as well as cognitive factors.

Consumers spend huge sums of money on weight-loss programs and products. Several factors have been proposed for why people are overweight. First, overweight persons may have become classically conditioned to eat. Second, overweight persons may eat more when under stress. Third, genetic factors may influence eating; overweight persons may have a low basal metabolic rate. This refers to the number of calories required at rest within a given period of time. Fourth, overweight persons may respond more strongly to external cues relating to food.

People who starve themselves until they loose dangerous amounts of weight have a condition known as anorexia nervosa. People who engage in repeated cycles of binge eating, followed by purging (through vomiting or laxatives) have a condition known as bulimia. Chapter 14 presents an extensive discussion of these conditions.

C.   Sexual Motivation: The Most Intimate Motive

Sexual motivation is a strong force in human behavior. In most species (other than humans), sexual hormones exert activational effects; sexual behavior does not occur or takes place with a low frequency in the absence of sexual hormones. Although sexual hormones play a role with humans, other bodily factors may play a more direct role. When sexually attracted to another person, chemical substances related to amphetamines or stimulants are produced.

The Kinsey reports were the only source of scientific information about sexuality until the 1960s. These reports found that there is great individual variation in sexual behavior. There are problems with the surveys -- people may not report their experiences accurately, and many persons refuse to participate in surveys involving reports of sexual activity. The research of Masters and Johnson was reported in the 1960s. This work is based on direct and systematic observation of actual sexual activity.

Based on the work of Masters and Johnson, it appears that we move through four phases during sexual behavior. In response to sexual stimuli, we may enter the excitement phase. At this time, the penis and clitoris are enlarged. During the following plateau phase, changes in sexual organs continue. In this phase there is increased muscle tension, respiration, heart rate, and blood pressure. During the orgasmic phase, there are contractions in the genital muscles and intense sensations of pleasure. The patterns of contractions and their timing is similar for males and females.

Following orgasm comes the resolution phase. With males, there is a reduction in sexual and physiological arousal. They also enter a refractory period during which they cannot be sexually aroused. Females may either return to an unaroused state or may experience additional orgasms if stimulation continues.

These basic patterns apply to all human beings. However, there are different cultural values about other aspects of sexuality such as the age at which sexual behavior should occur.

Sexual stimulation may be produced by direct contact or by naturally occurring odors. In one study, perfume containing vaginal secretions or copulins increased sexual activity in about 20% of males. Humans also respond to real or imagined erotic stimuli. In contrast to other species, humans can generate their own sexual arousal on the basis of erotic fantasies. In this and other ways, cognitive abilities play a major role in sexual motivation for humans.

About two percent of all adults are exclusively homosexual. About two or three percent of each sex are bisexual. There do not appear to be clear-cut answers about the basis of sexual orientation. This issue was discussed in depth in Chapter 2.

- **Beyond the Headlines: As Psychologists See It -- Can We Sniff Our Way to Emotional Health?**

    In this section, Baron discusses a set of experiments that seem to suggest humans, like many animals, can receive odorless chemical messages called pheromones. Supposedly, these chemicals activate only the vomeronasal organs (VNDs) of the opposite gender and produce a feeling of well-being.

    This is an interesting idea. However, Baron points out that this evidence seems to be published in newspapers — not in high-quality scientific journals. Therefore, caution in accepting these ideas is warranted.

D.   Aggressive Motivation: The Most Dangerous Motive

The desire to inflict harm on others is termed aggressive motivation. It often results in aggressive behavior. Most psychologists do not accept the view that aggression is an inherited and unavoidable human tendency. This is not to say it has no biological roots. Most psychologists believe that aggression is often elicited by external events. One hypothesis states that people experience a desire to harm others when these individuals have prevented them from obtaining what they want. This is termed the frustration-aggression hypothesis. This hypothesis is useful for understanding workplace violence. Frustration, however, does not appear to be the only cause of aggression. For example, aggression is often caused by direct provocation from others.

Exposure to violence in the media has also been found to increase aggression. Exposure has also been found to de-sensitize people to the harm produced by violence. Environmental conditions can increase aggression as well. For example, discomfort, such as heat, can trigger aggression directly or can trigger negative thoughts that lead us to become aggressive. There is also evidence that hormones, especially testosterone, play a role in aggression.

- **Exploring Gender and Diversity: Sexual Jealousy and Aggression: Some Surprising Gender Differences**

There may be gender differences in sexual jealousy. Men may experience more intense jealousy in response to sexual infidelity; whereas, women may experience more intense jealousy in response to emotional jealousy. According to sociobiology, the strong reaction of men to sexual infidelity occurs because they can never be perfectly certain that they are the fathers of their children. Therefore, they may be investing resources in another man's family. The strong reaction of women to emotional jealousy occurs because they need the assistance of the male to raise their children. These conclusions are not definite.

- **Research Methods: How Psychologists Study Aggression**

The study of aggression brings up the ethical issue of exposing participants to potentially dangerous situations. In the 1960s, Buss and Milgram developed procedures in which they temporarily deceived subjects into thinking that they could harm another person. Their procedures involved giving subjects the impression that another subject's errors on a learning task could be punished by several levels of shock. Of course, the learner was an assistant of the experimenter's and was never shocked. Aggression is measured by the real subjects' choice of shock-level intensity. Buss' research on this topic showed that aggression depends upon a number of societal factors (such as whether the learner was polite or rude) and the room temperature.

There has been some controversy about whether responses on this type of aggression machine really reflects aggression. For example, is this situation too artificial? However, the kinds of aggression seen in this setting is similar to aggression observed in natural settings. For example, males are more aggressive than females in both laboratory and natural settings. Therefore, this seems to be a useful method for studying aggression.

E.   Achievement Motivation and Cognitive Motivation: Two Complex Human Motives

Achievement motivation is the motive concerned with meeting standards of excellence and accomplishing difficult tasks. These motives are not directly derived from biological factors. Power motivation is the desire to be in charge and have status. One technique for measuring these motives involves responding to ambiguous stories -- the Thematic Apperception Test. Individuals high in achievement orientation tend to get higher grades in school. They also earn more rapid promotions, and are better at running their own businesses. High achievement oriented individuals prefer tasks of moderate risk or difficulty. Low achievement individuals prefer situations with either very low or high risk. High achievement oriented persons prefer feedback and like merit-based pay systems.

Need for cognition refers to a motive for engaging in effortful cognitive activities. Puzzles are attractive for persons high in this motive. There are differences in persons' reactions to persuasive communications based on this motive; persons high in need for cognition (NFC) tend to think carefully about arguments whereas persons low in NFC are influenced by factors such as how attractive the communicator is.

- **Exploring Gender and Diversity: Achievement Motivation and Economic Growth**

There are trends in which nations are economically dominant over time. Economists attribute such as labor costs and natural resources. Psychologists have argued that national differences in achievement motivation may contribute to these changes.

The average level of achievement motivation varies across cultures. In McClelland's classic research on this topic, he found that cultures differ on this dimension and that levels of achievement motivation are highly correlated with economic growth. These findings have been confirmed repeatedly. Of course, you should remember that correlations don't show causative relationships. So we can't be certain that differences in achievement motivation cause differences in economic growth.

F.   Intrinsic Motivation: How, Sometimes, to Turn Play Into Work

Activities that we perform mostly for pleasure are based on intrinsic motivation. When individuals are paid or rewarded for such intrinsic activities, their motivation or interest may be lowered. However, if the rewards are offered as a sign of recognition, or are large and satisfying, motivation may be maintained or enhanced. Research also finds that reductions in intrinsic motivation can be avoided by self-handicapping--providing explanations of poor performance.

Questions:

10-1.   What is emotion and what is motivation? _____

_____

_____

_____

10-2.   Why is the concept of motivation useful in explaining behavior? _____

_____

_____

_____

10-3.   Why has the concept of motivation replaced instinct in psychology? _____

_____

_____

_____

10-4.   What is the drive theory of motivation? _____

_____

_____

_____

10-5.   What is the arousal theory of motivation? _____

_____

_____

_____

10-6.   Why does expectancy theory take a cognitive perspective? _____

_____

_____

_____

10-7.   What is Maslow's hierarchy of needs, and what are the findings surrounding this view?

_____

_____

_____

10-8.   What are the factors involved in the regulation of caloric intake? _____

_____

_____

_____

10-9.   Why do some persons experience difficulty in regulating their caloric intake and body weight?

_____

_____

_____

10-10.   What is anorexia nervosa and bulimia? _____

_____

_____

_____

10-11.   What is the relationship between hormones and sexual behavior? _____

_____

_____

_____

10-12.   What are the basic facts about human sexual behavior? _____

_____

_____

_____

10-13. What are the factors that are thought to stimulate sexual arousal? _____

_____

_____

_____

10-14. What are the various views on the determinates of sexual preferences? _____

_____

_____

_____

10-15. What are the different views concerning the roots of aggression? _____

_____

_____

_____

10-16. What are the differences associated with achievement motivation, and how is it measured?

_____

_____

_____

10-17. What is need for cognition and what are its effects? _____

_____

_____

_____

10-18. What are the research findings concerning intrinsic motivation? _____

_____

_____

_____

II. Emotions: Their Nature, Expression, and Impact

L.O. 10.8:   Describe the nature of emotions.

L.O. 10.9:   Know the physiology of emotion.

L.O. 10.10:   Be able to describe how emotions are expressed.

L.O. 10.11:   Discuss the relationship between emotion and cognition.

L.O. 10.12:   Know the nonverbal cues associated with lying.

A.   The Nature of Emotions: Some Contrasting Views

Emotions are thought to involve three components. They include: (1) subjective cognitive states, (2) physiological changes within the body; and (3) expressive behaviors -- outward signs of these internal states or behaviors.

According to the Cannon-Bard theory, exposure to emotion related stimuli produces both the subjective experience of emotion and the accompanying physiological changes. The James-Lange theory of emotion proposes that subjective emotions are the result of changes within our bodies; recognition of these changes are responsible for emotional experience. Evidence in favor of the James-Lange theory comes from research on the facial feedback hypothesis -- changes in our facial expressions often produce shifts in our emotions. It is now evident that different emotions are accompanied by different patterns of physiological activity and outward expressions. In sum, consistent with the Cannon-Bard theory, emotional experiences often do occur in response to specific stimuli. However, consistent with James-Lange theory, they can be affected by changes in our bodily state.

The third important theory of emotion is the Schachter-Singer theory. According to this theory, emotional events produce internal arousal. We look to the environment for its base. From observed stimuli, we select a label for the arousal. This is known as the two-factor theory.

Support for the two-factor theory is seen in a study finding that males who met a female on a shaky suspension bridge rated her more sexually attractive than those who met her on a solid bridge. They interpreted their arousal in terms of the female instead of the bridge.

Opponent process theory assumes that emotional reactions to stimuli are automatically followed by an opposite reaction. In addition, repeated exposure to a stimulus causes the initial reaction to weaken and the opponent process to strengthen. Thus, emotional reactions occur in action-reaction cycles.

B.   The Physiology of Emotion

The physiological reactions that accompany emotions are regulated by the autonomic nervous system. The sympathetic nervous system readies the body for action. The parasympathetic nervous system is related to restoration of bodily resources.

Evidence indicates that different emotions are associated with different patterns of physiological reactions. Recently, evidence indicates that, although there are large individual differences associated with these patterns, positive feelings are associated with greater activation of the left hemisphere; negative feelings are associated with greater activation of the right hemisphere of the brain.

Lie detectors or polygraphs are used to determine if people are lying or telling the truth about an issue. These devices record several physiological reactions at once. They determine if a person's arousal level changes as a function of the type of question he/she is asked. Lie detectors yield uncertain results about whether a person is lying. First, lie detector tests measure only arousal. Second, a person's arousal can be influenced by many factors other than lying.

C.   The External Expression of Emotion: Outward Signs of Inner Feelings

Nonverbal cues are external and observable signs of internal emotional states. Persons reveal these states through several basic channels including facial expressions, eye contact, body movements, posture, and touching. Until recently, it was assumed that people have similar facial expressions when experiencing basic emotions such as anger, fear, surprise, happiness, sadness, and disgust. Generally, a high level of eye contact is seen as a sign of positive feelings or attraction. Avoidance of eye contact is a sign of negative feelings. Continuous gazing or staring is seen as a sign of hostility. However, recent research calls this assumption into question and suggests that interpretation of facial expressions are affected by the context in which the expression occurs. Baron points out that it is premature to make firm conclusions about this issue.

Nonverbal cues related to our posture and movements are called body language. A high level of body movement indicates arousal or anxiety. Different body orientations are associated with different emotional states. Body movements that provide specific information about emotions are called gestures.

Depending upon the context, touch can suggest such things as affection, sexual interest, caring, dominance, or even aggression. Interestingly, although context influences the meaning of touch, research indicates that touching someone in a manner that is considered acceptable for the current context generally produces positive reactions.

D.   Emotion and Cognition: How Feelings Shape Thoughts and Thoughts Shape Feelings

Research findings suggest that our current feelings can influence our cognitions. Our cognitions can also influence our current feelings. Affect can influence cognitions in several ways. First our current mood can influence how we evaluate ambiguous stimuli. Second, affect can influence memory. When we are in a positive mood it is generally easier to remember positive information. When we are in a negative mood it is generally easier to remember negative information. Third, people in a good mood are sometimes more creative.

Cognitions (thoughts) can also influence affect (feelings). This influence is discussed in the two-factor theory of emotion; our internal reactions are often interpreted through cognitive labels.

A second way cognition affects emotions is through the activation of schemas (cognitive representations) that contain strong affective components. For example, labeling a person as a member of some group may suggest he/she has traits that we may feel positively or negatively about. Thus, activation of stereotypes may exert powerful effects on our current feelings.

A third way our thoughts influence our affect is through our reactions to emotion-provoking events, such as anger-provocation. For example, anger can be reduced by distraction or apologies.

Lastly, our cognitive expectations can influence affect. These expectations affect the way we perceive events. For example, if you expect to like something, you may experience it as enjoyable.

Questions:

10-19. How does the Cannon-Bard theory differ from the James-Lange theory? _____

_____

_____

_____

10-20. What are the components of the Schachter-Singer theory, and what are some of the research findings surrounding this view? _____

_____

_____

_____

10-21. What are the assumptions of opponent-process theory? _____

_____

_____

_____

10-22. What are the physiological characteristics of emotion? _____

_____

_____

_____

10-23. How is emotion communicated through external expressions? _____

_____

_____

_____

10-24. What relationships exist between emotion and cognition? _____

_____

_____

_____

•   **Making Psychology Part of Your Life — How to Tell When Another Person is Lying: Nonverbal Cues and Detection of Deception**

Baron provides several cues that can help us detect when another person is lying. These include: (1) microexpressions - fleeting facial expressions; (2) interchannel discrepancies - inconsistencies among nonverbal cues; (3) paralanguage - nonverbal aspects of people's speech; (4) eye contact; and (5) exaggerated facial expressions.

YOUR NOTES:

MAKING PSYCHOLOGY PART OF YOUR LIFE: Key Terms and Concepts

Knowing the important concepts and key terms contained in this chapter is a very important part of mastering the material. We have presented a sample of these concepts below. Define each concept and check your definition with that presented in this chapter. It will also be beneficial for you to think of an example of each concept. Whenever possible, use your own personal experience to provide an example of each term below.

10-1.   **Achievement Motivation:** _____

        Example: _____

10-2.   **Affect:** _____

        Example: _____

10-3.   **Aggression:** _____

        Example: _____

10-4.   **Aggression Machine:** _____

10-5.   **Aggressive Motivation:** _____

        Example: _____

10-6.   **Arousal Theory:** _____

        Example: _____

10-7.   **Body Language:** _____

        Example: _____

10-8.   **Cannon-Bard Theory:** _____

10-9.   **Drive Theory:** _____

10-10. **Emotions:** _____

        Example: _____

10-11. **Expectancy Theory:** _____

10-12.   **Facial Feedback Hypothesis:** _____

Example: _____

10-13.   **Frustration:** _____

Example: _____

10-14.   **Gestures:** _____

Example: _____

10-15.   **Heterosexual (Sexual Orientation):** _____

Example: _____

10-16.   **Homeostasis:** _____

Example: _____

10-17.   **Hierarchy of Needs:** _____

10-18.   **Homosexual (Sexual Orientation):** _____

Example: _____

10-19.   **Hunger Motivation:** _____

Example: _____

10-20.   **Incentives:** _____

Example: _____

10-21.   **Instincts:** _____

Example: _____

10-22.   **Instinct Theory:** _____

10-23. **Interchannel Discrepancies:** _____

   Example: _____

10-24. **Intrinsic Motivation:** _____

   Example: _____

10-25. **James-Lange Theory:** _____

10-26. **Microexpressions:** _____

   Example: _____

10-27. **Motivation:** _____

   Example: _____

10-28. **Need for Cognition:** _____

   Example: _____

10-29. **Nonverbal Cues:** _____

   Example: _____

10-30. **Opponent-Process Theory:** _____

10-31. **Power Motivation:** _____

   Example: _____

10-32. **Schachter-Singer Theory (two-factor theory):** _____

10-33. **Sexual Jealousy:** _____

   Example: _____

10-34. **Sexual Orientation:** _____

10-35. **Thematic Apperception Test:** _____

10-36. **Two-Factor Theory (of emotion):** _____

10-37. **Work Motivation:** _____

        Example: _____

10-38. **Workplace Violence:** _____

        Example: _____

YOUR NOTES:

CHALLENGE: Develop Your Critical Thinking Skills

Recognizing Relationships Between Thoughts and Feelings: "Sad But Smart or Happy But Dumb?"

As discussed in your text, research suggests that moods significantly affect our information processing. Research suggests that we are less critical of information when we're in positive vs. negative moods. Thus, we seem to be "sad but smart -- happy but dumb." A critical thinker is aware of the influences of emotion on his/her thoughts. As an exercise toward recognizing these influences, chart your emotions for a few days and note your thoughts and behavior.

	Primary Mood	Your Thoughts	Your Behavior	Your Physiological Reactions
Day 1				
Day 2				
Day 3				
Day 4				
Day 5				

Assessment:

10-1.   Do you see any relationships among your mood, thoughts, and behavior?

10-2.   Were there any instances in which you made decisions that on second thought seemed less than perfect? If so, what was your mood state?

10-3.   Were there decisions that you made that were especially "good?" If so, what was your mood state?

<u>Alternative Exercise</u>

If you did not choose to track your moods for a week, retrospect on some of the decisions -- good and bad -- that you have made over the years. Use these "retrospections" to answer questions 1-4 above.

CHALLENGE: Taking Psychology With You

Effective Goal Setting

Goal setting is related to effective performance. Take this opportunity to use these guidelines in preparing for your next major class assignment (a paper or an exam). If you follow these guidelines, you will see their utility and will, hopefully, make them a part of your life!

10-1.   Set specific goals.

Indicate precisely what will be defined as adequate performance (e.g., how many pages a day you should read to be ready for the test).

10-2.   Set challenging but attainable goals.

Assess the difficulty level of your goals. Are they high enough that they stretch your ability, but not so high that you can't possibly reach them?

10-3.   Reward yourself for reaching each goal.

Identify the rewards you will give to yourself for reaching each goal.

10-4.   Become committed to your goals.

Assess your level of commitment to each goal. Adopt only those goals you are committed to reaching.

10-5.   Build feedback into the process.

How will you know when you've reached each goal?

CHALLENGE: Review Your Comprehensive Knowledge

SAMPLE TEST QUESTIONS

Once you have worked through the preceding sections, you should be ready for a comprehensive self-test. You can check your answers with those at the end of this section. An additional practice test is given in the supplementary section at the end of this study guide.

10-1.   One major problem with instinct theory of motivation is that the existence of the instinct is inferred from:
    a. physiological measures.
    b. observations.
    c. the behavior it was designed to explain.
    d. experimental analyses.

10-2.   Basal metabolic rate refers to:
    a. the number of calories a person consumes a day.
    b. the number of calories a person uses during activity.
    c. the number of calories the body requires at rest within a given period of time.
    d. the number of calories the body requires to maintain a stable weight.

10-3.   According to drive theory, behaviors will be repeated if they tend to:
    a. increase drives.
    b. have no effect on drives.
    c. decrease drives.
    d. initiate drives.

10-4.   The Kinsey reports found that:
    a. females were more sexually active than males.
    b. there was great individual variation in sexual behavior.
    c. only a minority of men and women have premarital sex.
    d. rates of homosexuality were higher than expected.

10-5.   Which of the following is **not** true of high achievement oriented individuals?
    a. high grades in school
    b. prefer difficult tasks
    c. succeed in running their own business
    d. rapid promotions

10-6.   If we are going to reward people for intrinsically motivated activities, it is best if these rewards:
    a. are a sign of recognition.
    b. are small.
    c. are unsatisfying.
    d. are external.

10-7.   The theory that holds that emotional stimuli produce both the experience of emotion and accompanying physiological changes is:
    a. James-Lange.
    b. Cannon-Bard.
    c. Schachter-Singer.
    d. Watson-Levin.

10-8.   The theory of emotion that asserts that different patterns of emotional activity are associated with different emotions is the:
    a. Cannon-Bard theory.
    b. James-Lange theory.
    c. Schachter-Singer theory.
    d. facial feedback theory.

10-9.   Research on the facial feedback hypothesis supports the _____ theory.
    a. James-Lange
    b. Cannon-Bard
    c. Schachter-Singer
    d. Watson-Levin

10-10.   What are the two factors that determine a person's emotional experience according to Schachter and Singer's two-factor theory?
a.   intensity of affect and behavior being performed
b.   intensity of affect and whether situation is positive or negative
c.   body gestures and transfer of excitation
d.   internal arousal and choice of label for this arousal based on external stimuli

10-11.   Research on emotions comparing Cannon-Bard and James-Lange theories have found support for:
a.   neither.   c.   only James-Lange.
b.   only Cannon-Bard.   d.   both.

10-12.   According to the opponent-process theory of emotion, the day following my graduation (a happy event), I may feel:
a.   sad.   c.   afraid.
b.   free.   d.   elated.

10-13.   At times, people experience a desire to harm others when they have been prevented by these people from obtaining what they want. This is called the _____ hypothesis.
a.   frustration-aggression   c.   frustration-catharsis
b.   opponent process   d.   goal blocking

10-14.   One technique of measuring achievement and power motives is the _____ test.
a.   Briggs-Storm test   c.   Strong-Davis test
b.   Thematic Apperception test   d.   Thematic Illusion test

10-15.   Opponent process theory assumes that repeated exposure to a stimulus causes the initial reaction to _____ and the opponent process to _____ .
a.   strengthen, weaken   c.   weaken, weaken
b.   weaken, strengthen   d.   strengthen, strengthen

10-16.   Which of the following is **not** a correct statement about Maslow's theory?
a.   Motives exist in a hierarchy.
b.   Motives at the bottom must be satisfied before those at the top.
c.   Deficiency needs include esteem needs.
d.   Self-actualization is a growth need.

10-17.   Which of the following is **not** a correct statement about why people may have a desire to overeat.
a.   It is learned.   c.   It is influenced by reactions to stress.
b.   It is influenced by basal metabolic rate.   d.   It is influenced by opioid barbiturates.

10-18.   Body movements that carry specific meanings in a given culture are called:
a.   microexpressions.   c.   body language.
b.   interchannel discrepancies.   d.   gestures.

10-19.   Which of the following theories of motivation include the role of incentives in producing motivation?
a.   expectancy theory   c.   drive theory
b.   arousal theory   d.   instinct theory

10-20.   Which of the following motives refers to the enjoyment of effortful cognitive activities?
a.   need for cognition   c.   need for power
b.   need for achievement   d.   need for thought

Answers and Feedback for Sample Test Questions:

10-1.   C   Using "instincts" as an explanation for behavior can be a circular form of explanation. For example, saying that a person was aggressive because he has an aggressive instinct is a problem because we are inferring the existence of this instinct from his behavior and then using it to explain his behavior. (p. 384-385)

10-2.   C   Basal metabolic rate refers to the number of calories the body requires at rest within a given period of time. Individuals differ in this rate. (p. 389)

10-3.   C   Behaviors tend to be repeated when they decrease aversive drive states. (p. 384)

10-4.   B   The Kinsey data show a basic theme: individual differences in sexual behavior are enormous. (p. 392)

10-5.   B   High achievement oriented individuals prefer tasks that are moderately difficult. (p. 403)

10-6.   A   Rewards that are seen as signs of recognition do not decrease intrinsic motivation for the activity. (p. 406-407)

10-7.   B   The Cannon-Bard theory of emotion suggests that emotion-provoking stimuli simultaneously elicit physiological arousal and the cognitive states we label as emotions. (p. 409)

10-8.   B   The James-Lange theory contends that emotion-provoking stimuli induce physiological reactions and that these form the basis for labeling emotions. (p. 409)

10-9.   A   This hypothesis states that facial expressions can influence our emotional states -- a view that is consistent with the theory that physiological reactions form the basis of labeling emotions (the James-Lange theory). (p. 410)

10-10.   D   According to Schachter-Singer theory, subjects emotional states are determined by both our internal state of arousal and the label we place on this feeling. (p. 410)

10-11.   D   There has been support for both of these theories of emotion. (pp. 410)

10-12   A   I may feel sad according to this view, because emotional reactions are followed automatically by an opposite reaction. Thus, feelings of happiness may be followed by feelings of sadness. (p. 410-411)

10-13.   A   According to the frustration-aggression hypothesis, aggression is caused by feelings of frustration that can be invoked, for example, by someone blocking my goals. (p. 397)

10-14.   B   The Thematic Apperception Test (TAT) is used to measure achievement and power motivation. (p. 402)

10-15.   B   This is the second assumption of opponent process theory. (p. 410-411)

10-16.   C   Esteem needs are **growth** needs. (p. 386-387)

10-17.   D   Opioid barbiturates are not implicated in obesity. (p. 389-390)

10-18.   B   Gestures are body movements which carry specific meanings. (p. 414)

10-19.   A   Expectancy theory assumes positive incentives "pull" (motivate) behavior. (p. 386)

10-20.   A   Need for cognition is the motive for engaging in effortful cognitive activities. (p. 402)

GLOSSARY OF DIFFICULT WORDS AND EXPRESSIONS

These terms from your text and this study guide were identified by students as potentially hard to understand. We have defined these terms and expressions.

Term or expression	Definition
A bout of	a period of
Ambiguous	uncertain; not clear
Banned	prohibited; prevented; not allowed
Bribe	something given, offered or promised in order to influence or persuade a person
Compel	force (a person or thing to do something)
Congruent	suitable; agreeing (with); consistent with
Conversion	changing one thing into another
Discerned	to make out or see
Distress	(case of) great pain, discomfort or sorrow
Elation	great happiness
Effective	having an influence
Frowning	draw the eyebrows together forming lines on the forehead
Gorge	narrow opening
Hikers	people who take very long walks
Mundane	dull; everyday; not special
Out on a limb	put oneself in a vulnerable position; taking a chance
Override	refuse to agree with, accept (a person's opinions, wishes, decisions, claims, etc.)
Overt	obvious; seen
Overwhelm	confuse; too much for a person to take
Paragon	model of a perfect person
Peak	highest point
Pendulum	weighed rod hung from a fixed point so that it swings freely
Pen poised	pen ready; being to write
Play a role	is involved in
Plunging	jumping into with force; getting involved in
Quest	dedicated effort; a special goal

Term or expression	Definition
Relish	have; enjoy something; with pleasure
Rubbing	move one thing backwards and forward on the surface of another
Shifts	changes in something
Skepticism	doubts about something
Soothing	making a person feel quiet or calm
Sorrow	cause of grief or sadness
Strenuous	using or needing a great effort; hard task
Striving for	trying to accomplish something; working toward a goal
Swaying	moving, first to one side and then to the other
Thwarting	obstruct; frustrate; keep from obtaining
Traits	characteristics; properties
Trigger	start something
Trivial	of small value or importance
Unverified	not proven
Wane	become weaker; going away

CHAPTER 11
INTELLIGENCE: COGNITIVE AND EMOTIONAL

INTEGRATED CHAPTER OUTLINE: Survey and Question

This section presents the major topics and ideas from the chapter. Use it as a tool for seeing how the components of the chapter fit together. At the end of each major topic, we have asked you a question that relates to the major learning objectives. If you can answer these questions, you have taken a major step toward mastering this material.

I. Intelligence: Contrasting Views of Its Nature

L.O. 11.1:   Compare and contrast the views on the nature of intelligence.

Psychologists generally agree that intelligence involves the ability to understand complex ideas, to adapt effectively to the environment, to engage in various forms of reasoning to overcome obstacles by careful thought, and to learn from experience. Many psychologists believe that people's relative position along this dimension predicts many important aspects of behavior, including how quickly a person can master new information and tasks and how quickly he/she will understand and adapt to new situations. Various measures of intelligence are related to important life outcomes but many other factors play a role.

A.   Intelligence: Unitary or Multifaceted

Some theorists feel that intelligence is a general, unified capacity. For example, researchers such as Spearman proposed that intelligence consists of a general ability to solve problems. Theorists who feel intelligence is composed of several distinct abilities believe intelligence is multifaceted. For example, Thurstone proposed that intelligence consists of seven distinct primary mental abilities. Among these were verbal meaning, number, and space.

B.   Gardner's Theory of Multiple Intelligence

Most theorists have focused on the intelligence of "normal" children. Gardner argued that this approach is limiting and that psychologists should study persons at the extreme; for example, geniuses, impaired persons, and those with special gifts. He argued that looking at this person allows us to see such kinds of intelligence as musical, intelligence, bodily-kinesthetic intelligence (like gymnasts possess), personal intelligence (the ability to get along with others), and emotional intelligence. He proposes that intelligence is multifaceted and we need to observe all to get a complete understanding.

C.   Sternberg's Triarchic Theory: The Value of Practical Intelligence

Sternberg's triarchic theory proposes that there are three distinct types of intelligence. Intelligence that is related to effectiveness in critical and analytic thinking is componential. This is associated with ability to think critically. The intelligence related to insight and the ability to develop new ideas is experiential.

Individuals high on this are good at combining seemingly unrelated facts. People who have practical sense have contextual or practical intelligence. They can quickly figure out what it takes to be successful at various tasks and how to accomplish various goals.

There is evidence that practical intelligence is different from the kind of intelligence necessary for academic success (componential intelligence). People readily distinguish between the two in their everyday lives. And growing evidence suggests componential intelligence peeks early in life whereas practical intelligence develops across the lifespan. Finally, there are instances in which people score high on one dimension and not the other.

Sternberg suggests that persons high in practical intelligence use tacit knowledge to solve problems. Tacit knowledge differs from academic knowledge in that it is (1) action-oriented, (2) it allows individuals to achieve personally-valued goals, and (3) it is usually acquired without direct help from others. Tacit knowledge is an important predictor of success in many areas of life.

II. Measuring Human Intelligence: From Tests to Underlying Psychological Processes and Beyond

L.O. 11.2:   Know how intelligence is measured.

L.O. 11.3:   Be able to discuss the neurological basis of intelligence.

The intelligence test was first developed by Binet and Simon. They selected items that children could answer without special training. Therefore, they used either new or unusual items or very familiar ones. In a later version, they grouped items by age. An item was placed at a particular level if about 75 percent of the children of that age could pass it correctly. It was adopted in the U.S. as the Stanford-Binet test and yielded a single score of intelligence or IQ.

A.   IQ: Its Meaning Then and Now

IQ stands for intelligence quotient. An IQ is obtained by dividing an individual's mental age by the chronological age and multiplying by 100. Mental age is determined by adding the number of items passed correctly on the test. One problem with this type of test is that at some point, mental growth levels off or stops while chronological age continues to grow. As a result, IQ appears to begin to decline with age. Now, IQ scores are considered differently. They are interpreted in relation to others of the same age.

B.   The Wechsler Scales

A major drawback of the Stanford-Binet is that it is predominantly verbal in content. To overcome this problem, Wechsler devised both verbal and nonverbal (or performance) items. Wechsler believed that differences between those two components reflected important diagnostic information. It was believed that differences between scores on the various subsets could be used to diagnose mental disorders. Research has yielded mixed results. Although not conclusive, children with learning disabilities sometimes score higher on picture completion and object assembly but lower on tests such as arithmetic, vocabulary, and information.

Individual tests of intelligence are costly. They are useful, however, for identifying children at the extreme ends of intelligence, such as those who suffer from mental retardation and those who are intellectually gifted. Mental retardation refers to considerably below-average intellectual functioning combined with difficulties in meeting everyday demands. There are four broad categories of mental retardation: mild, moderate, severe, and profound. Levels are determined by test scores and daily life success.

Mental retardation can be caused by genetic abnormalities, such as Down Syndrome or environmental factors such as inadequate nutrition or alcohol abuse by mothers during pregnancy.

The most comprehensive study of intellectually-gifted persons followed the lives of 1,528 children with IQs of 130 or above. As a group, these individuals experienced high levels of success in their occupations and personal lives.

C.   Group Tests of Intelligence

Group tests of intelligence can be administered to many persons at once. However, such tests have been criticized. Critics believe they are unfair in several respects to children from disadvantaged backgrounds.

In the history of these tests, they have been used to screen potential immigrants.

D.   The Cognitive Basis of Intelligence: Measuring Intelligence Through Processing Speed

Recently, psychologists have moved beyond the tests discussed above and have tried to identify the cognitive mechanisms and processes that underlie intelligence. Several such tests have been developed, including the Kaufman Assessment Battery for Children, the Kaufman Adult Intelligence Test, and the Woodcock-Johnson Test, which measures aspects of both fluid and crystallized intelligence.

General intelligence is called fluid intelligence. It involves the ability to form concepts, reason, and identify similarities. Specific knowledge gained from experience is called crystallized intelligence. For example, vocabulary tests involve crystallized intelligence. Fluid intelligence reaches its peak in early adulthood. Crystallized intelligence increases across the lifespan.

The speed with which people perform simple perceptual and cognitive tasks are often correlated with intelligence tests. These reaction time measures seem to reflect reasons why fluid intelligence increase as children grew older — the speed with which children can process information increases with age. Research by Fry and Hale (1996) with children supports this idea.

- **Research Methods: How Psychologists Study the Cognitive Basis of Intelligence**

    Because psychologists are interested in understanding and explaining, the study of underlying mechanisms of intelligence is important. The reaction time techniques described above are useful for this. But there are some drawbacks. Because these measures tap manual skills, such as button-pressing, as well as speed of mental processes, they may be affected by factors unrelated to intelligence.

    Researchers have begun to use inspection time, which reflects the minimum amount of time a particular stimulus must be present for a person to make an accurate judgment about it. This measure seems to be closely related to intelligence and it makes sense that the amount of time individuals require for the intake of new visual information would be a component of intelligence.

E.   The Neurological Basis of Intelligence: Intelligence and Neural Efficiency

According to a neuroscience approach, intelligence is related to rapid or efficient neural processing. There is research supporting this approach. First, in one study the speech of nerve impulses was correlated with scores on a written test of intelligence. Second, when asked to perform a complex cognitive task, persons scoring highest on written tests of intelligence expended less mental energy than those scoring lowest. Third, scores on a standard intelligence measure was related to the size of certain portions of the brain.

III.   Reliability and Validity: Basic Requirements for all Psychological Tests

L.O. 11.4:   Know how psychological tests are assessed for reliability and validity.

A.   Assessing Reliability: Internal Consistency and Test-Retest Reliability

To be useful, measuring devices must give the same result each time they are applied to the same person; that is, they must be reliable. To see if the items on the test are measuring the same thing, one can divide them in half to see if the scores are similar. This is split-half reliability and is a measure of internal consistency. A formula, termed coefficient alpha, considers all of the possible ways of splitting into halves the items on a test. Giving the test to the same group several times to determine the similarity of scores over time is test-retest reliability. Typically, the longer the time between testing intervals, the lower the reliability. To reduce practice effects, psychologists often use alternative forms of the same test.

B.   Validity: Do Tests Measure What They Claim to Measure?

The ability of a test to measure what it is supposed to is validity. The extent to which the items sample behaviors that are thought to be related to the characteristic in question is content validity. The type of validity related to whether differences in scores on the test are related to differences in behavior is criterion validity. The type of criterion validity in which scores on a test are used to predict later performance is predictive validity. The type of validity in which test scores are related to present behavior or performance is concurrent validity. Whether or not a test measures a concept or process in a theory is construct validity. Evidence for construct validity can be derived from convergent evidence. This evidence is obtained when, for example, scores on a particular health test are related to other accepted measures of health.

C.   Intelligence Testing and Public Policy: Are Intelligence Tests Fair?

On group tests of intelligence, African-Americans, Native Americans, and Hispanics score lower than those of European ancestry. This may reflect cultural bias for several reasons. First, children from minority or disadvantaged backgrounds may not have had the opportunity to acquire the knowledge necessary for a successful performance. Second, the tests may incorporate implicit European values about how to judge the correctness of answers. Therefore, they favor Europeans. This may reflect cultural bias in that these tests were developed for white middle-class children.

Attempts have been made to develop culture-fair tests that use items to which all groups have been exposed. One of these is the Raven Progressive Matrices test. Tests that measure general cognitive skills, such as processing speed, are promising in that they may lead to a culture-free test.

Questions:

11-1. Define intelligence and discuss whether it is best viewed as a unitary or multifaceted construct.

_____

_____

_____

11-2. Compare and contrast Gardner's theory of multiple intelligence and Sternberg's Triarchic theory of intelligence. _____

_____

_____

_____

11-3. What are the cognitive measures that are used to study intelligence? _____

_____

_____

_____

11-4. How is neural efficiency related to intelligence? _____

_____

_____

_____

11-5. What is test reliability and validity and what are the different types of reliability and validity?

_____

_____

_____

11-6. What are the sources of cultural bias in intelligence tests? _____

_____

_____

_____

11-7.   What are the practical applications of intelligence tests and what are the dangers involved in mis-using these tests? _____

_____

_____

_____

IV. Human Intelligence: The Role of Heredity and the Role of Environment

L.O. 11.5:   Discuss the evidence for the role of heredity and the environment in intelligence.

A.   Evidence for the Influence of Heredity

Human intelligence seems to be the result of both heredity and environmental factors. Evidence for heredity comes from the fact that the closer two people are related, the more similar their IQs. IQs of identical twins are more highly correlated than those of siblings. IQs of siblings are more highly correlated than those of cousins. [Remember: higher correlations indicate a stronger relationship between variables.]

The IQs of adopted children correlate more highly with those of their biological parents than their adoptive parents. However, in some cases IQs become increasingly similar to those of their adoptive parents. The IQs of identical twins reared apart correlate almost as highly as those of twins reared together. Twins reared apart are also similar in appearance and personality. On the basis of this research, psychologists have estimated that the heritability of intelligence (the proportion of the variance in intelligence within a given population that is attributable to genetic factors) ranges from about 35% in childhood to 75% in adulthood. Genetic factors appear to have an increasing impact with age. This may be the case because people are less affected by their families or their social origins as they grow older; they are more affected by their own characteristics. There is little doubt genetic factors play a role in intelligence throughout life.

B.   Evidence for the Influence of Environmental Factors

The worldwide gains in IQ studies of environmental deprivation and enrichment suggest the importance of environmental factors. Depriving children of certain forms of environmental stimulation early in life can reduce intelligence. Studies have shown that enrichment can improve intelligence. Removing children from sterile environments and placing them in a more favorable environment improved intelligence. Nutrition, family background, and the quality of education are environmental factors influencing intelligence and the longer students remain in school, the higher their IQs tend to be.

C.   Environment, Heredity, and Intelligence: Summing Up

Heredity and environment are both important in shaping intelligence. Research has led some psychologists to suspect that genetic factors may be more important than environmental factors within a given population. Nevertheless, even characteristics that are highly heritable can be influenced by the environment.

Questions:

11-8. What is the evidence for the role of heredity in intelligence? _____

_____

_____

_____

11-9. What is the evidence for the role of environmental factors in intelligence? _____

_____

_____

_____

11-10. How do genetic and environmental factors influence jointly the development of intelligence?

_____

_____

_____

V. Group Differences in Intelligence Test Scores: Why They Occur

L.O. 11.6:   Discuss the possible cause of group differences in I.Q. scores.

A.   Possible Causes of Group Differences in IQ Scores

In addition to the test biases discussed earlier, three other factors have received the most attention: socioeconomic factors, cultural factors, and genetic factors. A much larger proportion of minority groups live below the poverty line in the U.S. and other countries. Poverty is associated with many factors that adversely influence intelligence, such as poor nutrition, substandard schools and inadequate prenatal care. But this is only part of the story. When socioeconomic status is matched, there are still differences in the IQ scores of various ethnic groups.

Cultural differences, such as differences in emphasis in working alone vs. sharing, may contribute to the lower scores of certain ethnic groups. Differences in culture may influence the way school is experienced by children with different cultural backgrounds. African-American children may find school unpleasant because their culture has emphasized expressiveness and working together and schools dominated by the majority culture do not emphasize these dimensions.

A related factor is what has been termed membership in caste-like minority groups. Persons in minority groups may see their disadvantaged status as permanent and may grow up feeling helpless to change their fate. Therefore, they may reject academic achievement goals and other forms of behavior that is seen as "acting white," which in turn lowers scores.

- **Exploring Gender and Diversity: Genetic Factors and Group Differences in IQ Scores**

  In the controversial book, <u>The Bell Curve</u>, the authors argue the genetic hypothesis — the view that group differences in intelligence are related to genetic factors. Their argument is that intelligence is not changed by modifying the environment.

  Their argument is flawed because it rests on the assumption that group differences in intelligence are like individual differences in intelligence. This assumption is wrong. Environments in which members of various ethnic groups live are different; so it is a mistake to conclude that the environment does not have an effect.

B.   Gender Differences in Intelligence

There are no differences between males and females on standard IQ tests. There are a few subtle differences on certain components of intelligence: (1) females score higher on verbal abilities, (2) females score higher on college achievement tests in literature, spelling, and writing, (3) males score higher on visual-spatial tasks.

- **Beyond the Headlines: As Psychologists See It — Why Men Lose Keys and Women Find Them**

  In the "Beyond the Headlines" section, Baron discusses the possibility that differences in spatial ability reflect different kinds of tasks performed by men and women throughout history. Two psychologists (Silverman & Eals) have reasoned that hunters (males) need to be able to orient themselves in relation to things at a great distance; whereas gatherers (females) need to be able to remember locations of plants. So, men are better at visual tasks such as rotating objects and women remember locations better than men. Their research supports this reasoning.

Questions:

11-11.   What are the possible causes of group differences in IQ scores? _____

_____

_____

_____

11-12.   What are the gender differences in intelligence? _____

_____

_____

_____

VI.   Emotional Intelligence: The Feeling Side of Intelligence

L.O. 11.7:   Be able to discuss the nature of emotional intelligence.

A.   Major Components of Emotional Intelligence

Emotional intelligence can be defined as a cluster of traits or abilities relating to the emotional side of life. Goleman specifics five components: (1) knowing our own emotions, (2) managing our emotions, (3) motivating ourselves, (4) recognizing the emotions of others, and (5) handling relationships. We give examples of why each of these components are important below.

- Knowing our emotions is important because awareness of our feelings helps us make good decisions. Persons who are not aware of their feelings may not make good choices about such things as who to date or marry. They are also low in expressiveness, which hinders interpersonal relations.

- Managing emotions is important for both health and interpersonal relations. We need to regulate our emotional reactions to prevent depression and to get along well with others. Managing anger is discussed in the "Taking Psychology With You" section.

- Emotional intelligence helps us motivate ourselves by such means as pushing ourselves to work hard, remaining optimistic and enthusiastic, and delaying gratification.

- Recognizing others' emotions is an important interpersonal skill involving nonverbal cues. Unless we know how others feel, it is difficult to interact with them.

- Handling relationships, or interpersonal intelligence, is useful for negotiations and social coordination. This topic is discussed in more detail below.

B.   Emotional Intelligence in Action: Building Successful Intimate Relationships

Difficulties in long-term relationships often arise from differences between the sexes in emotional skills. Because of contrasting socialization practices, women are more skilled in detecting and expressing emotions. Both men and women can profit from work on their emotional intelligence. It also plays an important role in the business world.

Questions:

11-13. What are the five components of emotional intelligence? _____

_____

_____

_____

11-14. What role does emotional intelligence play in success and happiness? _____

_____

_____

_____

VII. Creativity: Generating the Extraordinary

L.O. 11.8:   Compare and contrast differing views of creativity.

L.O. 11.9:   Discuss the recent research on evidence for the confluence approach to creativity.

L.O. 11.10:   Know how you can use what you've learned to manage anger.

A.   Contrasting Views of Creativity

Creativity involves the ability to produce work that is both novel and appropriate. Cognitive psychologists focus on the basic processes, such as retrieval from memory, associations and synthesis. Social psychologists focus on environmental conditions that foster creativity and the traits that make people creative. The confluence approach appears to be a very useful approach to this topic.

The confluence approach is based on the idea that for creativity to occur, multiple factors must converge. Lubart's confluence model points to the importance of six distinct resources: (1) intellectual abilities, (2) knowledge, (3) certain styles of thinking, specifically a preference for thinking in novel ways and an ability to think globally, (4) personality attributes such as risk-taking and tolerance for ambiguity, (5) intrinsic task-focused motivation, and (6) an environment that is supportive of creative ideas.

B.   Recent Research on Creativity: Evidence for the Confluence Approach

There is support for the confluence approach. Creativity appears to require many factors and it is the case that people can be creative in one area and not another. Intellectual ability, thinking style, personality, and willingness to take risks have been shown to be related to creativity.

Questions:

11-15. What is creativity and how is it studied? _____

_____

_____

_____

11-16. What are the factors that the confluence approach consider to be essential for creativity?

_____

_____

_____

11-17. What evidence supports the confluence approach? _____

_____

_____

_____

- **Making Psychology Part of Your Life: Managing Anger: A Key Aspect of Emotional Intelligence**

Baron gives several steps that are useful in managing your anger — an important component of emotional intelligence. These include:

- Stop the process early
- Try a cool-off period
- Do something to get yourself off the anger track
- Seek positive explanations for the things others say or do that make you angry
- Don't rely on "catharsis"

MAKING PSYCHOLOGY PART OF YOUR LIFE: Key Terms and Concepts

Knowing the important concepts and key terms contained in this chapter is a very important part of mastering the material. We have presented a sample of these concepts below. Define each concept and check your definition with that presented at the end in your textbook. It will also be beneficial for you to think of an example of each concept. Whenever possible, use your own personal experience to provide an example of each term below.

11-1. **Confluence Approach:** _____

11-2. **Content Validity:** _____

11-3. **Creativity:** _____

Example: _____

11-4. **Criterion-Related Validity:** _____

Example: _____

11-5. **Cultural Bias:** _____

Example: _____

11-6. **Down Syndrome:** _____

11-7. **Emotional Intelligence:** _____

Example: _____

11-8. **Genetic Hypothesis:** _____

Example: _____

11-9. **Heritability:** _____

Example: _____

11-10. **Inspection Time:** _____

11-11. **Intelligence:** _____

Example: _____

11-12. **IQ:** _____

11-13. **Mental Retardation:** _____

Example: _____

11-14. **Practical Intelligence:** _____

11-15. **Processing Speed:** _____

Example: _____

11-16. **Raven Progressive Matrices:** _____

11-17. **Reliability:** _____

11-18. **Split-Half Reliability:** _____

Example: _____

11-19. **Stanford-Binet Test:** _____

11-20. **Tacit Knowledge:** _____

11-21. **Test-Retest Reliability:** _____

Example: _____

11-22. **Triarchic Theory:** _____

11-23. **Validity:** _____

CHALLENGE: Develop Your Critical Thinking Skills

Drawing Implications: Intelligence, Heritability, and Selective Breeding

Your text discusses some evidence that intelligence may be heritable. Demographic data over the last 20 years indicates that persons with higher IQs and more education tend to have fewer children. As an exercise in drawing implications from what you've learned about the heritability of intelligence, comment on the following:

11-1. If this trend continues, and if intelligence is heritable, then what might we expect to see in the future IQ levels of our population?

11-2. Consider your conclusion in light of the fact that heritable characteristics are still influenced by the environment. Does your conclusion change?

11-3. What are the political and socioeconomic issues that are suggested by this trend?

11-4. It has been suggested that "sperm banks" could be established that collect and sell sperm. Sperm from prominent individuals could be collected and sold. What are the ethical and practical implications of the existence of these banks for our population?

YOUR NOTES:

CHALLENGE: Taking Psychology With You

Baron provides a number of steps that help you improve your emotional intelligence by managing your anger. Try to recall a situation in which you handled anger well and a situation in which you didn't manager your anger as well. Then, complete the following exercise:

A. Well-managed situation: _____

_____

_____

_____

_____

1. What specific actions did you take that helped you handle your anger? _____

_____

_____

_____

B. Poorly managed situation: _____

_____

_____

_____

_____

2. What could you have done to handle this situation in a better way? _____

_____

_____

_____

CHALLENGE: Review Your Comprehensive Knowledge

SAMPLE TEST QUESTIONS

Once you have worked through the preceding sections, you should be ready for a comprehensive self-test. You can check your answers with those at the end of this section. An additional practice test is given in the supplementary section at the end of this study guide.

11-1. Psychological tests need to be:
    a. reliable and valid.
    b. reliable and difficult.
    c. reliable and consistent.
    d. valid and current.

11-2. Assessment of similarity of scores over time is called:
    a. split-half reliability.
    b. test-retest reliability.
    c. split-half validity.
    d. test-retest validity.

11-3. The ability of a test to measure what it is supposed to measure is its:
    a. predictive power.
    b. internal consistency.
    c. reliability.
    d. validity.

11-4. The type of validity in which test scores are related to present behavior is:
    a. content.
    b. predictive.
    c. concurrent.
    d. construct.

11-5. Spearman felt that intelligence consisted of:
    a. a general ability to reason, and solve problems.
    b. multiple types of intelligence.
    c. a composite of seven primary mental abilities.
    d. culturally determined skills.

11-6. Generally research indicates that the correlation of IQ scores is:
    a. lower than expected.
    b. higher for identical twins.
    c. higher among males.
    d. higher among fraternal twins.

11-7. According to Sternberg's triarchic theory, people who have practical sense have _____ intelligence.
    a. componential
    b. experiential
    c. contextual
    d. intuitive

11-8. Which of the following is not a factor that contributes to group differences in IQ?
    a. socioeconomic factors
    b. cultural factors
    c. personality
    d. genetic factors

11-9. Originally, IQ scores were obtained by dividing _____ age by _____ age and multiplying by 100.
    a. mental, chronological
    b. chronological, mental
    c. general, specific
    d. specific, general

11-10. It seems likely that the worldwide increase in IQ scores is due to:
    a. environmental factors.
    b. genetic factors.
    c. actual increase in intelligence.
    d. the ozone layer.

11-11. One major problem with the use of individual tests of intelligence is that they are:
    a. too difficult.
    b. culturally biased.
    c. too easy.
    d. not influenced by training.

11-12. The more closely two people are related, the _____ their IQs.
    a. lower
    b. higher
    c. more similar
    d. more different

11-13. According to Gardner's theory:
    a. there is one general type of intelligence.
    b. practical intelligence is most important.
    c. there are several important types of intelligence.
    d. none of the above

11-14. Which of the following statements is incorrect?
    a. Fluid intelligence involves the ability to form concepts, reason, and identify similarities.
    b. Specific knowledge gained from experience is called crystallized intelligence.
    c. Crystallized intelligence peaks around age 40.
    d. Fluid intelligence peaks in early adulthood.

11-15. Research has found that females perform better than males on all but one of the skills: Identify the skill that doesn't fit.
    a. verbal skills
    b. spelling
    c. spatial
    d. locating objects in the immediate environment

11-16. On two separate occasions, Ann took a test measuring an aspect of her personality and obtained very similar scores. In other words, the test has been shown to have:
    a. concurrent validity.
    b. predictive validity.
    c. test-retest reliability.
    d. split-half reliability.

11-17. In Sternberg's triarchic theory, the ability to formulate new ideas or to combine seemingly unrelated facts is referred to as:
    a. componential intelligence.
    b. experiential intelligence.
    c. contextual intelligence.
    d. crystallized intelligence.

11-18. The ability to read other's feelings is a component of
    a. emotional intelligence.
    b. fluid intelligence.
    c. crystallized intelligence.
    d. all of the above

11-19. Which is not one of Sternberg's three distinct types of intelligence?
    a. componential
    b. unitary
    c. experiential
    d. contextual

11-20. The minimum amount of time an individual needs in order to make a judgment about a particular stimulus is called:
    a. reaction time.
    b. intelligence quotient.
    c. reliability judgment.
    d. inspection time.

Answers and Feedback for Sample Test Questions:

11-1.   A   Reliability measures the extent to which a measuring device gives the same result each time it is applied to the same person. Validity refers to the ability of a test to measure what it is suppose to measure. Both are essential for a good psychological test. (p. 438-441)

11-2.   B   Test-retest reliability refers to the similarity of scores over time. (p. 439)

11-3.   D   See discussion of 11-1. (p. 440)

11-4.   C   Concurrent validity refers to how test scores are related to present behavior on performance. (p. 440-441)

11-5.   A   Spearman felt that intelligence consisted of a general ability to reason and solve problems. (p. 426)

11-6.   B   The correlation of IQ scores is generally highest for identical twins. (p. 450-453)

11-7.   C   Contextual intelligence refers to having practical sense. (p. 427)

11-8.   C   Personality factors are not discussed as related to group differences in IQ. This is an individual difference variable. (p. 448-450)

11-9.   A   Intelligence quotients are obtained by dividing an individual's mental age by his/her chronological age and multiplying by 100. (p. 431)

11-10. A   The worldwide gains in IQ suggest the importance of environmental factors. (p. 446)

11-11. B   Cultural bias is a serious problem for IQ tests. (p. 442)

11-12. C   The fact is that the more closely two people are related, the more similar their IQs. (p. 444)

11-13. C   There are several important types of intelligence for Gardner. (p. 426-427)

11-14. C   Crystallized intelligence increases across the lifespan. (p. 435-436)

11-15. C   In contrast to females, males are more likely to perform well on tasks involving spatial skills. (p. 451-452)

11-16. C   Test-retest reliability measures the extent to which a test measures the same on two occasions (see 11-1). (p. 439)

11-17. B   Experiential intelligence refers to the ability to develop new ideas and insight. (p. 427)

11-18. A   Emotional intelligence involves the ability to read others' emotions, as well as other components. (p. 453)

11-19. B   Componential, experiential, and contextual are the three distinct types of intelligence for Sternberg. (p. 427-429)

11-20. D   Inspection time replaced reaction time as a measure of processing speed. It is defined as stated by question #20. (p. 436)

GLOSSARY OF DIFFICULT WORDS AND EXPRESSIONS

These terms from your text and this study guide were identified by students as potentially hard to understand. We have defined these terms and expressions.

Term or expression	Definition
Androgynous	having both male and female qualities
Assessing	making a judgment; studying
Assets	advantages
Autocratic style	ruling style that doesn't consider the wishes of others
Bargain	good deal or fair price
Bewildered	puzzled; confused
"Big picture"	the complete view of an issue
Bogus	not real or truthful
Conversely	opposite to; in opposition to
Correlated	related to one another
Delaying gratification	putting off small rewards now in order to gain large ones later
Disparity	inequality; not equal
Drawbacks	disadvantages
Enhance	add to; make better, improve
Feedback	a response to a previous event; for example, a grade on a test
Hang-out	spend time socializing with; being around a place
Harsh	not easy or smooth; somewhat negative
Interpersonal	among two or more people
Kinship	family tie; being related to
Lasting gains	long-term gains; benefits that continue a long time
Launched	begun; started, initiated
Lifespan	how long you live; your lifetime
Mannerisms	behavior patterns; nonverbal behavior
Mildly	slightly
Minting	making coins; making something
Mirroring	reflecting; the same as
Modify	change

Term or expression	Definition
Multifaceted	
Neglect	pay little or no attention to
Novel	new; original; unexpected
Overt	done or shown openly; obvious
Pervasive	tending to spread through every part of; showing up everywhere
Purport	claim; suggest something in strong terms
Readily	very easily
Recruits	new member of a society, group, etc.
Refuted	proved to be wrong or mistaken
Share the burden	share the responsibility or weight
Steady	constant; on an even course
Subtle	not obvious
Tap	draw upon; use
Traits	characteristics
Vestiges	traces of; remaining parts of
Warrant	guarantee; assure
Yield	to give in or produce
Zeroing	concentrating on; pinpointing

CHAPTER 12
PERSONALITY:
UNIQUENESS AND CONSISTENCY IN THE
BEHAVIOR OF INDIVIDUALS

INTEGRATED CHAPTER OUTLINE: Survey and Question

This section presents the major topics and ideas from the chapter. Use it as a tool for seeing how the components of the chapter fit together. At the end of each major topic, we have asked you a question that relates to the major learning objectives. If you can answer these questions, you have taken a major step toward mastering this material.

I. Personality: Is It Real?

L.O. 12.1:   Be able to argue for and against the idea that there is stability in personality.

Personality is generally defined as the unique, but stable, set of characteristics that set people apart from others. A question exists about whether people do behave consistently across situations. We generally assume that people have traits that make them behave in similar ways across situations. One group of scientists has held that people do not have traits. Rather, behavior is the result of external factors. This view predicts that individuals behave inconsistently across different situations. Others believe that stable traits exist and that individuals behave consistently across time and settings. Many psychologists believe that both traits and situations are important. It is clear that behavior is influenced by both situational factors and personal dispositions. Such dispositions do appear to be relatively stable over time and across situations. Furthermore, a growing body of evidence suggests that some aspects of personality are influenced by genetic factors. Personality is "real."

II. The Psychoanalytic Approach: Messages From the Unconscious

L.O. 12.2:   Understand the psychoanalytic approach to personality.

A.   Freud the Person

Freud had a close relationship with his mother and a distant relationship with his father. Several persons have speculated on how these relationships may have affected his theories. As a young man, Freud was highly ambitious and wanted to be a medical researcher. He became discouraged in this field and entered private practice. During this time, he developed his theories. Freud was a powerful personality and attracted many followers -- some of whom later became dissenters.

B.   Freud's Theory of Personality

According to Freud, the human mind has three levels of consciousness. The part that holds our current and available thoughts is the conscious. Memories that can be brought to mind are part of the preconscious. The part that contains the thoughts, impulses, and desires of which we are not aware is the unconscious. This is the largest part of the mind. Freud believed that much of the unconscious contained thoughts or ideas that had been repressed because they were too anxiety provoking. These repressed thoughts were seen as responsible for some patient symptoms. One major goal of psychoanalysis is to bring repressed material to consciousness.

Freud proposed that personality has three parts. The id consists of our primitive innate urges. This part is unconscious and operates on the basis of the pleasure principle. The "reason" part of the personality or ego is concerned with holding the id in check until the impulses can be satisfied appropriately. It functions in accord with the reality principle. The third part of personality is our conscience or superego. It permits gratification of the id only when it is morally appropriate. The ego has to mediate between the conflicting aims of the id and superego.

Anxiety is experienced when unacceptable impulses get close to consciousness and close to the control limits of the ego. At this point, the ego may utilize one of several different defense mechanisms. All defense mechanisms serve to reduce anxiety. One defense mechanism channels unacceptable impulses into a socially acceptable action. This is called sublimation. Regression, rationalization, displacement, projection, and regression are other defense mechanisms.

According to Freud, there is an innate sequence of stages through which all human beings pass. These are known as the psychosexual stages of development. At each stage, pleasure is focused on a different body region. The concepts of libido and fixation are keys to understanding these psychosexual stages.

The instinctual life force that energizes the id is the libido. Fixation occurs if an excessive amount of energy is left at one stage of development. Fixation can result in psychological disorders.

Freud believed that events in the first few years of life determine adult personality. We supposedly pass through a series of psychosexual stages that reflect the id's focus on a part of the body to satisfy pleasure. During the oral stage, pleasure is sought through the mouth. During the anal stage, the id focuses on elimination. About age of four, we enter the phallic stage during which the genitals are the primary source of pleasure.

During the phallic stage, we presumably fantasize about relations with the opposite-sex parent. Freud called this the Oedipal complex for males. Boys fear castration; girls fear loss of love. For both genders, these fears are resolved by identifying with the same-sex parent. The male conflict was presumed to be resolved easier, resulting in stronger superego development in males. The idea that females experience penis envy is rejected by nearly all psychologists.

After resolution of the Oedipal conflict, sexual desires are repressed. We then enter the latency period. At puberty, we enter the genital stage when lust and affection are blended. Too much or too little gratification at one of these stages may lead to fixation and failure to develop normal adult personality.

C.   Research Related to Freud's Theory: Probing the Unconscious

Freud's ideas about the unconscious -- his contention that our feelings and behavior can be affected by information we aren't conscious of -- have been researched. Studies of the subliminal conditioning of attitudes is an example. This research investigates whether stimuli presented so briefly that we're not aware of their presence can influence attitudes. Results of several investigations suggest that this "below threshold" presentation does affect our attitudes.

D.   Freud's Theory: An Overall Evaluation

There have been many criticisms of Freudian theory. One criticism is that the theory is difficult to test. A second one is that several of his proposals are not consistent with present research findings. A third revolves around the way he collected his data through case studies. A fourth involves the fact that it can explain virtually all patterns of data after the fact. For these reasons, Freud's theory is not currently accepted, although it has influenced psychology.

Several of Freud's ideas have contributed to our understanding of people. One important idea is that behavior is affected by unconscious thoughts, motives, and memories. Another important idea is that anxiety does play an important role in many psychological problems. It can also be argued that his theories provided a framework that was useful before it was replaced by physiological accounts of the mind.

E.   Other Psychoanalytic Views: Freud's Disciples...and Defectors

Students of Freud who accepted many of his ideas are known as neo-Freudians. Most began by accepting his ideas, but later disagreed with some of his major assumptions. The views of these theorists are presented below.

Jung proposed a unique aspect of the unconscious -- the collective unconscious. He proposed that the material in the collective unconscious is shared by all humans: it is part of our biological heritage. Images that predispose us to perceive the external world in certain ways are called archetypes. The animus is the masculine side of females. The anima is the feminine side of males. Jung also believed that people are born with innate tendencies to be introverts or extroverts.

Karen Horney rejected Freud's idea of penis envy. She countered with her own suggestion that each gender has attributes that are admired by the other. For Horney, psychological disorders are not the result of fixation, but rather involve disturbed interpersonal relationships.

Adler suggested that people are motivated by feelings of inferiority that we develop in childhood. Personality development was viewed as stemming from efforts to overcome these feelings. This is termed "striving for superiority." In contrast to Freud, Adler emphasized the importance of social factors, and believed that birth order and family constellation are important factors influencing a person's style of life.

The theories of the neo-Freudians are subject to some of the same criticisms applied to Freud's view. For example, they are not based on the kinds of hard data science requires. But, importantly, they have been a bridge between the psychoanalytic approach and modern theories of personality.

Questions:

12-1. Why do some psychologists argue that "personality isn't real?" Is this position accepted?

_____

_____

_____

12-2.   What was Freud like as a person? _____

_____

_____

_____

12-3.   What are the different levels of consciousness proposed by Freudian theory? _____

_____

_____

_____

12-4.   What are the three personality structures proposed by Freud's theory? _____

_____

_____

_____

12-5.   How does the ego defend against unacceptable id impulses? _____

_____

_____

_____

12-6.   What are Freud's psychosexual stages of development? _____

_____

_____

_____

12-7.   What is the existing evidence concerning Freud's theory of personality? _____

_____

_____

_____

12-8.   What are the strengths and weaknesses of Freud's theory? _____

_____

_____

_____

12-9.   Summarize and evaluate the positions of the neo-Freudians. _____

_____

_____

_____

_____

III.   Humanistic Theories: Emphasis on Growth

L.O. 12.3:   Be able to discuss Roger's and Maslow's humanistic theories and evaluate the evidence for the humanistic approach.

Humanistic psychologists feel that human beings are basically good and emphasize the importance of personal responsibility, growth, and dignity. Only when obstacles interfere or block these positive tendencies do problems occur. A key goal of therapy is to remove these obstacles.

A.   Rogers' Self Theory: Becoming a Fully Functioning Person

Carl Rogers emphasized the positive traits of human beings. He proposed that, if left to their own devices, people (over the course of their lives) move toward becoming fully functioning persons. Their actions become increasingly dominated by constructive impulses. However, anxiety produced by a discrepancy between a person's self-concept and reality can block personal growth. To reduce anxiety, people develop defenses like distortion and denial. Distorted self-concepts develop because people feel that they must behave in certain ways in order to gain the approval of other people, such as parents. In this setting, gaining the positive regard of other people is conditional. To repair a distorted self-concept, Rogers proposes establishing a setting where positive regard is unconditional. This is the goal of client-centered therapy.

B.   Maslow and the Study of Self-Actualizing People

Maslow proposed that there is a hierarchy of needs, with satisfaction of the lower-order needs being necessary before higher-order ones develop. These needs are: physiological, safety, belongingness, esteem, and self-actualization. The last is similar to the esteem functioning person described by Rogers. Self-actualized people sometimes describe powerful feelings of unity with the universe and tremendous waves of power and wonder. These experiences are called peak experiences. According to Maslow, only a few people become self-actualized.

C.   Research Related to Humanistic Theories: Studying the Self-Concept

Unlike Freudian theory, humanistic theories can be tested scientifically. The self-concept, which is central to Roger's theory, has received the most attention. For example, research has looked at how our self-concept influences our perceptions and has examined how many components there are to our self-concept.

D.   Humanistic Theories: An Evaluation

Many of the ideas of humanistic psychology have entered the mainstream of psychology. Interest in the self and a positive view of people are two contributions of humanistic psychology. Criticisms of humanistic psychology center around their use of free will concepts, their loosely defined concepts and their overly optimistic assumptions about human nature.

Questions:

12-10. What are the basic assumptions about human nature that underlie all humanistic theories? ____

_____

_____

_____

12-11. Describe Rogers' humanistic theory. _____

_____

_____

_____

12-12. Describe Maslow's theory. _____

_____

_____

_____

_____

12-13. What is the self-concept and how is it studied? _____

_____

_____

_____

12-14. Why has humanism been praised and why has it been criticized? _____

_____

_____

_____

IV. Trait Theories: Seeking the Key Dimensions of Personality

L.O. 12.4:   Describe the trait theories of personality and evaluate the evidence for this approach.

A.   Allport's Central, Secondary, and Cardinal Traits

Trait theories of personality focus on identifying the key dimensions of personality. One approach for reducing the number of traits to a reasonable number is to look for clusters. Allport divided traits into secondary traits, central traits, and cardinal traits. Central traits are the 5-10 traits that best describe an individual; cardinal traits dominate a person's personality; secondary traits exert weak effects on behavior. At times a pattern of behavior that was acquired to satisfy one set of motives may be performed for a very different set of motives. This is called functional autonomy.

B.   Cattell's Surface and Source Traits

Using factor analysis techniques, Cattell identified 16 personality dimensions. He called these source traits and presumed that they underlie many other less important traits (surface traits).

C.   The "Big Five" Factors: The Basic Dimensions of Personality?

Recent findings suggest that there may be five key dimensions of personality. These dimensions are: extraversion, agreeableness, emotional stability, conscientiousness, and openness to experience.

These dimensions are often used by persons in describing themselves and are apparent to total strangers. They are useful in making judgments about others' personality.

D.   Research on Trait Theories: Effects of the "Big Five"

Studies indicate that the "big five" factors are related to important forms of behavior. One study finds that conscientiousness is a predictor of job performance and extraversion is related to job success. Thus evidence indicates that these factors are important and basic to personality.

D.   Trait Theories: An Evaluation

Most research in personality in recent years is based on the trait approach. However, the approach is not perfect. Several criticisms exist. First, it is descriptive in nature but doesn't explain how the traits develop or influence behavior. Second, although the five robust factor approach has come close to this goal, there is no universal agreement about what traits make up the basic parts of personality. However, we can conclude that the trait approach to personality is valuable.

- **Beyond the Headlines: As Psychologists See It**

   Is Patricia McColm a "Vexatious Litigant" or Just Accident Prone?

   The woman who is the subject of this headline has filed more than 30 lawsuits on her own behalf. This number of complaints is hard to believe. Perhaps she has decided to become a "professional litigant." What kind of person would choose such a lifestyle?

   Using the "big five" approach, we might say she's low in agreeableness and may also be low in emotional stability. Coupled with high intelligence and acting skill, we might see that these dimensions "set the stage" for this behavior. Of course, in the absence of measurement, this analysis is speculative.

Questions:

12-15. Compare and contrast the trait theories of Allport and Cattell. _____

_____

_____

_____

12-16. What are the five robust factors of personality? _____

_____

_____

_____

12-17. What are the strengths and weaknesses of the trait approach to the study of personality?

_____

_____

_____

V.   Learning Approaches to Personality

L.O. 12.5:   Describe and evaluate learning approaches to personality.

To answer the question "what accounts for the consistency and uniqueness of behavior?" Freud focused primarily on internal factors. In contrast, the behavioral or social learning approach focuses on the role of learning and experience. Skinner took a radical position and denied the importance of virtually any internal cause of behavior. Most psychologists now believe that internal factors are important. The social cognitive learning theory discussed reflects this view.

A.   Social Cognitive Theory: A Modern View of Personality

Bandura's social cognitive theory proposes that, in addition to operant and classical conditioning, observational learning is also important. Individuals do not respond automatically to external conditions. Rather, they plan, form expectancies, and so forth. In addition, humans also have the ability to self-regulate their own behavior and to strive for goals that are self-determined. Further, a person's thoughts and feelings, like self-efficacy, can influence performance.

Rotter's view shares similarities with Bandura in that he proposes that in addition to external factors, internal cognitive factors, like expectancies, must also be considered. He distinguished persons who believe they shape their own destinies (internals) and those that feel their outcomes are due to forces outside their control (externals).

B.   Research on the Learning Perspective

There is a lot of research on this perspective. As an example, Baron discusses the effects of self-efficacy (the belief in one's capacity to perform a specific task). This research has found that people with high self-efficacy perform well on many tasks. Self-efficacy can be increased and techniques designed to increase this belief are effective in countering the negative effects of job loss.

C.   Learning Approaches: An Evaluation

A key strength of the behavioral and social learning approach is that it is based on widely-accepted psychological principles. It also has practical implications. A criticism of early forms of this general approach is that they ignored cognitive factors. Another criticism is that they ignore inner conflicts and the unconscious. Modern learning theories insist that these issues are interpreted within the context of modern psychology.

Questions:

12-18. How does the learning approach account for the consistency and uniqueness of human behavior?

_____

_____

_____

12-19. Compare and contrast Bandura's and Rotter's social learning theories. _____

_____

_____

_____

12-20. Evaluate the social learning approaches to understanding psychology. _____

_____

_____

_____

VI.   Measuring Personality

L.O. 12.6:   Know how personality is measured.

A.   Objective Tests of Personality: Questionnaires and Inventories

Objective tests consist of questions or statements that measure personality. In some cases, they have face validity--it is easy to see what trait is being measured. In other cases, empirical keying is used--items are given to groups of people which are known to differ from one another and psychologists look to see whether these groups answer the questions differently. Examples of objective tests of personality are the

Minnesota Multiphasic Personality Inventory (MMPI), the Million Clinical Multiaxial Inventory (MCMI) and the Neo Personality Inventory (NEO-PI).

B.   Projective Tests of Personality: Of Inkblots and Images

Projective tests present individuals with ambiguous stimuli that can be interpreted in many ways. Since they are ambiguous, it is assumed that people's responses to them reflect their personalities.

The Rorschach test is an example of a projective test, using inkblots for interpretation. This test is controversial in terms of its reliability.

Question:

12-21. Compare and contrast objective and projective tests of personality. _____

_____

_____

_____

VII.   Key Aspects of Personality: A Sample of Recent Research

L.O. 12.7:   Provide a sample of recent personality research on self-esteem and self-monitoring.

L.O. 12.8:   Provide a sample of recent personality research on sensation-seeking.

L.O. 12.9:   Discuss the role of culture in determining personality.

L.O. 12.10:   Know how to relate the concept of self-monitoring to your personality.

A.   Two Aspects of the Self: Self-Esteem and Self-Monitoring

In recent years, psychologists have shifted their attention from "grand theories" to key aspects of personality. Research on self-esteem and self-monitoring reflects this trend.

Many theorists have suggested that our self-concept plays an important role in our total personality. The extent to which our self-evaluations are favorable or unfavorable defines our self-esteem. When these evaluations are favorable, people report fewer negative emotions, are less depressed, are better able to handle stress, and experience fewer negative health effects than those who are low in self-esteem. Differences in self-esteem may arise through processes of social comparison (comparing ourselves to others).

Self-monitoring is a personality trait involving sensitivity to social situations. Persons high in self-monitoring are sensitive to social settings and can adapt their behavior to the setting. These individuals are very good at reading others and make favorable impressions on others. In contrast, low self-monitors do not seem to be as sensitive to social demands; their behavior is more inner-directed. Low self-monitors show a higher degree of consistency in their behavior across situations.

B.   Sensation-Seeking: The Desire for Stimulation

Sensation-seekers desire new and exciting experiences. Differences in this desire may have biological origins. High sensation-seekers, in contrast to low sensation-seekers, pay more attention to unfamiliar stimuli, are better able to ignore irrelevant information, and may be better able to handle stress. They are also more likely to engage in substance abuse.

- **Exploring Gender and Diversity: Cultural Differences in Personality: Avoiding the Extremes**

  Culture does play a role in shaping personality. Persons in western nations seem to have an individualistic orientation; their self-concept on their own traits as unique individuals. Persons from Asian and African cultures often have a more collectivistic orientation; their self-concept is more strongly linked to group memberships.

  Cultural factors also influence personality measurements. Students from the U.S. are more likely to make extreme judgments on personality scales, perhaps because of their individualistic orientation.

  These findings indicate we should not overlook cultural differences in personality. But many aspects, such as the "big 5," seem to be universal.

- **Making Psychology Part of Your Life: Are You a High or Low Self Monitor?**

  Baron provides you with a self-test assessing self-monitoring. Self-knowledge is useful; it helps us make better choices and become better adjusted. This exercise should help you develop your self-knowledge. Take the test and discuss what you learned in the space provided on question 12-25.

Questions:

12-22. Compare and contrast the characteristics of persons with high and low self-esteem. _____

_____

_____

_____

12-23. Compare and contrast the characteristics of high and low self-monitors. _____

_____

_____

_____

12-24. What are the characteristics of high sensation seekers? _____

_____

_____

_____

12-25. What did you learn about your self-concept through the self-monitoring test? _____

_____

_____

_____

MAKING PSYCHOLOGY PART OF YOUR LIFE: Key Terms and Concepts

Knowing the important concepts and key terms contained in this chapter is a very important part of mastering the material. We have presented a sample of these concepts below. Define each concept and check your definition with that presented in the chapter. It will also be beneficial for you to think of an example of each concept. Whenever possible, use your own personal experience to provide an example of each term below.

12-1. **Agreeableness:** _____

Example: _____

12-2. **Anal Stage:** _____

12-3. **Anima:** _____

Example: _____

12-4. **Animus:** _____

Example: _____

12-5. **Anxiety:** _____

Example: _____

12-6. **Archetypes:** _____

Example: _____

12-7. **Cardinal Trait:** _____

Example: _____

12-8. **Central Traits:** _____

Example: _____

12-9. **Collective Unconscious:** _____

12-10. **Conscientiousness:** _____

Example: _____

12-11.   **Defense Mechanisms:** _____

Example: _____

12-12.   **Ego:** _____

12-13.   **Emotional Stability:** _____

Example: _____

12-14.   **Externals:** _____

Example: _____

12-15.   **Extroverts:** _____

Example: _____

12-16.   **Extroversion:** _____

Example: _____

12-17.   **Fixation:** _____

Example: _____

12-18.   **Fully-Functioning Persons:** _____

Example: _____

12-19.   **Functional Autonomy:** _____

Example: _____

12-20.   **Genital Stage:** _____

12-21.   **Humanistic Theories:** _____

Example: _____

12-22.   **Id:** _____

12-23.   **Internals:** _____

        Example: _____

12-24.   **Introverts:** _____

        Example: _____

12-25.   **Latency Stage:** _____

        Example: _____

12-26.   **Libido:** _____

12-27.   **Million Clinical Multiaxial Inventory (MCMI):** _____

12-28.   **MMPI:** _____

12-29.   **NEO Personality Inventory:** _____

12-30.   **Neo-Freudians:** _____

        Example: _____

12-31.   **Oedipus Complex:** _____

        Example: _____

12-32.   **Openness to Experience:** _____

        Example: _____

12-33.   **Oral Stage:** _____

        Example: _____

12-34.   **Peak Experience:** _____

        Example: _____

12-35. **Personality:** _____

Example: _____

12-36. **Personality Traits:** _____

Example: _____

12-37. **Phallic Stage:** _____

Example: _____

12-38. **Pleasure Principle:** _____

Example: _____

12-39. **Psychoanalysis:** _____

12-40. **Psychosexual Stages of Development:** _____

12-41. **Reality Principle:** _____

Example: _____

12-42. **Rorschach Test:** _____

Example: _____

12-43. **Secondary Traits:** _____

12-44. **Self-Actualization:** _____

Example: _____

12-45. **Self-Concept:** _____

Example: _____

12-46. **Self-Efficacy:** _____

Example: _____

12-47. **Self-Esteem:** _____

Example: _____

12-48. **Self-Monitoring:** _____

Example: _____

12-49. **Self-reinforcement:** _____

12-50. **Social Cognitive Theory:** _____

12-51. **Social Comparison:** _____

12-52. **Source Traits:** _____

Example: _____

12-53. **Striving for Superiority:** _____

Example: _____

12-54. **Sublimation:** _____

Example: _____

12-55. **Superego:** _____

12-56. **Trait Theories:** _____

Example: _____

12-57. **Unconditional Positive Regard:** _____

Example: _____

CHALLENGE: Develop Your Critical Thinking Skills

<u>Explaining Personality: Developing Alternative Accounts</u>

The critical thinker is able to recognize and formulate alternative explanations for the same event. By seeing "more than one side," he/she is in a position to take a more objective approach to problem-solving. Below, we provide you with a description of a person's behavior. As an exercise in developing your ability to "stretch your perspective," formulate an explanation for this person's behavior in terms of the theories of personality you have learned.

Situation:

Karen has never been married and has a hard time maintaining relationships with other persons. For example, she has been fired from her last two jobs because she got into arguments with her supervisors. Her parents were divorced when Karen was three and she lived with her grandmother until her grandmother died, when Karen was twenty. Since that time, she has lived alone. Although she desperately wants to have an active social life, she spends most of her time alone in her garden. Her garden is beautiful -- neat and colorful! She says she feels more comfortable with flowers than people. In her words, "I've never been rejected by a flower yet."

12-1.   How would Freud analyze Karen?

_____

_____

_____

_____

12-2.   In what stage of psychosexual development would Freud say Karen is fixated?

_____

_____

12-3.   Compare a Freudian account with that of a) Horney; b) Jung; c) Adler.

_____

_____

_____

_____

_____

12-4.   Formulate an explanation of Karen's behavior based on a humanistic theory.

_____

_____

_____

_____

12-4.   What would the Humanistic approach suggest about your personality development?

_____

_____

_____

_____

_____

_____

12-5.   What do you identify as your personality traits? Relate these traits to those suggested by the trait theorists.

_____

_____

_____

_____

_____

_____

12-6.   Can you explain how learning approaches would account for aspects of your personality development?

_____

_____

_____

_____

_____

_____

CHALLENGE: Review Your Comprehensive Knowledge

SAMPLE TEST QUESTIONS

Once you have worked through the preceding sections, you should be ready for a comprehensive self-test. You can check your answers with those provided at the end of this section. An additional practice test is given in the supplementary section at the end of this study guide.

12-1.   The part of the mind that contains the impulses which we are not aware of, according to Freud is the:
  a. conscious.
  b. preconscious.
  c. unconscious.
  d. subconscious.

12-2.   According to Freud, the part of our personality that functions on the basis of the reality principle is:
  a. the id.
  b. the ego.
  c. the superego.
  d. the conscious.

12-3.   According to Freud, adult personality is determined by what happens during:
  a. adulthood.
  b. the prenatal period.
  c. infancy.
  d. the psychosexual stages.

12-4.   For males, the conflict whose resolution is supposedly related to moral development is the _____ conflict.
  a. Oedipus
  b. oral
  c. anal
  d. genital

12-5.   The neo-Freudian who proposed the existence of the collective unconscious was:
  a. Adler.
  b. Jung.
  c. Horney.
  d. Fromm.

12-6.   The humanistic theorists emphasize:
  a. early development.
  b. personal responsibility.
  c. the unconscious.
  d. learning.

12-7.   Cattell used clustering techniques to identify _____ basic personality dimensions.
  a. 4
  b. 8
  c. 16
  d. 32

12-8.   Which neo-Freudian emphasized the importance of feelings of inferiority on personality development?
  a. Adler
  b. Jung
  c. Horney
  d. Fromm

12-9.   According to Rogers, healthy development of the self-concept requires:
  a. conditional regard.
  b. environmental blocking.
  c. control of emotions.
  d. unconditional positive regard.

12-10. Which of the following is **not** one of the five key dimensions of personality identified by recent research?
  a. Extroversion
  b. Agreeableness
  c. Intelligence
  d. Conscientiousness

12-11. In Bandura's theory, our perceived ability to carry out a desired action is called:
  a. self-reinforcement.
  b. self-efficacy.
  c. self-regulation.
  d. self-esteem.

12-12.   A defense mechanism that channels unacceptable impulses into a socially acceptable action is called:
    a. reaction formation.   c. regression.
    b. repression.   d. sublimation.

12-13.   The maintenance of patterns of behavior by motives other than the ones originally responsible for the behavior's occurrence is called:
    a. self-efficacy.   c. preventive maintenance.
    b. functional autonomy.   d. none of the above

12-14.   Which of the following statements is not a typical criticism of Freudian theory?
    a. the theory is difficult to test
    b. several of his proposals are inconsistent with research
    c. behavior is not affected by unconscious thoughts
    d. his data collection methods were not appropriate

12-15.   According to Jung, images that predispose us to perceive the external world in certain ways are:
    a. archetypes.   c. perceptual sets.
    b. conscious images.   d. defense mechanisms.

12-16.   According to Maslow, the basic needs are:
    a. physiological, safety, belongingness, esteem, and self-actualization.
    b. physiological, safety, and self-actualization.
    c. physiological, safety, esteem, and self-actualization.
    d. physiological, belongingness, and self-actualization.

12-17.   The Rorschach test is an example of:
    a. a projective personality test.   c. an ambiguous personality test.
    b. an objective personality test.   d. a reliable personality test.

12-18.   Which of the following is **not** a characteristic of high sensation-seekers?
    a. more likely to engage in high risk sports   c. less likely to withstand stress
    b. more likely to engage in substance abuse   d. operate best at high levels of arousal

12-19.   Which theory emphasizes the importance of generalized expectancies concerning internal or external control of outcomes?
    a. Rotter's social learning theory   c. Roger's self-theory
    b. Cattell's source trait theory   d. Maslow's need theory

12-20.   Which of the following is not a characteristic of high self-monitors?
    a. They are better at reading others.
    b. They are better at regulating their own behavior.
    c. They are better at making favorable impressions on others.
    d. They show more consistent behaviors across situations.

Answers and Feedback for Sample Test Questions

12- 1.   C   In Freud's theory, hidden impulses are in the unconscious. (p. 469)

12- 2.   B   The ego operates according to the reality principle. (p. 470)

12- 3.   D   The psychosexual stages essentially shape the adult personality. (p. 472-473)

12- 4.   A   For males, the resolution of the Oedipus complex results in the development of a conscience. (p. 473)

12- 5.   B   Jung proposed the collective unconscious. (p. 477)

12- 6.   B   Humanistic theories emphasize personal responsibility and free will. (p. 478)

12- 7.   C   Cattell identified 16 basic personality dimensions. (p. 484)

12- 8.   A   Adler emphasized feelings of inferiority on personality development. (p. 478)

12- 9.   D   Unconditional positive regard is essential for healthy personality development, according to Rogers. (p. 479-480)

12-10.   C   Intelligence is not one of the five key dimensions of personality. The "Big 5" are: extroversion, agreeableness, conscientiousness, emotional stability, and openness to experience. (p. 484)

12-11.   B   Self-efficacy is our perception of our ability to carry out a desired action. The higher such feelings, the better persons tend to do on a wide range of tasks. (p. 489)

12-12.   D   Sublimation is the defense mechanism that channels unacceptable impulses into acceptable actions. (p. 472)

12-13.   B   Functional autonomy is the term used by Allport to refer to this type of occurrence. (p. 483)

12-14.   C   In contrast to the other statements, Freud's theory is not subject to criticisms on the basis of this assumption. (p. 474-476)

12-15.   A   Archetypes are images that predispose us to perceive the world in a certain way. (p. 477)

12-16.   A   These are the five basic needs in Maslow's theory. (p. 480 and Chapter 10)

12-17.   A   The Rorschach test is a projective test involving the presentation of ambiguous inkblots. (p. 495)

12-18.   C   High sensation-seekers are more likely to withstand stress. (p. 497-498)

12-19.   A   Rotter's social learning theory emphasizes this factor. (p. 490)

12-20.   D   High self-monitors show **less** consistent behavior across situations. (p. 496-497)

GLOSSARY OF DIFFICULT WORDS AND EXPRESSIONS

These terms from your text and this study guide were identified by students as potentially hard to understand. We have defined these terms and expressions.

Term or expression	Definition
Ambiguous	open to many interpretations
Attuned	in touch with
Awkward	uncomfortable
Be neat	be clean cut; good grooming
Bestial	"beast-like"; primitive
Bridge	providing a connection
Broker	person who buys and sells for others
Clusters	groups of objects or items
Components	parts of something
Dam	barrier built to keep back water and raise its level
Dangling	hanging; on the edge
Dissenters	persons who argue against an idea
Factor analysis	a statistical procedure that reduces items into clusters that share something in common
Flee	escape; run away from
Gloat	selfish delight
Innately good	naturally good; inherently positive
Jagged rocks	rough uneven edges
Lose their temper	upset; angry
Mainstream	current
Maladaptive	not good for; against one's best interests
Obstacles	things that block or prevent progress
Once-cherished	once cared for
Overly dependent	too dependent; relies too much on others
Pampered	treated very well
Poised	self-confident
Professional litigant	someone who earns their living from filing lawsuits

Term or expression	Definition
Provocative	interesting; stimulating; sometimes controversial
"Set the stage"	provide the context for something
Sip	taking a very small quantity at a time
Slimy	covered with slime
Stemming from	originating or coming from; the source
"Stop-gap"	a temporary solution
Strive	try; reach for
Swig (beer)	a deep swallow; gulp
Traumatic	very upsetting
Trivial	of small value of importance
Toppled	caused it to fall
"Wing it"	trying to accomplish something without really being prepared for it

CHAPTER 13
HEALTH, STRESS, AND COPING

INTEGRATED CHAPTER OUTLINE: Survey and Question

This section presents the major topics and ideas from the chapter. Use it as a tool for seeing how the components of the chapter fit together. At the end of each major topic, we have asked you questions that relate to the major learning objectives. If you can answer these questions, you have taken a major step toward mastering this material.

I. Health Psychology: An Overview

L.O. 13.1: Provide an overview of the research methods health psychologists use to study health behavior.

The area of study that regards both psychological variables and health is health psychology. The field that combines behavioral and biomedical knowledge for the prevention and treatment of medical disorders is behavioral medicine. These fields have experienced rapid development over the past 20 years. This is probably due to the fact that many leading causes of death can be attributed to lifestyle.

Epidemiological studies involve large scale attempts to identify risk factors that predict the development of certain diseases. There are several reasons why these studies are important. First, illnesses often have multiple causes. Second, these studies often have a broad scope — they often involve the study of thousands of people across lengthy periods of time. Third, these studies have discovered patterns that exist between people's behaviors and important health outcomes. The Alameda County study is one of the best known examples of an epidemiological study.

Question:

13-1.   What is the aim of health psychology and why has it developed rapidly over the past 20 years?

_____

_____

_____

II. Stress: Its Causes, Effects, and Control

L.O. 13.2:   Describe the basic nature of stress.

L.O. 13.3:   Discuss the causes of stress.

L.O. 13.4:   Describe the major stressors that exist in the workplace.

L.O. 13.5:   Describe the major effects of stress.

A.   Stress: Its Basic Nature

Stressors are events or situations that cause stress. Events that are stressful have three characteristics. They are so intense that they produce overload. They produce incompatible tendencies to approach and avoid the same object or activity. They are beyond our limits of control or uncontrollable.

The sequence of responses to stress was termed the general adaptation syndrome by Selye. During the alarm stage the body prepares itself for action. In the resistance stage arousal is lower as the body continues to cope with the stressor. Continued exposure to the stressor may lead to the stage of exhaustion.

Cognitive processes are also important in stress. Among these are the individual evaluations or cognitive appraisals. Individuals experience stress to the extent that they perceive the situation as threatening to important goals (primarily appraisals) or that they are unable to cope with their demands or dangers (secondary appraisals).

B.   Stress: Some Major Causes

In general, individuals who have experienced stressful life events tend to have a high incidence of illness. The more stress individuals experience as a result of many minor problems or daily hassles, the poorer their psychological and physical health.

Hassles are minor sources of stress which can exert adverse effects on our health. After experiencing highly stressing events, people often experience a series or ripple of minor stressors. Major life events appear to sensitize people to minor negative events. In so doing, they increase the potentially harmful effects of these events.

Work overload is being asked to do too much. Work underload is being asked to do too little. Role conflict is having to deal with conflicting demands or expectations. Procedures for evaluating employees' performance are known as performance appraisal. All of these can be stressors at work.

A consideration of the person-environment (P-E) fit can reduce stress in the workplace. A "misfit" can increase in stress and stress-related illnesses. Social support and treatment aimed at improving workers' ability to cope with stress and change unhealthy practices can also reduce stress in the workplace.

C.   Stress: Some Major Effects

Stress may play a role in 50 to 70 percent of all illnesses, including heart disease, high blood pressure, hardening of the arteries, ulcers, and even diabetes. Research has shown that a variety of stressors, including disruptions in interpersonal relations, loneliness, academic pressure, daily hassles, and lack of social support, can interfere with the efficient operation of our immune system.

Lymphocytes and antibodies are white blood cells that are central to the immune system. Lymphocytes attack foreign substances (antigens) whereas antibodies combine with antigens and so neutralize them. Optimism, regular exercise, feelings of control and social support may reduce the negative effects of stress.

Some psychologists believe that the relationship between stress and performance takes the form of inverted U. A first, performance increases as stress increases, presumably because stress is arousing or energizing. Beyond some amount of stress, however, stress becomes distracting and performance drops.

The point at which stress starts to decrease performance is the inflection point. This point depends upon personal characteristics and the complexity of the task. For example, it takes less stress to interfere with a complex task than a simple one. Recent research suggests that even low levels of stress can interfere with task performance. There are several reasons why this is the case. First, even relatively mild stress can be distracting. Second, prolonged or repeated exposure to mild levels of stress can have negative effects on health and this may interfere with effective performance. Finally, many tasks performed by today's working people are very complex. Consequently, even relatively mild stressors can interfere with performance on these tasks.

People worn down by repeated exposure to stress at work are suffering from burnout. They often experience physical, emotional, and mental or attitudinal exhaustion. Attitudinal exhaustion is often called depersonalization and is associated with a cynical view, negative attitudes toward others, and a tendency to derogate self, jobs and life in general. Feelings of low personal accomplishments are also common. They may come from feeling useless or unappreciated. Burnout occurs when certain valued resources are lost, and when resources are inadequate to meet demands or do not yield the anticipated returns. Inflexible procedures and poor promotion opportunities are additional causes of burnout. The primary factor for burnout is stress.

Optimists are more resistant to stress than pessimists. Optimists use problem-focused coping and seek social support. Pessimists may give up the goal or deny the occurrence of stressful events. Table 13.2 in your text contains a summary of strategies.

In contrast to earlier work, recent research indicates that men and women differ very little in the amount of stress they report or in their coping strategies. They do, however, differ in the content of their respective problems. Asian students were more pessimistic and tended to use more problem avoidance and social withdrawal coping strategies than students of European descent.

Individuals who are hardy are also stress resistant. They have a high level of commitment to their work. They see change as a challenge. They have a sense of control over events in their lives.

Questions:

13-2.   What is the basic nature of stress, what is the general adaptation syndrome and the cognitive processes involved in stress? _____

_____

_____

_____

13-3.   What are the characteristics and effects of the major causes of stress? _____

_____

_____

_____

13-4.   How can stress in the workplace be reduced? _____

_____

_____

_____

13-5.   How can stress influence health? _____

_____

_____

_____

13-6.   How can stress influence burnout? _____

_____

_____

_____

13-7.   What are the individual characteristics that are related to the resistance from the effects of stress?

_____

_____

_____

III.   Understanding and Communicating Our Health Needs

L.O. 13.6:   Know how we perceive symptoms of illness.

L.O. 13.7:   Describe beliefs which influence when we seek medical advice.

L.O. 13.8:   Describe the major effects of stress.

A.   Symptom Perception: How Do We Know When We're Ill?

Sensations that reflect underlying medical conditions are symptoms. Persons who have few distractions in their lives are more likely to notice symptoms. Persons in a good mood report less symptoms than those in a bad mood. Our interpretations of symptoms are influenced by comparisons with others and our expectations.

B.   Health Beliefs: When Do We Seek Medical Advice?

The health belief model suggests that our willingness to seek medical help depends on the extent to which we perceive a threat to our health and believe that a particular behavior will reduce that threat. Perception of threat depends on our health values and our beliefs concerning susceptibility to illness and its seriousness. Perceived effectiveness depends on whether we believe actions will be effective or are worth the effort.

C.   Doctor-Patient Interactions: Why Can't We Talk To Our Doctors?

The most frequently observed communication skills of doctors are those dealing with mechanics of the illness. They infrequently display skills in the psychosocial aspect of the illness such as patient knowledge and emotional response. Good doctor-patient communication is related to successful treatment. Physicians' opinions regarding their role during medical examinations has changed from 1981 to 1994. In 1994, doctors were more likely to focus on medical issues whereas in 1981, they were more likely to focus on psychosocial issues.

Questions:

13-8.   What factors influence the reporting and interpretation of symptoms? _____

_____

_____

_____

13-9.   What is the health belief model of seeking medical advice? _____

_____

_____

_____

13-10.   What is the nature of the communication process between doctors and patients? _____

_____

_____

_____

13-11.   How has the opinion of doctors concerning their role during medical examinations changed from 1981 to 1994? _____

_____

_____

IV.   Behavioral and Psychological Correlates of Illness: The Effects of Thoughts and Actions on Health

L.O. 13.9:   Know the risky behaviors associated with illness and how diet and nutrition contribute to good health.

L.O. 13.10:   Understand how emotions impact health.

L.O. 13.11:   Be able to discuss the AIDS health crisis.

Families with high cancer rates have a diminished efficiency of the natural killer cells. Lifestyle features that affect our chances of becoming ill are risk factors. Cancer producing agents in our environment are carcinogens. Cancer is an illness in which rapidly growing abnormal cells overwhelm normal cells.

A.   Smoking: Risky for You and Everyone Around You

The largest preventable cause of illness and death in the U.S. (before age 65) is smoking, accounting for 434,000 deaths annually in the United States. Smoking seems to be influenced by genetic, psychosocial and cognitive factors. Some people appear to be biologically predisposed to nicotine. Nicotine alters the availability of certain neurotransmitter substances. These substances produce temporary improvements in concentration, recall, alertness, arousal, and psychomotor performance. Psychosocial factors include peer pressure and exposure to role models. Cognitive factors may influence people's tendency to continue smoking. People may continue to smoke because they are not prepared mentally to quit. People may proceed through a series of stages which reflect increasing levels of readiness to quit smoking. In the first stage (precontemplation stage), the smoker has no interest in quitting. During the contemplation stage, smokers begin to think about quitting, but do not take action. In the preparation stage, smokers prepare plans which they execute in the action stage. In the maintenance stage, former smokers expend effort to maintain their nonsmoking status.

- **Exploring Gender and Diversity: Smoking Around the Globe**

   Although the percentage of smoking related deaths is higher for males than females, there is a dramatic rise in smoking-related deaths among women and in other nations. One reason is because more women are entering high-pressure occupations. Second-hand smoke or passive smoke can also increase the incidence of respiratory and cardiovascular disease. Most exposure to passive smoke occurs at home.

B.   Diet and Nutrition: What You Eat May Save Your Life

Eating vegetables may reduce the risk of cancer. The regular consumption of broccoli and cauliflower may reduce the risk of colon and rectum cancer. Vitamin A inhibits the destruction of cells by carcinogens and dietary fiber may inhibit colorectal cancer. Diet is also a significant risk factor in the development of cardiovascular disease. Arteriosclerosis is the major cause of heart disease in the United States and is caused by the build up of cholesterol and other substances on arterial walls. High levels of blood or serum cholesterol is associated with increased risk of cardiovascular diseases.

Bad (LDL) cholesterol clogs arteries whereas HDL helps clear LDL from arteries and escorts it to the liver for excretion. The amount of cholesterol in our blood is affected by the amount of fat, especially saturated fat, and cholesterol in our diets.

More than 12 million Americans are severely overweight. Interventions to help these people work initially but typically do not last. Genetic, behavioral, and environmental factors play a role. According to self-determination theory, the type of motivation behind the decision to lose weight plays a key role in predicting success. Autonomous motivation occurs when people are motivated to lose weight for themselves whereas controlled motivation occurs when people feel forced to lose weight. In a recent study, people with autonomous motivation were more likely to maintain their weight loss than were those with controlled motivation.

C.   Alcohol Consumption: Here's to Your Health

Although moderate drinking may be associated with health benefits and increased earnings, consumption of alcohol is also related to many disorders such as cancer, cirrhosis of the liver, and impaired cognitive and sexual functioning.

Heavy drinking has been implicated as a risk factor for suicide. Drinking alcohol may interact with smoking to increase cancer risk.

D.   Emotions: Mood and Health

Inhibiting the expression of negative feelings can have detrimental effects on health. The expression of distress can aid recovery or survival of illness. Unexpressed anger has been related to high blood pressure or hypertension.

People who are competitive, hostile, aggressive, and impatient, show Type A behavior pattern. Those who are relaxed and easygoing are called Type B. Cynical hostility, and not the entire Type A pattern, appears to lead to increased heart disease. Cynical hostility is characterized by suspiciousness, resentment, anger, antagonism, and distrust of others. This tendency may develop early in life.

E.   AIDS: A Major Assault on Public Health

Acquired immune deficiency syndrome (AIDS) is a viral disease that reduces the immune system's ability to defend itself against disease. The cause of AIDS is HIV — human immunodeficiency virus. The estimated inculation period -- the time it takes for the disease to develop -- can be as long as ten years. See Figure 13.11 for a distribution of HIV infection worldwide. AIDS is usually fatal. An individual can be infected only if the virus is introduced into the bloodstream. Most HIV infections are acquired through unprotected sexual intercourse and infected blood or blood products. Worldwide, AIDS is transmitted primarily through heterosexual intercourse.

Prevention programs are the only effective means of combating AIDS. The Information-Motivation-Behavioral Skills (IMB) Model is useful in developing intervention programs. According to this model, people are more likely to perform HIV-preventive behaviors to the extent that they: (1) know how HIV is acquired and how to avoid it, (2) are motivated to perform HIV-preventive behaviors and omit risky ones, and (3) possess the skills necessary to perform relevant HIV-prevent behaviors. The IMB model is used in conjunction with elicitation research. This kind of research is performed to attain specific information about a target group.

- **Exploring Gender and Diversity: Women and AIDS**

  HIV infection rates among women are growing at an alarming rate. Sixty-five percent of women acquire HIV as a result of intravenous drug use. Unprotected sex with partners who may also use drugs or have multiple sexual partners are additional risk factors. The chances of male to female transmission of HIV are about 12 times greater than female to male transmission. The gender role of females, the skills required to ensure safe sex and the fear associated with negotiating safe sex with their partners are additional reasons why women are at greater risk than men. HIV-prevention programs that are consistent with the IMB model appear to increase self-reported HIV-prevention behaviors among females.

Questions:

13-12. What is the biological nature of cancer and how do risk factors influence cancer rates?_____

_____

_____

_____

13-13. What are the effects of smoking? _____

_____

_____

_____

13-14. What are the effects of passive smoke? _____

_____

_____

_____

_____

13-15. What are the effects of diet and nutrition on health? _____

_____

_____

_____

13-16. What are the effects of alcohol consumption on health? _____

_____

_____

_____

13-17. What is the influence of emotions and personality type on health? _____

_____

_____

_____

13-18. What are the nature and causes of AIDS? _____

_____

_____

_____

13-19. What factors influence the transmission and prevention of HIV? _____

_____

_____

_____

V.   Promoting Wellness: Developing a Healthier Lifestyle

L.O. 13.12:   Understand how sunlight can promote skin cancer.

L.O. 13.13:   Compare and contrast primary and secondary preventions of illness.

L.O. 13.14:   Know how you can use what you have learned to manage your stress.

Communities in which a large number of persons live to be more than 100 years old tend to have people who eat a high fiber diet, leafy green and root vegetables, fresh milk, fresh fruits, and low to moderate amounts of meat and animal fat. They maintain low to moderate levels of daily caloric intake and consume only moderate amounts of alcohol each day. Physical activity is a very important factor contributing to longevity and good health. Additional factors may be continued sexual activity and continued social involvement.

Techniques designed to reduce or eliminate illness are called primary prevention strategies. Techniques attempting to decrease the severity of illness by early detection are called secondary prevention strategies.

- **Beyond the Headlines: As Psychologists See It — "Just Catchin' Some Rays?"**

    People often disregard the evidence that over-exposure to sun causes cancer. This appears to occur for several reasons. First, a suntan makes people feel better about themselves and they believe it makes them more attractive to other people. Second, people believe that something negative is less likely to happen to them than to others — this is called the optimistic bias. Finally, people believe that skin cancer is a disease that affects older people.

A.   Primary Prevention: Decreasing the Risks of Illness and Injury

Limited success of mass media campaigns on health behavior may be due to the fact that most commercials promote unhealthy habits. A campaign on heart disease that combined the media and behavior therapy was quite effective. Beliefs may also influence our response to advertisements. Those who have a high fear of AIDS rate advertisements about AIDS as more effective than those with low fear.

Exercise can reduce coronary heart disease and premature death. However, only one in five Americans exercise sufficiently to reduce the risk of chronic disease and premature death. People who exercise have less than half the incidence of elevated cholesterol of those who do not. It can also improve our self-concept, alleviate feelings of depression and reduce anxiety. Exercise can also improve one's mood. An increase in mood may occur when companionship is associated with exercise or when it increases feelings of self-efficacy -- perceived confidence in one's ability to perform a behavior.

If starting and maintaining regular exercise, it is important to arrange the environment so that it supports the behavior and weakens competing behaviors. Supporting factors include cues that are a signal to exercise, rewards that maintain exercise and a strong social support network.

B.   Secondary Prevention: The Role of Early Detection in Disease and Illness

Use of available screening techniques could decrease the incidence of disease and the number of deaths due to disease. Early detection can decrease the incidence of cardiovascular disease and could significantly reduce the number of deaths due to cervical, colon, prostate, testicular, and breast cancer. Self-examination can be very helpful in the early detection of testicular and breast cancer.

Questions:

13-20.   What are the factors that appear to influence longevity and health? _____

_____

_____

_____

13-21.   Why are psychologists in favor of preventive strategies? _____

_____

_____

_____

13-22.   What is the use and effectiveness of primary prevention strategies such as health promotion in the mass media, control of alcohol consumption, and exercise? _____

_____

_____

_____

13-23.   What is the role of early detection in disease and illness? _____

_____

_____

_____

•   **Making Psychology Part of Your Life: Managing Stress — Some Useful Tactics**

One effective physiological technique of coping with stress is to reduce muscle tension by progressive relaxation. Another is exercise. A behavioral coping technique that involves efficient use of time is time management. Another effective cognitive coping technique is replacing negative appraisals with positive ones. This is called cognitive restructuring. A person's ability to cognitively restructure is aided by various sources of social support.

MAKING PSYCHOLOGY PART OF YOUR LIFE: Key Terms and Concepts

Knowing the important concepts and key terms contained in this chapter is a very important part of mastering the material. We have presented a sample of these concepts below. Define each concept and check your definition with that presented in the chapter. It will also be beneficial for you to think of an example of each concept. Whenever possible, use your own personal experience to provide an example of each term below.

13-1.   **Acquired Immune Deficiency Syndrome (AIDS):** _____

13-2.   **Cancer:** _____

13-3.   **Carcinogens:** _____

          Example: _____

13-4.   **Cardiovascular Disease:** _____

          Example: _____

13-5.   **Cognitive restructuring:** _____

          Example: _____

13-6.   **Epidemiological Studies:** _____

13-7.   **General Adaptation Syndrome:** _____

          Example: _____

13-8.   **Hardiness:** _____

          Example: _____

13-9.   **Hassles:** _____

          Example: _____

13-10.   **Health Belief Model:** _____

13-11.   **Health Psychology:** _____

13-12.   **Hypertension:** _____

      Example: _____

13-13.   **Lifestyle:** _____

      Example: _____

13-14.   **Meditation:** _____

13-15.   **Nicotine:** _____

13-16.   **Passive Smoke:** _____

13-17.   **Person-Environment (P-E) Fit:** _____

      Example: _____

13-18.   **Post Traumatic Stress Disorder:** _____

      Example: _____

13-19.   **Prevention Strategies:** _____

      Example: _____

13-20.   **Progressive Relaxation:** _____

13-21.   **Risk Factors:** _____

      Example: _____

13-22.   **Self-determination Theory:** _____

13-23.   **Serum Cholesterol:** _____

13-24.   **Social Norms:** _____

      Example: _____

13-25.   **Stress:** _____

Example: _____

13-26.   **Stressors:** _____

Example: _____

13-27.   **Type A Behavior Pattern:** _____

Example: _____

YOUR NOTES:

CHALLENGE: Develop Your Critical Thinking Skills

Thinking Critically about Health

The critical thinker is able to "stand back" and access how habits that may have developed over the years may have adverse effects on his/her health. As an exercise in this skill, take a look at your health habits. Then, think of ways you can do away with bad habits and substitute more healthy patterns of behavior.

13-1.   How often do you exercise? _____

_____

13-2.   Do you smoke? If so, what is maintaining this habit? _____

_____

_____

_____

13-3.   How often do you drink alcohol? _____

_____

13-4.   What problems do you see, if any, with your eating patterns? _____

_____

_____

_____

13-5.   Do you have a plan to handle the stress in your life? [See the application exercise.] _____

_____

_____

_____

13-6.   How can you improve your health habits? _____

_____

_____

_____

CHALLENGE: Taking Psychology With You

Finding Ways to Reduce Stress

Your textbook author provides you with examples of ways to cope with stress (see page 537-538). Below, we provide the major categories of coping techniques. For each category, list the techniques you presently use (and could use) to reduce the stress level in your life.

Physiological Coping Techniques

_____

_____

_____

_____

Behavioral Coping Techniques

_____

_____

_____

_____

Cognitive Coping Techniques

_____

_____

_____

_____

CHALLENGE: Review Your Comprehensive Knowledge

SAMPLE TEST QUESTIONS

Once you have worked through the preceding sections, you should be ready for a comprehensive self-test. You can check your answers with those at the end of this section. An additional practice test is given in the supplementary section at the end of this study guide.

13-1. The field that combines behavioral and biomedical knowledge for the prevention and treatment of medical disorders is:
  a. physiological psychology.
  b. behavioral medicine.
  c. bio-behaviorism.
  d. neuroscience.

13-2. The stage of the general adaptation syndrome when arousal is lowered as the body copes with the stressor is the:
  a. coping stage.
  b. resistance stage.
  c. alarm stage.
  d. exhaustion stage.

13-3. According to the cognitive appraisal perspective, stress occurs when people:
  a. are in the coping stage.
  b. are goal oriented.
  c. are in the resistance stage.
  d. feel unable to cope with demands.

13-4. People who have experienced a large number of stressful life events show:
  a. a high incidence of illness.
  b. a high level of stress resistance.
  c. hardiness.
  d. strong alarm reactions.

13-5. Being asked to do too many things in a short period of time is called work:
  a. conflict.
  b. overload.
  c. underload.
  d. incompatibility.

13-6. The negative effects of stress on health appears to result from its interference in the operation of our _____ system.
  a. nervous
  b. endocrine
  c. cardiovascular
  d. immune

13-7. Which of the following factors is **not** a factor that is likely to be a cause of burnout?
  a. being unappreciated
  b. feelings of control
  c. inflexible rules
  d. poor opportunities for promotion

13-8. Optimists tend to be more stress-resistant than pessimists. This may be due to optimists using _____ coping.
  a. problem-focused
  b. emotional
  c. denial
  d. psychological

13-9. The model which explains why people do not use medical screening devices is the _____ model.
  a. hardiness
  b. optimism
  c. health belief
  d. cognitive appraisal

13-10. Which is false?
  a. Men and women differ considerably in the amount of stress they report.
  b. Burnout occurs when certain valued resources are lost.
  c. Lymphocytes attack foreign substances.
  d. Antibodies neutralize antigens.

13-11.   Developing the smoking habit seems to be related to **all but one** of the following factors.
a.   biological susceptibility to nicotine   c.   peer pressure
b.   Type A behavior   c.   role models who smoke

13-12.   Which of the following is false?
a.   Individuals who have experienced stressful life events tend to have a high incidence of illness.
b.   Optimists are more resistant to stress than pessimists.
c.   Persons who have few distractions in their lives are more likely to notice symptoms than those who have many distractions.
d.   Smoking does not appear to be influenced by psychosocial factors.

13-13.   At times, individuals experience stress because they perceive the situation as threatening to important goals. This is termed:
a.   secondary appraisal.   c.   the general adaptation syndrome.
b.   primary appraisal.   d.   post-traumatic stress syndrome.

13-14.   Which **is true** of hardy individuals?
a.   They are not stress resistant.   c.   They do not have a sense of control.
b.   They see change as a challenge.   d.   They have a low level of commitment.

13-15.   Lifestyle features that affect our chances of becoming ill are termed _____ factors.
a.   risk   c.   punishment
b.   carcinogen   d.   individual

13-16.   Which is false?
a.   HDL cholesterol clogs arteries.
b.   Passive smoke has been associated with an increased risk of asthma attacks.
c.   Smoking can produce a temporary improvement in recall.
d.   Dietary fiber may inhibit colorectal cancer.

13-17.   Whish is false?
a.   Type As are competitive and impatient.
b.   The chances of male to female transmission of AIDS is 12 times greater than female to male transmission.
c.   Inhibiting negative feelings can have detrimental effects on health.
d.   Cynical hostility is not related to an increase in heart disease.

13-18.   The limited success of mass media campaigns on health behavior may be due to the fact that commercials:
a.   promote unhealthy habits.   c.   are not interesting.
b.   are too short.   d.   are not clear.

13-19.   An effective physiological technique of coping with stress is to reduce _____ by progressive relaxation.
a.   cognitive tension   c.   muscle tension
b.   cognitive appraisals   d.   time pressures

13-20.   Prevention strategies that are designed to increase early detection are called:
a.   preliminary   c.   primary
b.   tertiary   d.   secondary

Answers and Feedback for Sample Test Questions:

13-1.   B   Behavioral medicine is the field that combines behavioral and biomedical knowledge. (p. 504)

13-2.   B   The resistance stage is characterized by lowered arousal during coping. (p. 507)

13-3.   D   The cognitive appraisal view suggests that people feel stressed when they believe that they can't cope with demands. (p. 507-509)

13-4.   A   A high incidence of illness is expected when people have experienced a large number of serious events in an 18 month period. (p. 511 and 514-515)

13-5.   B   Overload is a source of stress and is characterized by being asked to do too many things during a short period of time. (p. 512)

13-6.   D   Stress appears to have a negative effect on our immune system, causing illness. (p. 514-515)

13-7.   B   Feelings of control, in fact, prevent burnout. (p. 516)

13-8.   A   Optimists appear to use problem-focused coping strategies, which increases their resistance to stress. (p. 517)

13-9.   C   Health belief models helps explain why people don't use screening devices. (p. 520)

13-10.   A   In contrast to earlier work, men and women do not appear to differ in the amount of stress they report or in their coping strategies. (p. 517)

13-11.   B   Type A behavior appears to be unrelated to smoking. (p. 524)

13-12.   D   Smoking is influenced by psychosocial factors. (p. 524)

13-13.   B   Primary appraisals involve the perception that a situation threatens important goals. (p. 508)

13-14.   B   Hardy individuals are stress resistant, have a sense of control, and have high levels of commitment. Therefore, options A, C, and D are false. Option B states that hardy individuals see change as a challenge: the only true statement. (p. 517-518)

13-15.   A   Risk factors are lifestyle features that affect our chances of becoming ill. (p. 522)

13-16.   A   HDL cholesterol helps clear LDL from arteries. (p. 527)

13-17.   D   Cynical hostility is a pattern of Type As that is related to an increase in heart disease. (p. 529)

13-18.   A   Many commercials promote unhealthy health habits. (p. 536)

13-19.   C   Decreasing muscle tension is an effective stress reduction technique. (p. 539)

13-20.   D   Secondary prevention strategies are designed to increase early illness detection. (p. 538)

GLOSSARY OF DIFFICULT WORDS AND EXPRESSIONS

These terms from your text and this study guide were identified by students as potentially hard to understand. We have defined these terms and expressions.

Term or expression	Definition
Aches	dull, continuous pain
Blatant	obvious and intentional
Boosting	increasing; raising up; supporting
Buffering	lessening; protecting; preventing from harm
Cope	manage; deal with effectively
Cueing	giving ideas on the behavior that is expected
Culprits	the ones to blame; the guilty ones
Depiction	describe in words; show in some way
Depleted	empty until little or nothing remains
Detrimental	harmful; having a bad effect
Disaster strikes	disaster hits; something very bad happens
Disseminating	distributing; giving out
Domain	area of topic or thought
Engulfing	swallow up; taking in
Hardy	strong; can handle lots of stuff
Hassles	things that bother you
Hectic	always busy
"Kick the habit"	quit the habit; stop doing something
Mutates	changes in form
Plight	difficulty; dilemma; small problem
Prompted	led; invoked; started
Queasiness	feeling of sickness; uneasy feeling
Rapport	a relationship; able to speak with very easily
Refrain	not do something; prevent
Remission	lessening or weakening of; going away

Term or expression	Definition
Resilience	being able to recover quickly
Scribbles	writes something quickly
Soar	quickly rise to the top
Sterling	exceptional
Take it in stride	not to be bothered by; deal with very easily
Tickle	to touch someone in a way that makes them laugh
Transient	temporary; not permanent
Trapped	unable to escape
Withstand	resist; cope with; deal with

CHAPTER 14
PSYCHOLOGICAL DISORDERS: THEIR NATURE AND CAUSES

INTEGRATED CHAPTER OUTLINE: Survey and Question

This section presents the major topics and ideas from the chapter. Use it as a tool for seeing how the components of the chapter fit together. At the end of each major topic, we have asked you a question that relates to the major learning objectives. If you can answer these questions, you have taken a major step toward mastering this material.

I. Changing Conceptions of Psychological Disorders

L.O. 14.1: Trace the different concepts of psychological disorders from ancient times to today.

Psychological disorders are maladaptive patterns of behavior and thought that cause the persons who experience them considerable distress. Although there is no single way of distinguishing between normal and abnormal behavior, most psychologists agree that all psychological disorders share four major features in common. First, these disorders cause distress in the people that experience them. They involve patterns of behavior or thought that are relatively atypical. Third, they are maladaptive in that they make it difficult for a person to meet the demands of their lives. Finally, psychological disorders are associated with behavior that is evaluated negatively by members of society.

A. The Ancient World: Of Demons and Humors

The earliest view of psychological disorders emphasized supernatural causes. Hippocrates, an ancient Greek physician, emphasized natural causes. The Romans generally accepted this view and the idea that psychological disorders result from natural causes was widely accepted.

B. The Middle Ages and the Renaissance: The Pendulum Swings

In the middle ages, abnormal behavior was, once again, attributed largely to supernatural forces. During the Renaissance, however, abnormal behavior was attributed to natural forces. However, up until the 1700s, patients were often kept in asylums. In these institutions patients were often shackled to walls and treated inhumanly.

Phillipe Pinel, the director of a major hospital for the insane in Paris, treated patients as sick people and produced improvements in their conditions. Similar actions by other physicians produced encouraging results and strengthened the view that abnormal behavior is the result of mental illness. This medical perspective is influential today and is the basis for the field of psychiatry.

C. The Psychodynamic Perspective

Freud proposed a psychodynamic perspective of psychological disorders. He proposed that anxiety occurs when the ego feels overwhelmed by the demands of the id. To protect itself, the ego uses defense mechanisms. The id is the repository of our primitive desires and demands instant gratification. The superego represents our conscience. The ego strives to maintain a balance between the impulses of the id and superego. The importance of Freud's theory is in his suggestion that unconscious thoughts or impulses play a role in abnormal behavior.

D.   The Modern Psychological Approach: Recognizing the Multiple Roots of Abnormal Behavior

The psychological perspective suggests that psychological disorders are better understood through studying processes such as learning, perception, and cognition. It further suggests that psychological disorders should be understood as resulting from the complex interplay between biological, psychological, and sociocultural factors. Finally, psychologists also attach considerable importance to cultural factors. Some disorders appear to be universal whereas others vary across cultures.

II.   Identifying Psychological Disorders: The DSM-IV

L.O. 14.2:   Know how the DSM-IV is used to identify psychological disorders.

The DSM-IV is a widely accepted classification system for identifying psychological disorders. In this manual, hundreds of disorders are described. These descriptions include information on diagnostic features or symptoms, associated features, and disorders and associated laboratory findings and physical examination signs. In addition, the DSM-IV classifies disorders along five axes. One relates to major disorders themselves, another to personality disorders, a third to general medical conditions relevant to each disorder, a fourth considers psychosocial and environmental problems, and a fifth relates to global assessment of current functioning.

This version of the DSM differs from past versions in several respects. In this version, psychologists had major input. In addition, this version is more firmly based on empirical evidence and takes greater efforts to consider the role of cultural factors. One major drawback of this manual is that it is primarily descriptive in nature. It does not provide an explanation of abnormal behavior.

•   **Research Methods: How Psychologists Study Psychological Disorders**

Although the Diagnostic and Statistical Manual of Mental Disorders-IV (DSM-IV) is an important guide to identify psychological disorders, it is not the only tool. Your author discusses four other important tools: assessment interviews, personality measures, assessment of brain disorders and behavioral assessment. In an assessment interview, a psychologist seeks information about a person's past and present behaviors, interpersonal relations and personality. The assessment of brain disorders is obtained through various measures. One is the Halstead-Reitan Neuropsychological Battery. This consists of many tests of auditory, visual, and psychomotor functioning. More direct evidence is obtained through various neuroimaging techniques discussed in Chapter 2. These include computerized axial tomography magnetic resonance imaging and positron emission tomography. With behavioral assessment, psychologists often focus on specific aspects of an individual's behavior(s) that led to the disorder. It may involve acquiring information on the antecedents and consequences of such behaviors. Antecedents are events or stimuli that precede the occurrence of such behaviors whereas consequences are the effects that these behaviors produce.

Questions:

14-1.   What are the basic features of the DSM-IV and how does it differ from previous versions?

_____

_____

_____

14-2.   What is the definition and what are the general characteristics of psychological disorders?

_____

_____

_____

14-3.   What are the biological/medical, psychodynamic, and modern perspectives of psychological disorders? _____

_____

_____

_____

III.   Mood Disorders: The Downs and Ups of Life

L.O. 14.3: Describe the mood disorders.

Swings in mood are normal. But for some persons, disturbances in mood are both extreme and prolonged. Extreme and prolonged disturbances in mood are called mood disorders. There are two major categories of this disorder: depressive disorder and bipolar disorders.

A.   Depressive Disorders: Probing the Depths of Despair

The criteria for the existence of depression include long periods of intense unhappiness, lack of interest in the usual pleasures of life, loss of energy, loss of appetite, disturbances of sleep and difficulties in thinking. If individuals experience five or more symptoms at once, they are classified as showing a major depressive episode. This is the most common psychological disorder and is more common among women.

B.   Bipolar Disorders: Riding the Emotional Roller Coaster

Bipolar depression includes wide swings in emotion. Individuals suffering from this disorder move between deep depression and mania -- a state in which they are extremely excited.

C.   The Causes of Depression: Its Biological and Psychological Roots

Depression tends to run in families, suggesting that there is a genetic component. The presence of low levels of the neurotransmitters serotonin and norepinephrine in depressed persons suggests a biochemical basis of depression.

While biochemical factors play an important role, psychological mechanisms are also involved. Some research suggests that depression is related to feelings of lack of control or helplessness.

Individuals suffering from depression appear to have negative self-schemas--negative conceptions of their sum traits, abilities, and behavior. In addition, depressed persons are prone to distorted thinking. Because they are often in a negative mood, they tend to notice, store, and remember information that is consistent with their negative mood. This type of mood dependent memory makes it likely for depressed persons to bring unhappy thoughts and memories to mind. Recent research suggests that tendency may occur at the unconscious as well as the conscious levels.

• **Exploring Gender and Diversity — Postpartum Depression: Why New Mothers Sometimes Get the Blues**

Between 20 and 30 percent of new mothers experience postpartum depression--they report symptoms of depression shortly after giving birth. Recent research suggests that postpartum depression is due to the stress associated with childbirth coupled with inadequate support from family and spouses. For example, the more help women received, the less depression they experienced. To the degree that infants were difficult in temperament and the mothers adopted less effective coping strategies, they experienced greater degrees of stress. And the greater their feelings of personal control and self-esteem, the less depression they experienced.

D. Suicide: When Life Becomes Unbearable

In the U.S., about 30,000 persons commit suicide each year and about 300,000 persons attempt suicide but don't succeed. Suicide rates vary by age and nation. The highest suicide rates occur among older people, but suicide has been on the rise among young persons for several decades. More attempts are made by women while more men actually succeed. It appears that persons attempt suicide for many different reasons. However, problems with relationships seem to be the most frequent reason. Suicide often occurs when individuals show some improvement after being in the depths of despair. Deeply depressed persons appear to lack the energy or will to commit suicide. Another signal to suicide plans involves a period of calm that follows considerable suffering or depression. Cognitive factors also provide clues to potential suicide. Persons who have not attempted suicide report that they are most frightened by loss of self-fulfillment and of the unknown and least frightened about loss of social identity. In contrast persons who have attempted suicide report about equal fear of each of these three fears as well as the fear of consequences to their family.

Questions:

14-5. What are the symptoms associated with depression? _____

_____

_____

_____

14-6. What are the characteristics of bipolar disorders? _____

_____

_____

_____

14-7. What are the biological and psychological differences between depressed and nondepressed persons?

_____

_____

_____

14-8.   What are the findings concerning suicide rates and the research concerning how it may be predicted?

_____

_____

_____

IV.   Anxiety Disorders: When Dread Debilitates

L.O. 14.4:   Describe the anxiety disorders.

When feelings of intense anxiety persist for long periods of time, one may be experiencing an anxiety disorder.

A.   Panic Attack: The Body Signals "Danger" But Is It Real?

Anxiety disorders take several different forms. Panic attacks are defined as brief periods of panic that have no specific cause. The symptoms include chest pains, nausea, feeling dizzy, shaking, fear of losing control, chills, hot flashes or numbness. For some persons, panic attacks are linked with specific situations. Agoraphobia is intense fear of specific situations in which individuals support that help will not be available should they experience an incapacitating or embarrassing event. These include fear of being in a crowd, car, being on a bridge, standing in line or merely leaving home. Biological factors and cognitive factors appear to play a role in these disorders.

B.   Phobias: Fear That is Focused

When people experience intense anxiety in the presence of an object or while thinking about it, they are said to have a phobia. These may be acquired by classical conditioning. Several factors appear to play a role in social phobias that involve social situation. These include childhood shyness, certain aspects of personality (e.g., being low in extraversion), and an early traumatic experience -- a social situation in which the individual felt uncomfortable and something negative happened.

C.   Obsessive-Compulsive Disorder: Behaviors and Thoughts Outside One's Control

Anxieties may sometimes lead to repetitive behaviors or compulsions. Recurrent thoughts or obsessions can also occur. This is known as the obsessive-compulsive disorder. Persons with this disorder cannot distract themselves from disturbing thoughts. Only by performing specific actions can they ensure their safety and reduce this anxiety.

D.   Posttraumatic Stress Disorder

Posttraumatic stress disorder describes an anxiety disorder in which a person persistently reexperiences a traumatic event in thoughts or dreams, persistently avoids stimuli linked with the trauma, and experiences persistent symptoms of increased arousal. This disorder can stem from various traumatic events including rape and accidents. The way we perceive events plays a key role in how we react to them.

Questions:

14-9.   What are the characteristics and potential causes of panic attacks? _____

_____

_____

_____

14-10. What are the nature and potential causes of the various phobias? _____

_____

_____

_____

14-11. What is the obsessive-compulsive disorder? _____

_____

_____

_____

14-12. What are the characteristics of the post-traumatic stress disorder? _____

_____

_____

_____

V.   Somatoform Disorders: Physical Symptoms Without Physical Causes

L.O. 14.5: Describe the somatoform disorders.

People who exhibit physical symptoms that have no underlying physical cause have somatoform disorders. A common type of this disorder involves an excessive fear of disease -- hypochondriasis. Another type involves reports of physical complaints -- somatization disorder. Another somatoform disorder is conversion disorder. People suffering from this disorder may experience blindness, deafness, and paralysis even though there is no underlying medical condition that would produce these symptoms. Conversion disorders are different from other somatoform disorders. First, in conversion disorders there are actual impairments. Second, psychological factors such as conflicts or other stressors appear to play a role in conversion disorder.

There are three interpretations for somatoform disorders. Freud believed that unacceptable conflicts are converted into various impulses. This conversion reduced the anxiety generated by the impulses and also gained attention and sympathy. While Freud's view is generally rejected it does appear to be accurate in one respect: people suffering from this disorder do appear to benefit from their disorder in terms of receiving sympathy and attention.

- **Beyond the Headlines: As Psychologists See It: Medical Masqueraders Unmasked**

Munchausen's Sufferers Use Ills to Get Attention

Munchausen's syndrome is a condition in which people travel from doctor to doctor claiming symptoms of a feigned ailment to gain attention for themselves. Munchausen's syndrome appears to be related to hypochondriasis. However, persons suffering from hypochondriasis are usually not faking whereas persons with Munchausen's syndrome know that there is nothing actually wrong with them.

Questions:

14-14. What are the different somatoform disorders? _____

_____

_____

_____

14-15. What is Munchausen's syndrome and how is it related to hypochondriasis? _____

_____

_____

_____

VI. Dissociative Disorders: When Memory Fails

L.O. 14.6: Describe the dissociative disorders.

When people have lengthy losses of memory or identity, they are said to experience dissociative disorders. They can take several different forms. Sudden disruptions of memory that occur without any clear-cut physical cause are called dissociative amnesia and seem to be caused by an active motivation to forget. This type of amnesia can be localized -- involves all events in a particular period, or selective -- involves some events in a particular period or generalized.

Persons suffering from dissociative fugue have a sudden disturbance of memory and are unable to recall their past. These individuals often adopt a new identity.

When a person appears to have two or more distinct personalities, they are said to have dissociative identity disorder (multiple personality disorder in earlier versions of the DSM). The origins of this disorder have proven difficult to determine.

Question:

14-15. What is the meaning of "dissociative disorder" and what are the different types of this disorder?

_____

_____

_____

VII.   Sexual and Gender Identity Disorders

L.O. 14.7:   Describe the sexual and gender identity disorders.

A.   Sexual Dysfunctions: Disturbances in Desire and Arousal

Sexual dysfunctions involve disturbances in sexual desire, arousal, or the ability to attain orgasm. These problems are classified according to when in the normal pattern of sexual activity they occur. Sexual desire disorders involve a lack of interest or aversion to sexual activities. Sexual arousal disorders involve erectile disorders in males and the absence of vaginal swelling and lubrication in females. Orgasm disorders involve the delay or absence of orgasm in both sexes and may also involve premature ejaculation in males.

B.   Paraphilias: Disturbances in Sexual Object or Behavior

Paraphilias exist when unusual images, acts, or objects are required for sexual arousal and performance. When individuals are aroused by inanimate objects, they have a fetish. Frotteurism exists when individuals have fantasies and urges involving touching a nonconsenting person. Preference for sexual activity with children is pedophilia. Those who are aroused by hurting others are sexual sadists. Those who are aroused by such treatment are sexual masochists.

C.   Gender Identity Disorders

Gender identity disorders exist when individuals desire to alter their primary and secondary sex characteristics. Individuals suffering from these disorders feel they were born with the wrong gender identity and seek a change. Many individuals who undergo a sex-change operation report increased happiness. Some persons, however, experience regrets and continued unhappiness, sometimes to the point that they commit suicide.

Questions:

14-16. What are the different types of sexual disorders? _____

_____

_____

_____

14-17. What are the different types of sexual disorders that involve disturbances in sexual objects or behavior? _____

_____

_____

_____

14-18. What are gender identity disorders? _____

_____

_____

_____

VIII. Eating Disorders

L.O. 14.8: Describe the eating disorders.

Eating disorders are disturbances in eating behavior that involve maladaptive and unhealthy efforts to control body weight.

A. Anorexia Nervosa: Carrying the Ideal of Being Slim to Extremes

When individuals refuse to maintain body weight at or above a minimal normal level they are said to have anorexia nervosa. This disorder is far more common among females than males.

B. Bulimia: the Binge-Purge Cycle

Bulimia nervosa involves alternating between binge eating and purging. Purging involves various forms of compensatory behaviors designed to avoid weight gain. Bulimics may be able to withstand the cycles of binge-purge due to reduced taste sensitivity, making purging less unpleasant. Therefore, although social pressures may contribute to the onset of this disorder, sensory factors (reduced sensitivity) may help strengthen and maintain it.

Question:

14-19. What are the characteristics of the two most common types of eating disorders? _____

_____

_____

_____

IX. Personality Disorders: Traits that Harm

L.O. 14.9: Describe the personality disorders.

Personality disorders are collections of extreme and inflexible traits that cause distress and adjustment problems to the persons who have them. The DSM-IV divides personality disorders into three distinct clusters. The first is described as involving odd, eccentric behavior or traits and includes three personality disorders: paranoid, schizoid, and schizotypal. A paranoid personality disorder involves strong feelings that others can't be trusted and delusions of persecution. A schizoid personality disorder is characterized by social detachment and emotional coldness. Contact with other persons is of little interest to persons with this disorder. A schizotypal personality disorder involves a pattern in which individuals are very uncomfortable in interpersonal relationships and at the same time, suffer from cognitive or perceptual distortions and eccentric behavior.

The second major cluster of personality disorders involves dramatic, emotional, and erotic forms of behavior. The personality disorders that fit into this cluster include: (1) borderline personality disorders--people who show tremendous instability in their interpersonal relationships, self-image, and moods; (2) histrionic personality disorders--people who need a great deal of attention from others; and (3) antisocial personality disorders--a disorder characterized by failure to conform to social norms, little or no concern for other people, deceitfulness, reckless disregard for their own and others' safety and irritability and aggressiveness. Persons with this disorder are often dangerous. Many factors appear to play a role in the origin of this disorder. These include: deficits in the ability to delay gratifications, disturbances in brain function including abnormalities in the neurotransmitter serotonin, and a reduced ability to experience negative emotions and to respond to warnings.

The third cluster involves anxious, fearful behavior including: (1) avoidant personality disorder--persuasive patterns of social inhibition, feelings of inadequacy, hypersensitivity to negative evaluation; (2) obsessive-compulsive disorder--preoccupation with orderliness and perfectionism; and, (3) dependent personality disorder--pervasive and excessive need to be taken care of.

Questions:

14-20. What are the characteristics of personality disorders? _____

_____

_____

_____

14-21. What are the characteristics and potential causes of the antisocial personality disorder? _____

_____

_____

_____

X. Substance-Related Disorders

L.O. 14.10: Describe the substance-related disorders.

Substance-related disorders involve the maladaptive use of various substances or drugs. They are divided into the categories of substance abuse and substance dependence. Substance abuse is diagnosed when individuals show one or more of the following problems: substance use resulting in failure to fulfill major obligations, substance use that is physically hazardous and/or repeated legal problems. Substance dependence is diagnosed when substance tolerance occurs, or people are unable to control their use, or people spend a great deal of time securing the substance.

XI. Schizophrenia: Out of Touch With Reality

L.O. 14.11: Be able to discuss schizophrenia.

L.O. 14.12: Know how you can help in the prevention of suicide.

Schizophrenia is a very serious and complex disorder involving hallucinations (e.g., hearing voices), delusions and several other symptoms. Oftentimes persons with this disorder must be removed from society, at least temporarily.

A.   The Nature of Schizophrenia

Schizophrenia involves a disruption in almost all aspects of psychological functioning. Reasoning is so strange that it is interpreted by others as incoherent. There are various symptoms of this disorder. First, they have disturbances of thought and language. They do not think or speak like others. Their ideas often seem totally unconnected and they often create words of their own. In some cases their words are completely jumbled into what is called a "word salad." This may result from the failure of schizophrenics to use selective attention. Schizophrenics often have delusions -- firmly held beliefs that have no basis in reality. False beliefs that one is extremely important are delusions of grandeur. Delusions of control are beliefs that one is under control of outside forces. Beliefs that others are "out to get you" are delusions of persecution.

Schizophrenics also show many signs of disturbed perceptions. Many report intense and vivid experiences with no basis in reality (hallucinations). The most common type of hallucination is auditory. In addition, schizophrenics often experience deficits in social perception -- their ability to recognize the emotions of others. A third symptom involves disturbances of emotion. A fourth is unusual motor actions -- such as staring at the floor for hours. Schizophrenia can also involve seriously impaired social behavior. Schizophrenia has been divided into positive symptoms (or Type I schizophrenia) and negative symptoms (or Type II schizophrenia). Positive symptoms involve the presence of something that is normally absent like hallucinations and delusions. Negative symptoms involve the absence of something that is normally present like emotion.

B.   Types and Phases of Schizophrenia

Schizophrenia is a chronic disorder: It lasts at least six months. Some experts believe schizophrenia involves three phases. In the prodormal phase, their functioning begins to deteriorate and they withdraw more and more from others. In the active or acute phase, positive symptoms are evident. In the residual phase, they again show fewer symptoms but still withdraw from others and continue to have bizarre thoughts.

Schizophrenia is divided into five distinct types. The disorganized schizophrenia is characterized by absence of affect and incoherence. Paranoid schizophrenia involves delusions of persecution and grandeur. The type of schizophrenia in which people vary from a frozen posture to an excitable state is catatonic schizophrenia. The undifferentiated type is characterized by many symptoms including delusions, hallucinations, and incoherence. The residual type occurs after prominent delusions and hallucinations are no longer present, but it does involve withdrawal, minimal affect, and no motivation.

C.   The Origins of Schizophrenia

It appears that genetic factors play a role in schizophrenia -- the closer the family relationship between people, the greater the odds of a person developing schizophrenia if one of the persons has the disorder. It does not appear that a single gene is responsible for this disorder. Rather, many genes and many environmental factors appear to work together to produce this disorder. One model that incorporates the assumption that genetic and environmental factors combine is the diathesis-stress model. This model assumes that genetic factors may predispose individuals to schizophrenia if they are exposed to certain kinds of stressful environmental conditions; if these stressful conditions are absent, schizophrenia will not occur.

It appears that some families create social environments that increase the likelihood of children developing schizophrenia. These families create a context that has high levels of conflict between parents or one in which one parent completely dominants the family. These environments also involve confusing and inconsistent patterns of communication. In such families, children are exposed to what is called a double-blind. A double-blind exists when children are encouraged to form intense relationships with one or both parents, but when they do, they are rejected.

Deficits in cognition may also be a factor in this disorder. Schizophrenics, especially with positive symptoms, demonstrate difficulty in ignoring irrelevant or distracting information. Those with negative symptoms appear to be underattentive to external stimuli.

Schizophrenia is associated with several types of brain dysfunctions. Some brain ventricles (fluid-filled spaces) are larger for schizophrenics than normal persons. This may reduce brain volume and produce abnormalities in the cerebral cortex. Decreased brain volume is related to increased hallucinations and reduced emotion among schizophrenics. Schizophrenics also show reduced activity in their frontal lobes relative to normal persons.

Biochemical factors also appear to be involved in schizophrenia. Some researchers have assumed that because antipsychotic drugs have been highly effective in treating schizophrenia, an understanding of how these drugs actually produced these effects would provide valuable evidence on the biochemical causes of schizophrenia. One hypothesis is that these drugs reduce dopamine levels. However, at this point, there is no clear evidence about dopamine's role in schizophrenia.

D.   Chronic Mental Illness and the Homeless

Many homeless persons suffer from psychological disorders. As many as one third have received care in hospitals but were released after drug therapy reduced their symptoms.

- **Making Psychology Part of Your Life: Preventing Suicide: How You Can Help**

    Baron outlines some basic steps for preventing suicide. These include:

    1.   Take all suicide threats seriously.
    2.   If someone mentions suicide, don't be afraid to discuss it.
    3.   Recognize the danger signs.
    4.   Discourage others from blaming themselves for failure to attain unrealistic standards.
    5.   If a friend or family member shows the danger signs described above, don't leave him or her alone.
    6.   Most important of all: Get Help!

Questions:

14-22. What is the general nature of schizophrenia as well as the major symptoms and types of this disorder?

_____

_____

_____

14-23. What are the findings concerning the origin of schizophrenia? _____

_____

_____

_____

14-24. How can you help prevent suicide? _____

_____

_____

_____

MAKING PSYCHOLOGY PART OF YOUR LIFE: Key Terms and Concepts

Knowing the important concepts and key terms contained in this chapter is a very important part of mastering the material. We have presented a sample of these concepts below. Define each concept and check your definition with that presented in the chapter. It will also be beneficial for you to think of an example of each concept. Whenever possible, use your own personal experience to provide an example of each term below.

14-1. **Agoraphobia:** _____

   Example: _____

14-2. **Anorexia Nervosa:** _____

   Example: _____

14-3. **Antisocial Personality Disorder:** _____

   Example: _____

14-4. **Anxiety:** _____

   Example: _____

14-5. **Anxiety Disorders:** _____

   Example: _____

14-6. **Assessment Interviews:** _____

   Example: _____

14-7. **Behavioral Assessment:** _____

14-8. **Bipolar Disorder:** _____

   Example: _____

14-9. **Bulimia Nervosa:** _____

   Example: _____

14-10. **Catastrophic Thinking:** _____

      Example: _____

14-11. **Catatonic Type:** _____

14-12. **Conversion Disorder:** _____

      Example: _____

14-13. **Delusions:** _____

      Example: _____

14-14. **Depression:** _____

      Example: _____

14-15. **Diagnostic and Statistical Manual of Mental Disorders - IV:** _____

14-16. **Diathesis-Stress Model:** _____

14-17. **Dissociative Amnesia:** _____

14-18. **Dissociative Fugue:** _____

14-19. **Dissociative Identity Disorder:** _____

14-20. **Dissociative Disorders:** _____

14-21. **Dopamine Hypothesis:** _____

14-22. **Eating Disorders:** _____

      Example: _____

14-23. **Gender Identity Disorder:** _____

14-24. **Hallucinations:** _____

14-25. **Halstead-Reitan Neuropsychological Battery:** _____

14-26. **Hypochondriasis:** _____

   Example: _____

14-27. **Learned Helplessness:** _____

   Example: _____

14-28. **Medical Perspective:** _____

   Example: _____

14-29. **Mood Disorders:** _____

   Example: _____

14-30. **Obsessive-Compulsive Disorder:** _____

   Example: _____

14-31. **Munchausen's Syndrome:** _____

14-32. **Panic Attack Disorder:** _____

   Example: _____

14-33. **Paraphilias:** _____

   Example: _____

14-34. **Personality Disorders:** _____

   Example: _____

14-35. **Postpartum Depression:** _____

   Example: _____

14-36. **Posttraumatic Stress Disorder:** _____

   Example: _____

14-37. **Psychiatry**: _____

14-38. **Psychological Disorders**: _____

     Example: _____

14-39. **Schizophrenia**: _____

     Example: _____

14-40. **Sexual Arousal Disorders**: _____

     Example: _____

14-41. **Sexual Desire Disorders**: _____

     Example: _____

14-42. **Somatization Disorder**: _____

     Example: _____

14-43. **Somatoform Disorder**: _____

14-44. **Substance-Abuse**: _____

     Example: _____

14-45. **Substance-Dependence**: _____

     Example: _____

14-46. **Substance-Related Disorders**: _____

     Example: _____

CHALLENGE: Develop Your Critical Thinking Skills

Societal Implications of Mental Illness

The critical thinker is able to recognize the implications of psychological research for society. Advances in our understanding of the causes of psychological research have increased our ability to treat psychological disorders, but they also create social and ethical issues that we must deal with. Stretch your ability to see the implications of psychological research by answering the following questions:

14-1.   As your text points out, there is evidence that genetic factors play a role in the occurrence of schizophrenia. Suppose that research confirms that this is the case. Further suppose that we are unable to treat this disorder. Should society pass laws prohibiting schizophrenics from having children?

14-2.   Baron points out that one important factor in homelessness is that many homeless persons suffer from psychological disorders, which interfere with their ability to function. It is estimated that as many as one-third previously received in-patient care, but were released when drug therapy reduced their symptoms. How might society better deal with this problem? Given that research suggests that effective treatments do exist for many of the disorders that some of the homeless suffer from, how can we get those in need of help into settings where they can receive it?

14-3.   Persons who have had psychological problems are often the targets of prejudice. For example, you may recall that the presidential campaign of Michael Dukakis was hurt by rumors that he had sought treatment for depression. Given what you have learned about psychological disorders, do you think that it is correct to use evidence that a person has had a psychological disorder as a basis for evaluating his/her suitability for positions of power? Why or why not? Would your answer change depending upon the nature of the psychological disorder? [Keep in mind that 50% of all persons have had a psychological disorder at some point during their lives.]

CHALLENGE: Taking Psychology With You

<u>Taking Steps to Prevent Suicide</u>

Baron provides you with some steps that can help prevent suicide. Although we don't like to think about it, there may be situations in which those we care about may contemplate such an act. We can help prevent this drastic act by following these simple steps. As an exercise in applying what you've learned, please think about (and write down) how you might use each of these steps.

Step 1. Take all suicide threats seriously.

What factors might lead us to ignore a person's threat? What can we do to minimize this possibility?

Step 2. Don't be afraid to discuss suicide with someone who mentions it.

Why do you think we hesitate to discuss this topic?

Step 3. Recognize the danger signs.

List and give examples of these danger signs.

Step 4. Discourage others from blaming themselves for failure to attain unrealistic standards.

Why is this important? Can you think of examples of when you or others are prone to this tendency?

Step 5. Don't leave a person alone who shows the danger signs of suicide.

In some cases, a person might insist that you do leave him/her alone. How would you handle this situation?

Step 6. Get help!

What resources do you have in your local community for getting help?

CHALLENGE: Review Your Comprehensive Knowledge

SAMPLE TEST QUESTIONS

Once you have worked through the preceding sections, you should be ready for a comprehensive self-test. You can check your answers with those at the end of this section. An additional practice test is given in the supplementary section at the end of this study guide.

14-1. This instrument assesses brain disorders. It considers many tests of auditory, visual, and psychomotor functioning.
   a. Diagnostic and Statistical Manual of Mental Disorders-IV
   b. Somatoform Battery
   c. Halstead-Reitan Neuropsychological Battery
   d. None of the above

14-2. The Greeks' view of abnormal behavior provided the basis of today's:
   a. psychodynamic perspective.   c. the psychological perspective.
   b. medical perspective.   d. the DSM-IV.

14-3. Which of Freud's views is most influential today in understanding abnormal behavior?
   a. his suggestion that the ego demands immediate gratification
   b. his suggestion that mental patients should be treated humanely
   c. his suggestion that psychological disorders are types of mental illnesses
   d. his suggestion that unconscious thoughts or impulses play a role in abnormal behavior

14-4. Which of the following perspectives suggests that abnormal behavior is best understood through studying subtle interactions between biological, psychological, and sociocultural factors?
   a. the psychological perspective   c. the psychodynamic perspective
   b. the biological/medical model   d. the descriptive approach

14-5. Which of the following statements **does not** accurately describe the use of the DSM-IV?
   a. It provides a useful tool for explaining abnormal behaviors.
   b. It provides a useful tool for describing abnormal behaviors.
   c. It classifies disorders along five axes.
   d. Its use may be subject to bias in making clinical judgments about the severity or presence of psychological disorders.

14-6. There are two major categories of mood disorders. They are _____ and _____ disorders.
   a. bipolar, euphoric   c. bipolar, unipolar
   b. euphoric, dysphoric   d. depressive, bipolar

14-7. The disorder that involves anxieties and repetitive behaviors is called:
   a. obsessive-compulsive.   c. panic.
   b. phobia.   d. generalized anxiety.

14-8. Lengthy losses of memory are known as _____ disorders.
   a. anxiety   c. dissociative
   b. personality   d. emotional

14-9. People who exhibit physical symptoms that have no underlying physical cause have _____ disorders.
   a. anxiety   c. dissociative
   b. organic   d. somatoform

14-10. When a person appears to have two or more distinct personalities, they are said to have which disorder?
    a. dysphoric   c. dissociative memory
    b. bipolar   d. dissociative identity

14-11. Schizophrenia has been divided into _____ distinct types.
    a. two   b. five
    b. four   c. eight

14-12. Which of the following has not been found to be associated with depression?
    a. genetic inheritance   c. high levels of neurotransmitters
    b. feelings of helplessness   d. negative self-schemas

14-13. Disorders that are associated with collections of extreme and inflexible traits that cause distress and adjustment problems are:
    a. somatoform disorders.   c. anxiety disorders.
    b. conversion reactions.   d. personality disorders.

14-14. This model assumes that genetic and environmental factors combine to produce schizophrenia.
    a. genetic-role model   c. confluence model
    b. schizophrenia model   d. diathesis-stress model

14-15. When schizophrenics believe they are under the control of outside forces they have delusions of:
    a. grandeur.   c. persecution.
    b. control.   d. power.

14-16. The type of schizophrenia that involves a frozen posture is:
    a. disorganized.   c. catatonic.
    b. paranoid.   d. undifferentiated.

14-17. This is a mood disorder in which individuals experience wide swings in emotion.
    a. bipolar disorder   c. dissociative disorder
    b. anxiety disorder   d. swing disorder

14-18. When individuals are very fearful of gaining weight and fail to maintain a normal body weight, they have:
    a. paraphilia nervosa.   c. bulimia nervosa.
    b. anorexia nervosa.   d. neologism nervosa.

14-19. A schizoid personality disorder is characterized by:
    a. physical symptoms that have no underlying cause.
    b. a desire to alter primary and secondary sex characteristics.
    c. social detachment and emotional coldness.
    d. multiple personalities.

14-20. Suicide attempts are more common among _____, while more _____ actually commit suicide.
    a. women; men   c. children; adults
    b. men; women   d. adults; children

Answers and Feedback for Sample Test Questions:

14-1.   C   The Halstead-Reitan Neuropsychological Battery is a brain assessment instrument. (p. 552)

14-2.   B   The Greeks believed that psychological disorders had natural causes. Focusing of attention to natural vs. supernatural causes of abnormal behavior led to the development of the biological/medical model. (p. 548)

14-3.   D   Freud's suggestion that unconscious thoughts play a role in abnormal behavior is seen as his major contribution. (p. 549)

14-4.   A   In contrast to the other perspectives listed in this question, the psychological approach concentrates on cognitive, learning, and perception processes as a basis for developing abnormal behavior. (p. 549-550)

14-5.   B   The importance of the DSM-IV is that it provides a tool for describing abnormal behavior. It does not explain behavior. (p. 551-552)

14-6.   D   Depression and bipolar disorders are the two forms of mood disorders. (p. 554-556)

14-7.   A   Obsessive-compulsive disorders are characterized by repetitive behaviors and irrational thoughts. (p. 563)

14-8.   C   Memory disorders are classified as dissociative disorders. (p. 567)

14-9.   D   Somatoform disorders involve physical symptomology, without corresponding physical causes. (p. 565)

14-10.   D   A person with dissociative identity appears to have two or more distinct personalities. (p. 567)

14-11.   C   Schizophrenia has been divided into five distinct types: Catatonic, paranoid, disorganized, undifferentiated, and residual. (p. 580)

14-12.   C   High levels of neurotransmitters are not associated with depression. The other characteristics are associated with depression. (p. 554-558)

14-13.   D   Personality disorders are associated with collections of traits (inflexible and long-standing) that cause distress. (p. 573)

14-14.   D   The diathesis-stress model incorporates the assumption that both genetic and environmental factors combine to produce schizophrenia. (p. 580)

14-15.   B   Delusions of control are characterized by feelings of being manipulated by outside forces. (p. 578)

14-16.   C   Catatonic schizophrenia is characterized by a frozen posture. (p. 580)

14-17.   A   Bipolar disorder is a mood disorder in which individuals experience wide swings in emotion. (p. 556)

14-18.   B   Anorexia nervosa is characterized by a fear of gaining weight. (p. 571)

14-19.   C   Social detachment and emotional coldness characterize the schizoid personality. (p. 574)

14-20.   A   Research suggests that more women attempt suicide, but more men actually commit suicide. (p. 559)

GLOSSARY OF DIFFICULT WORDS AND EXPRESSIONS

These terms from your text and this study guide were identified by students as potentially hard to understand. We have defined these terms and expressions.

Term or expression	Definition
Annoying	bothersome; irritating
Apprehension	fear; dread of something
Atrophy	decrease in size; shrink; the tissue dies
Bearable	tolerable; can deal with or cope with
Binge-purge	eating abnormally large amounts of food and then vomiting it up
Bizarre	strange; completely unexpected and abnormal
Charmed	enchanted, lucky
Clenched	press or clasp firmly together
Clinging	holding tight; grasping something very tightly
Clues	facts that suggests a possible answer to a problem
Continuum	range or spectrum; along some dimension
Cryptic	secret; with a hidden meaning; hard to figure out
Dazzling	sparkling; magnificent and wonderful
Deceitful	misleading; purposely concealing something
Delusion	false opinion or belief; not in contact with reality
Distractible	easily distracted; one's attention is on something else
Dungeons	dark, underground cells used as prisons
Feigned	faked or pretended
Giggling	laughing in a nervous and silly way
Grudges	feeling of resentment; holding something against someone
Harsh	cruel; treating unkindly
Heaves	raises; lifts up; a heavy object
Impassive	not displaying emotion; showing no feeling
Jumbled	mixed or confused
Lingerie	women's underwear
Mumbling	saying something that can be heard; garbled speech

Term or expression	Definition
Neologisms	meaningless words
Pierced ears	holes in ears made to wear earrings
Reckless	not thinking or caring about consequences or safety
Sex-change operation	surgery that changes a person from one gender to another
Shackled	chained or restricted
Shortcomings	failure to reach a standard or to develop properly
Shrieks	scream or yell
Slashing (their wrists)	cutting their wrists
Sprawled	spread out loosely and irregularly
Sprees	occasion of extravagant unusual spending of money
Spurious	false; not reliable or replicable
Subtle	not obvious or noticeable
Swelling	increasing in volume or thickness
Toil	working long/hard hours on something
Thug	criminal; person who performs illegal acts
Unhesitatingly	with a sense of certainty; not holding back
Vanish	disappear or make something go out of sight
Word salad	a jumble of words in a form that is not coherent or understandable

CHAPTER 15
THERAPY:
DIMINISHING THE PAIN OF PSYCHOLOGICAL DISORDERS

INTEGRATED CHAPTER OUTLINE: Survey and Question

This section presents the major topics and ideas from the chapter. Use it as a tool for seeing how the components of the chapter fit together. At the end of each major topic, we have asked you questions that relate to the major learning objectives. If you can answer these questions, you have taken a major step toward mastering this material.

I. Psychotherapies: Psychological Approaches to Psychological Disorders

L.O. 15.1: Compare and contrast the different approaches to therapy.

L.O. 15.2: Know the basis of psychodynamic therapy.

L.O. 15.3: Know the basis of behavior therapy.

L.O. 15.4: Know the basis of cognitive therapy.

L.O. 15.5: Know how humor may be useful in reducing depression.

Psychotherapies are procedures in which a trained person establishes a professional relationship with the patient in order to remove or modify existing symptoms, change disturbed behavioral patterns and promote personal growth and development.

A. Psychodynamic Therapies: From Repression to Insight

Psychodynamic therapies are based on the assumption that psychological disorders are caused primarily by the inner workings of personality. Psychoanalysis was developed by Freud and is the most famous psychodynamic therapy. Freud believed that the personality consists of three major parts. The id corresponds to "desire." The ego corresponds to "reason." The superego corresponds to "conscience." Freud suggested that psychological disorders stem from the repression of id impulses. To keep these impulses in check, individuals expend considerable psychic energy and use defense mechanisms to reduce feelings of anxiety. These hidden conflicts between the basic components of personality can, if left unresolved, interfere with normal psychosexual development.

The goal of Freud's psychoanalysis was to overcome repression by having the patient gain insight about hidden feelings. This would be accompanied by a release of emotion or abreaction. The most common psychoanalytic technique involves having the patient report everything that comes to mind or free associations. Dreams are also analyzed for their latent content, the actual motives symbolized in the dream. The therapist asks questions and provides suggestions. This is the process of interpretation. During the early part of the therapy the patient may show resistance. Later, intense feelings for the therapist or transference may develop.

347

The effectiveness of classical psychoanalysis is limited: It is costly and time-consuming and it is difficult to test. Its scientific base is weak, it is suitable only for people with good verbal skills, and it is not open to criticism. One of the major assumptions has not been supported -- once insight is acquired, mental health does not follow automatically. Modern forms of psychoanalysis are briefer than classical psychoanalysis. They also put more emphasis on ego functioning and less on unconscious conflicts; in addition, they also rely on social factors and the client's present life situation.

B. Humanistic Therapies: Emphasizing the Positive

For humanistic psychologists, psychological disorders arise because the environment interferes with personal growth and fulfillment. Unlike psychoanalysts, in this approach the therapist is primarily a guide or facilitator. The client must take responsibility for success.

According to Rogers, people have psychological problems when they lose contact with their own feelings and form a distorted self-concept. According to Rogers, individuals often acquire unrealistic conditions of worth -- they learn that they must be something other than what they are in order to be loved. Person-centered or client-centered therapy focuses on eliminating these unrealistic conditions of worth. This involves unconditional acceptance of the individual. A high level of empathy and an interest in the patient that is genuine are also critical components of this therapy.

The therapy developed by Perls that focuses on helping individuals become aware of themselves and their true current feelings is Gestalt therapy. This is a client-centered therapy that emphasizes self-awareness.

Humanistic therapies share the view that people have the capacity to reflect upon their problems, to control their own behavior, and to make choices that will lead to satisfying lives. All suggest that flaws in our self-concept produce psychological distress. All reject the Freudian idea that psychological disorders stem from repressed urges that must be forced from patients who are unwilling to gain self-insight.

Humanistic theories are criticized because they do not have a unified theoretical base. However, research findings tend to confirm Rogers' view that the gap between an individual's self-image and his or her ideal self plays a major role in maladjustment. Humanistic therapies have made lasting contributions.

C. Behavior Therapies: Psychological Disorders and Faulty Learning

Therapies that are based on the principles of learning and that focus primarily on individuals' current behavior are behavior therapies. Several are based on the type of learning that occurs when one stimulus comes to serve as a signal for the occurrence of the other (or classical conditioning). Many phobias may be acquired in this manner. To reduce these fears, various techniques, derived, at least in part, from the principles of classical conditioning have been used by behavioral therapists. One technique is flooding. This involves long exposure to the feared stimuli or some representation of it. Because the person is not allowed to avoid these stimuli, extinction of fear can occur. Systematic desensitization is another technique. In this technique, individuals first experience relaxation training. Then, while in a relaxed state, they are exposed to stimuli that elicit anxiety.

Therapies are also based on operant conditioning. This involves three basic steps: identifying undescribable behaviors, identifying the reinforcers that maintain these behaviors, and, then attempting to change the context so that reinforcement is no longer provided for these behaviors. Token economies have been established in hospitals whereby tokens can be exchanged for the performance of adaptive behavior. The results of token economies have often been impressive and support the utility of behavioral therapy.

The process through which behavior is influenced by exposure to others is modeling. Modeling has been used to change a wide range of behaviors such as sexual dysfunctions and it is based on observational learning (Chapter 5). Its most impressive application has involved its use in reducing various phobias. It has also been used to change the behavior of highly aggressive children and adolescents.

D. Cognitive Therapies: Changing Disordered Thought

The basic idea behind cognitive therapy is that psychological disorders come from faulty or distorted modes of thought. The approach by Ellis to change these is called rational emotive therapy. He holds that most problems come from irrational beliefs. Ellis believes irrational thoughts are often automatic reactions stemming from our strong desires for love, success, and a safe comfortable existence. They do not occur because we consciously choose them. Irrational beliefs escalate reasonable desires into "musts." Awfulizing or catastrophizing beliefs are irrational beliefs that if a certain event occurs or fails to occur, it will be a disaster. Ellis feels people should be forced to recognize this irrationality. Because people often are unwilling to give up their irrational beliefs, the therapist first identifies these beliefs and then tries to persuade the client to recognize the irrationality of these beliefs.

Beck's cognitive behavior theory assumes that depression results from illogical thinking about self, the world, and the future that is often maintained in the face of evidence that contradicts it. These illogical thoughts can lead to negative moods which, in turn, increase the probability of more negative thinking. He emphasizes the importance of mood dependent memory -- how our current moods influence what we remember and what we think about. Several tendencies foster depression. Seeing oneself as totally worthless because of a few setbacks is an example of overgeneralization. There is also a tendency to interpret positive experiences as exceptions to the general rule of failure and incompetence. The tendency to see the world as a dangerous place is an example of selective perception. There is a tendency to magnify the importance of undesirable events. All-or-more thinking involves the tendency to engage in absolutistic thinking.

Growing evidence indicates that changing or eliminating irrational beliefs can be effective in treating depression and other personal difficulties.

- **Beyond the Headlines: As Psychologists See It: Laughter -- The Best Medicine?**

  "Nursing the Funny Bone: Carol O'Flaherty Goes From Giving Shots to Needling Audiences"

  According to the incompatible response hypothesis, it is difficult, if not impossible, to experience two incompatible emotional responses like anger and humor. Because laughter is incompatible with depression, it may be possible to reduce depression by the use of humor. This is the major point of the described article about the self-described "nurse-humorist."

Questions:

15-1. What are the different types of psychotherapy and what are the two crucial features? _____

_____

_____

_____

15-2.   What is the basis and application of psychoanalysis? _____

_____

_____

_____

15-3.   What are person-centered and gestalt therapy? _____

_____

_____

_____

15-4.   How have classical conditioning and operant conditioning been applied to therapy? _____

_____

_____

_____

15-5.   What are the basic assumptions underlying the cognitive approach to therapy and the characteristics
of rational-emotive therapy? _____

_____

_____

_____

15-6.   How has Beck's cognitive-behavior therapy been used to treat depression? _____

_____

_____

_____

II.   Group Therapies: Working with Others to Solve Problems

L.O. 15.6:   Know how group therapies are used to aid people with problems.

A.   Psychodynamic Group Therapies

Psychoanalytic procedures have been modified to operate in group settings. This therapy is called
psychodynamic group therapy and its goal is to show clients how they actually behave and what hidden inner
conflicts lie behind their overt actions. Psychodrama is one form of this therapy in which group members
act in front of other group members. Techniques involve role reversal, in which group members switch
parts, and mirroring, in which they portray one another.

B. Behavioral Group Therapies

This therapy involves using the basic principles of learning to solve specific behavioral problems in a group setting. For example, individuals practice desired skills in front of and with others. Other people serve as positive reinforcers of desired behavior and can also serve as models for effective behavior.

C. Humanistic Group Therapies

Group therapy originated with humanistic psychologists. The Humanists developed encounter groups and sensitivity-training groups. By having group members talk about their problems, these therapies are designed to promote personal growth, increased understanding of self, and increased openness and honesty with others. Little formal research has been done on the effectiveness of this form of therapy.

D. Self-Help Groups: Help From Our Peers

Self-help groups, like alcoholics anonymous, bring individuals who share a problem together. They believe that those who share a problem have a unique understanding and can provide a different level of empathy for one another than those who have not experienced the problem.

Questions:

15-7.   What are the characteristics of the different types of group therapy? _____

_____

_____

_____

III. Therapies Focused on Interpersonal Relations: Marital and Family Therapy

L.O. 15.7:   Compare and contrast the various types of marital and family therapies.

L.O. 15.8:   Understand how psychologists assess therapy effectiveness.

The therapies discussed in the previous section all share in common the assumption that psychological disorders stem from processes operating within individuals. In contrast, therapies that focus on interpersonal relations assume that psychological disorders can only be fully understood in terms of the individual's social environment.

A. Marital Therapy: Spouses as the Intimate Enemy

Couple or marital therapy focuses on improving the communication skills of partners. This goal is attained through the use of role-playing techniques and through the use of videotapes that depict the couple's interaction. Poorly adjusted couples tend to make unfavorable attributions about the causes of their partner's behavior. Couple therapy attempts to help the partners recognize and change these attributional patterns.

B. Family Therapy: Changing Environments That Harm

Family therapy is based on the recognition that the gains people make through individual therapy often disappear when the person returns home.

One type of family therapy is family systems therapy. This therapy is built on the assumption that families are a dynamic system in which each member has a role. Relationships between family members are viewed to be more important in producing psychological disorders than factors operating within individuals. Once the social dynamics that are contributing to a particular disorder are identified, the therapist attempts to change these factors.

Another major family therapy approach is called problem-solving therapy. Although this approach views the dynamics within families as important, it concentrates on instituting well-defined changes within a family. There are four distinct problem solving phases: Defining the problem, generating alternative solutions to the problems, evaluating the alternative solutions, and implementing the solution.

In many cases family therapy is effective. However, as has been the case with many forms of therapy, research on family therapy has been somewhat informal.

• **Research Methods: How Psychologists Study the Effectiveness of Various Forms of Therapy**

Most psychologists consider the efficacy study to be the most powerful scientific test of a therapy's effectiveness. The efficacy study involves the fundamental requirements for conducting a valid experiment on virtually any topic in psychology (see Chapter 1). The efficacy study is made up of: at least one experimental group and one control group, random assignment of participants, rigorous controls, standardization of the experimental treatment, a fixed number of sessions, clear definition of the dependent variable, participants with one psychological disorder, and if raters are necessary, they must be trained and have no knowledge of whether participants were assigned to the experimental or to the control condition.

Questions:

15-8.   What are the basic assumptions of therapies focusing on interpersonal relations and the characteristics of marital family therapy? _____

_____

_____

_____

15-9.   Why is family therapy beneficial and what are the various kinds of family therapy? _____

_____

_____

_____

15-10. What are the basic characteristics of the efficacy study? _____

_____

_____

_____

IV. Psychotherapy: Some Current Issues

L.O. 15.9: Be able to discuss the current issues in psychotherapy.

Nearly 10 percent of the population in the U.S. have consulted a therapist. Negative attitudes toward psychotherapy have weakened considerably, but has not vanished. Psychotherapy is improving in its sophistication. Several current issues are discussed in this section.

A. Does Psychotherapy Really Work? Evidence From Efficacy and Effectiveness Studies

In 1952, Hans Eysenck published a paper indicating that psychotherapy is ineffective -- that about the same proportion of people improve with therapy as do without therapy. Several reviews of more than 500 studies indicate he was incorrect. Apparently, he underestimated the number of persons who improve after therapy and overestimated the number who improve without therapy. Further, people improve with more therapy. These conclusions are based on efficacy studies (see "Research Methods" above).

However, therapies are not practiced in efficacy studies as they are in actual therapy. There are several differences. In efficacy studies, psychotherapy continues for a fixed amount of time, only one type of therapy is used, participants are assigned to a type of therapy which they have not necessarily sought and participants have a single psychological disorder. This is not the case in actual practice. In actual practice, psychotherapy does not continue for a fixed amount of time, therapists often use more than one type of therapy, participants often pick their therapy, and participants often have more than one disorder. Furthermore, efficacy studies focus on improvements with respect for specific symptoms or disorders whereas in actual practice, psychotherapy is directed toward more general improvements.

Effectiveness research examines how individuals do under actual therapy — the actual conditions of treatment as they occur in real-life settings. Effectiveness research compliments efficacy studies. Consumer Reports magazine asked subscribers about the duration and frequency of therapy they had received and how much help they gained from therapy. Results indicated that therapy did help. Respondents perceived that they received the most help from psychologists, psychiatrists, and social workers. There are several criticisms of this study. It was based on self-reports, was somewhat informed in nature, and there was no control group — all participants were people who had received therapy. However, putting these fine points of design aside, it seems clear that evidence from this source says it is beneficial.

B. Are Some Forms of Therapy More Successful Than Others?

The various forms of therapy seem to produce roughly similar benefits. Therapies may be similarly effective because they all provide individuals with a special type of setting, an explanation for their problems, specific actions to cope more effectively with their problems, and a therapeutic alliance — a partnership in which powerful emotional bonds are forged between persons seeking help and their therapist. Two themes emerge from combining these similarities: Hope and personal control. Diverse forms of therapy may succeed because they all provide increased hope about the future and a sense of heightened personal control.

C. To Prescribe or Not To Prescribe: Psychology's "Drug Problem"

Should psychologists have prescription privileges — the right to prescribe drugs? Many psychologists believe that prescription privileges are neither necessary nor beneficial to the practice of psychology. Prescription privileges may change psychologists' scientific focus, would require additional training, might result in psychology being considered a junior branch of psychiatry, and might produce internal conflicts within psychology. Some psychologists would not wish to go back to school for additional training to allow them to write prescriptions. On the other side, prescribing drugs can be beneficial to treatment. Only time will tell the outcome of this debate.

D. The Necessity For Culturally-Sensitive Psychotherapy

Racial and ethnic factors can influence diagnosis and effective communication between therapist and client. Because of these issues, there is an attempt to make psychotherapies more culturally sensitive. Efforts are being made to employ a type of therapy that considers the client's cultural, economic, and educational background.

Questions:

15-10. What are the major findings concerning the effectiveness of psychotherapy? _____

15-11. What are issues concerning whether psychologists should have prescription privileges? _____

15-12. What are the important implications of including a multicultural perspective in psychotherapy?

15-13. What are the major findings concerning the effectiveness of psychotherapy? _____

V. Biologically Based Therapies

L.O. 15.10: Discuss the revolution in therapy that has come with the use of drugs.

L.O. 15.11: Be able to discuss the issue of whether there are ethnic differences in reactions to psychotropic drugs.

L.O. 15.12: Be able to describe the nature of electroconvulsive therapy.

L.O. 15.13: Be able to describe the nature of psychosurgery.

A. Drug Therapy: The Pharmacological Revolution

Drug therapy is by far the most common type of biological based therapy. Antipsychotic drugs, like chlorpromazine, are sometimes called major tranquilizers. They reduce the bizarre symptoms of a schizophrenia. They, however, do not cure schizophrenia. Persons on antipsychotic drugs often remain somewhat withdrawn and show reduced levels of affect. There are drawbacks to these drugs. They often produce fatigue and apathy. Further, many patients develop a side effect known as tardive dyskinesia -- a loss of motor control, especially in the face. Clozaril (clozapine) does not produce tardive dyskinesia, but it causes other problems.

Antidepressant drugs are effective in treating depression. There are three basic types: Tricyclics, selective serotonin reuptake inhibitors (SSRIs), and MAO inhibitors. They all exert their effects by influencing serotonin. Serotonin and norepinephrine are low in depressed persons. Prozac (fluoxetine) is a selective serotonin reuptake inhibitor that is very effective. However, it has side effects. A small percentage of persons taking this drug report suicidal thoughts whereas others report loss of sexual desire. More serious side effects, such as severe headaches, heart palpitations, stroke or even death, are found with MAO inhibitors. Because tricyclics, like Elavil (amitriptyline) and Toframil (imipramine) have less severe side effects, they are most commonly prescribed.

Lithium, usually administered as lithium chloride, is quite effective in treating manic-depressive disorder and is effective with 60 to 70 percent of such persons. This drug has serious side effects.

Anti-anxiety drugs or minor tranquilizers combat anxiety by inhibiting activity in the central nervous system. Benzodiazepines like Valium, Ativan, Xanax, and Librium are the most widely used. Because these substances remain in the body for long periods of time, long-term use can be very dangerous. They also produce dependency and their effects are magnified when taken with alcohol. Alcohol is sometimes used by people to combat anxiety. This is a dangerous practice.

Buspar (buspirone) is another anti-anxiety drug that does not produce the dependency associated with benzodiazepine. It can, however, produce dizziness, faintness, and mild drowsiness.

- **Exploring Gender and Diversity: Are There Ethnic Differences in Reactions to Psychotropic Drugs?**

  Physicians practicing in Asians countries prescribe lover doses of antipsychotic and antidepressant drugs than those prescribed in Europe and the United States. Nevertheless, the effects across countries are equivalent.

B.   Electroconvulsive Therapy

The therapy that involves the use of strong electric shock is electroconvulsive therapy. It involves placing electrodes on the patient's temples and delivering shocks of 70 to 130 volts for less than a second. They are continued until the patient has a seizure that lasts at least 30 seconds. It seems to be effective with severe depression and may help many persons who fail to respond to other forms of therapy. It is a therapy that should be used with extreme caution, only when other forms of therapy are ineffective.

C.   Psychosurgery

Surgical procedures on the brain to treat mental disorders are forms of psychosurgery. Prefrontal lobotomy, first used by Egas Moniz, is the technique that involved surgery on the prefrontal lobes and was used to control aggression. A major problem with this technique is unwanted side-effects. This procedure is not now in use. Evidence for the benefits of psychosurgery is uncertain and its use raises important ethical questions. New procedures involve more limited operations. In one procedure, a small connection between the brain and limbic system is severed. This may be effective in treating obsessive-compulsive disorder. Another procedure involves inserting tiny videocameras into the brain to guide laser surgery in repairing blood vessels. This is known as videolaserscopy. All forms of psychosurgery should be viewed as drastic measures.

Questions:

15-14. What is drug therapy and how effective is it? _____

_____

_____

_____

15-15. What is the basic procedure of electroconvulsive therapy and psychosurgery. _____

_____

_____

_____

15-16. What is the importance of gender and diversity for psychotherapy? _____

_____

_____

_____

VI.   The Prevention of Psychological Disorders: Bringing Psychology to the Community

L.O. 15.14: Understand the basis of primary, secondary, and tertiary prevention.

L.O. 15.15: Know how to choose a therapist that is right for you.

As drug therapy flourished, many patients were discharged from hospitals. Community mental health centers provided these persons with an environment for continued treatment. These centers provided aftercare treatment and emergency services. Emergency services are often delivered by satellite storefront clinics that remain open at night. Primary, secondary, and tertiary prevention are three types of prevention that can be distinguished.

A. Primary Prevention

These programs focus on the education of children and adults. The aim of primary prevention is to prevent new psychological problem from occurring.

B. Secondary Prevention

These programs attempt to detect psychological problems early. For example, diversion programs focus on juvenile offenders in the criminal justice system and aim to steer young offenders away from prison into more constructive lives.

C. Tertiary Prevention

These programs attempt to minimize the long-term harm associated with psychological disorders. These programs are especially helpful to persons released from state facilities after many years of confinement. In the Training in Community Living program, participants are out in the community, but are living in a protected environment, where they can learn the skills necessary for a successful life.

Questions:

15-17. What are community health centers?_____

_____

_____

_____

15-18. What are the goals of the different types of prevention programs? _____

_____

_____

_____

- **Making Psychology A Part of Your Life: How To Choose a Therapist: A Consumer's Guide**

  Effective help for psychological disorders is available. To start the process of looking for a therapist, you can contact the psychology department or student health center at any university, even if you are not a student there. You could also ask your physician or a member of the clergy or Mental Health Association for suggestions. Next, you should make sure that the therapist is well qualified and that their specialty matches your needs. At times, therapy can hurt. Some of the danger signs are: If you or other people are noticing that you are becoming more distressed, if you are asked to perform activities that are inconsistent with your morals and ethics, and if you are given exaggerated claims by the therapist.

Question:

15-19. Explain how to choose a therapist. _____

_____

_____

_____

MAKING PSYCHOLOGY PART OF YOUR LIFE: Key Terms and Concepts

Knowing the important concepts and key terms contained in this chapter is a very important part of mastering the material. We have presented a sample of these concepts below. Define each concept and check your definition with that presented in the chapter. It will also be beneficial for you to think of an example of each concept. Whenever possible, use your own personal experience to provide an example of each term below.

15-1. **Basic Mistakes:** _____

   Example: _____

15-2. **Beck's Cognitive Behavior Therapy:** _____

15-3. **Behavior Therapies:** _____

   Example: _____

15-4. **Biologically Based Therapies:** _____

   Example: _____

15-5. **Cognitive Therapy:** _____

   Example: _____

15-6. **Community Mental Health Centers:** _____

15-7. **Conditions of Worth:** _____

   Example: _____

15-8. **Drug Therapy:** _____

   Example: _____

15-9. **Efficacy Study:** _____

15-10. **Electroconvulsive Therapy:** _____

15-11. **Family Systems Therapy:** _____

   Example: _____

15-12. **Family Therapy:** _____

Example: _____

15-13. **Free Association:** _____

Example: _____

15-14. **Gestalt Therapy:** _____

Example: _____

15-15. **Humanistic Therapies:** _____

Example: _____

15-16. **Incompatible Response Hypothesis:** _____

Example: _____

15-17. **Marital Therapy:** _____

Example: _____

15-18. **Prescription Privileges:** _____

15-19. **Primary Prevention:** _____

Example: _____

15-20. **Problem-Solving Therapy:** _____

Example: _____

15-21. **Psychodynamic Therapies:** _____

Example: _____

15-22. **Psychosurgery:** _____

Example: _____

15-23. **Psychotherapies:** _____

15-24. **Rational Emotive Therapy:** _____

Example: _____

15-25. **Resistance:** _____

Example: _____

15-26. **Secondary Prevention:** _____

Example: _____

15-27. **Self-Help Groups:** _____

Example: _____

15-28. **Systematic Desensitization:** _____

Example: _____

15-29. **Tardive Dyskinesia:** _____

15-30. **Tertiary Prevention:** _____

Example: _____

15-31. **Token Economies:** _____

Example: _____

15-32. **Transference:** _____

Example: _____

CHALLENGE: Develop Your Critical Thinking Skills

Summarizing and Evaluating Evidence

Rather than passively accepting the recommendation of experts, the critical thinker is able to evaluate evidence that is related to a problem. This aids the person in assessing the strengths and weaknesses of various courses of action. As an exercise in developing this skill, complete the following analysis of biological intervention treatments using your text as a reference source:

15-1. Summarize the main ideas and key issues relating to the use of biological interventions (e.g., drugs) in the treatment of psychological disorders.

15-2. Identify and evaluate the evidence used to support each of the main ideas.

15-3. Assess the importance of this research to our society.

CHALLENGE: Taking Psychology With You

Smoking Cessation Programs

In this chapter, you learned about the various forms of therapy that are available. Although it takes years of education to practice these therapies, the information you have learned should enable you to understand the basic components. Practice applying this knowledge to the following situation.

Situation

Your best friend is a "smoker." She wants to quit, but hasn't been able to do so. Although you have urged your friend to seek help with this problem, she wants to try quitting on her own before seeking professional help. Can you use what you've learned to help her sketch-out a smoking cessation program?

Questions

15-1. What approach would you take from a humanistic perspective?

15-2. What procedures would you employ based on the behavioral view?

15-3. Could you make use of cognitive therapies to help your friend?

15-4. What are the strengths and weaknesses of each view?

CHALLENGE: Review Your Comprehensive Knowledge

SAMPLE TEST QUESTIONS

Once you have worked through the preceding sections, you should be ready for a comprehensive self-test. You can check, your answers with those at the end of this section. An additional practice test is given in the supplementary section at the end of this study guide.

15-1.   Procedures in which a trained person establishes a special relationship with the patient in order to bring about beneficial changes in the patient's thoughts, feelings, or behavior are:
    a. psychotherapies.   c. biologically-based therapies.
    b. drug therapies.   d. psychosurgeries.

15-2.   Which of the following is not one of the characteristics of psychoanalysis?
    a. empathy   c. transference
    b. free association   d. abreaction

15-3.   Freud suggested that psychological disorders stem from the _____ of id impulses.
    a. interpretation   c. transference
    b. repression   d. abreaction

15-4.   Which of the following is not one of the primary features of client-centered therapy?
    a. unconditional acceptance   c. genuine interest in patient
    b. free association   d. empathy

15-5.   The aim of primary prevention programs is to:
    a. minimize long-term harm.   c. provide behavior therapy.
    b. detect psychological problems.   d. prevent psychological problems.

15-6.   The basic assumption underlying cognitive therapies is that psychological disorders stem from:
    a. faulty modes of thought.   c. biological causes.
    b. repressed impulses.   d. faulty learning histories.

15-7.   Which of the following is not one of the assumptions of humanistic therapies?
    a. People have control over their own behavior.
    b. Flaws in self-concept produce psychological distress.
    c. People have the ability to make choices.
    d. The therapist must force repressed urges from patients.

15-8.   Most psychologists consider this study to be the most powerful scientific test of a therapy's effectiveness.
    a. efficacy study   c. interpretation study
    b. efficiency study   d. qualitative study

15-9.   In Beck's model of depression, seeing oneself as totally worthless because of one or two failure experiences is an example of:
    a. absolutistic thinking.   c. exceptions to the rule.
    b. overgeneralization.   d. selective perception.

15-10.   According to the cognitive therapy called rational emotive therapy, most psychological problems come from:
    a. rational beliefs.   c. frustrations.
    b. irrational beliefs.   d. childhood experiences.

15-11. Encounter groups and sensitivity-training groups are types of:
    a. behavioral group therapies.
    c. psychodynamic group therapies.
    b. humanistic group therapies.
    d. behavioral individual therapies.

15-12. This type of family therapy concentrates on instituting well-defined changes within the family.
    a. constructivistic family therapy
    c. communications approach
    b. psychodynamic family therapy
    d. problem-solving therapy

15-13. Synthetic drugs with antianxiety effects are called:
    a. major tranquilizers.
    c. barbiturates.
    b. minor tranquilizers.
    d. alcohol.

15-14. Patients taking antipsychotic drugs often experience a loss of motor control, especially in their face. This side-effect is called:
    a. selective paralysis.
    c. tardive dyskinesia.
    b. tricyclic dyskinesia.
    d. prozac.

15-15. This therapy is built on principles of learning and concentrates primarily in an individual's current actions:
    a. humanistic therapy
    c. cognitive therapy
    b. psychodynamic therapy
    d. behavior therapy

15-16. Electroconvulsive therapy (ECT) should be used with caution. However, it appears to be effective with severe:
    a. drug addictions.
    c. dissociative disorders.
    b. depression.
    d. alcohol addictions.

15-17. Which of the following is true of antipsychotic drugs?
    a. They do seem to relieve the major symptoms of schizophrenia.
    b. They do seem to eliminate the causes that underlie schizophrenia.
    c. They are not often associated with side-effects.
    d. They are sometimes known as minor tranquilizers.

15-18. This technique involves long exposures to the feared stimuli or some representation of it:
    a. shaping
    c. systematic desensitization
    b. fading
    d. flooding

15-19. The basic assumption underlying all interpersonal therapies is that psychological disorders can only be understood in terms of the individual's:
    a. learning history.
    c. relationship with his/her mother.
    b. mode of thinking about the world.
    d. social environment.

15-20. Which of the following drugs is helpful in treating manic-depressive disorder?
    a. barbiturates
    c. valium
    b. lithium
    d. Xanax

Answers and Feedback for Sample Test Questions:

15-1.   A   Psychotherapies involve establishing a special relationship with a trained person with the goal of bringing about beneficial changes in the client's thoughts, feelings, and/or behaviors. (p. 588)

15-2.   A   Empathy is a characteristic of client-centered therapy, not psychoanalysis. (p. 592)

15-3.   B   Repressed id impulses are the basis for psychological disorders, according to Freud. (p. 588-589)

15-4.   B   Free association is a characteristic of psychoanalysis, not client-centered therapy. (p. 589)

15-5.   D   Preventing psychological problems is the aim of primary prevention programs. (p. 619)

15-6.   A   Cognitive therapies assume that faulty modes of thinking underlie psychological disorders and, therefore, seek to change these patterns. (p. 596)

15-7.   D   Humanistic therapies do not force repressed urges from clients. They do, however, assume the other information given in this question. (p. 592)

15-8.   A   An efficacy study is a powerful scientific test of a therapy's effectiveness. (p. 607)

15-9.   B   Beck's model assumes that depressed individuals overgeneralize failure experiences. (p. 597)

15-10. B   Rational emotive therapy is based on the assumption that individuals often form irrational beliefs from objective information. (p. 597)

15-11. B   Humanistic group therapies often involve encounter groups and sensitivity-training groups. (p. 600)

15-12. D   Problem-solving therapy involves careful analysis of interaction patterns. (p. 604)

15-13. B   These drugs are known as minor tranquilizers. (p. 616)

15-14. C   Tardive dyskinesia is a side-effect of antipsychotic drugs in which patients experience a loss of motor control. (p. 615)

15-15. D   Behavior therapy is built on learning principles and focuses primarily on an individual's current behavior. (p. 593)

15-16. B   ECT is an effective treatment for depression. (p. 617)

15-17. A   Antipsychotic drugs do seem to relieve the major symptoms of schizophrenia. The other options in this question are not true. (p. 614-615)

15-18. D   Flooding involves long exposures to the feared stimuli or some representation of it. (p. 594)

15-19. D   Interpersonal therapies are based on the assumption that psychological disorders stem from problems in a person's social environment. (p. 602)

15-20. B   Lithium is quite effective in treating manic-depressive disorder. (p. 616)

GLOSSARY OF DIFFICULT WORDS AND EXPRESSIONS

These terms from your text and this study guide were identified by students as potentially hard to understand. We have defined these terms and expressions.

Term or expression	Definition
Acquaint	get to know; become familiar with
Akin	like; similar to something
Array of	variety of; many examples of
Attest	to give proof of, to indicate something is correct
Aversive	negative, unpleasant
Bear	carry, hold-up
Bizarre	strange, bold, unusual
Blurred vision	not clear; hard to see
Brace yourself	get ready; get ready for
Breakthrough	new discovery or finding
Carnage	killing of many people
Chores	everyday tasks usually around the house
Compelling	convincing, overpowering
Conjure up	create in the mind
Craving	strong desire to have something
Desensitization	reduce sensitivity
Dismal	gloomy; miserable
Disowned	no longer wishing to have any connection with
Distressed	do not have peace of mind
Drastic measure	actions that should be taken only as a last step, if at all
Drowsiness	feeling sleepy
Eclectic	selecting or employing individual elements from a variety of sources, systems or styles
Empathetic	an understanding person
Escalate	to increase or expand
Firm grip	strong hold
Forged	created

Term or expression	Definition
Gaps	break or opening in a wall, hedge, etc.
Harbor hostility	hide or conceal hostility
Hasty	hurried
Hushed tones	in a silent or quiet way
Inducing	persuade or influence; causing to happen
"Modes of thought"	styles of thinking
No matter how trivial	no matter how insignificant or small
Overt actions	behavior that can be observed or seen
Pitfalls	unsuspected snare or danger
Pop (as piece of gum)	put a piece of gum in the mouth
Relapse	fall back again; have another occurrence of something
Render	make; cause something to occur
Roughly	approximately; almost or approximated
Scope	range of action or observation; the extent of coverage
Strain	put pressure on
Strives to	makes an effort to; tries to; works toward
Stuttering	tendency to repeat rapidly the same sound or syllable
Sustain	maintain or keep going
Tantrums	fit of temper or anger
"Time will tell"	the answer will be known in the future
Underlie	form the basis of
Unflattering	not complimentary; insulting
Urges	immediate needs or an impulses that can be resisted
Wanderings	long travels; journeys
Whisper	speak in a very quiet voice
Wring	twist; squeeze

CHAPTER 16
SOCIAL THOUGHT AND SOCIAL BEHAVIOR

INTEGRATED CHAPTER OUTLINE: Survey and Question

This section presents the major topics and ideas from the chapter. Use it as a tool for seeing how the components of the chapter fit together. At the end of each major topic, we have asked you a question that relates to the major learning objectives. If you can answer these questions, you have taken a major step toward mastering this material.

I. Social Thought: Thinking about Other People

L.O. 16.1: Discuss how we understand the causes of others' behavior.

L.O. 16.2: Know how attribution processes are involved in victim blame.

L.O. 16.3: Discuss the various ways in which we process information about the social world.

L.O. 16.4: Be able to discuss the nature of attitudes and attitude change.

L.O. 16.5: Know how the peripheral route to persuasion can induce persons to act in careless ways.

A. Attribution: Understanding the Causes of Others' Behavior

Our attempts to understand the causes of others' behavior are known as attributions. One of the major concerns is whether the causes stem from internal or external factors. According to Kelley, we make attributions about the causes of others' behaviors by focusing on consistency, distinctiveness, and consensus factors. If a person acts in the same way over time, he/she has high consistency. If the person acts in the same way to other stimuli, he/she has low distinctiveness. If others react the same way as the person, there is high consensus.

We tend to attribute behavior to internal causes if consistency is high, consensus is low, and distinctiveness is low. We tend to attribute behavior to external causes if consistency is high, consensus is high, and distinctiveness is high. We tend to attribute behavior to a combination of these factors when consensus is low, but consistency and distinctiveness are high.

There are some basic sources of bias in the attribution process that produce deviations from the logic described above. The tendency to explain the behavior of others in terms of internal causes and to overlook external ones is the fundamental attribution error (also called the overattribution bias). This may occur because people do not pay attention to context or give it less importance. We start by assuming that a person's actions reflect his/her underlying personality and fail to adequately correct for the effects of the external world.

The tendency to interpret the causes of our behavior in a positive way is the self-serving bias. For example, we may attribute success to internal causes and failure to external causes. This may be based on a desire to enhance one's self-esteem and a desire to look good to others.

- **Exploring Gender and Diversity: Attribution and Rape: Blaming the Victim**

   Research relating to attribution has been applied to many real-world setting, including rape events. Rape victims are often held responsible for this crime. Research on this tendency suggests that our "belief in a just world" may be involved in this attributional pattern; we may think that world is fair, so people get what they deserve. Therefore, a woman who is sexually assaulted must have done something to deserve this.

B. Social Cognition: How We Process Social Information

Social cognition is an area of study concerned with understanding the processes through which we notice, interpret, remember, and use social information.

We tend to use various mental short-cuts or heuristics in making judgments. The tendency to believe that others share our views is the false consensus effect. It may occur because of the availability heuristic -- the easier it is to bring information to mind, the more important it is judged to be. Several factors play a role in this effect. The false consensus effect does not occur all of the time. People also desire to perceive themselves as unique when highly desirable attributes are involved.

We tend to pay attention to information that is unexpected or inconsistent with our expectations. Our attempts to understand inconsistent information often lead to better memory for these events. However, we also tend to downplay or discount inconsistent information, so it often has little influence on our social thought.

Research finds that we often engage in magical thinking — thinking that is based upon nonrational assumptions but that seems compelling to us. Several principles of magical thinking have been identified: (1) contagion — the idea that objects can pass properties to one another when they touch; (2) similarity — the idea that objects that resemble one another share fundamental properties, and (3) "thinking-makes-it-so" — the assumption that one's thoughts can achieve physical effects.

When we imagine events and outcomes that are different from the ones we actually experienced, we are engaging in counterfactual thinking. This kind of thinking often leads us to have more sympathy for persons who experience negative outcomes that follow their atypical behavior. This is the case, in part, because it is easier to imagine alternatives to unusual than to typical forms of behavior.

Research studying the kinds of "regrets" people have reveals interesting patterns. Regrets concerning our recent past tend to center around actions we took that turned out badly whereas regrets about our more distant past centers around actions we didn't take but wish we had. These tendencies may be related to differences in the ease with which we can rationalize actions we took — as time goes by, we can find reasons why we took certain actions but may not be able to explain away missed opportunities.

C. Attitudes: Evaluating the Social World

Attitudes can be defined as mental representations and evaluations of various aspects of the social world. They are composed of affective, cognitive, and behavioral components. Attitudes may be formed by such processes as operant and classical conditioning, as well as from observational learning.

Efforts at persuasion involve a source directing a message or communication to some target audience. The traditional approach was concerned primarily with the "who says what to whom with what effect?" Research generated from this approach has found that people who are experts are more persuasive than those who are not. Messages that do not appear to be designed to change our attitudes are more successful than ones that seem intended to manipulate us. The attractiveness and popularity of the source are also important factors in persuasion. Individuals who are low in self-esteem are often easier to persuade than persons high in self-esteem. When an audience holds attitudes contrary to the would-be persuader, it is often more effective to use a two-sided approach (i.e., it is better to present both sides of an issue). A one-sided approach is most effective when the audience holds attitudes that are already consistent with the would-be persuader. People who speak rapidly are generally more effective than those who speak slowly.

The cognitive approach is concerned primarily with the "why" of persuasion -- or what cognitive processes determine when someone is actually persuaded. When we carefully evaluate the arguments and are convinced by their logic, we are experiencing the central route to persuasion. This route is followed when the issues are important or personally relevant to recipients. Persuasion takes the peripheral route when we are not fully attending to the arguments and are influenced by persuasion cues -- information relating to the source's prestige, credibility or likability, or to the style and form of the message. This is likely to occur with issues that are relatively unimportant and not personally relevant to recipients, or when recipients are distracted. These routes are described by the elaboration likelihood model of persuasion.

When inconsistencies arise between attitudes, or between attitudes and behavior, an unpleasant feeling known as cognitive dissonance can occur. This produces a negative motivational state -- people experiencing it want to reduce cognitive dissonance. One way of reducing it is to change your attitudes or we can seek out information that supports our original attitude. Alternatively we can engage in trivialization -- concluding that our behavior or attitudes aren't important. We tend to take the tactic of reducing dissonance that is least effortful.

In many situations, we are forced to say or do something that is against our true attitudes. This is called forced compliance. The weaker the reasons individuals have for saying or doing things that are inconsistent with their attitudes, the stronger the dissonance generated; therefore, the greater the pressure for attitude change. This is known as the "less leads to more" effect. This effect is most likely to occur when individuals believe they have free choice and feel personally responsible for their actions.

Several experiments indicate that dissonance can indeed be an effective means for changing attitudes and behavior. In one study, dissonance theory was shown to predict which sexually-active participants would buy condoms. Those who made public commitments to engage in safe-sex and remembered times when they had not done so were more likely to purchase condoms than other participants in this study.

- **Beyond the Headlines: As Psychologists See It -- Persuasion Through Sexual Fantasies**

  Baron reports cases in which a man supposedly called three women late at night and in a sexy whisper persuaded them to unlock their doors, undress, put on blindfolds, and wait for him in bed. The man was charged with rape. How could these women have been so persuaded?

  Social psychologists would offer that the man was an expert at persuasion. He didn't choose these victims randomly. Rather, he observed them and carefully planned his approach to match the kind of fantasies he suspected the women had. He also framed his message so that they would respond without careful thought; in other words, he invoked the peripheral route to persuasion.

Questions:

16-1.   What are the topics that serve as the major focus of social psychology? _____

_____

_____

_____

16-2.   What is the definition of attribution and why is this an important topic for social psychologists to study? _____

_____

_____

16-3.   What are the conditions leading to internal and external causal attributions from Kelley's model?

_____

_____

_____

16-4.   Describe the various attributional biases, including the fundamental attribution error and the self-serving bias. _____

_____

_____

16-5.   What is the definition of social cognition? _____

_____

_____

_____

16-6.   Describe the errors we see in social thought, including the false consensus effect, magical thinking, and counterfactual thinking. _____

_____

_____

_____

16-7.   What are the effects of being exposed to information that is inconsistent with our expectations?

_____

_____

_____

16-8.   What is the definition of an attitude and how are they formed? _____

_____

_____

_____

16-9.   What are the conclusions concerning how we are influenced by source and message characteristics
in persuasion? _____

_____

_____

16-10.   What is the elaboration likelihood model of persuasion and what predictions does it make about when
we will be persuaded by rational arguments vs. superficial message characteristics? _____

_____

_____

16-11.   What is the role of cognitive dissonance in attitude change? _____

_____

_____

_____

16-12.   What are the practical implications of cognitive dissonance theory? _____

_____

_____

_____

II.   Social Behavior: Interacting With Others

L.O. 16.6:   Understand the nature of prejudice.

L.O. 16.7:   Know how psychologists study sexism.

L.O. 16.8:   Describe basic ways in which we influence other persons.

L.O. 16.9:   Discuss factors that lead us to help other persons.

L.O. 16.10:   Be able the discuss the psychological approach to understanding the nature of attraction and love.

L.O. 16.11:   Use the "Making Psychology Part of Your Life" exercise for insight into your feelings.

A.   Prejudice: Distorted Views of the Social World and Their Effects

Prejudice involves negative attitudes toward members of specific groups that are based solely on persons'
memberships in these groups. There are several perspectives on the origins of prejudice. (1) The realistic
conflict view suggests that prejudice arises out of economic competition between various groups. (2) The
social categorization view suggests that our tendency to divide the social world into distinct categories of "us"
versus "them" contributes to the development of prejudice. Persons in our own groups are perceived more

positively than are persons in outgroups. This tendency also affects our attributions such that we attribute positive behaviors of ingroup members to internal, stable factors but attribute similar behaviors of outgroup members to temporary, external factors, such as luck. (3) The fact that infants do not show prejudice suggests that it emerges through the process of social learning. (4) According to the cognitive perspective of prejudice, prejudice not only involves powerful emotional reactions, but also involves the ways we think about others and process various types of social information. The cognitive perspective emphasizes the role of stereotypes in prejudice. Stereotypes exert strong effects on the ways in which we process social information. For example, information relevant to a particular stereotype is processed more quickly than unrelated information. Stereotypes also determine what we remember about other persons and often lead to serious errors in judgment. The persistence of stereotypes seems to be related to their use in reducing the complexity of the social world and their contributions in protecting and enhancing our social identity.

How can we reduce prejudice? Increased contact between groups can sometimes reduce prejudice. This occurs only under the following conditions: (1) the groups are approximately equal in status, (2) the situation involves cooperation and interdependence so that the groups work toward shared goals, (3) contact between groups is informal, (4) existing norms favor group equality, and (5) the persons involved view one another as typical members of their respective groups. Research has found that procedures designed to shift or recategorize the boundaries between "us" and "them" can be a valuable approach to lessening prejudice. Finally, drawing attention or enhancing awareness of prejudice can sometimes lead to reductions.

- **Research Methods: How Psychologists Study Sexism -- and the "Glass Ceiling"**

Sexism -- prejudice based on gender - persists, often in subtle and hidden forms. Researchers have investigated the "glass-ceiling" for insights into sexism. Labor statistics support its existence, finding disproportionate numbers of females in high level jobs. But these statistics may result from other factors such as the length of time women have been in managerial positions. Researchers have used survey methods to assess whether men and women have the job-related experiences (developmental opportunities) to prepare them for top-level jobs. A few differences were found; women tended not to be given key assignments that increased their visibility or widened the scope of their responsibilities. These findings suggest the glass-ceiling is real and stems from subtle forms of discrimination.

B. Social Influence: Changing Others' Behavior

Social influence involves attempts by one or more persons to change the behavior of others. In many contexts, there are social rules or injunctive norms indicating how we should or ought to behave. Descriptive norms tell us what most people do in a situation. These rules exert pressure toward conformity -- toward thinking or acting like most other persons.

Compliance involves one person asking another to do something that he/she wants. There are various techniques for gaining compliance. Ingratiation involves efforts to increase one's appeal to a target person before asking that person to grant a request. This can be done by the use of agreement, emitting positive non-verbal cues, enhancing personal appearance, name dropping, self-deprecating remarks, and flattery.

Ingratiation tactics are based on attempts to induce compliance through attraction. In general, there are two basic strategies. Self-enhancing tactics are designed to enhance our personal appeal. Other-enhancing tactics involve flattery, showing interest in someone, or in agreeing with the person.

The strategy of going from a small request to a large one is the "foot-in-the-door" technique. This technique seems to be effective in increasing compliance. It seems to be related to changes in self-perception. People may see themselves as more helpful after the first request and act consistently with this perception in response to the large request.

The technique of beginning with a large request and switching to a small one after it is rejected is the "door-in-the-face" technique. The reduction in the size of the request places pressure on the other person to also make a concession or to "give in." This technique also leads to increased compliance. The "that's-not-all" approach throws something extra into the situation before the person has made a decision.

The "playing hard to get" and "fast-approaching deadline" compliance techniques are based on scarcity. "Playing hard to get" involves individuals trying to create an image that one is popular or in demand. This places pressure on a person to "say yes" to the popular requester. The "fast approaching deadline" technique involves establishing a cut-off point after which an opportunity is not available. As you can see, both techniques involve creating an illusion that something is valuable because it is scarce.

Social influence by demand is called obedience. In the classic but controversial Milgram study, in which people were told to shock another person, about 65 percent of participants showed total obedience. Similar findings have been obtained in studies conducted in Jordan, Germany, and Australia -- and with children as well as adults. An important factor in these results is that the person in authority relieves the subjects of responsibility for the actions. The experimenter possessed clear signs of authority and existing social norms suggest that authority figures are to be obeyed. The fact that increasing obedience is requested in a gradual manner is also important. These effects can be overcome if individuals are held responsible, witness others disobeying, and there is clear evidence that authorities are pursuing selfish goals. You should remember that, in this research, no one was actually shocked!

C. Prosocial Behavior: When We Help...And When We Don't

Prosocial behavior is defined as actions that benefit others without necessarily providing direct benefits to the helpers. Several possible motives for prosocial behavior have been identified. The empathy-altruism hypothesis suggests that we share the feelings or needs of people in trouble and this empathy moves us to help. In contrast, the negative state relief hypothesis suggests that seeing a person in trouble makes us feel bad and we help them in order to reduce our negative emotional feelings. A third view is based on the notion that we help people in order to increase the likelihood that genes similar to ours will be passed on. This genetic determinism hypothesis predicts that we will only help others who are similar to us. Evidence suggests that each of these motives may be involved in prosocial behavior.

What factors determine the likelihood that we will help? Studies have shown that as the number of bystanders to an emergency increase, helping decreases. This seems to be due to the assumption that others will help, known as diffusion of responsibility. Good moods will increase helping when it results in pleasant consequences. If helping stops the good feelings, tendency to help is reduced. A bad mood can reduce helping if the potential helpers concentrate on their own needs or misfortunes. Sometimes a bad mood can increase helping because it provides negative state relief. This can occur when persons can observe the positive effects of helping and can praise themselves for having helped.

Reactions to being helped are not always positive. Our culture emphasizes independence and being helped runs counter to this value. Sometimes being helped puts us in a negative light.

D. Attraction and Love

Friendship or liking is often increased by the close physical distance between people, known as propinquity. This may lead to repeated exposure and familiarity, which in turn leads to more liking. Similarity also leads to increased liking. One possibility is that similarity provides validation for our views. In addition, the more others like us, the more we tend to like them. This may be because we enjoy receiving positive evaluations and dislike negative ones. This tendency is so strong that it can even occur in situations where we believe that the assessments are inaccurate or represent attempts at flattery. Physical attractiveness is another factor influencing attraction. It is a factor for both men and women, although the effects appear to be stronger for males.

Romantic love involves strong feelings of attraction and sexual desire. According to one approach, three conditions must be met for a person to conclude that they are in romantic or passionate love: a) it requires the experience of strong emotional arousal, b) a suitable object, and c) the concept of romantic love must be present in the culture. Passionate love is dominated by strong physical attraction whereas companionate love emphasizes commitment and concern for the loved-one's well-being. Attachment to one's parents may serve as a forerunner to love. In addition, love may serve the purpose of bonding for reproduction and childcare.

Several factors may contribute to troubled relationships. These include jealousy, the discovery of dissimilarities, boredom, and self-defeating patterns of behavior. These factors contribute to the dissolution of relationships.

- **Making Psychology Part of Your Life: Are Your in Love? One Way of Telling**

  In this section, Baron provides a questionnaire that measures several components of romantic love. Approach the test as an example of such scales, but interpret the results with caution (as you should all self-tests). [See page 662 in your text for the "Love Test."]

Questions:

16-13.   What are the different views on the origins of prejudice and discrimination? _____

_____

_____

_____

16-14.   What methods can be used to reduce prejudice and its impact? _____

_____

_____

_____

16-15.   How do descriptive and injunctive norms create pressures to conform? _____

_____

_____

_____

16-16.   When is conformity a "good thing" and when is it undesirable? _____

_____

_____

_____

16-17. What is compliance and what is the role of friendship and liking in this process? _____

_____

_____

_____

16-18. What are the techniques for gaining compliance that involve commitment, reciprocity, and scarcity?

_____

_____

_____

16-19. What is obedience and what are the factors that increase the extent of obedience to authority?

_____

_____

_____

16-20. What are the motives for prosocial behavior? _____

_____

_____

_____

16-21. What are the factors that influence the likelihood of helping? _____

_____

_____

_____

16-22. Why are reactions to being helped not always positive? _____

_____

_____

_____

16-23. What factors influence our attraction to other person? _____

_____

_____

_____

16-24.   What is "romantic love"? _____

_____

_____

_____

16-25.   What factors may cause love to fade over time? _____

_____

_____

_____

YOUR NOTES:

MAKING PSYCHOLOGY PART OF YOUR LIFE: Key Terms and Concepts

Knowing the important concepts and key terms contained in this chapter is a very important part of mastering the material. We have presented a sample of these concepts below. Define each concept and check your definition with that presented in the chapter. It will also be beneficial for you to think of an example of each concept. Whenever possible, use your own personal experience to provide an example of each term below.

16-1. **Attitudes:** _____

Example: _____

16-2. **Attribution:** _____

Example: _____

16-3. **Bystander Effect:** _____

Example: _____

16-4. **Central Route to Persuasion:** _____

Example: _____

16-5. **Cognitive Dissonance:** _____

Example: _____

16-6. **Cognitive Perspective on Persuasion:** _____

Example: _____

16-7. **Companionate Love:** _____

Example: _____

16-8. **Compliance:** _____

Example: _____

16-9. **Conformity:** _____

Example: _____

16-10.   **Consensus:** _____

     Example: _____

16-11.   **Consistency:** _____

     Example: _____

16-12.   **Contact Hypothesis:** _____

     Example: _____

16-14.   **Counterfactual Thinking:** _____

     Example: _____

16-15.   **Diffusion of Responsibility:** _____

     Example: _____

16-16.   **Distinctiveness:** _____

     Example: _____

16-17.   **Door-in-the-face Technique:** _____

     Example: _____

16-18.   **Elaboration Likelihood Model:** _____

16-19.   **Foot-in-the-door Technique:** _____

     Example: _____

16-20.   **Forced Compliance:** _____

     Example: _____

16-21.   **Fundamental Attribution Error:** _____

     Example: _____

16-22. **Ingratiation**: _____

      Example: _____

16-23. **Interpersonal Attraction**: _____

      Example: _____

16-24. **Less-Leads-to-More Effect**: _____

      Example: _____

16-25. **Magical Thinking**: _____

      Example: _____

16-26. **Obedience**: _____

      Example: _____

16-27. **Peripheral Route to Persuasion**: _____

      Example: _____

16-28. **Persuasion**: _____

      Example: _____

16-29. **Prejudice**: _____

      Example: _____

16-30. **Propinquity**: _____

      Example: _____

16-31. **Prosocial Behavior**: _____

      Example: _____

16-32. **Realistic Conflict Theory**: _____

16-33. **Recategorization:** _____

       Example: _____

16-34. **Repeated Exposure Effect:** _____

       Example: _____

16-35. **Romantic Love:** _____

       Example: _____

16-36. **Self-Serving Bias:** _____

       Example: _____

16-37. **Social Categorization:** _____

       Example: _____

16-38. **Social Cognition:** _____

       Example: _____

16-39. **Social Influence:** _____

       Example: _____

16-40. **Social Norms:** _____

       Example: _____

16-41. **Stereotypes:** _____

       Example: _____

CHALLENGE: Develop Your Critical Thinking Skills

I.   Introspection: Prejudice and Discrimination

Unfortunately, prejudice and discrimination are common in our social world. Rather than denying this fact, it is useful to recognize the instances in which we have been both victims and instigators of prejudice and discrimination. A critical thinker is able to recognize instances in which he/she has been affected by these social forces. Recognizing these instances is the first step toward reducing these negative forms of social behavior. As an exercise in developing these skills, look within yourself and your past experiences (i.e., introspect) for instances in which prejudice and discrimination have affected your thought and behavior.

16-1.   List the social labels that can be applied to you (e.g., male, female). _____
        _____
        _____
        _____

16-2.   When has prejudice touched your life? Have you ever felt "put-down," excluded or discriminated against because you were in any of the social groups you listed above? Describe an occasion. _____
        _____
        _____
        _____
        _____

16-3.   Describe your feelings about the occasion described above. _____
        _____
        _____
        _____

16-4.   Have you ever felt that anyone responded to you based on assumptions that they made concerning your social group (what you are) vs. your individual characteristics (who you are)? If so, describe an occasion.
        _____
        _____
        _____

16-5.   If you answered "yes" to question 4, describe the feelings you experienced in this occasion. _____
        _____
        _____
        _____

16-6.   Have you ever felt that you responded to another person based upon his/her social group membership? If so, please describe an occasion. _____

_____

_____

_____

16-7.   Do you ever feel as if you are prejudiced? For example, have you ever had immediate prejudice reactions -- regardless of how you then acted? If so, describe an occasion. _____

_____

_____

_____

16-8.   If you answered "yes" to either question 6 or 7, speculate on why you had these reactions. Does the material you've learned in this chapter give you insight into the reason? _____

_____

_____

_____

16-9.   Have you ever felt that others responded to you as if you were prejudiced? If so, describe an occasion.

_____

_____

_____

16-10. If you answered "yes" to question 9, how did this make you feel? _____

_____

_____

_____

16-11. After completing questions 1-10, you may want to ask your friends and/or classmates these questions. You may be surprised to find that many people feel they have been both victims and instigators of prejudice. How might you use the information you've learned to reduce prejudice in your social world?

_____

_____

_____

_____

_____

II. Magical thinking is a style that is in opposition to critical thinking. Baron describes several types of magical thought. As an exercise in recognizing occurrences in your own experience, provide some examples of each type of magical thought. Recognizing these may help you avoid the pitfalls of falling into this style of thought.

A. Principle of contagion -- Definition: _____

_____

_____

Examples: _____

_____

_____

_____

B. Principle of similarity -- Definition: _____

_____

_____

Examples: _____

_____

_____

_____

C. Principle of "thinking-makes-it-so" -- Definition: _____

_____

_____

_____

Examples: _____

_____

_____

_____

CHALLENGE: Taking Psychology With You

<u>Attribution</u>

As an exercise in seeing how the research on attribution discussed in your text applies to you, complete the following questionnaires:

Questionnaire I

16-1. From the following, circle the trait that is most applicable to the President of the United States.

1. a. trustworthy	b. untrustworthy	c. depends on the situation
2. a. friendly	b. unfriendly	c. depends on the situation
3. a. intelligent	b. not intelligent	c. depends on the situation
4. a. insincere	b. sincere	c. depends on the situation
5. a. humorous	b. serious	c. depends on the situation
6. a. anxious	b. calm	c. depends on the situation
7. a. easy going	b. stubborn	c. depends on the situation
8. a. conscientious	b. unconscientious	c. depends on the situation
9. a. agreeable	b. disagreeable	c. depends on the situation
10. a. unattractive	b. attractive	c. depends on the situation

16-2. From the following list, circle the trait that is most applicable to you.

1. a. trustworthy	b. untrustworthy	c. depends on the situation
2. a. friendly	b. unfriendly	c. depends on the situation
3. a. intelligent	b. not intelligent	c. depends on the situation
4. a. insincere	b. sincere	c. depends on the situation
5. a. humorous	b. serious	c. depends on the situation
6. a. anxious	b. calm	c. depends on the situation
7. a. easy going	b. stubborn	c. depends on the situation
8. a. conscientious	b. unconscientious	c. depends on the situation
9. a. agreeable	b. disagreeable	c. depends on the situation
10. a. unattractive	b. attractive	c. depends on the situation

16-3. Count the number of times you circled "depends on the situation" when you made judgments about the President vs. yourself. Record the tally below:

<u>The President</u>   <u>You</u>

<u>Analysis</u>: Did you circle "depends on the situation" more often when describing your characteristics vs. those of the President? If so, you demonstrated the **fundamental attribution error** -- our tendency to explain others' actions in terms of dispositional (internal) factors vs. seeing the situation factors that may influence others' behavior.

Source: Suggested by R. E. Nisbett Attribution Scale.

Questionnaire II

16-1. Imagine the following situation: You have just received an A+ on your psychology exam. To what extent do you think your grade was affected by:

a. the amount you studied for the exam. (Mark the scale point that corresponds with your feeling.)

    Not at all   1   2   3   4   5   6   7   a great deal

b. the difficulty of the exam.

    Not at all   1   2   3   4   5   6   7   a great deal

c. your talent for psychology.

    Not at all   1   2   3   4   5   6   7   a great deal

d. the instructor's grading standards.

    Not at all   1   2   3   4   5   6   7   a great deal

16-2. Imagine the following scenario: You have just received a failing grade on your psychology exam. To what extent do you think that your grade was affected by the following:

a. the amount you studied for the exam. (Mark the scale point that corresponds with your feeling.)

    Not at all   1   2   3   4   5   6   7   a great deal

b. the difficulty of the exam.

    Not at all   1   2   3   4   5   6   7   a great deal

c. your talent for psychology.

    Not at all   1   2   3   4   5   6   7   a great deal

d. the instructor's grading standards.

    Not at all   1   2   3   4   5   6   7   a great deal

Analysis:

1. Tally the numbers you placed on the scales for items A and C and items B and D in scenario 1 and 2.

    A & C = _____   2. A & C = _____

    B & D = _____   B & D = _____

    What pattern do you see? Did you tend to place higher numbers for options A and C in scenario 1 vs. scenario 2? And did you give higher numbers to B & D in scenario 2 vs. 1? _____

    _____

    _____

    _____

    _____

2. Options A and C represent internal causal dimensions and options B and D represent external causal dimensions. If you made more internal vs. external causal attributions for scenario 1 vs. 2, you demonstrated what's known as "the self-serving bias" -- our tendency to take credit for positive behavior or outcomes by attributing them to internal causes, but to blame negative ones on external causes.

    Source: Suggested by B. Weiner attribution scale.

YOUR NOTES:

CHALLENGE: Review Your Comprehensive Knowledge

SAMPLE TEST QUESTIONS

Once you have worked through the preceding sections, you should be ready for a comprehensive self-test. You can check your answers with those presented at the end of this section. An additional practice test is given in the supplementary section at the end of this study guide.

16-1. According to Kelley, if a person reacts the same way to a given stimulus or situation on different occasions (i.e., across time), he/she exhibits:
a. low distinctiveness.
b. high consistency.
c. high consensus.
d. low covariation.

16-2. According to Kelley, we tend to attribute behavior to external causes if consistency is _____, distinctiveness is _____, and consensus is _____.
a. high, low, low
b. high, high, high
c. low, low, low
d. low, high, high

16-3. The fundamental attribution error is the tendency to explain the behavior of others in terms of _____ causes.
a. internal
b. external
c. stable
d. unstable

16-4. The tendency to interpret the causes of our behavior in a positive way is the:
a. fundamental attribution error.
b. basis of most gender differences.
c. illusory correlation.
d. self-serving bias.

16-5. The tendency to overestimate the extent to which we are similar to others is the _____ effect.
a. false consensus
b. priming
c. illusory correlation
d. false uniqueness

16-6. Advertisements that are designed to sell by having a basketball "star" endorse the products use the:
a. peripheral route to persuasion.
b. central route to persuasion.
c. counterfactual thinking route to persuasion.
d. foot-in-the-door technique.

16-7. The central route to persuasion refers to:
a. the careful processing of arguments.
b. the impact of persuasion cues on attitude change.
c. attitude change that occurs because an individual recognizes inconsistencies between their attitudes and behavior.
d. persuasion induced by fear.

16-8. When we imagine events and outcomes that are different from the ones we actually experienced, we are engaging in:
a. counterfactual thinking.
b. internal attributions.
c. high distinctiveness thinking.
d. illusory correlation.

16-9. The view of prejudice that suggests that prejudice stems from competition between social groups over valued commodities or opportunities is the:
a. realistic conflict theory.
b. cognitive dissonance theory.
c. social learning theory.
d. social categorization perspective.

16-10. This view suggests that prejudice results from our tendency to divide the social world into "us" versus "them."
  a. conflict
  b. social categorization
  c. social learning
  d. cognitive dissonance

16-11. This view of prejudice emphasizes the role of stereotypes.
  a. realistic conflict
  b. peripheral cue
  c. learning
  d. cognitive

16-12. According to dissonance theory, the _____ the obvious pressure for attitude change, the _____ the pressure to change one's own view.
  a. more stable, more stable
  b. greater, weaker
  c. greater, greater
  d. less stable, less stable

16-13. Finding that people are more likely to help others who are similar to themselves would be most consistent with the _____ approach to prosocial behavior.
  a. empathy-altruism
  b. negative state relief
  c. positive mood
  d. genetic-determinism

16-14. The foot-in-the-door technique seems to be effective because it produces changes in:
  a. self-image.
  b. attitudes.
  c. motivation.
  d. self-confidence.

16-15. In the door-in-the-face technique, the first request is a _____ one and the second request is a _____ one.
  a. large, small
  b. small, large
  c. large, large
  d. small, moderate

16-16. Bystanders may not help in emergencies because they presume others will help. This is known as:
  a. pluralistic ignorance.
  b. nonempathy.
  c. diffusion of responsibility.
  d. division of impact.

16-17. An important factor in getting participants to obey in the obedience studies is that the person in authority relieves the participant of:
  a. responsibility.
  b. negative emotion.
  d. awareness.
  d. empathy.

16-18. Increased contact between groups can sometimes reduce prejudice, especially if several conditions are met. Which of the following is not one of the conditions?
  a. the groups are approximately equal in status
  b. existing norms favor equality
  c. the persons involved view one another as atypical members of their respective groups
  d. the groups work toward shared goals

16-19. This type of love emphasizes commitment and concern for the loved-one's well-being.
  a. passionate love
  b. companionate love
  c. responsible love
  d. motivated love

16-20. The view that love occurs as a method for promoting a bond that is necessary for prolonged child care is consistent with:
  a. evolutionary theory.
  b. learning theory.
  c. cognitive dissonance theory.
  d. the negative state relief hypothesis.

Answers and Feedback for Sample Test Questions:

16-1.   B   If a person acts in the same way to a stimulus over time, he/she has high consistency. (p. 627)

16-2.   B   We tend to attribute behavior to external causes if consistency is high, consensus is high, and distinctiveness is high. (p. 627)

16-3.   A   The tendency to explain the behavior of others in terms of internal causes and to overlook external ones is the fundamental attribution error. (p. 628)

16-4.   D   The tendency to interpret the causes of our behavior in a positive way is the self-serving bias. (p. 628)

16-5.   A   The false consensus effect refers to the tendency to overestimate the extent to which we are similar to others. (p. 631)

16-6.   A   Persuasion is taking the peripheral route when we are not fully attending to the arguments and are influenced by information related to such things as the source's prestige. A basketball "star" has prestige for many persons. (p. 638)

16-7.   A   The central route involves careful processing of information. (p. 637)

16-8.   A   Counterfactual thinking occurs when we imagine events and outcomes that are different from the one we actually experienced. (p. 634)

16-9.   A   The realistic conflict theory contends that prejudice stems from competition over valued resources. (p. 643)

16-10. B   The social categorization view suggests that an "us" versus "them" distinction contributes to prejudice. (p. 643)

16-11. D   The cognitive perspective emphasizes the role of stereotypes. (p. 644)

16-12. B   According to cognitive dissonance theory, the greater the obvious pressure for attitude change, the weaker the pressure to change one's own attitude or view. This follows from the less-leads-to-more effect and research on forced compliance. (p. 639-640)

16-13. D   The genetic determinism hypothesis states we are likely to help similar others in order to get our genes into the next generation. (p. 654)

16-14. A   The foot-in-the-door technique seems to be effective because of changes in self-perception in that people may see themselves as more helpful after complying to the first request. (p. 649)

16-15. A   The door-in-the-face technique begins with a large request and switches to a small one after the large request is rejected. (p. 650)

16-16. C   Bystanders may not help in emergencies because the presence of other individuals leads to a diffusion of responsibility. (p. 655)

16-17. A   An important factor in the obedience studies is that the authority figure relieves the participant of responsibility. (p. 652)

16-18. C   The persons involved should view one another as <u>typical</u> (not atypical) members of their respective groups. (p. 645-646)

16-19. B   Companionate love emphasizes commitment and concern for the loved-one's well-being. (p. 660)

16-20. A   Evolutionary theory emphasizes the role that feelings and behaviors play in ensuring reproductive success.
        (p. 660-661)

YOUR NOTES:

GLOSSARY OF DIFFICULT WORDS AND EXPRESSIONS

These terms from your text and this study guide were identified by students as potentially hard to understand. We have defined these terms and expressions.

Term or expression	Definition
Bigots	people who are strongly partial to their own religion, race or group; people who are prejudiced
Clerk	a person who works in an office performing such tasks as keeping records
Clumsy	lacking physical coordination, skill or grace
Compelled	forced or made to happen
Concession	to give in or let someone have what they want
Curtailed	to cut short
Disproportionate	either more than or less than would be expected based on, for example, population frequencies
Drought	state that occurs due to lack of water
Empathy	sharing the feelings of others
"Ethnic cleansing"	killing members of an ethnic group in order to make one's own group safe from their influence
Flattery	excessive praise
Fled	left in a hurry
Frown	drawing the eyebrows together forming lines on the forehead; an expression of displeasure
"Glass-ceiling"	a barrier against women advancing in some organizations that prevents them from attaining top organizational positions
Hypocrisy	the feeling that you are not acting in a way that matches your beliefs
Inept	awkward, incompetent; lacking sense or reason
Jargon-studded paper	paper filled with words that are common to a particular field
Law-abiding citizens	citizens who respect the law
Murky	unclear
Negligence	carelessness; inattention to one's responsibilities
Onslaught	overwhelming
Pleas for aid	desperate calls for help
Plight	unfortunate situation
Prevail	to win or overcome difficulties

Term or expression	Definition
Reluctant	hesitant
Resiliency	marked by the ability to recover; toughness
Shudder	to shake from fear
Slick	smooth; slippery
Sorting	to arrange; to put in order
Succumb	to give in
Unsettling	uneasy; something that makes you uncomfortable
Valued commodities	things that can be exchanged for increased status or comfort or that are important for survival

CHAPTER 17
PSYCHOLOGY AND THE WORLD OF WORK:
INDUSTRIAL/ORGANIZATIONAL PSYCHOLOGY
AND HUMAN FACTORS

INTEGRATED CHAPTER OUTLINE: Survey and Question

This section presents the major topics and ideas from the chapter. Use it as a tool for seeing how the components of the chapter fit together. At the end of each major topic, we have asked you questions that relate to the major learning objectives. If you can answer these questions, you have taken a major step toward mastering this material.

I. Industrial/Organizational Psychology: Studying Behavior in Work Settings

L.O. 17.1: Be able to describe the theories and techniques of work motivation.

L.O. 17.2: Know the psychological factors operative in performance appraisal.

L.O. 17.3: Be able to discuss whether napping may be a positive workplace practice.

L.O. 17.4: Understand the prevalence, causes, and effects of job satisfaction.

L.O. 17.5: Know how psychologists study job satisfaction.

L.O. 17.6: Be aware of new forms and strategies in career development.

L.O. 17.7: Discuss the research on effective leadership.

With the exception of sleep, most adults spend most of their time in work-related activities. Work is also a key part of our self-concept. Given its importance, this topic, the fields of industrial/organizational and human factors have evolved to study behavior in work settings. Industrial/organizational psychology focuses on all aspects of behavior in work settings and on the nature of work settings themselves. Human factors psychology attempts to discover and apply information about human abilities and limitations to the design of tools, systems, tasks, jobs, and working environments. These two related fields are considered in this chapter.

A. Work Motivation: Theories and Techniques

A motivated work force is a crucial component of an organization's success. Industrial/organizational psychologists believe that we need to understand the basic nature of motivation in order to address the issue of how to motivate employees. Several views of motivation have been proposed. As you recall from Chapter 10, expectancy theory suggests that motivation is a function of: (a) our belief that effort will result in improved performance (expectancy); (b) our belief that good performance will be recognized and rewarded (instrumentality); and (c) the perceived value of the rewards we expect to receive (valence). This view has been confirmed in the workplace.

Goal-setting theory recognizes the important role that setting goals has on motivation. Research on goal-setting suggests that goals are more effective when: (a) they are specific; (b) they are challenging; (c) they are attainable; and (d) people are committed to the goals. Goals are thought to increase motivation because: (a) they increase attention to the task; (b) they increase effort; and (c) they increase persistence. In addition, a goal helps clarify required levels of performance, which helps a person develop effective task strategies.

Individuals' beliefs that they are being treated fairly at work is an important determinant of motivation. Equity theory addresses this issue and begins with the new idea that we socially compare to similar others in our environment. It suggests that we compare the ratio of what we receive (inputs) and what we contribute (outcomes) to the corresponding input-outcome ratios of similar others in the workplace. If these ratios are equal, we perceive our treatment as fair; when they are unequal, a state of inequity exists. Over-reward equity exists when we think we are getting relatively more reward than others. When this occurs, we usually explain it away and assume we deserve more reward (a form of self-serving bias). Inequity interferes with work motivation when we feel under-rewarded. In this case, individuals may take one of several steps. They may: (a) attempt to increase their outcomes (e.g., ask for a raise); (b) leave the relationship (e.g., quit); or,(c) reduce their inputs -- expend less effort on the job. Research also suggests that feelings of inequity may result in theft.

From the theories discussed above, industrial/organizational psychologists have developed several practical ways for increasing motivation. Goal-setting can greatly increase motivation and performance. Job design programs have been developed that attempt to make jobs more interesting and appealing.

The ones that have received the most attention are job enlargement and job enrichment programs. Job enlargement programs involve expanding jobs to include a larger number of tasks. This is especially useful when job requirements are repetitive and dull. Job enrichment involves giving employees more tasks that require higher levels of skill and responsibility. Electronic performance monitoring, in which companies monitor employees' performance through access to their computers are controversial but are becoming more common. Such monitoring produces effects similar to those produced by the presence of an audience-social facilitation. Research in this area shows that such effects can be either positive or negative. They can be used to provide immediate and accurate feedback to employees about their performance. Critics contend that computer-monitoring poses an invasion to privacy, produces stress, and lowers morale. Results of research investigating this practice have been mixed -- it is clear they should be used with caution.

B.   Performance Appraisal: Tying Rewards to Performance

Most organizations have procedures to evaluate performance and link these evaluations with rewards. Providing feedback about employee's performance is a crucial part of the workplace. But it is a process that is subject to error. What you have learned about memory and social cognition will help you understand the sources of error in this process (see Chapters 6, 7, and 16).

Errors in attribution can lead us to evaluate persons with identical levels of performance quite differently. We tend to assign higher ratings to persons whose performance stems from high motivation and effort than to talent or past experience. We also tend to attribute the successful performance of persons we like vs. dislike to internal factors.

Halo effects occur when overall impressions shape specific judgments. If our impressions of a person are favorable, we see everything he or she does in a positive light. If our impression is unfavorable, we tend to perceive the person's actions in a negative light.

Leniency errors occur when we tend to inflate the evaluations of most employees (e.g., give almost everyone an "outstanding" rating). This makes it impossible to differentiate among these persons for raises, promotions, and other benefits.

Affective reactions are sources of error and bias. We are influenced by whether we like or dislike the person we are evaluating. Stereotypes -- cognitive frameworks consisting of knowledge and beliefs about specific social groups -- can provide sources of error in performance appraisal. They can lead a person to process information in terms of stereotypic knowledge, rather than in terms of the person's individual behavior. Clear evidence exists that demonstrates the role of gender stereotypes in applicant selection and in conceptions of the "ideal." In addition there are tendencies to inflate ratings of persons similar to us.

Industrial/organizational psychologists have found several techniques which can be used to enhance the accuracy of performance appraisal. These include keeping accurate ratings. Making "diary notes" can reduce the impact of a faulty memory on appraisals. The rating format is often important. Using behaviorally anchored rating scales (those which define acceptable and unacceptable behaviors) may be a useful format. Using frame of reference training in which evaluators meet and together examine various examples of on-the-job performance until they agree on the criteria for good performance is also useful.

- **Beyond the Headlines: As Psychologists See It -- Sleeping on the Job: Can It Have Potential Benefits?**

    An increasing number of companies are experimenting with the practice of promoting taking short naps at work. There is scientific evidence that this is a good idea. As we learned in Chapter 4, sleep researchers have found that the "down period" between 2:00 and 5:00 p.m. can be helped by a short nap. Manufacturers have developed a "Relax and Refresh Chair" that allows people to program the length of their nap.

C.   Work-Related Attitudes: The Prevalence, Causes, and Effects of Job Satisfaction

Work-related attitudes have long been a topic of research in I/O. Although most persons report being satisfied with their jobs, they are not equally satisfied with all aspects of their work. There are individual differences in job satisfaction that may be related to job type, age, gender, and personality factors.

The causes of job satisfaction can be grouped into two categories: (1) work-related influences and (2) person-related influences. Factors which fall into these categories are listed below:

Work-Related Influences	Person-Related Influences
The reward system	Self-esteem level
Perceived quality of supervision	Status level
Decision-making processes	Seniority
Level of work and social stimulation	Type A/Type B personality
Nature of work setting	Person-Job fit

The relationship between job satisfaction and work-related behavior is complex. Job dissatisfaction is modestly related to employee withdrawal -- absenteeism and voluntary withdraw. The relationship is modest because other factors, such as economics and affective dispositions, influence absenteeism and turnover. In addition, job satisfaction is only modestly related to job performance. This may be the case because some jobs may be structured so that there is little room for variation. It may also be the case that both satisfaction and performance are caused by a third factor, such as rewards. However, recent research suggests that the overall level of satisfaction within an organization does influence the organization's overall success. It is suggested that satisfaction may influence the extent to which persons engage in organizational citizenship behaviors (e.g., cooperation), which are related to the success of the entire organization.

D.   Careers: New Forms, New Strategies

There have been many changes in the assumptions people need to make about their careers. "Single-job" careers are largely a thing of the past and people need new strategies and approaches if they are to attain success. Baron discusses what research has contributed to our understanding of these new challenges. We have summarized the major points below:

(1)   View jobs as opportunities for learning new skills, rather than in terms of pay or job-length. This allows you to map out a career strategy.

(2)   It is useful to move from job to job within a company -- job rotation. This builds skill and is related to promotion and salary growth.

(3)   Find a mentor who can help you avoid pitfalls and provide support.

•   **Exploring Gender and Diversity: Race, Gender, and Mentoring**

There is some evidence that women and minorities are at a disadvantage in obtaining a mentor, and this can have adverse effects on their careers. This may be due to the effects of similarity -- most potential mentors are white males. Women also report less willingness to serve as mentors and male managers fear that a close relationship with a female employee might be misperceived as a romantic relationship. Other factors may also be involved; but it is clear that this is another barrier faced by women and minorities.

E.   Leadership: Patterns of Influence Within Groups

•   **Research Methods: How Psychologists Study Job Satisfaction**

Because job satisfaction is a type of attitude, it can't be "seen" directly. The most common method to measure job satisfaction is through questionnaires, such as the Job Descriptive Index (JDI) and the Minnesota Satisfaction Questionnaire (MSQ). These instruments deal with aspects of the job such as the work itself, pay, promotional opportunities, supervision, and co-workers (the JDI). Critical incident techniques, in which employees describe events related to their work that they have found especially satisfying or dissatisfying are also used. Confrontational meetings are also used.

Leadership is the process through which one member of a group influences other group members toward the attainment of specific group goals. This section focuses on who becomes an effective leader and the factors that make a leader effective.

The great person theory of leadership suggests that leaders possess key stable traits that set them apart from others. Recent research suggests that a leader's traits do matter. Flexibility seems to be the most important trait. In addition leaders have high levels of drive, self-confidence, creativity, and leadership motivation. Leadership styles also matter. The extent to which a leader adopts either a democratic or autocratic approach, and the extent to which she or he focuses on personal relationships or task performance, are basic dimensions of leadership style. No single style is best. Different leadership styles are required across situations.

History is filled with leaders who have exerted profound influence on others. These leaders are termed transformational or charismatic leaders. These leaders tend to have traits that set them apart from others.

However, growing evidence suggests that it is the reactions they invoke from followers that is exceptional. Thus, these kinds of leaders are characterized by a special leader-follower relationship.

Charismatic leaders engage in a number of common behaviors that create a special relationship with subordinates. (1) They possess and transmit a vision of the future; (2) they offer a clear road map for attaining the vision; and (3) they define the purpose of their movement in a way that gives meaning and purpose to the actions they request (framing).

Transformational leadership is a "two-edged sword." It can be used for beneficial purposes or it can be used for selfish, illegal or immoral purposes.

Questions:

17-1. What is the subject matter of human factors and industrial/organizational psychology? _____

_____

_____

_____

17-2. Describe the major theoretical approaches to work motivation. _____

_____

_____

_____

17-3. Describe the techniques used to enhance worker motivation. _____

_____

_____

_____

17-4. Discuss the strengths and weaknesses of computer-monitoring systems. _____

_____

_____

_____

17-5. Discuss the errors that can influence performance appraisals. _____

_____

_____

_____

17-6.   Outline the various ways of reducing errors in performance appraisals. _____

_____

_____

_____

17-7.   What are causes, effects, and prevalence of job satisfaction? _____

_____

_____

_____

17-8.   Describe the research concerning the relationship between job satisfaction and performance.

_____

_____

_____

17-9.   How have careers changed in recent decades and what are the new strategies for career success discussed in your text? _____

_____

_____

17-10. Define "leadership" and discuss the characteristics that promote effective leaders. _____

_____

_____

_____

II. Human Factors: Designing for Effectiveness, Health, and Safety

L.O. 17.8:   Know how human factors research has lead to designs for effective visual displays.

L.O. 17.9:   Know how human factors research has lead to designs for effective controls.

L.O. 17.10: Know how human factors research has lead to designs for effective tools and equipment.

L.O. 17.11: Know how you can use effective impression management techniques for improving your interview skills.

The field of human factors or ergonomics uses knowledge about human abilities and limitations to help design tools and equipment that are both convenient and safe for human use. This section focuses on examples of this work.

A.   Visual Displays: Principles and Applications

Some kinds of visual displays are easier to read than others. Several basic principles are discussed: (1) Pointers moving against a fixed scale are easier to read than the opposite. (2) Ease of reading is increased by displaying increases in units in terms of "up" or "higher" vs. "down" or "lower." (3) Displays in which scale markings are clear and easy to read are effective. (4) Different colors for different zones (e.g., "caution" -- yellow) are useful.

B.   Effective Controls: "What Happens When I Turn This Dial?..."

Confusing or misleading controls are common. Several principles have been found to guide the production of clearer controls. For example, compatibility -- the degree to which relationships are consistent with expectations (e.g., knobs turn in a clockwise fashion) -- is an important design principle.

C.   Designing Tools and Equipment: Two Concrete Examples

Human factors research has come to the rescue of letter carriers, who carry heavy loads with considerable discomfort and risk of injury. A better mailbag supported at the waist by a belt or having two pouches supported by both shoulders was developed.

Problems of extensive keyboard use have also been addressed. A new tilt-down keyboard that puts less pressure on the wrist has been developed.

Questions:

17-11. What are the important principles for constructing a visual display? _____

_____

_____

_____

17-12. What are the factors associated with designing good controls? _____

_____

_____

_____

17-13. Discuss the two examples of how research in human factors has been used to solve workplace problems. _____

_____

_____

_____

• **Making Psychology Part of Your Life -- Impression Management in Job Interviews: The Fine Art of Looking Good**

Clearly, getting the "right job for you" is an important goal of life. Information that we have learned on impression management or self-presentation (efforts by individuals to enhance the impressions they make on others) can help us meet this goal. Baron provides some tips based on the findings of this research.

1.   Do your homework! Find out as much as you can about the company.
2.   Dress and groom appropriately.
3.   Engage in self-enhancing tactics in moderation.
4.   Engage in other-enhancing tactics in moderation.
5.   Concentrate on jobs for which you are qualified.
6.   Practice, practice, practice!

MAKING PSYCHOLOGY PART OF YOUR LIFE: Key Terms and Concepts

Knowing the important concepts and key terms contained in this chapter is a very important part of mastering the material. We have presented a sample of these concepts below. Define each concept and check your definition with that presented in the chapter. It will also be beneficial for you to think of an example of each concept. Whenever possible, use your own personal experience to provide an example of each term below, whenever possible.

17-1. **Behaviorally Anchored Rating Scales:** _____

   Example: _____

17-2. **Careers:** _____

   Example: _____

17-3. **Compatibility:** _____

   Example: _____

17-4. **Critical Incident Technique:** _____

   Example: _____

17-5. **Electronic Performance Monitoring:** _____

   Example: _____

17-6. **Equity Theory:** _____

   Example: _____

17-7. **Frame-of-Reference Training:** _____

   Example: _____

17-8. **Goal-Setting Theory:** _____

   Example: _____

17-9. **Great Person Theory:** _____

   Example: _____

17-10. **Human Factors:** _____

Example: _____

17-11. **Industrial/Organizational Psychology:** _____

Example: _____

17-12. **Job Descriptive Index:** _____

17-13. **Job Design:** _____

Example: _____

17-14. **Job Enlargement:** _____

Example: _____

17-15. **Job Enrichment:** _____

Example: _____

17-16. **Rotation:** _____

17-17. **Job Satisfaction:** _____

Example: _____

17-18. **Leader:** _____

Example: _____

17-19. **Minnesota Satisfaction Questionnaire:** _____

Example: _____

17-20. **Organizational Citizenship Behavior:** _____

Example: _____

17-21. **Performance Appraisals:** _____

   Example: _____

17-22. **Social Facilitation:** _____

   Example: _____

17-23. **Transformational Leaders:** _____

   Example: _____

17-24. **Visual Displays:** _____

   Example: _____

YOUR NOTES:

CHALLENGE: Develop Your Critical Thinking Skills

Assessing Leadership Styles

As your text points out, the capacity of leaders to be flexible -- to recognize what actions or styles of leadership are required in a given situation -- is a key component of effective leadership. This exercise provides an opportunity for assessing your style of leadership. As we have noted, a critical thinker is able to assess his/her characteristics in an open way.

If you are presently in a leadership role, answer the following questions in relation to your present approach. If you are not in this role, answer the questions with reference to how you would approach this role. Choose either A or B within each question, depending upon which statement best applies to you.

1.   Do you think of yourself as (a) a manager or boss, or (b) as a sponsor and team leader?   ____

2.   Do you (a) follow the chain of command, or (b) deal with anyone to facilitate the job?   ____

3.   Do you (a) work within a set structure, or (b) change structures in response to needs?   ____

4.   Do you (a) make most of the decisions yourself, or (b) include others in decision-making?   ____

5.   Do you (a) keep most of the relevant information to yourself, or (b) share information freely?   ____

6.   Do you think of yourself as (a) a specialist in your area, or (b) a generalist who tries to   ____
     master a wide array of disciplines within your field?

7.   Do you (a) demand long hours, or (b) demand that your subordinates get results?   ____

Go back over your responses and count the number of questions that you marked "A" and the number of questions that you marked "B." If you marked more "A" responses than "B," your style may be indicative of a less flexible leadership approach. If you marked more "B" than "A" responses, your style is more consistent with the flexible approach.

CHALLENGE: Taking Psychology With You

How Satisfied Are You With Your Job?

Many students work while they go to college or work during vacation periods. Some of the features of these jobs may be quite positive while others may be somewhat negative. For the items listed below, indicate whether you are dissatisfied or satisfied with these in your present job. (If you do not have a job now, you can rate your last job.)

1. Pay   _____ satisfied   _____ dissatisfied

2. Job security   _____ satisfied   _____ dissatisfied

3. Promotion opportunities   _____ satisfied   _____ dissatisfied

4. Recognition for good work   _____ satisfied   _____ dissatisfied

5. Physical working conditions   _____ satisfied   _____ dissatisfied

6. Relations with other workers   _____ satisfied   _____ dissatisfied

7. Opportunity for growth or learning _____ satisfied _____ dissatisfied

8. Degree of responsibility   _____ satisfied   _____ dissatisfied

9. Company policies   _____ satisfied   _____ dissatisfied

10. Quality of supervisors   _____ satisfied   _____ dissatisfied

11. Nature of work   _____ satisfied   _____ dissatisfied

12. Opportunities for achievement   _____ satisfied   _____ dissatisfied

Now indicate on the following scale how satisfied you are with your job.

Very satisfied   Satisfied   Neutral   Dissatisfied   Very dissatisfied

Scoring:

Add up the number of times you check satisfied and the number of times you check dissatisfied on Items 3, 4, 7, 8, 11, and 12. Write these numbers under "Motivation Score." Do the same for Items 1, 2, 5, 6, 9, and 10 and write the scores under "Maintenance Score." Do these scores relate to your job satisfaction? If you are very satisfied with your job, you probably have a high motivation score for satisfied. This means that your job is providing you the stimulation necessary to motivate you. If you are very dissatisfied, you probably have a high dissatisfaction score for Maintenance. This means that your job is probably not providing you with a context that maintains your level of satisfaction. According to some researchers, motivation factors create job satisfaction and maintenance factors prevent job dissatisfaction.

Motivators score: Maintenance score:

_____ Satisfied   _____ Dissatisfied   _____ Satisfied   _____ Dissatisfied

CHALLENGE: Review Your Comprehensive Knowledge

SAMPLE TEST QUESTIONS

Once you have worked through the preceding sections, you should be ready for a comprehensive self-test. You can check your answers with those at the end of this section. An additional practice test is given in the supplementary section at the end of this study guide.

17-1. The field of psychology that is focused on applying information about human abilities and limitations to design is known as:
     a. industrial/organizational psychology.   c. design psychology.
     b. professional psychology.   d. human factors.

17-2. Which of the following theories emphasizes the importance of a person's beliefs about whether effort will result in improved performance?
     a. expectancy theory   c. equity theory
     b. goal-setting theory   d. personal equity theory

17-3. Which of the following is not an effective guideline suggested by goal-setting theory?
     a. set specific goals   c. set far-reaching goals
     b. provide feedback   d. increase the probability that goals will be accepted.

17-4. Equity theory suggests that a person will feel he/she has been unfairly treated when:
     a. he/she receives low pay.
     b. he/she receives high pay.
     c. he/she receives more pay than others.
     d. his/her ratio of inputs to outcomes is unequal to that of others.

17-5. According to equity theory, a person who experiences underpayment inequity in the workplace may engage in all but one of the following kinds of activities.
     a. steal from his/her employers   c. engage in self-serving biases
     b. reduce his/her effort   d. ask for a raise

17-6. Which of the following is **not** good advice for approaching careers in today's job market?
     a. view a job as a learning opportunity   c. develop a "mentor"
     b. develop a career strategy for the long-term   d. avoid job rotation programs

17-7. If I give Karen a positive appraisal on her first evaluation because I thought she'd be a "top-notch" performer on her interview, I may be making an error based on:
     a. attributional errors.   c. the leniency error.
     b. the halo effect.   d. self-serving biases.

17-8. We tend to assign higher ratings to persons who we think perform well because of:
     a. their high motivation and effort.   c. their past experiences.
     b. their talents.   d. their skills in impression management.

17-9. Which of the following is **not** a technique which can enhance the accuracy of performance appraisals?
     a. keep "diary notes"
     b. refer to the original notes you took during the employee's interview
     c. use behaviorally-anchored rating scales
     d. use frame-of-reference meetings

17-10. Which of the following is **not** a work-related cause of job satisfaction?
    a. reward systems
    b. decision-making processes
    c. quality of supervision
    d. employee's level of self-esteem

17-11. Which of the following is a **correct** statement about the relationship between job satisfaction and work-related behavior?
    a. The overall level of satisfaction within an organization influences the overall success of an organization.
    b. Job satisfaction is strongly related to absenteeism.
    c. Job satisfaction is strongly related to voluntary turnover.
    d. Job satisfaction is strongly related to job performance.

17-12. The statement "a leader is born, not made" is most consistent with the _____ theory of leadership.
    a. normative
    b. great-person
    c. behavioral
    d. situational-leadership

17-13. Which of the following traits seems to be the most important for the ability to adopt a number of leadership styles?
    a. extroversion
    b. flexibility
    c. intelligence
    d. persistence

17-14. Research suggests that charismatic leaders do all but one of the following.
    a. motivate followers through fear-tactics
    b. possess and transmit a vision of the future
    c. give meaning and purpose to the actions they request
    d. offer a clear road map for attaining the visions they promote

17-15. Which of the following is **not** a basic principle of visual display design?
    a. Pointers moving against a fixed scale are harder to read than the opposite.
    b. Gradiation in scale should be clear and easy to read.
    c. Use clockwise directions to indicate increments in scale.
    d. Different colors should be used for different zones.

17-16. Which of the following theories of motivation suggests that people will work hard when they believe extra effort will improve their performance?
    a. expectancy theory
    b. equity theory
    c. goal-setting theory
    d. need theory

17-17. A leader who invites input and participation in decision-making from their followers would be called:
    a. an autocratic leader.
    b. a permissive leader.
    c. a democratic leader.
    d. a transformational leader.

17-18. Which of the following is the technique for measuring job satisfaction in which participants describe events relating to their work that they find especially satisfying or dissatisfying?
    a. the JDI
    b. the MSQ
    c. behaviorally anchored rating scales
    d. the critical incident technique

17-19. In expectancy theory, our belief that good performance will be recognized and rewarded is called:
    a. an expectancy
    b. valence
    c. instrumentality
    d. equity

17-20. This field of psychology is focused on all aspects of behavior in work settings and on the nature of work settings themselves.
      a. industrial/organizational
      b. social
      c. cognitive
      d. personality

Answers and Feedback for Sample Test Questions:

17-1. D   Human factors is the area which deals with these applications. (p. 668)

17-2. A   Expectancy theory includes the belief that effort will result in improved performance (expectancy) in its analysis of motivation in the workplace. (p. 670)

17-3. C   Goal theory suggests that we should set difficult, but attainable goals. (p. 670-671)

17-4. D   Equity theory suggests that we compare our input-outcome ratio to that of others in order to determine whether we are being treated fairly. (p. 673-674)

17-5. C   Self-serving biases are most often seen under conditions of over-payment inequity. (p. 673-674)

17-6. D   Job rotation programs increase success likelihood by enlarging a person's skills to include tasks requiring higher or more diverse levels of skill and responsibility. Therefore, they should be approached as learning opportunities. (p. 689-690)

17-7. B   The halo effect occurs when overall impressions shape our specific judgments. In this case, my overall positive impression of Karen on her interview may have generalized to my assessment of her early performance. (p. 679)

17-8. A   Research shows that we evaluate persons more positively when we make attributions that their performance reflects effort and motivation. (p. 679-680)

17-9. B   Referring to your initial notes is not recommended. It may increase your chances of making an error due to the "halo effect" (see discussion of #17- 7). (p. 679-681)

17-10. D   The employee's level of self-esteem is a person-related influence of job satisfaction. (p. 684-686)

17-11. A   Surprisingly, job satisfaction is only modestly related to turnover, absenteeism, and performance. However, it is related to the overall success level of the organization. It is suggested that satisfaction may influence the extent to which persons engage in organizational citizenship behaviors, which may not be typically assessed in individual measurements. (p. 686-687)

17-12. B   The great-person theory of leadership suggests that leaders possess stable key traits that set them apart from others. (p. 692)

17-13. B   Research suggests that "flexibility" is associated with effective leadership. This is most likely the case because different leadership styles are required across situations. (p. 693)

17-14. A   Although some charismatic leaders may use fear tactics, not all share this characteristic. In contrast, all charismatic leaders share the characteristics listed in options B - D. (p. 695-696)

17-15. A   Ease of reading is increased (not decreased) by displaying pointers moving against a fixed scale. (p. 697)

17-16. A   This belief is a component of expectancy theory. (p. 670)

17-17. C   Democratic leaders invite and permit participation in decision. (p. 693)

17-18. D   Critical incident techniques are used as described. Once these incidents are recorded, psychologists look for common themes. (p. 688)

17-19. C Instrumentality is the term used to describe this belief. (p. 670)

17-20. A Industrial/organizational is the field that focuses on all aspects of behavior in work settings and on the nature of work settings themselves. (p. 668)

GLOSSARY OF DIFFICULT WORDS AND EXPRESSIONS

These terms from your text and this study guide were identified by students as potentially hard to understand. We have defined these terms and expressions.

Term or expression	Definition
Adverse	negative
Barrier	something blocking or standing in the way of a goal
Bias	inclination or tendency
Blinking	shining on and off
Brink	on the edge
Cramped	kept in a narrow space
Dim	not a lot of light
Dingy	dirty-looking
Far-fetched	unlikely; hard to believe
Flashy	very noticeable
Gauges	instruments for measuring distance, speed, etc.
Glance	quick look
Hardships	circumstances that cause suffering
Hauled	moved by force
"I stuck it out"	I persisted even though I didn't want to
Leniency	treated in an easy way
Meddling	intruding into other people's businesses
Mentor	a more experienced individual who advises and helps a person
Muddled	in a state of confusion
Nap	a short period of sleep
Oversee	supervise, watch, manage
Pitfalls	dangers or mistakes one can make
Sake	for the benefit of
Sparingly	in low quantity, in small amounts
Stale air	air that is not fresh
Subordinates	people directed in work by other persons

Term or expression	Definition
The last straw	addition to a task that makes it intolerable
"top-notch"	very good, the best, superior
Unbearable pain	pain that cannot be tolerated

SUPPLEMENTAL PRACTICE TESTS

This section provides you with additional practice quizzes for each chapter. Review these after you have finished studying for your exam. If you find you cannot correctly answer eight or more questions, you should review the material in the chapter. But be sure and go back to the material in the chapter that discusses any of the questions you missed. The page number in the text where this material can be found is indicated at the end of each question. The answers for each quiz can be found at the end of this section. Good luck!

CHAPTER 1
PSYCHOLOGY: A SCIENCE AND A PERSPECTIVE

PRACTICE QUIZ 2

1- 1. This method asks individuals to describe what is going on in their minds: (p. 6)
    a. introspection   c. behavioral
    b. consciousness raising   d. signal to noise

1- 2. A radical spokesperson for the behavioral view: (p. 7)
    a. Watson   c. Wundt
    b. James   d. Freud

1- 3. One of the major changes in psychology in recent years has been the increased interest in: (p. 12)
    a. parapsychology.   c. multi-cultural issues.
    b. animal behavior.   d. perception.

1- 4. The characteristics that define a field as scientific are: (p. 16)
    a. adherence to the key values and standards.
    b. the topics under investigation.
    c. the use of particular scientific procedures.
    d. the use of naturalistic observation.

1- 5. A detailed study of a few individuals is the _____ method. (p. 24)
    a. natural observation   c. survey
    b. case   d. common sense

1- 6. One problem with the survey method is that it may be: (p. 25)
    a. time consuming.
    b. non-representative of larger groups to whom the findings are generalized.
    c. too manipulative.
    d. difficult to use.

1- 7. This view focuses on the possible role of inherited tendencies in various aspects of behavior: (p. 10)
    a. behavioral   c. evolutionary
    b. cognitive   d. psychodynamic

1- 8. An important theme in psychology centers around the following question: To what extent are various aspects of our behavior determined by inherited tendencies, and to what extent are they learned? This is usually known as the _____ question. (p. 8)
    a. rational versus rational   c. nature-nurture
    b. confirmation   d. stability versus change

1- 9. In an experiment, the factor that is measured is called the _____ variable. (p. 29)
    a. independent   c. control
    b. dependent   d. stimulus

1-10. This view focuses on personality and unconscious processes (p. 10)
    a. psychodynamic   c. behavioral
    b. socio-cultural   d. evolutionary

CHAPTER 2
BIOLOGICAL BASES OF BEHAVIOR:
A LOOK BENEATH THE SURFACE

PRACTICE QUIZ 2

2- 1.   Information is carried to the cell body by: (p. 45)
      a. dendrites.   c. glial cells.
      b. axons.   d. dopamine.

2- 2.   A change in electric charge is called: (p. 46)
      a. dynamic state.   c. action potential.
      b. steady-state stage.   d. resting potential.

2- 3.   When the neuron is stimulated it lets _____ charged _____ enter. (p. 46-47)
      a. positively, ions   c. positively, proteins
      b. negatively, ions   d. negatively, proteins

2- 4.   When a drug mimics a transmitter it is a(n): (p. 53)
      a. ion.   c. antagonist.
      b. agonist.   d. ion.

2- 5.   Opiate-like substances produced by the brain during times of pain or vigorous exercise are: (p. 51)
      a. analgesics.   c. glutamic acid.
      b. endorphins.   d. aspartic acid.

2- 6.   The part of the autonomic nervous system that readies the body for use of energy is the _____ division. (p. 57)
      a. central   c. parasympathetic
      b. sympathetic   d. somatic

2- 7.   The part of the brain involved in eating and drinking is the: (p. 63)
      a. midbrain.   c. cerebellum.
      b. hypothalamus.   d. medulla.

2- 8.   Damage to the right hemisphere of the occipital lobe results in an inability to: (p. 65)
      a. point to objects.   c. to see objects in the left visual field.
      b. to name objects.   d. identify features in the right visual field.

2- 9.   The procedure that involves the injection of small amounts of radioactive forms of glucose is: (p. 60)
      a. electroencephalography (EEG).   c. magnetic resonance imaging (MRI).
      b. event-related potentials (ERP)   d. positron emission tomography (PET).

2-10.   This plays a major role in emotion and motivated behavior: (p. 63)
      a. cerebellum   c. limbic system
      b. midbrain   d. none of the above

CHAPTER 3
SENSATION AND PERCEPTION:
MAKING CONTACT WITH THE WORLD AROUND US

PRACTICE QUIZ 2

3- 1.   This theory of pain suggests that the spinal cord contains a mechanism that can block transmission of pain to the brain: (p. 101)
   a. gate-control
   b. trichromatic
   c. signal detection
   d. pain-control

3- 2.   The fact that rewards and costs affect our ability to detect stimulation is part of the _____ theory. (p. 86)
   a. discrimination.
   b. threshold analysis.
   c. signal detection.
   d. utility.

3- 3.   The threshold that refers to how much change is required for a physical stimulus to be perceived as noticeably different is called a _____ threshold. (p. 87)
   a. sensitivity
   b. variation
   c. detection
   d. difference

3- 4.   The receptors in the eye that are involved in color vision are the: (p. 89)
   a. ganglion cells.
   b. blind spot.
   c. rods.
   d. cones.

3- 5.   Cells in the visual system that respond to length, width, and shape are: (p. 95)
   a. simple.
   b. complex.
   c. hypercomplex.
   d. geometric.

3- 6.   Which of the following best explains why we first feel cold when we dive into a swimming pool but then feel it is just right a few minutes later? (p. 88)
   a. sensory adaptation
   b. sensory threshold
   c. sensory deprivation
   d. signal detection theory

3- 7.   The theory that holds that sounds of different pitch cause different rates of neural firing is: (p. 99)
   a. place.
   b. frequency.
   c. neuronal.
   d. pitch differential.

3- 8.   When we take the apparent distance of an object into account in determining its size, we are using the _____ principle. (p. 115)
   a. size constancy.
   b. relative size.
   c. size-distance invariance.
   d. distance-size perspective.

3- 9.   Theories that propose that pattern recognition is based on simple perceptual abilities are called: (p. 120)
   a. prototype.
   b. top-down.
   c. bottom-up.
   d. feature.

3-10.   The fact that perceived size of an object remains the same when the distance is varied, even when the size of the image it casts on the retina changes greatly is called: (p. 115)
   a. the law of closure.
   b. size constancy.
   c. shape constancy.
   d. law of similarity.

CHAPTER 4
STATES OF CONSCIOUSNESS

PRACTICE QUIZ 2

4- 1.   Which of the following is **not** one of the characteristics of REM sleep? (p. 142-143)
    a. occurs only in adults
    b. accompanied by rapid eye movements
    c. muscular relaxation occurs
    d. individuals dream during REM sleep

4- 2.   Fluctuations in our bodily rhythms that occur throughout the day are called: (p. 132)
    a. circadian rhythms.
    b. nocturnal myoclonus rhythms.
    c. ultradian rhythms.
    d. REM rhythms.

4- 3.   The drugs that reduce activity in the nervous system are: (p. 159)
    a. opiates.
    b. amphetamines.
    c. hallucinogens.
    d. barbiturates.

4- 4.   If I believe that the effects of hypnosis are due to persons' playing a social role as "hypnotized subjects," I am adopting the _____ view of hypnosis. (p. 151)
    a. learning
    b. neodissociational
    c. social-cognitive
    d. Freudian

4- 5.   The belief that dreams reflect aspects of our memories and waking experiences is most compatible with the _____ view. (p. 148)
    a. physiological
    b. behavioral
    c. psychodynamic
    d. cognitive

4- 6.   Which of the following is the sleep disorder in which individuals are overcome by uncontrollable periods of sleep during waking hours? (p. 146)
    a. insomnia
    b. somnambulism
    c. narcolepsy
    d. apnea

4- 7.   As we fall to sleep there is an increase in: (p. 142)
    a. beta waves.
    b. alpha waves.
    c. delta waves.
    d. macro waves.

4- 8.   Increased tolerance for one drug that develops as a result of taking another drug is called: (p. 157)
    a. physiological tolerance.
    b. cross-tolerance.
    c. carry-over effect.
    d. tolerance.

4- 9.   Which of the following is not one of the basic facts about dreams? (p. 147)
    a. Everyone dreams.
    b. External events can be incorporated into dreams.
    c. They occur during REM sleep.
    d. They last only an instant.

4-10.   The procedure that is designed to produce an altered state of consciousness in which awareness and contact with the external world is reduced is called: (p. 165)
    a. hypnosis.
    b. apnea.
    c. delta states.
    d. meditation.

CHAPTER 5
LEARNING: HOW WE'RE CHANGED BY EXPERIENCE

PRACTICE QUIZ 2

5- 1.   The type of learning that involves pairing unconditioned and conditioned stimulus is: (p. 173-174)
     a. vicarious.   c. classical.
     b. operant.   d. emotional.

5- 2.   The tendency of stimuli similar to the conditioned stimulus to produce conditioned reactions is called: (p. 175)
     a. stimulus generalization.   c. spontaneous recovery.
     b. response generalization.   d. extinction.

5- 3.   Which of the following statements about conditioned taste aversion is false? (p. 177-178)
     a. It is a type of conditioning.
     b. The UCS must occur within a few minutes of the CS.
     c. It can occur in a single trial.
     d. The UCS is usually an internal cue.

5- 4.   Conditioned reinforcers acquire their reinforcing quality by association with: (p. 185)
     a. negative punishment.   c. aversive stimuli.
     b. primary reinforcers.   d. secondary reinforcers.

5- 5.   The _____ is in effect when preferred activities reinforce behavior. (p. 185)
     a. matching law   c. contrast principle
     b. Premack principle   d. opponent principle

5- 6.   The process through which a conditioned stimulus gradually loses the ability to evoke conditioned responses when it is no longer followed by the unconditioned stimulus is called: (p. 175)
     a. extinction.   c. instinctual drift.
     b. spontaneous recovery.   d. natural resemblance.

5- 7.   The reinforcement schedule in which some period of time which varies around an average value must elapse before a response will yield reinforcement is called: (p. 191)
     a. fixed interval.   c. fixed-ratio.
     b. variable-interval.   d. variable-ratio.

5- 8.   The reinforcement schedule which leads to brief pauses after the delivery of the reward is called: (p. 191)
     a. fixed-interval.   c. variable-interval.
     b. fixed-ratio.   d. variable-ratio.

5- 9.   A person is exposed to this schedule of reinforcement when he/she is free to alternate continuously between two or more responses, each having its own schedule. (p. 192)
     a. fixed-interval   c. variable-interval
     b. concurrent   d. variable-ratio

5-10.   A child learning to share his/her toys by exposure to adult sharing behavior (e.g., giving to the Salvation Army) is an example of: (p. 202)
     a. positive reinforcement.   c. instrumental conditioning.
     b. classical conditioning.   d. observational learning.

CHAPTER 6
MEMORY: OF THINGS REMEMBERED AND FORGOTTEN

PRACTICE QUIZ 2

6- 1. The earliest systematic study of memory was done by: (p. 214)
a. Pavlov.
c. Watson.
b. Freud.
d. Ebbinghaus.

6- 2. Finding that it is easier to recall information that matches our current mood is: (p. 227)
a. mood dependent memory.
c. mood matching memory.
b. mood congruent memory.
d. episodic memory.

6- 3. Which portion of the brain is though to be involved in implicit memory? (p. 246-247)
a. hippocampus
c. diencephalon
b. cerebellum
d. occipital lobe

6- 4. Our general abstract knowledge about the world is known as: (p. 217)
a. semantic memory.
c. episodic memory.
b. long-term memory.
d. procedural memory.

6- 5. The memory system that holds information that is being used in consciousness is known as: (p. 219-220)
a. short-term memory.
c. sensory memory.
b. long-term memory.
d. parallel memory.

6- 6. Each item in short-term memory can represent several other pieces of information. This is called: (p. 221)
a. grouping.
c. retrieval.
b. encoding.
d. chunking.

6- 7. What are the two basic components of STM? (p. 221)
a. sensory register and phonological loop
c. phonological store and rehearsal mechanism
b. semantic and episodic memory
d. none of the above

6- 8. Information enters LTM from STM by means of: (p. 224)
a. elaborative rehearsal.
c. retrieval.
b. shallow encoding.
d. cues.

6- 9. Loss of memory for events that occur after an accident is called: (p. 244)
a. retrograde amnesia.
c. Korsakoff's syndrome.
b. phobic amnesia.
d. anterograde amnesia.

6-10. The memory disorder that develops from prolonged alcohol abuse is: (p. 247)
a. Alzheimer's disease.
c. Ebbinghaus syndrome.
b. Korsakoff's disease.
d. infantile amnesia.

CHAPTER 7
COGNITION: THINKING, DECIDING, COMMUNICATING

PRACTICE QUIZ 2

7- 1. Mental frameworks for categorizing diverse items as belonging together are called: (p. 257)
    a. categories.   c. concepts.
    b. frameworks.   d. schemas.

7- 2. Concepts that can be clearly defined by a set of rules are _____ concepts. (p. 258)
    a. artificial   c. intuitive
    b. natural   d. semantic

7- 3. A person who doesn't think of using a coin as a screwdriver may be experiencing: (p. 279)
    a. a framing effect.   c. a means-end analysis.
    b. functional fixedness.   d. a representativeness heuristic.

7- 4. A source of error in reasoning that leads us to assume we are better at predicting events than we really are is the: (p. 264)
    a. hindsight effect.   c. perseverance effect.
    b. availability heuristic.   d. confirmation bias.

7- 5. If people were perfectly rational decision-makers, choice would be based on: (p. 267)
    a. expected utility.   c. confirmation strategies.
    b. heuristics.   d. emotion.

7- 6. Overestimation of chances of being a victim of a violent crime can be understood as an example of the _____ heuristic. (p. 268)
    a. informational   c. representativeness
    b. availability   d. perseverance

7- 7. You could conclude from the research described in your text that escalation of commitment would increase when: (p. 271-272)
    a. subjects make decisions in groups.   c. subjects feel they are not responsible for decisions.
    b. subjects make decisions as individuals. d. subjects feel they are responsible for decisions.

7- 8. My uncle only remembers things that fit with his political views. His behavior is consistent with: (p. 264)
    a. the hindsight effect.   c. the "know it all" effect.
    b. the framing effect.   d. the confirmation bias.

7- 9. Problem solving strategies suggested by experiences are: (p. 276)
    a. trial-and-error.   c. algorithms.
    b. heuristics.   d. inducers.

7-10. For symbols to be a language, they must meet all but one of the following criteria. Which one is not a criterion? (p. 282)
    a. transmission of meaning
    b. combination into an infinite number of sentences
    c. be logically interrelated
    d. meaning of sentences must be independent of context

CHAPTER 8
HUMAN DEVELOPMENT I: THE CHILDHOOD YEARS

PRACTICE QUIZ 2

8- 1.   Development begins when the sperm fertilizes the: (p. 298)
    a. embryo.   c. uterus.
    b. ovum.   d. fetus.

8- 2.   Differences between persons of different ages stemming from the contrasting social or cultural conditions in which they grew up are called: (p. 306-307)
    a. cross-sectional differences.   c. teratogens.
    b. cohort effects.   d. personality effects.

8- 3.   Which of the following statements is not true concerning the milestones of motor development? (p. 303)
    a. At birth, the child can raise his/her chin from the ground.
    b. At about 6 months, the child can sit alone.
    c. At about 1 year, the child can walk alone.
    d. At about 7 months, the child can stand by holding onto furniture.

8- 4.   Susan is doing developmental research in which she is studying a single group of subjects when they are two years old, then 4 years old and finally six years old to determine whether they change. Which method is Susan using? (p. 306-307)
    a. the cross-sectional method   c. the age-transfer method
    b. the case-study method   d. the longitudinal method

8- 5.   The stage at which children are egocentric and have difficulty with the principle of conservation is: (p. 310)
    a. formal operations.   c. preoperational.
    b. concrete operations.   d. sensorimotor.

8- 6.   Which of the following Piagetian concepts refers to the process of changing schema as a result of experience? (p. 309)
    a. accommodation   c. adaption
    b. assimilation   d. preoperation

8- 7.   The judgment of actions in terms of self-chosen moral principles occurs at the _____ level of morality. (p. 318-319)
    a. preconventional   c. postconventional
    b. conventional   d. abstract

8- 8.   The most common form of attachment is the _____ type. (p. 324)
    a. avoidant   c. secure
    b. insecure   d. ambivalent

8- 9.   Harlow's research on attachment with monkeys led to the conclusion that the important factor was: (p. 327)
    a. contact comfort.   c. instrumental conditioning.
    b. classical conditioning.   d. need reduction.

8-10.   Beliefs about the expected behavior of males and females are called: (p. 330)
    a. sex stereotypes.   c. sex differences.
    b. gender roles.   d. gender schemas.

CHAPTER 9
HUMAN DEVELOPMENT II:
ADOLESCENCE, ADULTHOOD, AND AGING

PRACTICE QUIZ 2

9- 1.   The period in adulthood during which the functioning of the reproductive system changes greatly for both males and females is called: (p. 359-360)
- a. menopause.
- b. primary aging.
- c. climacteric.
- d. secondary aging.

9- 2.   The first stage in Erikson's psychosocial development theory is: (p. 349)
- a. integrity vs. despair.
- b. initiative vs. inferiority.
- c. trust vs. mistrust.
- d. identity vs. role confusion.

9- 3.   According to Levinson, the two key components of early adults' life structure are: (p. 366)
- a. financial and emotional independence.
- b. mentor and dream.
- c. trust and integrity.
- d. self-absorption vs. generativity.

9- 4.   According to Erikson, the last crisis of adult life centers around the issue of: (p. 356)
- a. intimacy vs. isolation.
- b. integrity vs. despair.
- c. identity vs. role confusion.
- d. generativity vs. self-absorption.

9- 5.   Which of the following concepts is most important to the life-event models of adult development? (p. 356)
- a. a biological clock
- b. a social clock
- c. the social crisis
- d. physical development

9- 6.   Physical or biological changes related to disease, injury, or abuse of the body are called: (p. 360)
- a. secondary aging.
- b. primary aging.
- c. the biological clock.
- d. lifestyle aging.

9- 7.   The genetically-determined upper limit to a lifespan may be set by: (p. 373)
- a. a biological clock.
- b. a social clock.
- c. disease.
- d. physical.

9- 8.   According to Levinson, we follow an underlying pattern or design throughout our lives that constantly evolves as we move from one era to another. This is called the: (p. 364-365)
- a. climacteric.
- b. transition structure.
- c. social clock.
- d. life structure.

9- 9.   Which of the following factors would not be important to explanations of aging from genetic theories? (p. 373)
- a. teleomeres
- b. free radicals
- c. lipofusins
- d. ultraviolet light

9-10.   In Kübler-Ross's views, feelings of depression are often replaced by _____ in the dying process. (p. 374)
- a. anger
- b. denial
- c. acceptance
- d. bargaining

CHAPTER 10
MOTIVATION AND EMOTION

PRACTICE QUIZ 2

10- 1. Identify the theory of motivation that stresses physiological needs. (p. 384)
    a. instinct theory
    b. drive theory
    c. expectancy theory
    d. behavior theory

10- 2. Expectancy theory holds that behaviors are motivated by expectations of: (p. 386)
    a. control.
    b. stimulation.
    c. positive incentives.
    d. grooming.

10- 3. Which of the following describes the typical sequence of phases of female sexual behavior described by Masters and Johnson? (p. 393)
    a. resolution, orgasmic, excitement, plateau
    b. excitement, plateau, orgasmic, resolution
    c. excitement, resolution, plateau, orgasmic
    d. resolution, excitement, plateau, orgasmic

10- 4. In Maslow's theory, a person who is motivated to move out of a dangerous neighborhood would be influenced by: (p. 386)
    a. growth needs.
    b. deficiency needs.
    c. self-actualization needs.
    d. incentive needs.

10- 5. Which of the following is **not** thought to be a consequence of exposure to violence in the media? (p. 398)
    a. increase aggression
    b. learning of new ways to aggress
    c. sensitize people to the harm produced by violence
    d. learning that aggression often leads to success

10- 6. The desire to harm a person who has prevented you from obtaining what you want is most consistent with the _____ view of aggression. (p. 397)
    a. biological
    b. frustration-aggression
    c. social-learning
    d. depression-aggression

10- 7. According to your text, emotions involve all but one of the following: (p. 407)
    a. subjective cognitive states.
    b. instincts.
    c. physiological changes.
    d. expressive behaviors.

10- 8. External rewards do not necessarily decrease motivation if such rewards are: (p. 406-407)
    a. seen as a bribe.
    b. seen as contingent on performance.
    c. seen as signs of recognition.
    d. seen as desirable.

10- 9. The _____ is thought to play a role in both eating and satiety (knowing when we've had enough to eat). (p. 387)
    a. hypothalamus
    b. temporal cortex
    c. brain stem
    d. thalamus

10-10. The needs at the top of Maslow's hierarchy of needs are _____ needs. (p. 386)
    a. safety
    b. social
    c. self-actualization
    d. deficiency

CHAPTER 11
INTELLIGENCE: COGNITIVE AND EMOTIONAL

PRACTICE QUIZ 2

11- 1.   If one divides a test in half to determine whether scores in both halves are similar, one is assessing: (p. 439)
a. split-half reliability.
b. test-retest reliability.
c. split-half validity.
d. test-retest validity.

11- 2.   This type of intelligence involves the ability to form concepts, reason, and identify similarities. (p. 435)
a. practical
b. crystallized
c. fluid
d. none of the above

11- 3.   Which of the following is not one of the types of intelligence proposed by Sternberg in his triarchic theory? (p. 427-429)
a. componential
b. experiential
c. contextual
d. intuitive

11- 4.   According to triarchic theory of intelligence, people who are good at combining seemingly unrelated facts have _____ intelligence. (p. 427-429)
a. componential
b. experiential
c. contextual
d. intuitive

11- 5.   Which of the following is <u>not</u> a finding that suggests intelligence is related to neural functioning and brain structures? (p. 437-438)
a. scores on standardized tests are correlated with nerve conduction velocity.
b. scores on standardized tests are correlated with limbic functioning.
c. scores on standardized tests are correlated with the size of portions of the brain.
d. scores on standardized tests are correlated with efficiency in brain functioning.

11- 6.   A person who is very good at organizing his/her day-to-day life may be high in: (p. 427-429)
a. componential intelligence.
b. experiential intelligence.
c. fluid intelligence.
d. practical intelligence.

11- 7.   What was the first individual test of intelligence? (p. 430)
a. Wechsler scale
b. Sternberg scale
c. Henmon-Nelson test
d. Stanford-Binet test

11- 8.   This test contained verbal and performance items: (p. 431-432)
a. Wechsler scales
b. Stanford-Binet test
c. Thurstone scales
d. none of the above

11- 9.   Which of the following would not be considered as evidence for a genetic influence on intelligence? (p. 444-448)
a. finding that the more closely related persons are, the higher the correlation in their IQ
b. finding a worldwide increase in IQ scores
c. finding a high correlation between identical twins' IQs who were separated at birth
d. the outcomes of research on adopted children

11-10.   Developing a new use for discarded tea bags would be an example of: (p. 458)
a. creativity.
b. emotional intelligence.
c. tacit knowledge.
d. componential intelligence.

CHAPTER 12
PERSONALITY:
UNIQUENESS AND CONSISTENCY IN THE
BEHAVIOR OF INDIVIDUALS

PRACTICE QUIZ 2

12- 1.   In Freud's theory, the stage at which male children supposedly fantasize about sexual relations with their parents is the _____ stage. (p. 473)
a. phallic
b. genital
c. oral
d. latency

12- 2.   The part of our personality concerned with morality is the: (p. 470)
a. id.
b. ego.
c. superego.
d. preconscious.

12- 3.   According to Maslow, our highest need is for: (p. 480)
a. acceptance.
b. safety.
c. self-actualization.
d. esteem.

12- 4.   Which of the following is a characteristic of low sensation-seekers? (p. 497-498)
a. They show stronger orienting responses to stimuli.
b. They have better abilities to ignore irrelevant stimuli.
c. They are less likely to engage in substance abuse.
d. They are better able to tolerate stress.

12- 5.   For Freud, a defense mechanism whereby a person forgets or pushes thoughts from consciousness is: (p. 472)
a. projection.
b. regression.
c. repression.
d. sublimation.

12- 6.   _____ occurs when an excessive amount of libido energy is tied to a particular stage. (p. 472)
a. projection
b. distortion
c. transference
d. fixation

12- 7.   According to Jung, inherited images that shape our perception of the external world are called: (p. 477)
a. archetypes.
b. the collective unconscious.
c. animus.
d. defense mechanisms.

12- 8.   Which theorists would most likely agree with this statement: "All human beings possess the capacity to become fully-functioning persons. Problems arise when distortions in our self-concepts interfere with our personal growth." (p. 479-480)
a. Freud
b. Adler
c. Rogers
d. Jung

12- 9.   Recent findings suggest that there may be _____ key dimensions of personality. (p. 485)
a. 2
b. 5
c. 7
d. 10

12-10.   Bandura's social learning theory suggests that there are three important forms of learning. They are: (p. 489)
a. classical, operant, and observational.
b. classical, operant, and instrumental.
c. operant, internal, and external.
d. classical, operant, and internal.

CHAPTER 13
HEALTH, STRESS, AND COPING

PRACTICE QUIZ 2

13- 1. The sequence of responses to stress noted by Selye is called the general _____ syndrome. (p. 507-508)
    a. stressor   c. adaptation
    b. alarm   d. coping

13- 2. If you feel stressed because you perceive that important goals are being threatened, you are acting consistent with the _____ perspective of stress. (p. 507-508)
    a. cognitive appraisal   c. goal orientation
    b. cognitive adaptation   d. general adaptation

13- 3. Epidemiological studies involved _____ scale attempts to identify _____. (p. 506)
    a. large, heart disease   c. large, risk factors
    b. large, lymphocytes   d. small, health beliefs

13- 4. If you are experiencing burnout, which of the following is not likely to be one of your symptoms? (p. 516-517)
    a. emotional exhaustion   c. feelings of underload
    b. feelings of low personal accomplishment   d. physical exhaustion

13- 5. Prevention strategies that are designed to reduce or eliminate illness: (p. 534)
    a. secondary   c. adaptation
    b. tertiary   d. primary

13- 6. The largest preventable cause of illness and death in the U.S. (before age 65) is: (p. 524)
    a. poor diet.   c. smoking.
    b. lack of exercise.   d. stress.

13- 7. Type A individuals are most likely to suffer an increased risk of heart disease if they also exhibit: (p. 529)
    a. pessimism.   c. cynical hostility.
    b. introversion.   d. burnout.

13- 8. Which is false? (p. 527)
    a. People believe that a suntan makes them more attractive to other people.
    b. Beliefs may influence our response to advertisements.
    c. LDL helps clear HDL from arteries.
    d. Major life events appear to sensitize people to minor negative events.

13- 9. Time management is an example of: (p. 539)
    a. a physiological coping technique.   c. a belief coping technique.
    b. a cognitive coping technique.   d. a behavioral coping technique.

13-10. The personality type that is characterized by high levels of commitment and a sense of control over events is called: (p. 517-518)
    a. optimism.   c. pessimism.
    b. hardiness.   d. Type B.

CHAPTER 14
PSYCHOLOGICAL DISORDERS: THEIR NATURE AND CAUSES

PRACTICE QUIZ 2

14- 1.   This type of depression can occur after childbirth: (p. 558)
    a. flux
    b. postpartum
    c. postbirth
    d. preparent

14- 2.   Susan washes her hands an average of 100 times a day. She says she cannot control this activity and can't stop even though her skin is sore as a result of this activity. Susan may have (p. 563)
    a. a somatoform disorder.
    b. a dissociative disorder.
    c. an obsessive-compulsive disorder.
    d. a psychogenic disorder.

14- 3.   Identify the rare disorder in which a single person seems to possess two or more distinct personalities. (p. 567)
    a. multiple personality disorder
    b. dissociative identity disorder
    c. dissociative amnesia
    d. dissociative fugue

14- 4.   When people have losses of memory beyond ordinary forgetfulness, they are said to experience: (p. 567)
    a. a somatoform disorder.
    b. a dissociative disorder.
    c. an obsessive-compulsive disorder.
    d. a psychogenic disorder.

14- 5.   Jay has no feeling in his leg although multiple tests reveal no physical cause that would produce this symptom. Interestingly, he shows little concern over his paralysis. Jay may be experiencing: (p. 565)
    a. fugue.
    b. hypochondriasis.
    c. a conversion disorder.
    d. reaction formation.

14- 6.   This is a condition in which people travel from doctor to doctor claiming symptoms of a feigned ailment. (p. 566)
    a. Ralston disorder
    b. Munchausen's syndrome
    c. Halstead syndrome
    d. hypochondriasis

14- 7.   A person who for no apparent reason suddenly becomes dizzy, short of breath, fearful, and anxious may be experiencing: (p. 560)
    a. a phobia.
    b. a panic attack.
    c. a somatization disorder.
    d. a conversion disorder.

14- 8.   The dysfunction exists when unusual images, acts or objects are required for sexual arousal and performance: (p. 570)
    a. histrionics
    b. fugue
    c. paraphilias
    d. hypochondriasis

14- 9.   This eating disorder is associated with binge eating and purging. (p. 586)
    a. anorexia nervosa
    b. frotteruism
    c. obsessive-dissociation
    d. bulimia nervosa

14-10.   The type of schizophrenia that involves delusions of persecution and grandeur is: (p. 580)
    a. disorganized.
    b. catatonic.
    c. paranoid.
    d. undifferentiated.

CHAPTER 15
THERAPY:
DIMINISHING THE PAIN OF PSYCHOLOGICAL DISORDERS

PRACTICE QUIZ 2

15- 1.   Which of the following is not one of the problems of classical psychoanalysis? (p. 590-591)
 a. weak scientific base
 b. not suitable for sophisticated patients with good verbal skills
 c. time-consuming
 d. costly

15- 2.   Which of the following assumptions is not shared by all humanistic approaches to therapy? (p. 592)
 a. the view that people can reflect on their problems
 b. the view that people are unwilling to reflect on their problems
 c. the view that people can control their behavior
 d. the view that flaws in self-understanding cause problems

15- 3.   The therapy developed by Perls that focuses on awareness and understanding of one's own feelings: (p. 592)
 a. person-centered.   c. ego analysis.
 b. existential.   d. Gestalt.

15- 4.   Which of the following is **not** an important factor in Ellis' rational-emotive therapy? (p. 597)
 a. dealing with irrational beliefs   c. identifying self-defeating cycles of maladaptive behavior
 b. overcoming "awfulizing" tendencies   d. unconditional positive regard

15- 5.   What is the major goal of Rogers' client-centered therapy? (p. 592)
 a. eliminating distorted patterns of thought
 b. eliminating faulty learning histories
 c. eliminating unrealistic conditions of worth in a therapeutic environment of unconditional positive regard
 d. eliminating repressed id impulses through the use of free association

15- 6.   The hypothesis that is based on the notion that it is difficult if not impossible to have two opposite emotions at once to the same stimulus is: (p. 598)
 a. attribution.   c. aversive conditioning.
 b. incompatible response.   d. activation.

15- 7.   This systems is used in some hospitals and is based on the principles of operant conditioning: (p. 595)
 a. aversive conditioning.   c. token economy.
 b. desensitization.   d. counterconditioning.

15- 8.   This technique is used in therapies in which individuals are exposed to others behaving in an adaptive manner: (p. 595)
 a. systematic desensitization   c. attributional analysis
 b. modeling   d. flooding

15- 9.   The benzodiazepines like, Valium, seem to have their effects by depressing activity in the _____ system. (p. 616)
 a. circulatory   c. immune
 b. hormonal   d. central nervous

15-10. A basic assumption underlying various behavior therapies is that a psychological disorder is the result of: (p. 593)
a. unresolved unconscious conflict.   c. failure to achieve self-actualization.
b. low self-esteem.   d. faulty learning.

CHAPTER 16
SOCIAL THOUGHT AND SOCIAL BEHAVIOR

PRACTICE QUIZ 2

16- 1. We tend to attribute behavior to internal causes if consistency is _____, distinctiveness is _____, and consensus is _____. (p. 627)
    a. low, high, high
    b. high, low, low
    c. high, high, high
    d. low, low, low

16- 2. Overestimating the role of dispositional causes in our attributions is the: (p. 628)
    a. fundamental attribution error.
    b. self-serving bias.
    c. availability heuristic.
    d. false consensus effect.

16- 3. The tendency to assume that more people agree with our views than is actually the case is called: (p. 631)
    a. magical thinking.
    b. counterfactual thinking.
    c. the fundamental attribution error.
    d. the false consensus effect.

16- 4. For the person on the peripheral route, persuasion will often occur if: (p. 638)
    a. strong, convincing arguments are used.
    b. careful attention is given to the arguments.
    c. cognitive dissonance is aroused.
    d. the person is distracted to prevent focusing on the content of the arguments.

16- 5. When individuals notice that attitudes they hold and their behavior are inconsistent, they often experience a negative emotional state known as: (p. 639)
    a. commitment.
    b. cognitive dissonance.
    c. false consensus.
    d. forced compliance.

16- 6. The fact that infants do not show prejudice supports the idea that prejudice is due to: (p. 643-644)
    a. realistic conflict.
    b. social learning.
    c. mutual interdependence.
    d. social categorization.

16- 7. What percentages of subjects obeyed completely in Milgram's obedience study in which they were asked to shock another person? (p. 651)
    a. 25
    b. 40
    c. 65
    d. less than 10%

16- 8. Falling in love with "the boy/girl next door" reflects the influence of _____ on attraction. (p. 657)
    a. propinquity
    b. similarity
    c. mood
    d. attractiveness

16- 9. If you are in a bad mood, you should be more likely to help when you think helping is likely to: (p. 654)
    a. be observed by others.
    b. be costly.
    c. unpleasant.
    d. relieve the negative mood.

16-10. The belief that your thoughts can influence the likelihood of an event you're not a part of is an example of: (p. 632)
    a. the foot-in-the-door effect.
    b. counterfactual thinking.
    c. mere exposure effect.
    d. magical thinking.

CHAPTER 17
PSYCHOLOGY AND THE WORLD OF WORK:
INDUSTRIAL/ORGANIZATIONAL PSYCHOLOGY AND HUMAN FACTORS

PRACTICE QUIZ 2

17- 1. The type of rating scale which is based on the view that one must have a clear idea of what actions constitute good and poor performance is called: (p. 680-681)
a. distributional ratings.
b. likert scales.
c. behaviorally anchored-scales.
d. semantic differential scales.

17- 2. The view that individuals are motivated by their beliefs about how fairly they are being treated at work is most consistent with: (p. 673-674)
a. equity theory.
b. expectancy theory.
c. goal-setting theory.
d. drive theory.

17- 3. A person who experiences under-reward equity may resolve her feelings by: (p. 673-674)
a. attempting to decrease her outcomes.
b. attempting to increase her input.
c. reducing her input.
d. none of the above

17- 4. The tendency to allow our overall impressions to shape our specific judgments is known as the: (p. 679)
a. halo effect.
b. leniency error.
c. fundamental attribution error.
d. self-serving bias.

17- 5. Which of the following is a "person-related" influence on job satisfaction? (p. 686)
a. self-esteem
b. reward system
c. decision-making process
d. supervision quality

17- 6. This dimension of leadership involves the extent to which leaders dictate how followers should carry out their assigned tasks. (p. 693)
a. autocratic-democratic
b. social exchange
c. task-person orientation
d. directive-permissive

17- 7. Cafeteria-style benefit plans in which people choose benefits that they want would be related to the _____ factor in expectancy theory. (p. 670)
a. instrumentality
b. expectancy
c. feedback
d. valence

17- 8. Job satisfaction seems to have a strong influence on: (p. 686-687)
a. absenteeism.
b. turnover.
c. the organization's overall success.
d. job performance.

17- 9. Lateral moves between jobs in a given organization characterize _____ programs. (p. 677)
a. job enrichment
b. job design
c. job training
d. job enlargement

17-10. Which of the following groups of employees face barriers due to problems of obtaining mentors in the workplace? (p. 691)
  a. women and minorities
  b. older workers
  c. younger workers
  d. all of the above

Answers For Practice Quizzes:
Note any particular topics that you need to review in the space provided beside each chapter.

Chapter 1:
Answers: 1a; 2a; 3c; 4a; 5b; 6b; 7c; 8c; 9b; 10a

Chapter 2:
Answers: 1a; 2c; 3a; 4b; 5b; 6b; 7b; 8c; 9d; 10c

Chapter 3:
Answers: 1a; 2c; 3d; 4d; 5c; 6a; 7b; 8c; 9c; 10b

Chapter 4:
Answers: 1a; 2a; 3d; 4c; 5d; 6c; 7c; 8b; 9d; 10d

Chapter 5:
Answers: 1c; 2a; 3b; 4b; 5b; 6a; 7b; 8b; 9b; 10d

Chapter 6:
Answers: 1d; 2b; 3d; 4a; 5a; 6d; 7c; 8a; 9d; 10b

Chapter 7:
Answers: 1c; 2a; 3b; 4a; 5a; 6b; 7d; 8d; 9b; 10c

Chapter 8:
Answers: 1b; 2b; 3a; 4d; 5c; 6a; 7c; 8c; 9a; 10b

Chapter 9:
Answers: 1c; 2c; 3b; 4b; 5b; 6a; 7a; 8d; 9a; 10c

Chapter 10:
Answers: 1b; 2c; 3b; 4b; 5c; 6b; 7b; 8c; 9a; 10c

Chapter 11:
Answers: 1a; 2c; 3d; 4b; 5b; 6d; 7c; 8a; 9b; 10a

Chapter 12:
Answers: 1a; 2c; 3c; 4c; 5c; 6d; 7a; 8c; 9b; 10a

Chapter 13:

Answers: 1c; 2a; 3c; 4c; 5d; 6c; 7c; 8c; 9d; 10b

Chapter 14:
Answers: 1b; 2c; 3b; 4b; 5c; 6b; 7b; 8c; 9d; 10c

Chapter 15:
Answers: 1b; 2b; 3d; 4d; 5c; 6b; 7c; 8b; 9d; 10d

Chapter 16:
Answers: 1b; 2a; 3c; 4d; 5b; 6b; 7c; 8a; 9d; 10d

Chapter 17:
Answers: 1c; 2a; 3c; 4a; 5a; 6d; 7d; 8c; 9d; 10a